International and Comparative Law in the Asia Pacific

International and Comparative Law in the Asia Pacific is an ambitious and timely series dedicated to exploring the dynamic and multifaceted landscape of legal systems across the Asia Pacific. The series aims to provide a comprehensive and scholarly examination of the legal traditions, contemporary practices, challenges, and law reforms in jurisdictions across the Asia Pacific, offering valuable insights into their convergence and divergence within the broader context of international and comparative law. This series will also delve into specific areas of law, offering in-depth analyses and comparative perspectives that highlight the unique legal landscapes of individual countries while also identifying common trends and regional patterns.

The primary objectives of this series are multifaceted and aim to:

1. Bridge the Gap Between International and Domestic Law: Enhance understanding and foster dialogue among legal scholars, practitioners, and policy-makers by exploring the interaction between international law and the diverse legal systems of the Asia Pacific.
2. Advance Comparative Legal Research: Develop the field of comparative law by conducting in-depth analyses that highlight the similarities and differences among legal systems in the Asia Pacific. This will provide a foundation for understanding how various countries address similar legal issues.
3. Promote Harmonisation of Laws: Facilitate the harmonisation of laws across the Asia Pacific by identifying common legal principles and encouraging the adoption of best practices. This objective aims to support regional integration and cooperation.
4. Examine Dispute Resolution and Propose Law Reforms: Assess various dispute resolution mechanisms, including arbitration, mediation, and judicial reforms. The objective is to evaluate the effectiveness of these mechanisms in providing justice and resolving conflicts in diverse legal contexts.
5. Foster Legal Scholarship and Education: Promote the development of legal scholarship and education in the Asia Pacific by providing a platform for high-quality research and discussion. This will support the academic and professional growth of legal experts in the region.

Shu Zhang · Jie Luo · Peng Guo

Technology, Legal Education and Legal Profession in China and Australia

Opportunities and Challenges

Springer

Shu Zhang
Deakin Law School
Deakin University
Melbourne, VIC, Australia

Jie Luo
Law School
Zhongnan University of Economics
and Law
Wuhan, China

Peng Guo
Swinburne Law School
Swinburne University of Technology
Melbourne, VIC, Australia

ISSN 3059-2178 ISSN 3059-2186 (electronic)
International and Comparative Law in the Asia Pacific
ISBN 978-981-96-1638-1 ISBN 978-981-96-1639-8 (eBook)
https://doi.org/10.1007/978-981-96-1639-8

This Springer imprint is published by the registered company Springer Nature Singapore Pte Ltd.
The registered company address is: 152 Beach Road, #21-01/04 Gateway East, Singapore 189721, Singapore

Contents

About the Authors

Dr. Shu Zhang is a Senior Lecturer in Commercial Law at Deakin Law School, Deakin University (Australia), and coached Deakin Law School's Vis Moot team. Prior to joining Deakin Law School, Dr. Zhang was a Postdoctoral Fellow at the Chinese International Business and Economic Law Initiative, Law School, University of New South Wales (Australia). Her research interests include international commercial law, dispute resolution, and international arbitration, as well as comparative contract law. She also completed internships at both the Australian Centre for International Commercial Arbitration (ACICA) and the Chinese International Economic and Trade Arbitration Commission (CIETAC). She is also admitted to practise in New South Wales, Australia. She obtained her Ph.D. in Law from the University of New South Wales (Australia), and her LLM, LLB, and B.A. in Economics (Double Degree) from Peking University (China). She has published various manuscripts in leading journals in this area, such as the *Journal of Contract Law*, *Vindobona Journal of International Commercial Law and Arbitration* and *China Quarterly*.

Dr. Jie Luo is an Associate Professor at the Law School of the Zhongnan University of Economics and Law. She obtained a MA in Law from the University of East Anglia, a Ph.D. in International Law from Wuhan University, and a Ph.D. in Private Law from University of Paris-Sud. Her main research interests lie in international trade law, comparative law, and law and technology. She is the principal investigator for several research projects, and she has published books and articles in leading law journals globally.

Dr. Peng Guo is a Lecturer in Law at the Swinburne University of Technology. He has worked across several Australian universities and has held visiting positions at different universities in Europe and Asia. He has received scholarships and fellowships awarded by renowned research institutions and international organisations, including, but not limited to, the Max Planck Institute for Comparative and International Private Law, the International Institute for the Unification of Private Law (UNIDROIT), the Swiss Institute of Comparative Law and the European Union.

His research interests lie in comparative contract law, international sale of goods, international commercial arbitration, and technology and legal education.

Part I
Australia

Chapter 1
Australia: Overview of the Australian Legal System

This chapter introduces the fundamental aspects of the Australian legal system as a background to the discussion of legal education and the legal profession in subsequent chapters. The discussion in Sect. 1 begins from a brief historical review of the development of the current Australian legal system from its colonial past. It proceeds with the main features of the Australian political and legal framework, as governed by the *Australian Constitution*, in Sect. 2. Finally, Sect. 3 briefly examines the three branches of the Australian government and their functions under the rule of law: the legislative branch, the executive government, and the court system.

1.1 A Brief History of Australian Legal System

The Australian legal system is shaped by British colonial influence. The arrival of the First Fleet at Botany Bay, Sydney Cove, on 26 January 1788 marked the beginning of British colonisation in Australia. The European settlers brought English common law and established a legal framework based on British political and legal principles.

New South Wales was established as the first English colony, followed by Victoria and other colonies. English common law was received in those colonies on their establishment. The development of legal institutions in Australia also developed following the English model, and in particular, the Westminster system. A court system gradually developed in the colonies, claiming independence from the legislative and administrative branches of the government.

To clarify the applicability of the English law, the Imperial Parliament passed the *Australian Courts Act* (Imp) in 1828. It provided that all laws and statutes in force in England on 25 July 1828 that were applicable to the situations in the then colonies of New South Wales (including the current geographic areas of New South Wales, Victoria, and Queensland), and Van Diemen's Land, were deemed to be in force in these colonies. Following the same rationale, English law was deemed to

S. Zhang et al., *Technology, Legal Education and Legal Profession in China and Australia*, International and Comparative Law in the Asia Pacific,
https://doi.org/10.1007/978-981-96-1639-8_1

be received in Western Australia,[1] South Australia,[2] the Northern Territory,[3] and the Australian Capital Territory.[4] The courts in the colonies were authorised to determine the applicability of a particular law.

The colonial governments gradually obtained the power to make their own law, subject to the English law-maker's power to invalidate Australian laws inconsistent with English law under the doctrine of repugnancy. The *New South Wales Act 1823* (Imp) created a Legislative Council and conferred on the Governor the power to enact laws with the advice of the Legislative Council, which marked the transition from the colonies towards a constitutional state. Further, in 1825, an Executive Council was created along with Governor Darling. The *Australian Courts Act 1828* (Imp) further increased the size of the Legislative Council and provided for trial by jury. The *Australian Constitutions Act (No 1) 1842* (Imp) further expanded the Legislative Council, with two-thirds of its members to be elected. It also removed the Governor from the legislature and only maintained its role to give or withhold royal assent to the passed Bills. The *Australian Constitutions Act (No 2) 1850* (Imp) marked the independent self-governed status of the colonies, conferring the legislative bodies in the colonies to remodel their own constitutions. Following this move, the colonies promulgated their own constitutions, such as the *New South Wales Constitution Act 1855* (Imp). Along with the development of the colonies, the application of the doctrine of repugnancy was restricted through the *Colonial Laws Validity Act 1865* (Imp).[5] In the colonial era, the ultimate court of appeal in Australia was the Judicial Committee of the Privy Council in London.

The *Australian Constitution* commenced on 1 January 1901, reflecting the colonies' intention to assert independence from Britain. It reflected the important features of the Australian legal system, including the Westminster style bicameral federal legislature. Despite this, a full independence is only recognised after further moves in the twentieth century. Following the *Balfour Declaration 1926*, the *Statute of Westminster 1931* (Imp) provided that the British Parliament would not pass legislation applicable to the dominions unless upon request. It further repealed the doctrine of repugnancy. This legislation was formally adopted in Australia in 1942.[6] In 1985, the Commonwealth Parliament passed the *Australia (Request and Consent) Act 1985* (Cth) to request the British government to relinquish any residual power over Australia. Upon this request, the *Australia Acts 1986* (Cth), (UK), declared that no UK law should extend to the Commonwealth, States, and Territories of Australia,

---

[1] On 1 June 1829, as recognised in the *Interpretation Act 1984* (WA) s 73.

[2] On 28 December 1836, as recognised in *Acts Interpretation Act 1915* (SA) s 48.

[3] On 1 January 1911 when the Territory *was proclaimed;* see *Northern Territory Acceptance Act 1910* (Cth) s 7.

[4] On 1 January 1911 when the Territory *was proclaimed;* see *Seat of Government Acceptance Act 1909* (Cth) s 6.

[5] *Colonial Laws Validity Act 1865* (Imp) s 3.

[6] *Statute of Westminster Adoption Act 1942* (Cth), which provides that the *Statute of Westminster 1931* (Imp) was deemed to have effect on 3 September 1939.

and terminated the final channel of appeal to the Privy Council. This signalled the full independence of the Australian legal system.

Influenced by its colonial history, the Australian legal system adopts the common law tradition. A distinctive feature of this tradition is reflected in the doctrine of *stare decisis* which recognises the binding force of precedent.

1.2 Australian Constitution

The *Australian Constitution*, or the *Commonwealth of Australia Constitution Act 1900*, is the foundation of the Australian legal system. As previously noted, the Constitution entered into effect on 1 January 1901. It established a united federal government, or the Commonwealth government, over all States and Territories. It shapes the three key branches of the government: the legislature, the executive, and the judiciary, under the principle of separation of powers. The features of the government, especially the separation of powers, are similar to the British ones, reflecting the colonial history of Australia. The *Australian Constitution* reflects important constitutional principles such as separation of powers among different branches of the government, responsible government, and rule of law.[7]

According to the *Australian Constitution*, the federal government is at the pinnacle of the semi-autonomous governments of six States (New South Wales, Victoria, Queensland, Western Australia, South Australia, and Tasmania) and two Territories (Northern Territory and Australian Capital Territory). The governing power is divided between the federal government and the State and Territory governments.[8]

Chapter I of the *Australian Constitution* lays down the rules governing the federal legislature, the Parliament. Chapter II introduces the executive government. Chapter III governs the judicature. Chapter IV governs finance and trade matters. Chapter V specifies the role of States under the Constitution. Chapter VI governs the matters relating to new States. Chapter VII deals with miscellaneous matters, while Chapter VIII, with only one provision (s 128), deals with the alteration of the Constitution.

1.3 Legislature, Executive, and Judicature in Australia

Each government, at both federal and State/Territory levels, has three branches: legislature, executive, and judicature. Thus, there are legislatures and judicatures at both federal and State/Territory levels in Australia. The powers are therefore divided between these two levels.

---

[7] Hamer et al. (2024, 59–62).

[8] See, e.g., *Australian Constitution* s 51, as discussed below.

1.3.1 Legislature

The legislative branch of the government makes the law. In Australia, most legislature, or Parliament, adopts a bicameral system and has two houses. A Bill needs to pass both houses to become law. In Queensland, Northern Territory, and the Australian Capital Territory, however, there is only one house in their Parliament.

The legislative power is divided between the federal and State/Territory Parliaments. Sections 51–52 of the *Australian Constitution* provide the matters on which the Commonwealth Parliament can make law. Most of the legislative powers of the Commonwealth Parliament and the State and Territory Parliaments are concurrent; however, according to s 109 of the *Australian Constitution*, in case of any inconsistency, the Commonwealth legislation shall prevail. In addition, the Commonwealth Parliament may also override Territory legislation under s 122 of the *Australian Constitution*. Other than those limitations, the States and Territory Parliaments retain its legislative power for the peace, welfare, and good government of its own.

1.3.2 The Executive Government

The executive branch of the government administers and implements the law. At the federal level, it includes the Governor-General, the Prime Minister, the Ministers, the government departments, the defence force, the police, and other public or private entities supporting the government. The Prime Minister and the Ministers are collectively considered as the Federal Executive Council. A regulatory framework on the executive bodies is established by law, including the *Australian Constitution*, as well as the *Public Governance, Performance and Accountability Act 2013* (Cth).

1.3.3 Judiciary

The judicial branch exercises the judicial power of the State. According to the principle of the separation of powers, this is distinct from the law-making and executive powers.[9] The *Australian Constitution* provides the structure of the Australian judicial system. There are two types of systems of courts in Australia, the federal system and the State/Territory court system. Thus, there are eight court systems in each States and Territories, as well as the Federal Court system. However, all court systems respect the High Court of Australia as top of the hierarchy. The *Australian Constitution* provides rules governing the judicature, and in particular, the High Court of

---

[9] *R v Kirby; Ex Parte Boilermaker's Society of Australia* (1956) 94 CLR 254, 273.

Australia. It includes the appellate and original jurisdiction of the Court,[10] as well as the appointment, tenure, and remuneration of judges.[11]

The Federal Court system consists of the High Court of Australia, the Federal Court of Australia, and the Federal Circuit and Family Court of Australia.[12] The High Court of Australia is the highest in the hierarchy. It hears matters dealing with the application and interpretation of the *Australian Constitution*. It also hears final appeals in civil and criminal matters from all federal and State and Territory court systems. The Federal Court of Australia hears various federal law matters, such as corporation law, industrial relations, native title, and taxation. It also hears appeals from the Federal Circuit and Family Court but not family matters. The Federal Circuit and Family Court of Australia consist of Division 1, which is the previous Family Court of Australia and deals with family law cases, and Division 2, which is the previous Federal Circuit Court of Australia and deals with both family and general law cases. Family law cases are filed with Division 2 first and may progress to Division 1 if needed. The Federal Circuit and Family Court of Australia sits in every State and Territory except in Western Australia, where the family law cases are dealt by State courts instead.

The Local Court system in each State and Territory follows a similar hierarchy. Taking the court system in the New South Wales as an example, the highest court is the Supreme Court of New South Wales which has the supervisory jurisdiction over other State courts and tribunals in New South Wales. It includes the Common Law Division, the Equity Division, Court of Criminal Appeals (which is the highest court for criminal matters in New South Wales), and Court of Appeal (which is the highest court for civil matters in NSW).[13] Under the Supreme Court of New South Wales, there are District Court, Local Court, Land and Environment Court, Children's Court, Coroner Court, Drug Court, NSW Civil and Administrative Tribunal, Industrial Relations Commission, and the Dust Diseases Tribunal.[14] The District Court of the New South Wales is immediately below the Supreme Court of New South Wales, which deals with indictable criminal offences (excluding murder, treason, and piracy) and civil claims from AUD $100,000 to $750,000, all motor accident cases, and appeals from the Local Court. All criminal cases and most civil cases will begin in the Local Court of New South Wales and will be referred to the District or Supreme Court if needed. The New South Wales Civil and Administrative Tribunal is a consolidation of all specialist tribunals in New South Wales, dealing with various matters such as tenancy, building and construction matters, guardianship, and administrative review of government decisions. Other specialist courts and tribunals deal with specific

---

[10] *Australian Constitution 1900* (Cth) ss 73–76.

[11] Ibid s 72.

[12] 'Courts', *Attorney-General's Department* (Web Page) <https://www.ag.gov.au/legal-system/courts>.

[13] 'About Us', *Supreme Court of New South Wales* (Web Page) <https://supremecourt.nsw.gov.au/about-us.html>.

[14] 'New South Wales Courts and Tribunals', *NSW Government* (Web Page, 3 December 2023) <https://courts.nsw.gov.au/about-us/about-the-courts-and-tribunals.html>.

issues, such as the application of planning and environmental law; workplace and industrial disputes; care and protection of children and young people under 18 years; and investigation of deaths and related matters.

Chapter 2
Legal Education in Australia

This chapter demonstrates the fundamentals of the legal education in Australia. Section 1 provides an overview. Section 2 introduces and examines the development and features of Australian law schools. Section 3 introduces the main degrees, certificates, diplomas, and other courses offered by the Australian law schools. Section 4 examines the curriculum in the delivery of the degrees. Sections 5–8 discuss other main aspects of law students' activities, such as clinical legal education, Work Integrated Learning (WIL), extracurricular activities, as well as the clerkships and internships which enhance the career development for future lawyers.

2.1 An Overview of the Legal Education in Australia

The Australian legal education landscape is made up of both undergraduate and postgraduate pathways, each marked by distinct learning objectives. Law students are challenged to develop comprehensive legal knowledge, critical thinking and analysis skills, and a sense of professional ethical responsibility as prescribed in the Australian Law School Standards.[1] Law schools, as governed by the Council of Australian Law Deans ('CALD') and the Australian Law Schools Standards Committee ('ALSSC'),[2] seek to equip future legal professionals with the skills, knowledge and ethics required to thrive in the legal profession. As it currently stands, there are 42 law schools across 38 universities offering law degrees, each offering students a glimpse into the legal

[1] Council of Australian Law Deans (2020, 12).

[2] Evans et al. (2017, 16).

S. Zhang et al., *Technology, Legal Education and Legal Profession in China and Australia*, International and Comparative Law in the Asia Pacific,
https://doi.org/10.1007/978-981-96-1639-8_2

profession. According to a 2019 report by the Council of Australian Law Deans, there were about 15,000 students enrolled in Australian law schools.[3]

2.2 Australian Law Schools

2.2.1 Overview

Legal education first began in Australia in New South Wales during the eighteenth and nineteenth centuries, where the English system of legal education, along with the rules for admission and practice, was adopted.[4] In its infancy, the legal education system in Australia primarily followed the apprenticeship model from England[5] and it was not until the introduction of the *Barristers Admission Act 1848* (NSW) that educational requirements for aspiring barristers were introduced.[6]

The first law school was opened in 1855 at the University of Sydney with Melbourne University's law school following in 1857, and the University of Adelaide in 1883.[7]

Over the last 25 years, there has been a significant increase in the number of law schools and law students, beginning with what some scholars refer to as an avalanche of law schools.[8] Unprecedented growth in legal fraternity resulted in the establishment of 23 additional law schools in the period of 1989–2013, despite the 1987 *Pearce Report*[9] recommending that no further law schools be established in Australia.[10] This growth continued, and presently, as already noted, there are 42 law schools within 38 universities across Australia that offer a law degree, as noted in the tables below.[11]

---

[3] Council of Australian Law Deans (2019) 2018 Data Regarding Law Schools Graduate Numbers and Outcomes. <https://cald.asn.au/wp-content/uploads/2023/11/Updated-Factsheet-Law_Students_in_Australia-20-04-2019.pdf>.

[4] Chief Justice Robert French, 'Legal Education in Australia—A Never Ending Story' (Speech, Australasian Law Teachers' Association Conference, 4 July 2011) 14 <https://www.hcourt.gov.au/assets/publications/speeches/current-justices/frenchcj/frenchcj04july11.pdf>.

[5] James (2000, 965, 966).

[6] *Barristers Admission Act 1848* (NSW) cited in Chief Justice French (n 18) 15.

[7] Ibid 16.

[8] Evans et al. (n 16) 15.

[9] Dennis Pearce, Enid Campbell and Don Harding, 'Australian Law Schools: A Discipline Assessment for the Commonwealth Tertiary Education Commission' (Final Report, Australian Government Publishing Service, 1987).

[10] Barker (2013, 153).

[11] Raz et al. (2020, 1–2); Council of Australian Law Deans, 'Australia's Law Schools' *Council of Australian Law Deans* (Web Page) https://cald.asn.au/home/deans-law-schools/.

SA	TAS	NT	ACT
Flinders University University of Adelaide University of South Australia	University of Tasmania	Charles Darwin University	Australian National University (ANU College of Law, ANU Law School) University of Canberra
WA	**NSW**	**VIC**	**QLD**
Curtin University Edith Cowan University Murdoch University University of Notre Dame University of Western Australia	Australian Catholic University Charles Sturt University Macquarie University Southern Cross University University of Newcastle University of New England University of New South Wales University of Notre Dame University of Sydney University of Technology Sydney Western Sydney University University of Wollongong	Australian Catholic University Deakin University La Trobe University Monash University RMIT University Swinburne University of Technology Victoria University University of Melbourne	Bond University Central Queensland University Griffith University James Cook University Queensland University of Technology Southern Cross University University of Queensland University of Southern Queensland University of the Sunshine Coast

2.2.2 Regulation of Law Schools

The Australian Law Schools Standards ('the Standards') govern law schools, in conjunction with the *Higher Education Standards Framework (Threshold Standards) 2021*[12] ('HES Framework') and the Australian Qualifications Framework[13] (administered by the Tertiary Education Quality and Standards Agency ('TEQSA')) and the *Higher Education Support Act 2003* (Cth).[14] The Australian Law School Standards are wide ranging and cover educational matters and infrastructure requirements, as well as values and missions for law schools.[15] The Standards were created to provide

[12] *Higher Education Standards Framework (Threshold Standards) 2021* (Cth).

[13] 'Australian Qualifications Framework' *Australian Qualifications Framework* (Web Page, 2016) <https://www.aqf.edu.au/framework/australian-qualifications-framework/>.

[14] *Higher Education Support Act 2003* (Cth).

[15] Council of Australian Law Deans (n 17) 1.

a self-regulatory framework to enhance the quality of Australian law schools and to complement educational accreditation requirements.[16]

The Australian Government does not prescribe a national curriculum for legal education; however, it provides a national standard for learning outcomes in higher education.[17] The TEQSA evaluates the standards and quality of education through the application of the Australian Qualifications Framework, which lays down six learning thresholds for Bachelor of Laws and Juris Doctor law programs.[18] The six Threshold Learning Outcomes for a Bachelor of Laws ('TLOs') include:

1. Knowledge (TLO 1);
2. Ethics and Professional Responsibility (TLO 2);
3. Thinking Skills (TLO 3);
4. Research Skills (TLO 4);
5. Communication and Collaboration (TLO 5); and
6. Self-management (TLO 6).[19]

The TEQSA audits law schools for compliance with the six TLOs. As such, the Australian Law School Standards should be read in conjunction with the prescribed higher education learning outcomes.

2.3 Degrees

2.3.1 Bachelor of Laws

The Bachelor of Laws, otherwise known by its Latin (*Legem Baccalaureus)* abbreviation LLB, is the most common law degree in Australia. The LLB is an undergraduate degree to be completed after secondary school studies.[20] The Bachelor of Laws can be undertaken as a single degree, combined degree, or as a graduate entry bachelor program. Traditionally, the Bachelor of Laws takes four years of full-time study to complete[21] and provides students with the foundational legal knowledge required for legal practice.

---

[16] Ibid 2.

[17] Black and Black (2018, 53.

[18] 'Australian Qualifications Framework', *Tertiary Education Quality and Standards Agency* (Web Page) <https://www.teqsa.gov.au/how-we-regulate/acts-and-standards/australian-qualifications-framework/>.

[19] Council of Australian Law Deans, *Bachelor of Law Standards: Learning and Teaching Academic Standards Statement* (December 2010), 10. I couldn't find a CALD document but could find: Sally Kift, Mark Israel and Rachel Field, *Learning and Teaching Academic Standards Project: Bachelor of Laws: Learning and Teaching Standards Statement December 2020* (Australian Learning & Teaching Council, 2011) <https://cald.asn.au/wp-content/uploads/2024/04/LLB-TLOsKiftetalLTASStandardsStatement2010-TLOs-LLB2.pdf>.

[20] Raz, Loh and Fevereux (n 25) 3.

[21] Ibid.

Each university entry requirements may vary, as each law school has purview to set their own entry requirements. Universities will also set a minimum Australian Tertiary Admissions Rank ('ATAR'). An ATAR is a ranking of students' academic achievements in comparison with other students in their cohort.[22] For law degrees, minimum ATAR requirements are often quite high, for example Monash University requires an ATAR 95.05.[23] However, other universities like James Cook University only require an ATAR of 75.[24] In addition to the requirement of a certain ATAR, universities may also set a minimum score for certain subjects like English (i.e. a study or subject score of at least 30) and impose English language requirements.[25] Some universities, like the University of New South Wales, may also require an admissions test in addition to a high ATAR.[26]

2.3.2 *Combined Degrees*

The Bachelor of Laws may be taken in conjunction with another degree, which is known as a combined or double degree. This allows students to simultaneously undertake two undergraduate degrees at the same time. Students completing a double degree will often complete these degrees in five years, which is shorter than completing each degree separately.[27]

Admission requirements for combined degrees are slightly different, for example if a student wanted to combine the Bachelor of Laws from Monash University mentioned above, the minimum ATAR requirement may be slightly different.[28] In addition to the requirement of a 30-subject score in English, students will also require a subject score of at least 25 in Mathematical Methods or Specialist Mathematics and a subject score of 25 in Chemistry or Physics.[29] This degree is also 6 years, as opposed to 4 years in straight law.[30]

---

[22] Ibid 6.

[23] 'Law (Honours) Monash University', *Victorian Tertiary Admissions Centre* (Webpage) https://delta.vtac.edu.au/coursesearch/#/course/28/2802838.

[24] 'Bachelor of Laws' *James Cook University Australia* (Webpage) <https://www.jcu.edu.au/courses/bachelor-of-laws/>.

[25] Raz, Loh and Fevereux (n 25) 6.

[26] 'Bachelor of Laws', *UNSW Sydney* (Webpage) <https://www.unsw.edu.au/law-justice/study/undergraduate/bachelor-laws/>.

[27] Raz, Loh and Fevereux (n 25) 6.

[28] 'Laws (Honours)/Engineering (Honours)' *Victorian Tertiary Admissions Centre* (Webpage) <https://delta.vtac.edu.au/coursesearch/#/course/28/2802832>.

[29] Ibid.

[30] Ibid.

2.3.3 Juris Doctor

The Juris Doctor, or JD, is the postgraduate equivalent of the Bachelor of Laws and is a Masters-level program.[31] The Juris Doctor was first offered by the University of Queensland in 1996, as a postgraduate professional degree much like the American model of legal education.[32] It is a three-year program and is only open to students who have successfully completed an undergraduate degree.[33]

Historically, some law schools required a LSAT (Law School Admission Test) for admission to a Juris Doctor program, in addition to a GPA (Grade Point Average) or WAM (Weighted Average Mark) requirement. The LSAT is a standardised test made up of six sections, five multiple choice, and one writing task.[34] However, universities like the University of Melbourne no longer require an LSAT for admission to the Juris Doctor.[35]

2.3.4 Other Law Degrees and Law Courses

In addition to the LLB and JD courses offered by law schools, there are also various courses and degrees in the law discipline in Australia. They can be divided into three main categories:

First, qualifications equivalent to a law school degree that makes students eligible for admission. A typical example is the Diploma in Law offered jointly by the Legal Profession Admission Board ('LPAB') in New South Wales and University of Sydney.[36] It offers "a readily accessible legal education and a flexible means of entry to the legal profession".

The second type of courses are coursework-based ones, but not meeting the purpose of admission. It might be a preliminary introduction to law, or a more advanced course specialising in specific areas of law. For example, the University of Sydney offers a Master of Laws and Graduate Diploma in Laws by coursework programs on various specialised areas: administrative law and policy; business law; criminology; environmental law; health law; international law; labour law and relations; taxation.[37]

---

31 Raz, Loh and Fevereux (n 25) 3.

32 Black and Black (n 31) 52.

33 Raz, Loh and Fevereux (n 25) 3.

34 Ibid 9–10.

35 'JD intake FAQs' *Melbourne Law School* (Webpage) <https://law.unimelb.edu.au/study/jd-intake-faqs/>.

36 'Course Overview', *The University of Sydney* (Web Page) <https://lec.sydney.edu.au/why-study-with-the-law-extension-committee/course-overview/>.

37 'Master of Laws', *The University of Sydney Law School* (Web Page) <https://www.sydney.edu.au/law/study-law/postgraduate/masters.html>.

Finally, there are research-based courses, namely Master of Laws by research and Doctor of Philosophy programs, offered by Australian law schools. Students are required to complete a research thesis in pursuing these degrees.

2.4 Curriculum

2.4.1 Australian Law School Standards

The Australian Law Schools Standards outline under standards 2.2 and 2.3 the required curriculum design and content for law schools. These curriculum requirements, according to the explanatory note, should be read in conjunction with the TLOs for the Bachelor of Laws and Juris Doctor to ensure that law schools meet the national tertiary education requirements set out by the HSE Framework.[38] The TLOs are not addressed in the accreditation process for law schools, thus making Standard 2 particularly important.[39]

(a) *Standard 2.2: Curriculum Design and Educational Methods*

Standard 2.2 emphasises that law schools must have a curriculum and teaching methods aligned with the educational goals of the law program, promoting active student engagement and critical analysis of legal concepts.[40] It also requires the provision of appropriate instruction, whether through physical, virtual, or blended means, to facilitate the development of the knowledge, understanding, and skills as specified in Standard 2.2.3.[41] Additionally, the standards encourage law schools, as far as is practicable, to offer experiential learning opportunities, such as clinical programs, internships, workplace experience, and pro bono community service, to enhance the practical skills and real-world experience of their students.[42]

The language used in this standard indicates that law schools should have consideration to the use of a variety of teaching methods. These teaching and learning methods should include blended learning, as well as a variety of seminars, lectures, workshops, and group activities to name a few.[43] The references to blended or virtual learning, as well the broad meaning of learning and teaching methods, accommodate the increased use of technology across the higher education sector.[44]

Additionally, the Standards reflect the HSE Framework which can be seen in Standard 2.2.1. In particular, the HSE Framework requires that "teaching and learning activities are arranged to foster progressive and coherent achievement of expected

---

[38] Council of Australian Law Deans (n 15) 14.

[39] Ibid 17.

[40] Ibid Standard 2.2.1–2.2.2.

[41] Ibid.

[42] Ibid 2.2.4.

[43] Ibid 15–16.

[44] Ibid 16.

learning outcomes throughout each course of study".[45] This is consistent with the above, 2.2.1 of the Standards, as law schools are required to demonstrate how the curriculum, as well as teaching and learning methods, promotes educational outcomes.[46]

(b) *Standard 2.3: Curriculum Content*

Standard 2.3 discusses the comprehensive requirements for the curriculum of law schools in Australia.[47] This standard requires that the curriculum includes coverage of all of the academic requirements that are necessary for admission to practise as a lawyer in Australia.[48] In general, the curriculum seeks to develop the knowledge, understanding, skills, and principles required to understand legal principles and the context in which legal issues arise.[49] More specifically, the curriculum requires law schools to equip students with knowledge and understanding of fundamental legal doctrines, fundamental areas of substantive law, sources and development of the law, and concepts of legal theory.[50]

Other areas the Standard mentions specifically include providing students with a deep understanding of the broader social, political, historical, and cultural contexts in which legal issues arise, international and comparative perspectives on Australian law, the principles of ethical conduct, and the role and responsibility of lawyers, including pro bono obligations and the inclusion of Aboriginal and Torres Strait Islander perspectives on and intersections with the law.[51] The Standards also place a strong emphasis on the intellectual and practical skills needed for research, analysis, problem-solving, effective communication, and an awareness of ethical responsibility.[52]

The above curriculum requirements reflect a diverse and expansive range of topics which reflect not only the skills required for the purpose of admission to practise, but also the diversity of motivations for studying law.[53] Not all students completing a law degree wish to pursue legal practice, as such law schools must cater to this as well as the diversity of their students.

Importantly, law schools are required to foster Aboriginal and Torres Strait Islander cultural competencies and promote the inclusion of Indigenous perspectives in legal education.[54] This was a new addition to the curriculum in 2020. When considering law as a discipline, it is important that law students receive a well-rounded

---

[45] *Higher Education Standards Framework (Threshold Standards)* (n 26) 3.1.3.

[46] Council of Australian Law Deans (n 15?) 15.

[47] Ibid 2.3.

[48] Ibid 2.3.1.

[49] Ibid 2.3.1–2.3.2.

[50] Ibid 2.3.3(a).

[51] Ibid.

[52] Ibid 2.3.3(b)-(d).

[53] Ibid 17.

[54] Ibid 17–18.

education informed by many perspectives and the broader contexts in which legal issues arise.[55]

2.4.2 *The Priestley 11*

In addition to the above, the Australian Law School Standards prescribes that the law school curriculum must cover all topics required for the purposes of admission to legal practice in Australia including eleven prescribed areas of knowledge known as the Priestley 11.[56] The educational requirements for admission to practise are uniform across all States and Territories,[57] with applicants required to complete an accredited full-time (or equivalent) law degree. The degree also must cover the Priestly 11, which is a set of eleven law subjects including:

- Criminal Law and Procedure;
- Tort Law;
- Contract Law;
- Property Law;
- Equity;
- Company Law;
- Administrative Law;
- Federal and State Constitutional Law;
- Civil Dispute Resolution;
- Evidence; and
- Ethics and Professional Responsibility.[58]

These subjects were chosen by the Law Admissions Consultative Committee in 1992 as the minimum academic study requirements for legal practice.[59] Universities and institutions offering LLB and JD programs are required to cover all aspects of the Priestley 11 for accreditation purposes.

(a) *Criminal Law and Procedure*

When teaching criminal law, law schools must cover a series of topics including the basics of criminal law, the definition of crime, the elements of crime, and the

---

[55] Kift, Israel and Field (n 33) 8.

[56] Council of Australian Law Deans (n 15) Standard 2.3.1.

[57] See *Court Procedure Rules 2006* (ACT) r 3605; *Legal Profession Admission Rules 2015* (NSW), (Vic), (WA) r 5: *Legal Profession Admission Rules 2007* (NT) r 4: *Court (Admission) Rules 2004* (Qld) r 6; *Rules of the Legal Practitioners Education and Admission Council 2018* (SA) r 7: *Legal Profession (Board of Legal Education) Rules 2021* (Tas) r 4.

[58] See *Court Procedure Rules 2006* (ACT) r 3605; *Legal Profession Admission Rules 2015* (NSW), (Vic), (WA), sch 1; *Legal Profession Admission Rules 2007* (NT) sch 3; *Court (Admission) Rules 2004* (Qld) r 9AA(1)(a); *Rules of the Legal Practitioners Education and Admission Council 2018* (SA) app A; *Legal Profession (Board of Legal Education) Rules 2021* (Tas) sch 1.

[59] Ebejer (2022, 2–6).

aim of criminal law and its general doctrines.[60] Numerous elements of criminal procedure must be covered. This consists of topics such as classification of offences, processes to compel appearance, bail, preliminary examination, and trial of indictable offences.[61] Students must also sufficiently understand a number of offences, for example non-fatal offences against the person, homicide, offences against property, and their respective defences.[62] Finally, law schools have the flexibility to choose from the following topics: attempts, participation in crime, drunkenness, mistake, and strict responsibility.[63]

Should law schools wish to deviate from the above requirement, they must satisfy the guideline for criminal law and procedure. This guideline suggests that topics should provide students with a breadth of knowledge on the general doctrines of criminal law and examine property offences and offences against the person, various defences, and the elements of criminal procedure.[64]

(b) *Torts*

The prescribed areas of knowledge require the following topics to be taught when teaching the law of torts. The topics include negligence (and its defences), a representative range of torts and their respective defences, concurrent liability, compensation schemes, and damages.[65]

Should law schools wish to depart from the above list of topics, the guidelines require that lecturers cover the following topics in sufficient depth and breath. These topics include the tort of negligence as well as a range of other torts which consideration given to defences and damages as well as methods for compensation for accidental injury.[66] Some examples of other torts that may be covered include concurrent liability, defamation, economic torts, nuisance, breach of statutory duties, and compensation schemes.[67]

(c) *Contract Law*

When studying contract law, law students are required to have an understanding of contract formation (including the components of capacity, formalities, privity, and consideration), construction of contracts and their content, vitiating factors, discharge, remedies for breach of contract, and assignment.[68]

Due to the breadth and detail of contract law topics, some variation is expected in the guidelines.[69] However, at a minimum, law schools are required to ensure

---

[60] *Legal Profession Admission Rules 2015* (NSW), (Vic), (WA) sch 1, s3 (a)–(g).

[61] Ibid s3(i).

[62] Ibid s3(d)-(f).

[63] Ibid s3(h).

[64] Ibid s3.

[65] Ibid s4(a)–(e).

[66] Ibid s4.

[67] Ibid.

[68] Ibid s5(a)–(f).

[69] Ibid s5.

that students have a broad understanding of the theory of contracts, as well as acquiring knowledge of the formal requirements for concluding contracts, capacity, the content and interpretation of contracts, their performance and discharge, and available remedies for breach of contract.[70]

(d) *Property Law*

In order to meet the requirements of the prescribed areas of knowledge, when designing property law units law schools must cover a range of topics from the foundational principles of property law to the creation and enforceability of proprietary interests.[71] These topics must include the possession, seisin, title, the nature and type of proprietary interests, remedies in equity and law, registration under statute, acquisition and disposal of proprietary interests, concurrent ownership, proprietary interests in land owned by another third party, and mortgages.[72]

Should law schools wish to structure their unit differently to the above requirements, the guidelines prescribe that, at a minimum, topics should include the nature and type of proprietary interest in chattels and land, their creation and enforceability in equity and at law.[73] Statutory schemes for registration under general law and Torrens land must also be covered.[74] Law schools may also cover a variety of topics including fixtures, concurrent interests in property, and further in-depth study into matters including the sale of land, leases, mortgages, easements, and restrictive covenants, to name a few.[75]

(e) *Equity*

In the study of equity and equitable doctrines, law schools must cover a range of topics from the nature of equity to the elements of trust law.[76] It is required that half of the course be devoted to equity and the other half to trusts.[77] When teaching the law of equity, law schools should provide comprehensive coverage of the nature of equity, equitable rights, titles and interests, equitable assignments, estoppel, fiduciary obligations, unconscionable transactions, and equitable remedies.[78] In addition to the aforementioned topics, law schools must also sufficiently cover topics of trust law, with reference to various types of trusts, the creation of trusts, and variation of trusts.[79] Particularly, the duties, rights and powers of trustees, breach of trust, remedies for breach of trust, and the rights of beneficiaries.[80]

---

[70] Ibid.

[71] Ibid s6(a)–(j).

[72] Ibid.

[73] Ibid s6.

[74] Ibid.

[75] Ibid.

[76] Ibid s7(1)–(2).

[77] Ibid.

[78] Ibid s7(1)(a)–(g).

[79] Ibid s7(2).

[80] Ibid.

If law schools wish to depart from the above requirements, the guidelines prescribe that such breach and depth must be given to the elements of trust law and equitable doctrines.[81] With respect to trusts, law schools must ensure they cover topics such as the various kinds of trusts, rights, powers and duties of trustees, and the consequences of breach of trust.[82] When covering equitable doctrines, law schools may cover fiduciary obligations, equitable assignments, unconscionability and confidential information, as well as the remedies of specific performance, injunctions, declaration, and damages in equity.[83] The guidelines also prescribe that half of the course is to be devoted to trusts and the other half to equitable doctrines.[84]

(f) *Company Law*

The guidelines for the prescribed area of knowledge stipulate that law schools must, in the studies of company and corporations law, analyse the incorporation of companies as well as its effects of incorporation, the management and control of the company, methods of financing (including by the issue of shares and by debt), and the processes of winding up a corporation.[85]

Alternatively, law schools can choose to teach the following curriculum of topics which includes topics such as the corporate personality, the process of incorporation, the corporate personality, company contracts, the administration of companies, the management of the business of companies, directors' and officers' duties and liabilities, share capital and membership, members' remedies, company credit and security arrangement, and the winding up of corporations.[86]

(g) *Administrative Law*

During the study of administrative law, law schools must ensure that they cover topics ranging from the theory of administrative law to specifics of the Commonwealth and State avenues for judicial review.[87] Other topics that are required to be taught include the organisation and structure of the administration, common law and statutory avenues for judicial review, grounds for judicial review, statutory review, the Administrative Appeals Tribunal (known as the "AAT"), which has been replaced by the Administrative Review Tribunal on 14 October 2024, crown immunity, remedies, and freedom of information.[88]

With regard to administrative law, the guidelines advise that should law schools wish to pursue other topics, that the depth and breadth of topics should not only

[81] Ibid s7.

[82] Ibid.

[83] Ibid.

[84] Ibid.

[85] Ibid s8.

[86] Ibid s8(a)–(j).

[87] Ibid s9(a)–(i).

[88] Ibid; https://www.art.gov.au/about-us/accountability-and-reporting/administrative-appeals-tribunal.

embrace traditional common law remedies for judicial review, but also cover a wide range statutory regimes at both a State and Commonwealth level.[89]

(h) *Federal and State Constitutional Law*

Constitutional law units are required to address a number of topics.[90] These topics include State constitutions and their constitutional systems, the *Commonwealth Constitution* and its constitutional system, the operation of different institutions of government known as the legislature, executive and judiciary, the relationship between the different institutions, the concept of the separation of powers, and the relationship between the different levels of government.[91]

The guidelines advise that where law schools stray from the above required topics, students are required to have a depth of knowledge on major principles of the *Commonwealth Constitution*, and their relevant State or Territory Constitution, including the relationship between their respective State or Territories laws and Federal/Commonwealth laws.[92] Additionally, law schools must ensure students have a general understanding of the scope of the *Commonwealth Constitution* and their State or Territory Constitution.[93] The guidelines do, however, specify that some topics, especially in the Commonwealth sphere, require further depth of study due to the treatment of specific heads of power.[94]

(i) *Civil Dispute Resolution*

The Priestley 11 guidelines require that law schools cover a wide range of civil procedure and dispute resolution topics. The topics should cover the process of dispute resolution from the determination of jurisdiction, whether it be through court adjudication under an adversarial system or alternative dispute resolution methods, to the commencing of proceedings through to the handing down of a judgment, subsequent appeals, and enforcement.[95] Additionally, law schools must cover the costs of litigation and the use of costs to control litigation, the joinder of claims and parties to avoid the multiplicity of proceedings, pleadings and other defining questions for trial, the evidential processes relating to evidence including discovery, interrogatories, and subpoenas, disposition without trial, the compromise of litigation, extra-judicial determination of issues arising in the course of litigation, and the obligations of practitioners and parties when resolving disputes.[96]

Alternatively, the guidelines recommend that if law schools wish to cover alternative topics they should examine the fundamental rules and aspects of civil procedure

---

89 Ibid s9.

90 Ibid s10.

91 Ibid s10(a)–(e).

92 Ibid s10.

93 Ibid.

94 Ibid.

95 Ibid s11(a)–(m).

96 Ibid.

and alternative dispute resolution in their State or Territory.[97] This should encompass the study of jurisdiction, the commencement of legal proceedings and service of documents, the formulation of pleadings, and the enforcement of judgements.[98] Law students should have an understanding of the foundational elements and mechanisms that govern civil dispute resolution.

(j) *Evidence*

When teaching evidence law, law schools must have regard for introducing the relevant sources of evidence law and procedure, the different forms of evidence, evidentiary rules and principles, lawyer-client privilege, judicial warnings, comment, and directions, and exclusions and limitations on evidence (both mandatory and discretionary).[99]

Some areas of evidence law require further depth and analysis. These areas are the introductory principles of evidence, the forms of evidence and evidentiary principles and rules. With regard to the introductory principles of evidence, this also refers to the principles underpinning accusatorial justice, fair trials, proof and adversarialism, and issues of evidence that must be addressed before trial such as disclosure, notices, and requests.[100] During the study of the forms of evidence, there should be a particular focus on witnesses, including the competence and compellability of witnesses, the examination of witnesses, vulnerable witnesses, the accused as a witness, and the privilege against self-incrimination.[101] The curriculum should also include documentary evidence, proof of contents, and real evidence.[102] Finally, during the study of the rules and principles of evidence, a particular focus should be given to the relevance of evidence, original evidence, hearsay evidence, opinion evidence, admissions of guilt, confessions, coincident evidence, credibility evidence, and character evidence.[103]

(k) *Ethics and Professional Responsibility*

The educational requirements for professional responsibility and ethics include a practitioner's professional and personal conduct, in relation to their duties to the law, the courts, to their clients (including duties relating to the holding of money in trust), and to fellow practitioners.[104]

At a minimum, the topics covered should, as per the guidelines, sufficiently cover areas such as the pertinent rules concerning a practitioner's paramount duty to the law and the Courts, as well as their duty to clients and fellow practitioners, and a basic overview of the principles relating to the holding of money on trust.[105]

---

[97] Ibid s11.

[98] Ibid.

[99] Ibid s12(a)–(f).

[100] Ibid s12(a)(i)–(iii).

[101] Ibid s12(b)(i)–(iii).

[102] Ibid.

[103] Ibid s12(c)(i)–(vii).

[104] Ibid s13(a)–(d).

[105] Ibid s13.

2.4.3 *TLOs—Bachelor of Laws*

The Threshold Learning Outcomes, otherwise referred to as TLOs, were developed in line with the Australian Qualifications Framework. For the Bachelor of Laws, there are six TLOs which are consistent with the academic requirements for admission to practise.[106] As per the AQF, a graduate from a Bachelor of Laws should develop a "set of knowledge, skills, and the application of the knowledge and skills a person has acquired and is able to demonstrate as a result of learning".[107]

(a) *TLO 1: Knowledge*

Graduates of a Bachelor of Laws demonstrate a sufficient understanding of the fundamentals of legal knowledge and the Australian legal system.[108] This body of knowledge includes the underlying concepts and principles of the Australian legal system, the broader contexts where legal issues may arise, the values and principles of justice, and the role of layers in ethical legal practice.[109]

(b) *TLO 2: Ethics and Professional Responsibility*

Bachelor of Laws graduates, upon completion of their degree, should have an understanding of legal professional responsibility. This includes an understanding of ethical decision-making and the differing approaches to ethical decision-making, the ability to recognise ethical issues that may arise in a professional context, how to respond and reflect upon ethical issues, and the professional responsibility of laws to promote justice and service to the community.[110] Graduates should also demonstrate their developing ability to exercise professional judgement.[111]

(c) *TLO 3: Thinking Skills*

Upon graduating from a Bachelor of Laws graduates will be able to effectively identify and articulate legal issues, apply legal reasoning to legal issues, research appropriate responses to legal issues, engage in critical analysis, make reasoned judgements when considering alternative perspectives, and think creatively when approaching legal issues and responding appropriately to legal issues.[112]

(d) *TLO 4: Research Skills*

Following the completion of a Bachelor of Laws, graduates must be able to demonstrate both intellectual and practical skills needed to effectively conduct research.[113]

---

[106] Kift (n 33) 1.

[107] Australian Qualifications Framework (n 27 or n 32?) 85.

[108] Kift (n 33) 10.

[109] Ibid.

[110] Ibid.

[111] Ibid.

[112] Ibid.

[113] Ibid.

This includes the skills required to identify, research, evaluate, and synthesise relevant factual, legal, and policy issues.[114]

(e) *TLO 5: Communication and Collaboration*

Graduates are required to develop effective collaboration and communication skills throughout their Bachelor of Laws.[115] This means that graduates will be able to communicate to both legal and non-legal audiences in a way that is effective, appropriate, and persuasive, as well as collaborate effectively in groups.[116]

(f) *TLO 6: Self-Management*

At the time of graduation, Bachelor of Laws graduates should be able to learn and work independently and reflect on their own capabilities and performance.[117] This includes assessing and making use of feedback as appropriate to support both personal and professional development.[118]

2.4.4 TLOs—Juris Doctor

The TLOs prescribed for the Juris Doctor differ slightly than those of the Bachelor of Laws; however, to the extent that they overlap, the LLB TLOs and JD TLOs should be interpreted consistently.[119] Much like the Bachelor of Laws, there are 6 TLOs for the Juris Doctor and they are as follows.[120]

(a) *TLO 1: Knowledge*

Graduates of the Juris Doctor should be able to demonstrate an advanced understanding of complex areas of legal knowledge and the Australian legal system.[121] This body of knowledge includes the underlying concepts and principles of the Australian legal system, the broader contexts where legal issues may arise, the values and principles of justice, and the role of layers in ethical legal practice.[122] Additionally, graduates should be able to identify and understand contemporary developments in law and professional practice.[123]

---

[114] Ibid.

[115] Ibid.

[116] Ibid.

[117] Ibid.

[118] Ibid.

[119] Council of Australian Law Deans, *Juris Doctor Threshold Learning Outcomes* (March 2012) 2.

[120] Ibid 3.

[121] Ibid.

[122] Ibid.

[123] Ibid.

(b) *TLO 2: Ethics and Professional Responsibility*

Students graduating from the Juris Doctor will be able to demonstrate an advanced understanding and approach to ethical decision-making.[124] These skills should allow Juris Doctor graduates to demonstrate an ability to exercise professional judgement, recognise and reflect upon ethical issues that may arise in a professional context, to respond to ethical issues that may arise, and recognise and reflect upon the professional responsibility of legal professionals to promote justice and service the community.[125]

(c) *TLO 3: Thinking Skills*

Upon graduating from a Juris Doctor graduates must demonstrate an ability to effectively identify and articulate legal issues, apply legal reasoning to legal issues, research and generate appropriate jurisprudential and practical responses to legal issues, engage in critical analysis, make reasoned choices and judgements when considering alternative perspectives, and show sophisticated cognitive and creative reasoning skills when approaching legal issues and generating appropriate responses.[126]

(d) *TLO 4: Research Skills*

Graduates of a Juris Doctor program will demonstrate the practical and intellectual skills required to justify and interpret theoretical propositions, legal methodologies, conclusions, and professional decisions.[127] Graduates will also be able to identify, research, evaluate, and synthesise relevant factual, legal, and policy issues.[128]

(e) *TLO 5: Communication and Collaboration*

Graduates are required to develop effective collaboration and communication skills throughout their Juris Doctor.[129] This means that graduates will be able to communicate to both legal and non-legal audiences in a way that is effective, appropriate, and persuasive, as well as collaborate effectively in groups.[130]

(f) *TLO 6: Self-Management*

Graduates will be required to demonstrate a high level of autonomy, accountability, and professionalism upon graduating from their Juris Doctor program.[131] This requires graduates to independently reflect on their own capabilities and performance, while assessing and making use of feedback as appropriate to support both personal and professional developments.[132]

---

[124] Ibid 3–4.

[125] Ibid.

[126] Ibid 4.

[127] Ibid.

[128] Ibid.

[129] Ibid.

[130] Ibid.

[131] Ibid.

[132] Ibid.

2.5 Clinical Legal Education

Clinical Legal Education ('CLE') refers to a method or model of teaching and learning about the law that involves students acting for clients in the handling of real legal matters.[133] A significant number of law schools offer CLE opportunities to their students through law clinics.[134] Whether it takes the form of an in-house clinic, clinics run by a law school, or internships, CLE programs allow for students to participate in supervised legal practice.[135]

CLE programs are distinguished from Practical Legal Training programs or other legal work, as there is a dimension of community service and social justice.[136] According to Evans et al., clinical programs operated by law schools promote a focus on community service, professional ethical responsibility, and engagement in professional activities.[137] This occurs as there is greater responsibility placed on students as they are working on unpredictable legal issues generated by crisis circumstances.[138] As such, it becomes clear that the experiential framework of clinical legal education has more of a focus on professional development and social justice than other law placements or work-integrated leaning experiences.

CLE programs allow for students to have a substantial contribution to legal matters while being supervised by practising lawyers. For example, law students can get involved in a number of different kinds of supervised work, including:

- analysing client problems and giving legal advice;
- meeting with clients and witnesses to gather information;
- reviewing and preparing legal documents, such as contracts, wills, or legal briefs;
- negotiating with opposing parties or their lawyers;
- representing clients in administrative hearings, in court or before other tribunals in which the students have been granted a case-specific right of audience or the right to appear on behalf of a client;
- fact investigation;
- legal research for policy or law reform; and
- developing materials for community legal education and presenting a legal seminar.[139]

Law students involved in law clinics will work closely with their supervising practising lawyer as well as an academic educator.[140] Where the law clinic is offered in a for credit subject capacity, the academic education will coordinate the experience, facilitate alignment to the curriculum, and ensure academic learning objectives are

133 Evans et al. (n 16), 40.

134 Fletcher (2019, 3).

135 McNamara (2020, 70).

136 Evans et al. (n 16) 12.

137 Ibid.

138 Ibid 13.

139 McNamara (n 149) 70.

140 Fletcher (n 148) 3.

met.[141] Students may also be required to submit assessments such as reflections to be assessed by the academic educator.[142] Law clinics have been endorsed by the CALD and are reflected within the Australian Law School Standards.

The key benefit of CLE is that students become responsible for a client's file or a specific legal task, which allows for deeper learning.[143] Students are often participating as a lawyer, rather than an observer or assistant which creates a more meaningful learning experience.[144] Experience-based learning, like a CLE program, generates opportunities and challenges for law students by broadening and deepening their learning experience.[145] Sustained exposure to legal work in clinical programs provides law students with an enriching experience that fosters ethical and reflective practice, as well as exposing them to professional engagement activities.[146]

2.6 Work Integrated Learning

Work Integrated Learning ('WIL') refers to a law school program that requires law students as a formal part of their studies to engage with workplace and communities.[147] WIL is an approach to learning that provides students with a rich and contextualised learning experience by allowing students to engage in their learning.[148] By requiring students to engage in legal services through a workplace, law schools are encouraging their students to gain new knowledge and capabilities, as well as master skills that are considered essential for future legal practice.[149] WIL, much like other practical learning programs, provides law students with opportunities to challenge their impressions from law school of what practice is actually like and provides them with experience in a legal workplace.[150]

In the Bradley Review of Australian Higher Education, the federal government acknowledged that universities must prepare their graduates for the world of work.[151] WIL, as an educational approach, is used by law schools in response to this sentiment. It is not the only method of addressing these concerns, with some law schools utilising clinical legal education. Pre-admission supervised practice, like in a WIL program

[141] Ibid.

[142] Ibid.

[143] Evans et al. (n 16) 42.

[144] Ibid 42.

[145] Ibid 12.

[146] Ibid.

[147] Ibid 25.

[148] Ibid.

[149] Ibid.

[150] Ibid 43.

[151] Denise Bradley et al., 'Review of Australian Higher Education (Final Report, Department of Education, Employment and Workplace Relations, December 2008) <https://apo.org.au/sites/default/files/resource-files/2008-12/apo-nid15776.pdf>.

or practical legal training, can enhance law graduates' skills in order for graduates to transition seamlessly between novice lawyers to autonomous legal practitioners.[152]

While WIL is similar to CLE, clinical legal education is distinct in many aspects.[153] Both approaches expose law students to the practical aspects of legal workplaces and provide students with an opportunity to reinforce knowledge of legal theory.[154] At the most basic level, WIL programs are less structured than CLE and have a limited focus on linking experience to academic components of law degrees.[155] Additionally, CLE is distinct as its focus is primarily on social justice concerns, equity, and access to justice, while WIL focuses on law students engaging in a workplace while completing their studies.[156] The approach of a WIL program is more on vocational skills and the "how to" of practising law, while a CLE program focuses more on strengthening the academic phase of legal education through expose to real clients.[157]

2.7 Extracurricular Activities

Learning is not limited to the classroom. As such law students are encouraged to engage in opportunities to participate in extracurricular activities to learning practical and useful skills.[158] Extracurricular activities offer law students an opportunity to learn, practise, and demonstrate their legal skills.[159] These opportunities can vary from engaging with law students' societies, to competitions and mooting.

2.7.1 Law Societies

Law societies are often student-run groups at universities aimed at assisting law students with their studies and setting them up for success as future legal professionals. Law students' societies plan and execute various events throughout the school year and have become a key part of the law school experience.[160] Law societies recognise that participation and involvement outside of the classroom can broaden a law student's educational experience in a way that is both intellectually stimulating and socially rewarding. This is done through providing experiences to build both student

[152] McNamara (n 149) 31.
[153] Evans et al. (n 16) 43.
[154] Ibid 43.
[155] Ibid 25–26.
[156] Ibid 25.
[157] Evans et al. (2012, 4–5).
[158] Raz, Loh and Fevereux (n 25) 40.
[159] Ibid.
[160] Ibid 45.

and professional networks.[161] Student law societies also offer information sessions, competitions, and social events. Law students are not limited to being involved with their university's law school society. Students can become involved with the national Australian Law Students' Association.[162] The Australian Law Students' Association provides unique opportunities to connect with interstate law students.[163]

Additional to law student societies, students have the opportunity to receive provisional or student membership to professional law societies such as the Law Society of New South Wales or the Legal Institute of Victoria.[164] Professional law societies, like the Law Society of New South Wales, provide law students with resources as to volunteer opportunities, clerkship and graduate program recruitment, and even mentoring.[165]

2.7.2 *Volunteering and Pro Bono*

Getting involved in volunteering and pro bono work provides law students with an interesting opportunity to work directly with clients while completing their studies.[166] Pro bono comes from a Latin phrase meaning "for the public good", and in the context of legal services refers to the provision of legal services for a significantly reduced fee or for free with no expectation of commercial return.[167] As a law student, pro bono work refers to providing legal services as a volunteer (often without reimbursement or academic credit) to assist disadvantaged communities by increasing their access to justice.[168] Some law schools have clinical legal education programs, community legal centres or volunteer law clinics, which provide their students with access to pro bono or volunteer work and receive academic credit.[169]

Pro bono work, whether it is through a law clinic or community legal service, gives law students the opportunity to work directly with clients and engage in practical legal work.[170] Engaging in volunteer legal work, students are exposed to legal work which may lead to a passion in social justice issues but also add meaning to their

[161] Ibid.

[162] See 'Welcome to ALSA', *Australian Law Students' Association* (Web Page, 2022) <https://alsa.asn.au/>.

[163] Raz, Loh and Fevereux (n 25) 45.

[164] See 'Law Students', *The Law Society of New South Wales* (Web Page, 2023) <https://www.lawsociety.com.au/Legal-Communities/Law-Students>; 'Membership Categories: Student Membership' *Law Institute of Victoria* (Web Page, 2023) <https://www.liv.asn.au/Web/Content/Membership/Membership/Member_Category/Student.aspx>.

[165] See 'Law Students' (n 178).

[166] Raz, Loh and Fevereux (n 25) 44–5.

[167] See 'Definition of Pro Bono' *Australian Pro Bono Centre* (Web Page, 2023) <https://www.probonocentre.org.au/information-on-pro-bono/definition/>.

[168] Raz, Loh and Fevereux (n 25) 45.

[169] Ibid.

[170] Ibid.

career choice.[171] According to the Australian Pro Bono Centre, the participation of law students in community legal services not only increases access to justice by increasing the capacity of community legal organisations to deliver free legal services, but also inculcates the students involved with a personal commitment to social justice and practical legal environment skills.[172]

2.7.3 Competitions

Law competitions are a great extracurricular activity for law students to get involved with, as it allows them to demonstrate their legal research and communication skills.[173] There are several different kinds of legal competitions, each usually modelled from scenarios and challenges a legal professional may face.[174] These include client interviewing, negotiation, witness examination, paper presentations, and mooting.[175]

(a) *Client Interviewing*

Client interviewing usually involves a team of two students and a "client" to simulate the first meeting between lawyer and client.[176] The students are required to gather as much information from their potential client and at the conclusion of the "appointment" should be able to advise their client of next steps.[177] This competition requires law students to think quickly and critically in order to identify gaps in the client's narrative and respond with pointed questions in order to fully ascertain the relevant facts.[178] This exposes law students to the realty of the solicitor-client relationship.

(b) *Negotiation*

Negotiation competitions often require a pair of students to engage with an opposing party on behalf of their clients in order to reach some form of an agreement.[179] The competition scenario can either be based on a transactional matter or settlement negotiation in a dispute.[180] The two opposing teams will receive an

---

171 Ibid.

172 'Pro Bono Partnership Models: A Practical Guide to What Works – Chapter 18: Law Students', *Australian Pro Bono Centre* (Web Page, December 2022) <https://www.probonocentre.org.au/whatworks/part-3/chap-18/>.

173 Raz, Loh and Fevereux (n 25) 46.

174 Ibid.

175 Ibid.

176 Ibid 47.

177 Ibid.

178 Ibid.

179 Ibid.

180 Ibid.

identical copy of the facts of the scenario, but also a unique set of confidential facts including instructions from the client.[181] Depending on the competition, the negotiation will go for 50 min with an additional 10 min reflection for both teams.[182]

(c) *Witness Examination*

Competitions involving witness examination will often follow the same structure as that of a real trial. The competition aims to build trial advocacy skills by having one team represent the plaintiff and the other the defendant seeking to establish their client's case.[183]

(d) *Paper Presentations*

In a paper presentation competition, students will conduct a 15-min presentation on an academic article of their writing.[184] The length and topic of the article will vary depending on the competition, but often students will write a piece ranging from 2500 to 5000 words and will be required to answer questions from the judges.[185]

(e) *Mooting*

Mock trials, often referred to as moots, are one of the most common law student competitions.[186] A moot, by definition, is a mock tribunal, court, or arbitral hearing where two student teams will present written and oral submissions before an arbitrator, judge, or tribunal member.[187] Mooting competitions will simulate a court proceeding where students are required to apply their theoretical knowledge of the law while having an opportunity to practise written and oral advocacy skills.

2.8 Clerkships/Internships

Internships and clerkships are the best way law students can gain experience in the legal profession while studying.[188] Clerkships and internships can provide law students with insight into the realities of the legal profession by exposing them to a real law firm environment and clients.[189] Internship programs will vary by provider and, however, can provide law students with a valuable educational experience.[190] Legal internships can be found in law firms, government agencies, non-for-profit

[181] Ibid.

[182] Ibid.

[183] Ibid 48.

[184] Ibid.

[185] Ibid.

[186] Ibid 49.

[187] Cassimatis and Billings (2016) [1.20].

[188] Raz, Loh and Fevereux (n 25) 55.

[189] Ibid.

[190] Ibid 55.

organisations, and even internationally.[191] The benefits for law students completing an internship or clerkship are that they provide access to graduate programs while also providing training in research, the application of the law and how to work with clients.[192]

The Summer clerkship programs are one of the most important career-development opportunities for Australian law students. Students usually apply for the clerkship during the winter break in their penultimate year (July and August) and, if selected, do the clerkship in the upcoming summer. Every law firm's program operates differently with regard to the number of students offered the placement and priority offers for graduate positions; however, these processes are often governed by the State's relevant law society. The Law Society of New South Wales and the Legal Institute of Victoria release clerkship program guidelines each year to provide a framework for clerkship (and graduate) recruitment processes to ensure fairness and consistency among signatories.[193] Students are required to fill in the application forms for each opportunity and may be invited to interviews, career events, and online tests, during the selection process.

Once selected, students will usually be required to complete a full-time 4-week program run by law firms over university break periods.[194] These programs are often the most direct pathway to graduate programs in the major law firms.[195]

In addition to the local clerkship opportunities, students may also conduct clerkship overseas. The Hong Kong clerkships, for example, are considered as attractive career opportunities for Australian students who actively pursue an international career path.[196]

2.9 Graduation

In order to be eligible to graduate, law students must:

(a) Satisfy all academic and course requirements of their degree. This includes any placements, practical components, and internships;

---

[191] Ibid.

[192] Ibid 167.

[193] 'Clerkship Recruitment Program', *The Law Society of New South Wales* (Web Page) <https://www.lawsociety.com.au/Legal-Communities/Law-Students/Clerkship-Recruitment-Program>; Law Institute of Victoria (2024), <https://www.liv.asn.au/download.aspx?DocumentVersionKey=31f602a6-4dae-406b-80b7-2c90c530f938>.

[194] Ibid 167. Can't use ibid here as previous fn has more than one citation. LIV document only goes to page 12.

[195] Ibid 56. Can't use ibid here as previous fn has more than one citation.

[196] 'Admission in Hong Kong', *Melbourne China Law Society* (Web Page) <https://themcls.org/international-opportunities/hongkong-2/#:~:text=Hong%20Kong%20Clerkships&text=Clerkship%20is%20essentially%20a%20legal,and%20culture%20at%20the%20firm>.

(b) Complete all assessments and achieve the number of credit points required by their degree; and
(c) Pay all outstanding fees to their university, including subject fees and library fines.[197]

[197] Raz, Loh and Fevereux (n 25) 66.

Chapter 3
Legal Profession in Australia

This chapter provides a comprehensive overview of the legal profession in Australia. It introduces the main features of the Australian legal profession from the following perspectives. Section 1 provides an overview of the legal profession in Australia. Section 2 illustrates the process of being admitted as the crucial step of entering the legal profession. Section 3 further discusses the common roles in the profession, solicitors and barristers, and the rules and guidelines governing their practice. Section 4 focuses on the foreign lawyer's rights and limits to practise in Australia. Section 5 examines the roles, practices, and pathways for traditional career choices in the legal profession, including private practice, academia, judges and judicial officers, government, as well as in-house or corporate counsels. Section 6 turns to non-traditional career options and paths in the legal profession. Section 7 examines the ethical obligations of practising lawyers, taking solicitors as an example.

3.1 An Overview of the Australian Legal Profession

The legal profession in Australia is comprised of a diverse array of legal practitioners from solicitors to barristers, judges to legal academics, and paralegals to legal executives. According to the Australian Census Data, in 2021 there were 122,958 people employed in legal services, with 69,704 of those people being solicitors, 13,923 judges and judicial professionals, and 8,848 barristers.[1]

The profession, much like the legal education landscape, has seen significant growth over the past decade.[2] In 2022, there were over 90,000 solicitors practising nationally. This is a 57% increase in the number of practising solicitors over the

[1] Australian Bureau of Statistics, *Census of Population and Housing: Income and Work Data Summary 2021* (12 October 2022) Table 11 Occupation.

[2] Urbis, *2022 National Profile of Solicitors* (Report No 6, 23 April 2023) 7.

S. Zhang et al., *Technology, Legal Education and Legal Profession in China and Australia*, International and Comparative Law in the Asia Pacific,
https://doi.org/10.1007/978-981-96-1639-8_3

previous 10 years, with only 32,752 solicitors in 2011.[3] Similar growth is also seen in the number of barristers, with only 7800 practising barristers in 2011, and almost 9000 currently as noted above.[4]

The legal landscape in Australia is multifaceted and dynamic as it is made up of so much more than just practising solicitors, barristers, and judges. By examining the roles of different legal professionals, we gain a deeper understanding of the many career paths available for aspiring legal professionals.

In order to be admitted as a lawyer in Australia, candidates must be admitted to the Supreme Court of their State or Territory. Further, in order to practise law, they should obtain a practising certificate from the law society (as solicitors) or bar association (as barristers) of their State or Territory.[5]

In Australia, the difference between solicitor and barrister is maintained, but the detailed rules in different States and Territories are different. Solicitors need to be registered with the law societies of a State or Territory. Barristers needs to be registered with the bar associations of a State or Territory. The latter specialises in representing clients in court. In some States and Territories, practising lawyers can practise as both solicitors and barristers. However, in Victoria, a practitioner can only choose one.

The legal profession is governed by the State and Territory legislation dealing with the legal profession. To increase the consistency among different jurisdictions in Australia, a uniform Act had been drafted.[6] New South Wales, Victoria and Western Australia adopted the *Legal Profession Uniform Law* by their own *Legal Profession Uniform Law Application Act* (2014 in NSW and Victoria; 2022 in Western Australia). Other States and Territories still maintain their own legislation: *Legal Profession Act 1981* (SA), *Legal Profession Act 2006* (ACT), *Legal Profession Act 2006* (NT), *Legal Profession Act 2007* (Tas), and *Legal Profession Act 2007* (Queensland).

[3] Ibid.

[4] See 'Barristers' Commonwealth Government Jobs and Skills, Labour Market Insights' (Web Page, 10 September 2021) <https://labourmarketinsights.gov.au/occupation-profile/barristers?occupationCode=2711#:~:text=The%20median%20age%20of%20Barristers,all%20jobs%20average%20of%2048%25>.

[5] Raz, Loh and Fevereux (n 25) 83.

[6] *Legal Profession Uniform Law 2014*.

3.2 Admission

3.2.1 Admission Requirements

The admission process for law graduates is regulated independently by each State and Territory, and the applicant should apply for admission within the State or Territory they intend to practise law in.[7] Generally, those seeking admission must meet a number of educational, character-based, and training requirements. These prerequisites include their age (18 years old and over), an approved academic qualification, approved practical legal training (or supervised legal training in some States), and suitability of character.[8]

Some States prescribe specific additional requirements for admission. For example, under rrs 12 and 12A of the *Supreme Court (Admission) Rules 2004* in Queensland, all applicants must publish a notice of intention to apply to practise in the *Queensland Law Reporter*.[9]

The admission authority in each jurisdiction is as follows:

State/territory	Admission authority	Court
ACT	Legal Practitioners Admission Board	Supreme Court of the Australian Capital Territory
NSW	Legal Profession Admission Board	Supreme Court of New South Wales
VIC	Victorian Legal Services Board	Supreme Court of Victoria
QLD	Queensland Legal Practitioners Admissions Board	Supreme Court of Queensland
NT	Legal Practitioners Admission Board	Supreme Court of Northern Territory
SA	Legal Practitioners Education and Admission Council	Supreme Court of South Australia
WA	Legal Practice Board	Supreme Court of Western Australia
TAS	Board of Legal Education	Supreme Court of Tasmania

(a) *Educational Requirements*

There is complete uniformity in Australia regarding the academic requirements for admission to the legal profession as a solicitor. When applying to practise, applicants must, according to the *Uniform Legal Profession Rules* (Vic), (NSW), and (WA),

[7] See *Court Procedure Rules 2006* (ACT); *Legal Profession Admission Rules 2015* (NSW), (Vic), (WA): *Legal Profession Admission Rules 2007* (NT): *Supreme Court (Admission) Rules 2004* (Qld); *Rules of the Legal Practitioners Education and Admission Council 2018* (SA); *Supreme Court Civil Rules 2006* (SA); *Supreme Court Civil Supplementary Rules 2014* (SA); *Legal Profession (Board of Legal Education) Rules 2021* (Tas); *Supreme Court Rules 2000* (Tas).

[8] Raz, Loh and Fevereux (n 25) 84–6.

[9] *Supreme Court (Admission) Rules 2004* (Qld) r 12; *Legal Profession Act 2007* (Qld) s 34.

demonstrate understanding and competence in the stipulated areas of knowledge.[10] The educational requirements of admission include that applicants have completed a 3 year full-time (or equivalent) law degree,[11] the law degree must include the Priestley 11 subjects, and the student has completed a practical legal training course or supervised legal training in a workplace.[12]

The admission authority in each State and Territory maintains a list of accredited academic courses. They also review the law courses offered by higher education institutions from time to time to make sure that the content of the courses, especially the relevant subjects covering the Priestley 11, complies with the accreditation purpose. A list of accredited academic courses and institutions offering those courses in selected States and Territories is given below; other States or Territories did not display such a list on their website.

Legal professionals can be admitted in more than one State and Territory.

State/ territory	PLT providers
ACT[13]	• Australian National University—LLB and JD • University of Canberra—LLB and JD
NSW[14]	• LPAB—Diploma in Law • University of Sydney—LLB and JD • University of New South Wales—LLB and JD • Macquarie University—LLB and JD • University of Technology Sydney—LLB and JD • University of Wollongong—LLB • University of New England—LLB and JD • Southern Cross University—LLB • University of New Castle—LLB and JD/GDLP and JD • Western Sydney University—LLB and JD • University of Notre Dame—LLB • Top Education Group (Trading as Australian National Institute of Management and Commerce)—LLB • Australian Catholic University—LLB • Charles Sturt University—LLB and LLB/BCrimJustice

(continued)

[10] *Legal Profession Admission Rules 2015* (NSW), (Vic), (WA), r 5.

[11] *Court Procedure Rules 2006* (ACT) r 3605; *Legal Profession Admission Rules 2015* (NSW), (Vic), (WA) r 5: *Legal Profession Admission Rules 2007* (NT) r 4: *Supreme Court (Admission) Rules 2004* (Qld) r 6; *Rules of the Legal Practitioners Education and Admission Council 2018* (SA) r 7: *Legal Profession (Board of Legal Education) Rules 2021* (Tas) r 4.

[12] *Court Procedure Rules 2006* (ACT) r 3607D; *Legal Profession Admission Rules 2015* (NSW), (Vic), (WA), r 6: *Legal Profession Admission Rules 2007* (NT) r 5: *Supreme Court (Admission) Rules 2004* (Qld) r 7; *Rules of the Legal Practitioners Education and Admission Council 2018* (SA) rr 8–9: *Legal Profession (Board of Legal Education) Rules 2021* (Tas) r 7.

[13] 'Coming to the Bar', *ACT Bar Association* (Web Page) <https://www.actbar.com.au/coming-to-the-bar/>.

[14] 'Accredited Law Courses', *Legal Profession Admission Board* (Web Page, 6 December 2023) <https://www.lpab.justice.nsw.gov.au/Pages/admission-lawyer/accredited-law-courses-plt-providers.aspx>.

(continued)

State/ territory	PLT providers
VIC[15]	• Australian Catholic University—LLB • Deakin University—LLB and JD • La Trobe University—LLB and JD • Monash University—LLB and JD • RMIT University—LLB and JD • Swinburne University—Dual Award LLB and Leo Cussen Centre for Law • The University of Melbourne—JD • Victoria University—LLB
QLD[16]	• Australian Catholic University • University of Queensland • Queensland University of Technology • Griffith University • James Cook University • Bond University • University of Southern Queensland • Central Queensland University • University of the Sunshine Coast • Southern Cross University (Gold Coast Campus)—courses are approved for admission in New South Wales
WA[17]	• Curtin University—LLB • Edith Cowan University—LLB • Murdoch University—LLB • The University of Notre Dame—LLB • The University of Western Australia—JD

There are a number of accredited practical legal training providers listed in the table below.

State/ territory	PLT providers
ACT	• Australian National University College of Law School of Legal Practice • College of Law • Leo Cussen Centre for Law
NSW	• College of Law • University of Newcastle • University of New South Wales • University of Technology Sydney

(continued)

[15] 'Academic', *Victorian Legal Admissions Board* (Web Page, 27 June 2024) <https://www.lawadmissions.vic.gov.au/qualifications-and-training/academic>.

[16] 'Studying Law', *Queensland Law Society* (Web Page, 2023) <https://www.qls.com.au/Pages/Your-legal-career/Studying-law>.

[17] 'Admission', *The Supreme Court of Tasmania* (Web Page) <https://www.supremecourt.tas.gov.au/practitioners/admission/>.

(continued)

State/ territory	PLT providers
VIC	• Australian National University College of Law School of Legal Practice • College of Law • Leo Cussen Centre for Law • Australian College of Applied Professions (in conjunction with Legal Institute of Victoria)
QLD	• Bond University • College of Law • Leo Cussen Centre for Law • Queensland University of Technology
NT	• Australian National University College of Law School of Legal Practice • Bond University • College of Law • Flinders University of South Australia • University of Technology Sydney • Queensland University of Technology
SA	• College of Law • Flinders University of South Australia • Leo Cussen Centre for Law • University of Adelaide
WA	• College of Law • Curtin University • Leo Cussen Centre for Law • The Piddington Society Inc
TAS	• University of Tasmania Centre for Legal Studies

Alternatively, some jurisdictions in Australia allow for law graduates to complete a supervised legal training known as a traineeship or articles of clerkship. Supervised legal training commonly involves the completion of a minimum of 12 months supervised training program which has been approved by the admission board and meets an appropriate level of understanding and competence.[18] It is important to note that supervised traineeships or articles of clerkship are not available in New South Wales, South Australia, and Tasmania.[19]

(b) *Good Fame and Character Requirements*

The "good fame and character" requirement (as well as the "fit and proper person" test in some jurisdictions) is the basic suitability requirement for admission to the legal profession.[20] The Supreme Court is required to ensure that any person admitted to legal practice is of good fame and character and has a responsibility to the public and the profession to ensure that applicants are worthy.[21]

---

[18] See 'Supervised Legal Training', *Victorian Legal Services Board* (Web Page, 20 September 2022) <https://www.lawadmissions.vic.gov.au/qualifications-and-training/supervised-legal-training>.

[19] Ebejer (n 73) 27.

[20] Raz, Loh and Fevereux (n 25) 85.

[21] GE Dal Pont, *Lawyers' Professional Responsibility* (Thomson Reuters, 7th ed, 2021) [2.30].

In *Frugtniet v Board of Examiners*, the Supreme Court of Victoria expressed that:

> The requirement… that the applicant be a fit and proper person, means that the applicant must have the personal qualities of character which are necessary to discharge the important and grace responsibilities of being a barrister and solicitor. A legal practitioner, upon being admitted to practice, assumes duties to the courts, to fellow practitioners as well as to clients. At the heart of all those duties is a commitment to honesty and, in those circumstances when it is required, to open candour and frankness irrespective of self interest or embarrassment. The entire administration of justice in any community which is governed by law depends upon the honest working of legal practitioners who can be relied upon to meet high standards of honesty and ethical behaviour... The level and extent of trust placed in what legal practitioners say or do is necessarily high and the need for honesty is self evident and essential.[22]

There are a number of factors that are relevant to the good fame and character requirements. These can include:

- Previous criminal behaviour;
- Previous improper conduct in the course of education (academic misconduct);
- Previous improper conduct in the course of employment;
- Previous professional disciplinary proceedings and sanctions;
- Previous issues with taxation and social security debts;
- Previous disciplinary action as a lawyer in a different jurisdiction (domestic or foreign);
- Health issues, including mental instability; and
- Previous bankruptcy or history as an officer of a company that has been wound up or under administration.[23]

It is at the discretion of the admission boards and Supreme Court to consider whether an applicant is of good fame and character to be admitted.

Once a legal professional is admitted in one of the Australian jurisdictions, they are generally eligible to apply for a practising certificate in other jurisdictions and in Federal Courts. However, the interstate regulators might have specific rules governing the moving of practitioners; it is always prudent to check with both authorities to ensure compliance with those rules.

3.2.2 Foreign Legal Professionals' Admission to Practise Local Law

Foreign lawyers can become eligible for admission in Australian States, Territories, and the Commonwealth. In order to do so, they must first apply to one of the admission authorities mentioned above for an assessment of whether their academic and legal training qualifications would meet the admission tests. In most cases, the authorities would identify some additional subjects or training they need to complete

---

[22] *Frugtniet v Board of Examiners* [2002] VSC 140, [10].

[23] See Dal Pont (n 232) [2.60]–[2.85]; Raz, Loh and Fevereux (n 25) 85.

at Australian institutions in order to meet the admission tests. Such assessment will be based on the Uniform Principles for Assessing the Qualifications of Overseas Applicants for Admission to the Australian Legal Profession.[24] For legal professionals who had been trained and admitted in New Zealand, their qualifications will be recognised under the *Trans-Tasman Mutual Recognition Act 1997* (Cth).

Generally, in order to be admitted in Australia, a foreign legal professional should have:

(a) completed a tertiary course leading to legal practice in the applicant's home jurisdiction, which is substantially equivalent to a three-year full-time law course that leads to admission to the legal profession in Australia;
(b) successfully completed subjects, either as part of that course or otherwise, which are substantially equivalent to the areas of study which Australian applicants must successfully complete before being admitted to the legal profession in Australia;
(c) acquired and demonstrated an appropriate understanding of, and competence in, certain skills, practice areas, and values, which are substantially equivalent to the skills, practice areas, and values which Australian applicants must acquire and demonstrate an understanding of and competence in, before being admitted to the legal profession in Australia; and
(d) undertaken, or been exempted from, the International English Language Testing System Academic Module ('IELTS') test within two years before seeking admission, and obtained minimum scores of 8.0 for writing, 7.5 for speaking, and 7.0 for reading and listening, in the components of that test.[25]

An admitting authority may dispense with one or more of the requirements referred to in items (b) and (c) in the case of an experienced practitioner from an overseas jurisdiction if it considers that the applicant's experience is sufficiently relevant, substantial, and current to justify a dispensation.[26]

3.3 Practising as a Solicitor and Barrister

Once admitted as a lawyer, one must apply for a practising certificate to practise as a solicitor and/or barrister. A practitioner who practises law should hold a current practising certificate when engaging in relevant legal practice. The practising licence is to be renewed annually at the beginning of every financial year, with a fee to be paid yearly.

---

[24] Law Admissions Consultative Committee, *Uniform Principles for Assessing the Qualifications of Overseas Applicants for Admission to the Australian Legal Profession* (Legal Profession Admission Board, 2015).

[25] Ibid Art 1.

[26] Ibid.

The practising certificates are issued by the authorities below:

State/territory	Practising certificate issuing authorities
ACT	• ACT Law Society • ACT Bar Association
NSW	• The Law Society of New South Wales • The New South Wales Bar Association
VIC	• The Legal Services Board of Victoria
QLD	• Queensland Law Society • The Bar Association of Queensland
NT	• The Law Society of Northern Territory
SA	• The Law Society of South Australia
WA	• The Legal Services Board of Western Australia
TAS	• Law Society of Tasmania

There are various types of practising certificates issued by the authorities. For example, the Law Society of New South Wales provides for five types of practising certificates for solicitors. Practitioners holding different categories of practising certificates are authorised to engage in different types of legal work, as indicated below.[27] Other issuing authorities provide for similar categorisations of practising certificates.

Category	Authorised activities
Principal of a law practice	The holder is authorised to engage in legal practice as a principal of a law practice and also as an employee of a law practice, corporate legal practitioner or government legal practitioner and also as a volunteer at a community legal service, or otherwise on a pro bono basis
Employee of a law practice	The holder is authorised to engage in legal practice as an employee of a law practice and also as a corporate legal practitioner or government legal practitioner and also as a volunteer at a community legal service, or otherwise on a pro bono basis
Corporate legal practitioner	The holder is authorised to engage in legal practice as a corporate legal practitioner or government legal practitioner and also as a volunteer at a community legal service, or otherwise on a pro bono basis
Government legal practitioner	The holder is authorised to engage in legal practice as a government legal practitioner or corporate legal practitioner and also as a volunteer at a community legal service, or otherwise on a pro bono basis
Volunteer	The holder is authorised to engage in legal practice both as a volunteer at a community legal service and otherwise on a pro bono basis only

[27] 'Practising Certificate Conditions', *The Law Society of New South Wales* (Web Page) <https://www.lawsociety.com.au/practising-law-in-NSW/working-as-a-solicitor-in-NSW/your-practising-certificate/conditions>.

During a fixed-term period, usually 18 months or 2 years depending on the specific requirement of the jurisdiction,[28] there will be a condition imposed on the practising certificate of newly admitted lawyers that they will need to practise law under supervision. This might not apply to barristers or Australian-registered foreign lawyers in some jurisdictions who may be exempted upon application.

Depending on the specific circumstances, there might be further conditions imposed by the relevant law and rules, e.g. the *Legal Profession Uniform Law* and the *Legal Profession Uniform General Rules* in relevant jurisdictions, or discretionary conditions imposed by the relevant certificate issuing authorities. Common conditions include, for example, that the holder must comply with continuing professional development requirements under the *Legal Professional Uniform Law* and *Legal Profession Continuing Professional Development (Solicitors) Rules*;[29] that a principal must complete a Practice Management Course before being authorised to be a principal of a law practice;[30] the holder is authorised to receive trust money on behalf of a law practice, or they are not authorised to receive trust money on their own account.[31]

According to the URBIS's report, there are 90,239 practising solicitors in Australia. A solicitor is subject to the relevant rules applicable to solicitors. It includes, for example, the *Legal Professional Uniform Law*, the *Legal Profession Uniform General Rules 2015*, and the *Legal Profession Uniform Legal Practice (Solicitors) Rules 2015*.[32]

Lawyers have the option to pursue admission to the bar as a barrister. The admission requirements to practise as a barrister are not uniform across Australia; however, in every jurisdiction to become a barrister you must be admitted as an Australian legal practitioner first.[33] Further requirements and relevant authority for each jurisdiction are as follows:

---

[28] See, e.g., Legal Profession Uniform Law (NSW) s 49.

[29] See, e.g., *Legal Professional Uniform Law* (NSW) s 52, and the *Legal Profession Uniform Continuing Professional Development (Solicitors) Rules 2015* (NSW).

[30] *Legal Professional Uniform Law* (NSW) s 53; *Legal Profession Uniform General Rules 2015* (NSW) r 16(b)(ii).

[31] See, e.g., *Legal Professional Uniform Law* (NSW) s 47(2).

[32] *Legal Profession Uniform Legal Practice (Solicitors) Rules 2015*.

[33] Ebejer (n 56) 58.

State/ territory	Authority	Requirements
ACT	Australian Capital Territory Bar Association	• Completion of the Bar Exam in NSW • "Readers" Course"[34]
NSW	New South Wales Bar Association	• Completion of the Bar Exam in NSW • Become a "Reader" • Completion of the 12-month bar practice course[35]
VIC	Victorian Legal Services Board	• Completion of the Entrance Exam in VIC • Completion of an 8 to 9 week "Readers" Course • Work supervised under an approved mentor for 9 months[36]
QLD	Bar Association of Queensland	• Completion of Bar Exam • Completion of 6-week Bar Practice Course[37] • Completion of a pupillage program for 12 months[38]
SA	Legal Practitioners Education and Admission Council	• Hold an unrestricted practising certificate • Completion of the South Australian Bar readers course over 20 weeks • Completion of a 3-month Reading Program with a mentor • Seek approval to sign the bar roll[39]
WA	Legal Practice Board	• At present, there are no formal pupillage and/or bar entry examination requirements in Western Australia[40]
TAS	Board of Legal Education	• There is no requirement for a bar examination in Tasmania • Those seeking to become a barrister must complete a pupillage for two years[41]

Senior barristers may hold titles of King's Counsel ('KC'), or previously Queen's Counsel ('QC') prior to the passing of Queen Elizabeth II in 2022, or Senior Counsel ('SC'), recognising their outstanding performance over a long period of time and reputation in administering justice. In some States and Territories, for example, the title of KCs or QCs is no longer used. The KCs or SCs are appointed by internal groups within the Bar upon application. This is also referred as "taking silk" because the Counsels with titles wear silk gowns of a particular design in the courtroom as

---

[34] 'Coming to the Bar' (n 224).

[35] 'Admission', *New South Wales Bar Association* (Web Page) <https://nswbar.asn.au/becoming-a-barrister/admission>.

[36] 'Becoming a Barrister', *Victorian Bar* (Web Page) <https://www.vicbar.com.au/public/about/becoming-barrister>.

[37] 'Qualifications Overview', *Bar Association of Queensland* (Web Page, 2023) <https://qldbar.asn.au/baq-cms/barrister-qualifications>.

[38] Ebejer (n 73) 60.

[39] Ibid.

[40] 'Prerequisites and Professional Obligations', *WA Bar Association* (Web Page, 2023) <https://www.wabar.asn.au/coming-to-the-bar/prerequisites-and-professional-obligations/>.

[41] 'Becoming a Barrister' *The Law Society of Tasmania* (Web Page, 2023) <https://www.lst.org.au/home/membership-and-legal-practice/practising-in-the-law/becoming-a-barrister/>.

a privilege. Counsels who do not hold a title are referred to as Counsels or junior Counsels.

Having once obtained the practising certificate in a State or Territory, one can also register their name in the Register of Practitioners kept by the Chief Executive and Principal Register of the High Court of Australia, and practise in the Federal Courts with the same capacity they are entitled to practise in States and Territories. Detailed guidance is provided by the High Court of Australia.[42]

3.4 Foreign Lawyers in Australia

Other than being admitted as an Australian lawyer, foreign legal practitioners can also practise foreign law on a "fly-in, fly-out" basis, which provides them a temporary opportunity to come to Australia and provide legal services for their clients for a maximum period of 90 days within any 12-month period of time, as long as they do not establish a commercial presence. They can practise foreign law to the extent that they are entitled to practise law in their home country and/or another foreign jurisdiction. An appropriate visa will need to be arranged for a foreign lawyer to do so. Currently, there is no requirement for foreign lawyers acting in this way to register with a regulatory body.

Foreign lawyers wishing to practise foreign law in Australia exceeding the time limit mentioned above, or wishing to establish an office in Australia, will need to register with a State or Territory authority as an Australian-registered foreign lawyer. The registration certificate is issued upon application, with a fee to be paid, evidence of the legal practitioner's engagement in legal practice overseas, and potentially, sufficient coverage of professional indemnity insurance.[43] The registration certificate is issued and renewed every financial year. Once registered in one of the Australian jurisdictions, they will be able to practise foreign law in all other Australian jurisdictions. They are allowed to practise law of foreign jurisdictions in which they are qualified, as well as international law. While Australian-registered foreign lawyers cannot practise Australian law, they may coordinate with Australian lawyers or employ Australian lawyers.

Australian-registered foreign lawyers are subject to the same professional, ethical, and practice standards as Australian lawyers.

---

[42] 'Register of Practitioners', *High Court of Australia* (Web Page) <https://www.hcourt.gov.au/registry/register-of-practitioners>.

[43] See, e.g., 'Foreign Laws and Lawyers', *Victorian Legal Services Board + Commissioner* (Web Page) <https://lsbc.vic.gov.au/lawyers/practising-law/practising-certificates/foreign-laws-and-lawyers>.

3.5 Traditional Careers in Law

Following the completion of a law degree, graduates are no longer limited to seeking admission to practise and working in a law firm. Law students are able to leverage their skills to enter the job market. While there is little data outlining the educational outcomes for law students, the Council of Australian Law Deans suggest that 75% of law graduates gain full-time employment within the first four months after graduating from university.[44] In some circumstances, this employment may not be within the legal profession; however, this indicates that a law degree equips graduates with the skills required to secure employment across a number of fields.[45]

3.5.1 Private Practice and Law Firms

Following the completion of a law degree, most follow the traditional course of action and seek opportunities in the private sector as solicitors.[46] In this regard, UBRIS produced the National Profile of Solicitors in 2011 and has since tracked the development of solicitors, mainly in the private section, in Australia.[47] In 2022, 67% of all solicitors worked in private practice; larger proportion of solicitors work in the private sectors consistently in all States, while in the Australian Capital Territory and the Northern Territory a larger portion work in the government. Entering private practice provides lawyers with excellent training and often provides pathways for continued professional development.[48] Depending on the different practices, lawyers will be exposed to a variety of clients and matters which allows them to expand their legal knowledge.[49]

Those who enter private practice might choose different types of practice they would like to join. The *Legal Profession Uniform Law* defines the "law practice" as a sole practitioner, a law firm, a community legal service, an incorporated legal practice, or an unincorporated legal practice.[50] Further definitions of the different categories of practices are listed below.

Practice	Definition (Legal Profession Uniform Law)
Sole practitioner	An Australian legal practitioner who engages in legal practice on his or her own account;

(continued)

[44] Council of Australian Law Deans (n 17) 1.
[45] Ibid.
[46] Raz, Loh and Fevereux (n 25) 162.
[47] Urbis (n 213).
[48] Raz, Loh and Fevereux (n 25) 162.
[49] Ibid.
[50] *Legal Profession Uniform Law 2014* (NSW) s 6.

(continued)

Practice	Definition (Legal Profession Uniform Law)
Law firm	A partnership consisting only of (a) Australian legal practitioners or (b) one or more Australian legal practitioners and one or more Australian-registered foreign lawyers;
Community legal service	An organisation (whether incorporated or not) that (a) holds itself out as (i) a community legal service; (ii) a community legal centre; or (iii) an Aboriginal and Torres Strait Islander Legal Service; Whether or not it is a member of a State or Territory association of community legal centres, and whether or not it is accredited or certified by the National Association of Community Legal Centres; and (b) is established and operated on a not-for-profit basis; and (c) provides legal or legal-related services that (i) are directed generally to people who are disadvantaged (including but not limited to being financially disadvantaged) in accessing the legal system or in protecting their legal rights or (ii) are conducted in the public interest;
Incorporated legal practice	A corporation that satisfies the following criteria (a) it is (i) a company within the meaning of the Corporations Act or (ii) a corporation, or a corporation of a kind, approved by the Council under section 114 or specified in the Uniform Rules for the purposes of this definition; (b) it has given notice under section 104 that it intends to engage in legal practice in Australia and that notice is still operative; (c) the legal services it provides or proposes to provide are not limited to either or both of the following services (i) in-house legal services for the corporation or a related entity; (ii) services that are not legally required to be provided by an Australian legal practitioner and that are provided by an officer or employee who is not an Australian legal practitioner; (d) it is not excluded by the Uniform Rules from being an incorporated legal practice But does not include a community legal service;

(continued)

(continued)

Practice	Definition (Legal Profession Uniform Law)
Unincorporated legal practice	An unincorporated body or group that satisfies the following criteria (a) it is (i) a partnership or (ii) an unincorporated body or group, or an unincorporated body or group of a kind, approved by the Council under section 114 or specified in the Uniform Rules for the purposes of this definition; (b) it has given notice under section 104 that it intends to engage in legal practice in Australia and that notice is still operative; (c) the legal services it provides or proposes to provide are not limited to either or both of the following services (i) in-house legal services for the unincorporated body or group; (ii) services that are not legally required to be provided by an Australian legal practitioner and that are provided by an officer or employee who is not an Australian legal practitioner; (d) it is not excluded by the Uniform Rules from being an unincorporated legal practice But does not include (e) a law firm; (f) a community legal service; or (g) an incorporated legal practice

It is notable that while partnerships are the commonly known structure of law firms there are some large practices which choose the form of a company, which is allowed in Australia. This reform had been raised by the Trade Practices Commission as early as in 1994[51] and was supported by scholarly discussions.[52] Some law firms are even listed on the Australian Securities Exchange, such as Slater and Gordon (ASX: SGH), Af Legal Group Ltd (ASX: AFL), and Shine Justice Ltd (ASX: SHJ).

It is also worth mentioning that most private law practices are sole practices. In the 2022 URBIS report, of 16,514 practices, 84% are sole practices. Only 70 law practices had more than 20 principals, representing less than 1% of the total practices, but hiring 19% of solicitors in total.[53]

There are various terms to describe law firms, for example, top-tier firms and boutique firms, international law firms or local firms, although in Australia the boundary between these two is less clear along with merger and partnership between Australian leading firms and international firms. There were the "Big Six" law firms, which were considered as the largest and most influential Australian law firms since the creation of a national market in 1981, before which law practices had been restricted to run their business within a State or Territory only. The Big Six firms were: Allens Arthur Robinson; Black Dawson; Clayton Utz; Freehills; Mallesons Stephen Jaques; and MinterEllison. In the 2010s, however, there were major mergers and partnerships made by those firms. Since then, Allens Arthur Robinson rebranded

[51] Trade Practices Commission, 'Study of the Professions: Legal' (Final Report, March 1994).

[52] Ramsay (1994).

[53] Urbis (n 213) 29.

as Allens and operates in association with the leading UK firm Linklaters LLP; Blake Dawson merged with the UK firm Ashurst LLP and rebranded as Ashurst Australia; Freehills merged with the UK firm Herbert Smith and is now a part of Herbert Smith Freehills; Mallesons Stephen Jaques merged with the Chinese firm King and Wood and is now a part of King and Wood Mallesons. Other than those firms, there are also international firms running their businesses in Australia, such as Clifford Chance, White and Case and Baker and McKenzie; and reputable local firms such as Corrs Chambers Westgarth and Gibert + Tobin.

In law firms and other private practices, roles are typically broken down into areas of specialisation known as practice groups. These areas can include corporate law, commercial litigation, insurance law, employment law, and taxation law to name a few. Graduates who enter a law firm will often gain exposure to different practice groups, as well as a variety of issues, processes, and legal and commercial considerations.[54]

3.5.2 *Academia and Teaching*

Law graduates seeking an alternative to practise may consider a career in academia. In the current legal education landscape, academic roles are considered a professional and competitive career choice.[55] There are many pathways into academia. This often includes undertaking a Master's degree in law or a PhD, or even beginning with a casual or short-term position as a tutor.[56]

Positions in academia vary, with only 65.1% of lecturers engaged in full-time employment.[57] For graduates seeking to enter academia full-time, postgraduate study in a research-based Master of Laws can assist in securing a role as an academic.[58] Most academic positions require candidates to have completed a PhD and have a track record of quality published research papers.[59] Recruitment is highly competitive.

Following the practice in the Australian tertiary education industry, the full-time continuing roles for law academics usually include lecturers, senior lecturers, associate professors, and professors. Law academics are usually required to provide consistent publication of high-quality research outputs with leading academic journals and publishers, capacity to teach law subjects, especially those within the scope of the Priestley 11, communication skills with colleagues, students, and stakeholders, as well as participation of administrative tasks within the law schools.

While being an academic and working in academia is more than writing papers and research, law graduates who wish to enter academia career pathways should be

54 Raz, Loh and Fevereux (n 25) 166.

55 Ibid, 144.

56 Ibid, 96–97.

57 Ibid, 144.

58 Ibid.

59 Ibid.

skilled in analysis and interpretation and demonstrate a wide understanding of the law.

3.5.3 Courts, Judges, and Judicial Officers

Judges play important roles in the judicial system and hear civil and criminal proceedings in the courts. Depending on the jurisdiction, they are usually appointed by a State or federal Governor or Attorney-General. Depending on their roles and responsibilities, they are further divided into judges, magistrates, etc. In order to be eligible for an appointment as a judge, one must complete a law degree and become a lawyer for a certain number of years. Broadly speaking, coroners and judicial registrars might also be considered as judicial officers.

The operation of the courts, including the capacity and performance of judges, are overseen by Judicial Commissions in some of the States and Territories. The *Judicial Officers Act 1986* (NSW) established the Judicial Commission of New South Wales which was the first in Australia. It organises and supervises continuing education and training of judicial officers, and deals with complaints against judicial officers. Similarly, the Judicial Commission of Victoria handles complaints in relation to judicial officers and VCAT members in Victoria.[60] There had also been a public consultation for the establishment of a Federal Judicial Commission in 2023 in response to the Australian Law Reform Commission's 2021 report, *Without Fear or Favour: Judicial Impartiality and the Law on Bias*.[61]

Following the 1977 constitutional referendum that introduced the judicial retirement ages for the Australian federal judiciary, federal judges must retire when they reach the age of 70.[62] Following this move, States and Territories also introduced retirement ages and limits on post-retirement employment for their judges and judicial officers, as listed below. Most of them followed the federal practice of a retirement age of 70 but some jurisdictions adopted the retirement requirement with some variations.[63]

[60] 'Complaints', *Judicial Commission of Victoria* (Web Page, 2024) <https://www.judicialcommission.vic.gov.au/complaints/>.

[61] 'Scoping the Establishment of a Federal Judicial Commission', *Attorney-General's Department* (Web Page) <https://consultations.ag.gov.au/legal-system/federal-judicial-commission/>.

[62] *Australian Constitution* (Cth) s 72, following the *Constitution Alteration (Retirement of Judges) Act 1977* (Cth).

[63] See further Blackham (2016).

State or territory	Retirement age[64]	Source
Australian Capital Territory	Judges and Magistrates: 70	*Supreme Court Act 1933* (ACT) s 4(3) *Magistrates Court Act 1930* (ACT) s 7D
New South Wales	Judicial Officers and Magistrates: 75 Non-judicial members of the Industrial Relations Commission: 65	*Judicial Officers Act 1986* (NSW) s 44
Victoria	Supreme Court and County Court Judges: 70 or 72 Associate Judges and Magistrates: 70	*Constitution Act 1975* (Vic) s 77; *County Court Act 1958* (Vic) s 14(1) *Supreme Court Act 1986* (Vic) s 104 *Magistrates' Court Act 1989* (Vic) s 12(a)
Queensland	Judges and Magistrates: 70	*Constitution of Queensland 2001* (Qld) s 60(2); *District Court of Queensland Act 1967* (Qld) s 14; *Supreme Court of Queensland Act 1991* (Qld) s 21 *Magistrates Act 1991* (Qld) s 42(d)
Northern Territory	Judges and Magistrates: 70	*Supreme Court Act 1979* (NT) s 38 *Magistrates Act 1977* (NT) s 7
South Australia	Judges and Magistrates: 70	*Supreme Court Act 1935* (SA) s 13A(1); *District Court Act 1991* (SA) s 16(1) *Magistrates Act 1983* (SA) s 9(1)(c)
Tasmania	Supreme Court Judges and Magistrates: 72	*Supreme Court Act 1887* (Tas) s 6A(1) *Magistrates Court Act 1987* (Tas) s 9(4)(a)
Western Australia	Judges: 70 Magistrates: 65	*District Court of Western Australia Act 1969* (WA) s 16; *Judges' Retirement Act 1937* (WA) s 3(1) *Magistrates Court Act 2004* (WA) sch 1 cl 11(1)(a)

There are several career paths within the judiciary for solicitors, barristers, and law graduates. The judicial system employs a number of legal professionals in a variety of different functions. These include Judge's Associateships, registrars, and magistrates to name a few.

Some career paths in the judiciary involve a rigours selection process. For example, a magistrate in New South Wales is appointed by the Governor of New South Wales pursuant to the *Local Court Act 2007*[65] in accordance with the Attorney-General's recommendations,[66] while others, including a Judge's Associateship, can be secured by law graduates.

[64] This does not include the limit on post-retirement employment of judges. In some jurisdictions, retired judges can be appointed as acting judges for an extended period of time. For example, in New South Wales, they can be appointed as Acting Judges until age 77; see *Supreme Court Act 1970* (NSW), ss 37(4)-(4A).

[65] *Local Court Act 2007* (NSW) s 13.

[66] See 'Chief Magistrate and Other Judicial Officers', *Local Court New South Wales* (Web Page, 24 August 2023) <https://www.localcourt.nsw.gov.au/about-us/chief-magistrate.html>.

The role of Judge's Associateship involves working closely with a Judge and will often vary based on the court in which the judge sits.[67] As a Judge's Associate, the candidate will work closely with the Judge and will often work as both a professional and personal confidential aide.[68] Associateships provide law graduates with an in-depth insight into the court system and the administration of justice. The duties completed in these roles will differ from judge to judge but will often involve everything from legal research to liaising directly with the courts, barristers, and other professional associations.[69] While these positions are usually only 12-month contracts, those who complete these roles will gain unique perspectives on court matters and advocacy.[70]

3.5.4 Government

Public service and government agencies offer a wide range of employment opportunities to legally educated individuals. For example, in 2015 9.6% of all solicitors worked in government roles as public service lawyers[71] and in 2022 this number was closer to 12%.[72] A career in government as a legal professional is considered to be fulfilling and rewarding, with the specialisation options being endless.[73]

As a legal professional, a person may be employed by a government agency to act in a legal capacity or as a public servant who has legal training. The government sector requires legal staff for their operation, with roles focused in legislation interpretation, policymaking, legal compliance, litigation, and regulatory enforcement to name a few.[74] High-profile public service and government positions are often filled by former lawyers.[75] A significant proportion of former Australian Prime Ministers and Cabinet Ministers have been lawyers or have a professional background in the law, including Julia Gillard, Sir Robert Menzies, and Malcom Turnbull to name a few.[76] Several federal government departments recruit lawyers and legal professionals. They are as follows:

- Attorney-General's Department;
- Australian Appeals Tribunal;
- Australian Communications and Media Authority;

[67] Raz, Loh and Fevereux (n 25), 153.

[68] Ibid 154.

[69] Ibid.

[70] Ibid.

[71] Urbis, *2014 Law Society National Profile* (Report, Law Society of New South Wales, April 2015).

[72] Urbis (n 213) 24.

[73] Raz, Loh and Fevereux (n 25) 155.

[74] Ibid 164.

[75] Ibid.

[76] Ibid.

- Australian Competition and Consumer Commission;
- Australian Crime Commission;
- Australian Government Solicitor (within the Australian Government Attorney-General's Department);
- Australian Human Rights Commission;
- Australian Institute of Criminology;
- Australian Law Reform Commission;
- Australian Prudential Regulation Authority;
- Fair Work Commission;
- Family Court of Australia;
- Federal Court of Australia;
- Office of Director of Public Prosecutions.

3.5.5 In House/Corporate

In-house lawyers are legal professionals who are employed directly by a corporation or business.[77] In-house lawyers are different from their counterparts in law firms as they have responsibility for one client, their employer. Lawyers employed within corporations are often tasked with a range of issues from commercial transactions, risk management, business decisions, and regulatory policy compliance.[78] Due to the nature of the role, in-house lawyers partner with their corporation by balancing commercial imperative and business goals with legal requirements. Lawyers in corporations will handle a variety of matters and are often commercial law generalists. These roles are primarily focused on commercial advisory and will often brief out work to law firms when litigation or disputes arise.[79]

3.6 Alternative Legal Careers

Law students are no longer limited to a traditional career as a solicitor, barrister, or academic. The legal ecosystem is evolving, and with it so does the potential career outcomes for law students. NewLaw careers, as it has been referred to as by the College of Law and the Legal Centre of innovation, are multidisciplinary careers for legal professionals that are on the rise. This can include careers from consultancy to Legal Technologist and to Legal Operations Professional to name a few.[80]

---

[77] Ibid 169.

[78] Ibid.

[79] Ibid 170.

[80] 'Career Options for Lawyers', *College of Law* (Web Page) <https://www.collaw.edu.au/your-career/career-options-for-lawyers>.

Delivery of legal services has changed due to technological innovation requiring a multidisciplinary approach with both technical and legal skills.[81] The area of legal technology continues to grow, especially after the COVID-19 pandemic, and as such so does demand for these roles.[82] Technology such as artificial intelligence is changing the legal profession and creating new alternative career paths for law students.[83] A career in legal technology could involve positions and roles such as legal technologist, data scientist, privacy engineer, and legal technology entrepreneur to name a few.[84] As this area grows, law firms and corporations are seeking candidates who can innovate and champion these new technologies which have created alternative career options for legal graduates who may not want to pursue legal practice.[85]

3.6.1 Consultancy

One common alterative career path for legal professionals is consultancy. Consultants are usually individuals who have expert knowledge in a particular area and are often considered independent professionals.[86] Consultancy gives legally trained individuals an opportunity to work on specific tasks and projects in the capacity of a legal expert, while maintaining flexibility and greater control of their career than their private practice counterparts.[87] Consultancy can take many different forms and may even lend itself to allowing Australian legal practitioners to practise in other countries. With the rise of global and international law firms, some are seeking Australian legal professionals as law consultants.[88]

3.6.2 Legal Operations Professional

The role of Legal Operations Professional is an intersection of legal services and other professional services such as project management, technology, and finance.[89] Legal

---

[81] Ryan et al. (2021, 377).

[82] Ibid.

[83] See College of Law (2023, 6) <https://www.collaw.edu.au/resources/2021/01/21/alternative-careers-where-else-can-your-law-degree-take-you>.

[84] Ibid 7.

[85] Ibid 6.

[86] Ibid 145. There are only 16 pages in this download.

[87] Ibid.

[88] Ibid.

[89] 'The Legal Operations Role is Indispensable to Today's Law Firms as Well as to Legal Departments', *College of Law* (Web Page, 27 August 2020) <https://www.collaw.edu.au/news/2020/08/27/the-legal-operations-role-is-indispensable-to-today-s-law-firms-as-well-as-to-legal-departments>; Centre for Legal Innovation 'What are NewLaw Careers?' (YouTube, 26 May 2022, 00:00:00–1:00:10) <https://youtu.be/q3uzjjgOkBo>.

operations bridge the gap between legal services and the operation of a business.[90] The work of a Legal Operations Professional covers a vast range of topics from discussing client-based solutions, financial management and reporting, managing the implementation of new technologies, and process mapping to increase efficiency.[91] The heart of a Legal Operations Professional role is utilising different roles, skills, and methodologies to find solutions to operations-based problems and implementing solutions whether that is process reviewing or implementing a piece of legal technology.[92]

3.6.3 *Legal Data Analyst*

A Legal Data Analyst provides technical and insightful analysis of legal data and information to inform legal decision-making and strategies to serve both a law firm and its clients.[93] They utilise data analytical skills to understand the impact of a particular matter or issue by using data to break down a legal problem and communicate solutions through a technology lens.[94] Law firms and other legal professionals capture rich data and information that has historically only been analysed for financial decision-making, while legal data analysts are able to review this previously unreviewed intellectual capital to optimise output and provide further insights for decision-making at an executive level.[95] In order to curate and analyse this rich data, data analysis utilises predictive analytics, data mining, and even machine learning.[96]

3.6.4 *Legal Technologist*

The term Legal Technologist is broad and encapsulates many things.[97] The role of a Legal Technologist involves setting a technology strategy for a law firm or in-house legal team and delivering projects to increase process efficiency, to optimise the experience of both the client and the lawyer, and to increase the quality of legal

---

[90] Centre for Legal Innovation, 'The Role of a Legal Operations Professional' (YouTube, 26 May 2022, 12:20:00–12:42:00) <https://youtu.be/LDB_17lZdVg>.

[91] Ibid 8:50:00–18:30:00.

[92] Ibid 17:10:00–18:20:00.

[93] Centre for Legal Innovation, 'The Role of a Legal Data Analyst' (YouTube, 26 May 2022, 04:00:00–06:25:00) <https://youtu.be/Sg72dgp-HoM>.

[94] Ibid 05:37:00–06:25:00.

[95] Ibid 08:14:00–09:04:00.

[96] Ryan et al. (n 292) 376.

[97] Centre for Legal Innovation, 'The Role of a Legal Technologist' (YouTube, 26 May 2022, 01:12:00–01:49:00) <https://youtu.be/Z2tAm2jM_hM>.

services delivered.[98] A Legal Technologist role involves bridging the gap between technology and the law by equipping legal professionals with tools to improve their practice to make legal services more accessible.[99] Legal Technologists utilise their understanding of the legal landscape and technology to find solutions to transform the way in which legal solutions are delivered.[100] The role of Legal Technologist has been created as a result of the increasing introduction of technology to the legal profession and is an intermediary between technology and the law.[101] As technology continues to innovate the legal profession, there is growing demand for technical skills paired with legal knowledge leading to roles such as Legal Technologist becoming an alternative career path for law students.[102]

3.6.5 Client Experience Designer

Being a Client Experience Designer is about improving the experience of both employees and clients through client journey mapping.[103] This involves proactively gathering information and data on the impressions and feelings of both clients and employees to analyse customer interactions to improved legal services through client-focused legal design.[104] Following the data gathering, Client Experience Designers work to implement and operationalise solutions, be it through technology, further training for staff or new client-centric strategies to create long-term improvement in client experience.

3.6.6 Knowledge Manager

A Knowledge Manager plays a pivotal role in the management of systems, organisational knowledge, and innovation of a legal practice. This can involve keeping up to date with new technologies, running training sessions on both general areas of law and changes or updates to legislation, and producing marketing documents.[105] A Knowledge Manager supports innovation and the continuous improvement of a

---

[98] Ibid.

[99] 'What Does a Legal Technologist Do?', *Josef* (Web Page, 15 April 2021) <https://joseflegal.com/blog/new-job-what-is-a-legal-technologist/>.

[100] Ibid.

[101] Bullows (2021, 258, 259).

[102] Ryan et al. (n 292) 377.

[103] Centre for Legal Innovation, 'The Role of Client Experience Designer' (YouTube, 26 May 2022, 01:16:00–03:12:00) <https://youtu.be/l5fVpfjj0Ac?si=ByqLafHS6fVGIL9c>.

[104] Ibid.

[105] Centre for Legal Innovation, 'The Role of a Knowledge Manager' (YouTube, 26 May 2022, 01:15:00–08:12:00) <https://youtu.be/vq553SWEib8?si=z3U_XKOM7VxgfGTS>.

legal practice. Knowledge Managers can have both technological and legal expertise which can be utilised to optimise existing processes and find creative solutions to address clients' needs and issues.[106]

3.7 Legal Ethics

In Australia, there are a number of sources of legal ethics for legal professionals. These include, but are not limited to, common law, contract law, tort, fiduciary obligations, equity, and the regulatory framework (consisting of legislation, regulations, and professional conduct rules).[107]

3.7.1 General Law

On a basic level, the common law plays a significant role throughout a lawyer's professional life. The general law governs a lawyer's relationship with their clients, the court, and third parties. This includes:[108]

- At the time of admission, a person must meet the suitability requirement of "good fame and character" and "fit and proper person" as set down by the common law;[109]
- The contractual relationship between lawyer and client also attracts a duty of care in tort;[110]
- The lawyer-client relationship will also attract fiduciary duties, with the law of equity requiring a lawyer to ensure they disclose costs relating to legal services, prescribing conditions where a lawyer can act where a conflict of interest may arise and requiring a lawyer to maintain client confidence and privilege;[111]
- Lawyers must exercise reasonable care, and where a lawyer fails to maintain that standard concurrent liability arises in tort and contract;[112]
- The lawyer's paramount duty to the court and the administration of justice; and[113]
- The duties that a lawyer owes to third parties that they come in contract with during the provision of legal services.[114]

---

[106] Ryan et al. (n 292) 375.

[107] Ebejer (n 73) 3.

[108] Dal Pont (n 232) [1.95].

[109] Ebejer (n 73) 3.

[110] Ibid.

[111] Ibid.

[112] Ibid.

[113] Ibid.

[114] Ibid 4.

3.7.2 Regulatory Framework

In addition to the general law, there is a strong regulatory framework which regulates and governs the behaviour and ethical conduct of lawyers. The framework is made up of legislation, regulations, and professional conduct rules in each State and Territory.

The below table outlines the regulatory framework by jurisdiction.[115]

State/ territory	Statute	Regulations	Professional conduct rules
ACT	Legal Profession Act 2006 (ACT)	Legal Profession Regulation 2007 (ACT)	Legal Profession (Solicitors) Conduct Rules 2015 (ACT)
NSW	*Legal Profession Uniform Law Application Act 2014* (NSW)	*Legal Profession Uniform Law Application Regulations 2015* (NSW)	Legal Profession Uniform Law Australian Solicitors Conduct Rules 2015 (NSW); *Legal Profession Uniform General Rules 2015* (NSW); *Legal Profession Uniform Law Australian Conduct (Barristers) Rules 2015* (NSW)
NT	*Legal Profession Act 2006* (NT)	*Legal Profession Regulations 2007* (NT)	*Rules of Professional Conduct and Practice 2005* (NT)
VIC	*Legal Profession Uniform Law Application Act 2014* (NSW)	*Legal Profession Uniform Law Application Regulations 2015* (NSW)	*Legal Profession Uniform Law Australian Solicitors Conduct Rules 2015* (NSW); *Legal Profession Uniform General Rules 2015* (NSW); *Legal Profession Uniform Law Australian Conduct (Barristers) Rules 2015* (NSW)
QLD	*Legal Profession Act 2007* (Qld)	*Legal Profession Regulation 2007* (Qld)	*Australian Solicitors Conduct Rules 2012* (Qld)
SA	*Legal Practitioners Act 1981* (SA)	*Legal Practitioners Regulations 2014* (SA)	*Australian Solicitors Conduct Rules 2011* (SA)
WA	*Legal Profession Uniform Law Application Act 2014* (WA)	*Legal Profession Uniform Law Application Regulations 2015* (WA)	*Legal Profession Uniform Law Australian Solicitors Conduct Rules 2015* (WA); *Legal Profession Uniform General Rules 2015* (WA); *Legal Profession Uniform Law Australian Conduct (Barristers) Rules 2015* (WA)

(continued)

[115] Ebejer (n 73) 4–5.

(continued)

State/ territory	Statute	Regulations	Professional conduct rules
TAS	*Legal Profession Act 2007* (Tas)	*Legal Profession Regulations 2018* (Tas)	*Legal Profession (Solicitors Conduct) Rules 2020* (Tas)

As mentioned previously in Chapter 3, New South Wales, Victoria, and Western Australia adopted the *Legal Profession Uniform Law 2014*. Section 427(2) of the law empowers the Law Council of Australia to develop Uniform Rules, which lead to the making of the *Australian Solicitors' Conduct Rules* ('ASCR') for those jurisdictions, as well as the *Legal Profession General Rules and the Australian Conduct (Barristers) Rules*. Taking the ASCR as an example, it is a uniform set of rules providing for ethical and professional principles governing all aspects of solicitors, including their relations with clients, courts, other practitioners, regulatory authorities, and other stakeholders. The ASCR are developed by the Law Council of Australia as a collaboration of 16 law societies and bar associations and law firms as the constituent bodies of the Law Council. The ASCR was adopted in New South Wales and Victoria in 2015 and in Western Australia in 2022 following the adoption of the *Legal Profession Uniform Law*. The ASCR for non-Uniform Law jurisdictions were also adopted in South Australia in 2011, in Queensland in 2012, in Australian Capital Territory in 2016, and in Tasmania in 2010, with some variations. The Law Council of Australia also reviews the ethical rules from time to time and publishes commentary to improve the application and implementation of these rules across Australia.[116] Only the Northern Territory maintained its own ethical rules for legal professionals.

3.7.3 Ethical Obligations: ASCR as an Example

Given the wide acceptance of the ASCR in Australia, we provide for a brief overview of its contents to demonstrate the ethical requirements for legal practitioners in Australia. The following summary is provided on the basis of the content of the *Legal Profession Uniform Law Australia Solicitors' Conduct Rules 2015* (NSW). The objective of the set of rules, as indicated in section 1.3, is "to assist solicitors to act ethically and in accordance with the principles of professional conduct established by the common law and these Rules". The operational rules contain 43 rules, covering various aspects of the solicitors' conducts. Rule 1 established the scope of the application of this rule, covering both Australian solicitors and Australian-registered foreign lawyers acting in the manner of a solicitor. Rule 2 provides for the

[116] 'Australian Solicitors' Conduct Rules', *Law Council of Australia* (Web Page) <https://lawcouncil.au/policy-agenda/regulation-of-the-profession-and-ethics/australian-solicitors-conduct-rules>.

purpose and effect of the rules; in particular, it clarifies that a breach of the Rules may be considered as unsatisfactory professional conduct or professional misconduct and may lead to disciplinary action by the regulatory authority.

Further rules include fundamental duties (rr 3–6), relations with clients (rr 7–16), advocacy and litigation (rr 17–29), Relations with other persons (rr 30–35), and law practice management (rr 36–43).

(a) *Fundamental Duties*

A solicitor owes a paramount duty to the court and the administration of justice, which prevails in case of inconsistencies between this duty and any other duties.[117] In addition, a solicitor also has other fundamental ethical duties, such as that they should act in the best interests of a client while representing the client; be "honest and courteous" in legal practice; deliver legal service in the manner that is "competently, diligently, and as promptly as reasonably possible"; avoid any compromise to their integrity and professional independence; and comply with the law and ethical rules.[118] Solicitors should not engage in conduct demonstrating that they are "not a fit a proper person to practise law", or is likely "to be prejudicial to, or diminish the public confidence in the administration of justice", or "bring the profession into disrepute" to a material degree.[119] In case that a solicitor has given an undertaking in the course of legal practice, they should honour that undertaking and ensure the timely and effective performance of the undertaking.[120]

(b) *Relation with Clients*

When dealing with clients, solicitors should provide them with clear and prompt legal advice to help them understand relevant issues and make informed decisions throughout their case. They should also inform clients and instructing solicitors about alternatives to fully contested adjudication, unless they reasonably believe that these options had already been well understood and informed decisions are being made.[121] Solicitors should follow a client's lawful, proper, and competent instructions.[122] They should not disclose any confidential information in relation to the client obtained during their engagement except to specific individuals associated with the law practice, or under specific circumstances exempted from the duty, e.g. with the client's authorisation, required by law, to prevent serious crime or imminent harm.[123]

Further, one of the solicitor's most important duty to the client is to avoid, and manage, conflict of interest situations. Solicitors and legal practice should avoid conflicts between duties owed to previous and current clients; for example, if they

---

[117] *Legal Profession Uniform Law Australian Solicitors' Conduct Rules 2015* (NSW) s 2.3.

[118] Ibid s 2.4.

[119] Ibid s 2.5.

[120] Ibid s 2.6.

[121] Ibid s 2.7.

[122] Ibid s 2.8.

[123] Ibid s 2.9.

are in possession of material confidential information in relation to a previous client, they must not act for a current client if the disclosure of such confidential information is detrimental to the previous client, unless the previous client has given informed consent, or an effective information barrier has been established.[124] They should also avoid conflicts between the duties owed to two or more current clients. Specifically, there is a duty of loyalty that they should avoid acting for two or more clients in the same or related matters if the clients might have adverse or conflicted interests, unless each client is aware of the situation and gives informed consent. Further, under a duty of confidentiality, if confidential information from one client is detrimental to their case if disclosed to another client, the solicitor and the practice should not act for both clients unless there is informed consent for disclosure, or an effective information barrier is maintained.[125] Finally, in the circumstance of short-term legal assistance, if a solicitor believes that it is not practical to screen for conflicts due to the specific circumstances, they should disclose the nature of the service to the client, ensure that there are not actual or potential conflicts between the duties owed to the client and one or more other clients, and that informed consent is given. However, if the client's interest is conflicting with a current client, or the solicitor has confidential information from a previous or current client, the disclosure of which would cause harm to those clients, the solicitor must not provide or cease to provide short-term legal assistance.[126] Solicitors should also not represent a client if it conflicts with their own interests unless otherwise allowed by the rules. They should not encourage clients or third parties to confer benefits beyond fair remunerations, and should avoid actions leading to such benefits. Borrowing money from clients and former clients who still rely on their service is strictly prohibited unless the client falls into specific categories of borrowers. Their activities as executors of wills, or receptions of benefits from third parties related to client dealings, are also scrutinised under ethical and transparent requirements.[127]

Once a solicitor is designated with responsibilities regarding a client's matter, they should ensure the completion of the service unless the client otherwise agrees, or they discharge the law practice, or the law practice terminates the engagement "for just cause and on reasonable notice", or the engagement is ended by operation of law. In particular, in case of serious criminal offences, the client's failure to make satisfactory arrangements for payment will usually not justify the termination of the engagement, unless reasonable notice being given, allowing the client to arrange such payment, and the registrar of the court is notified. If the client is legally assisted, and such aid is withdrawn or terminated, solicitors or the law practice may terminate the engagement by giving reasonable written notice, allowing the client to make alternative arrangement for payment of future costs.[128]

---

[124] Ibid s 2.10.

[125] Ibid s 2.11.

[126] Ibid s 2.11A.

[127] Ibid s 2.12.

[128] Ibid s 2.13.

Solicitors should handle client documents in a reasonable matter. They should ensure that upon completion or termination of their engagement, the client or an authorised person receives all client documents (or copies of electronic documents) as soon as reasonably possible if the client so requests, unless an effective lien exists. Client documents may be destroyed after seven years from the engagement's completion or termination unless there are specific client instructions or legal obligations to retain them.[129] When a solicitor claims a lien for unpaid legal costs on client documents crucial for ongoing legal proceedings, if another solicitor is representing the client, the first solicitor must provide the documents to the second solicitor if the second solicitor agrees to hold the documents under the lien and maintains reasonable security for the unpaid costs; or the first solicitor agrees to arrangements for the second solicitor to secure payment upon completion of the proceedings. Alternatively, the first solicitor must deliver the documents to the client upon receiving reasonable security for the unpaid costs.[130] A solicitor must not charge for the storage of client documents, files or other properties unless client consent is obtained.[131]

(c) *Advocacy and Litigation*

In court-related activities, solicitors should also act ethically and not jeopardise the administration of justice. They should act independently, disinterestedly, and exercise their own forensic judgement while taking into account the client's and instructing solicitor's instructions and shall not act as a mere mouthpiece for the client or the instructing solicitor. This includes, for example, that they can choose strategies such as focusing on the real issues, presenting the case efficiently, and informing the court of any opposing legal authority, while not failing their duty to the client. They should not express personal opinions regarding the merits or evidence when making submissions to the court and cannot act as surety for the bail of a client.[132] They must not deal with a court on terms of informal personal familiarity in the presence of any parties and solicitors that would reasonably give rise to the impression that they have special favour with the court.[133]

In particular, the solicitor owes duties to the court that they should not deceive, or knowingly or recklessly mislead the court. If a solicitor becomes aware of a misleading statement being made by them, they must correct it promptly. However, they are not responsible for correcting errors made by the opposing party.[134] This duty also extends to the proper handling of information, evidence, and authorities supporting their cases. When seeking *ex parte* interlocutory relief, a solicitor must disclose all relevant factual or legal matters within their knowledge, including those that could oppose the relief. If a solicitor knows of relevant matters protected by privilege, they should always seek the client's waiver of that privilege for disclosure. If

---

129 Ibid s 2.14.

130 Ibid s 2.15.

131 Ibid s 2.16.

132 Ibid s 2.17.

133 Ibid s 2.18.

134 Ibid s 2.19, rr 19.1–19.3.

the privilege is not waived, the solicitor should inform the client of the consequences and notify the court accordingly. A solicitor must inform the court of any binding authority, and in case of no binding authority, any authority decided by an Australian appellate court, and relevant legislation against the client's case when appropriate. However, a solicitor need not disclose adverse authorities if the opponent indicates they will withdraw their case or consent to judgement, unless the appropriate time for disclosure has already arrived or passed.[135] If new relevant information arises after a judgement has been reserved but remains pending, the solicitor must inform the court, either through a letter or by requesting the relisting of the case for further argument. A solicitor need not inform the court of matters that makes inadmissible evidence admissible if the court has already ruled it out without calling on the defence. A solicitor should not question a prosecution witness about a client's prior convictions if the prosecution is unaware of them. Solicitors must inform the court of any misapprehensions regarding the effect of an order. If the opposing party in civil proceedings makes a concession regarding evidence, case law, or legislation contrary to the true position by mistake, the solicitor must alert the opponent and inform the court if necessary.[136]

The ethical obligation also requires solicitors to handle clients' and witnesses' misconduct in court properly. If they learn that a client, or their witness, acts in a manner compromising the administration of justice, such as lying materially or procuring other people to lie to the court, falsifying documents or procuring falsified documents, or suppressing or procuring other people or supress material evidence in the trial, the solicitor should refuse to take part in the case unless the client authorise them to inform the court the above circumstances, and do so promptly upon the authorisation.[137] In a criminal case, if a client confesses guilt to the solicitor but pleads not guilty, the solicitor may continue the representation but should not falsely suggest another person committed the offence, or present a case inconsistent with the confession. Alternatively, they can use strategies such as that the prosecution did not discharge its burden of proof to prove the commitment of the crime, or argue on the basis of a legal reason that bars a conviction, etc. However, if the client insists on giving evidence denying guilt or asserting their innocence, the solicitor must cease the representation.[138] In the case that a client intends to disobey a court order and informs their solicitor, the solicitor must advise against it and warn the client of the consequences and should not assist the client in actioning and concealing the disobedience. They may inform the court or opponent of such intention of their client if the client authorise them to do so, or if they believe on reasonable grounds that the client's conduct constitutes a threat to someone's safety.[139]

Solicitors are obligated to use the court process and privilege responsibly. This includes that they should ensure that their legal advice to invoke court powers is

---

[135] Ibid s 2.19, rr 19.4–19.7.

[136] Ibid s 2.19, rr 19.8–19.12.

[137] Ibid s 2.20, r 20.1.

[138] Ibid s 2.20, r 20.2.

[139] Ibid s 2.20, r 20.3.

justified by available evidence, supports the client's case on its merits, and is not intended to harass someone or gain an unfair advantage from someone.[140] Allegations made under privilege must similarly be substantiated by reasonable grounds and must not be aimed at embarrassing others.[141]

When drafting court documents or making submissions and opening and closing addresses, solicitors must only allege facts they believe are supported by adequate evidence.[142] This is particularly so regarding the making of serious allegations, including claims of criminality, fraud, and other serious misconduct, which would require solid evidence-based factual grounds for belief, and must be made with the client's informed consent regarding the potential consequences if such allegations are not proved.[143] They should also handle issues of credibility of evidence and witnesses in cross-examination, in accusing other people committing serious misconduct, and examination of vulnerable witnesses (e.g. victims of domestic or family violence, sexual assault, indecent assault) with great caution.[144]

The ethical obligation also includes that a solicitor should deal with the opponent fairly. They should not knowingly make false or misleading statements in relation to the case, and if any such statements had been made, take all necessary steps to correct them as soon as they are aware of it.[145] They must not make ex parte communication with the court concerning the substance of the case except in ex parte application or hearing and the opponent has been given proper notice, unless the court had first communicated in such manner, or the opponent has given consent in advance. In that situation, the solicitor should inform the opponent in a timely manner of the content of the communication.[146] They should inform the opponent as soon as possible of an intention to apply for adjournment on behalf of their client of the fact and grounds of such an application, and must try to inform the court promptly with the opponent's consent.[147]

The ethical obligations apply to the handling of witnesses and evidence comprehensively in order to maintain the integrity of the submission of evidence in court proceeding. Solicitors should not take any step to prevent or discourage witnesses from conferring with opponents or being interviewed by others involved in the proceedings. However, they do not violate this rule by informing a witness that they are not obligated to confer or be interviewed, nor by advising them on confidentiality obligations.[148] They should not advise or suggest that a witness provide false or misleading evidence, nor should they coach a witness on how to answer questions. They can still encourage honesty, testing the witness's version of events,

[140] Ibid s 2.21, r 21.1.

[141] Ibid s 2.21, r 21.2.

[142] Ibid s 2.21, r 21.3.

[143] Ibid s 2.21, r 21.4.

[144] Ibid s 2.21, rr 21.5–21.9.

[145] Ibid s 2.22, rr 22.1–22.2.

[146] Ibid s 2.22, rr 22.5–22.7.

[147] Ibid s 2.22, r 22.8.

[148] Ibid s 2.23.

or pointing out inconsistencies in their evidence, as long as they do not prompt the witness to provide testimony contrary to their true beliefs.[149] A solicitor must not meet with more than one lay witness at the same time regarding potentially contentious issues that could influence the witnesses' evidence, unless special circumstances justify such an arrangement. However, this rule does not apply when conferring with multiple clients regarding court undertakings, admissions, amendments of pleadings, or compromises.[150] A solicitor must not confer with a witness they have called while the witness is under cross-examination, unless the cross-examiner has given prior consent or if they believe on reasonable grounds that special circumstances necessitate the conference. In the latter case, the solicitor should, if possible, inform the cross-examiner beforehand or notify them as soon as possible afterwards.[151] If it is apparent, or known, that a solicitor will need to provide material evidence on contested issues in a case, they should not represent the client as an advocate during the hearing. Additionally, neither the solicitor, their associates, nor their law practice may continue to represent the client if it would compromise the administration of justice.[152] Finally, the solicitor should not publish, or take steps towards the publication of, materials concerning the ongoing proceedings if it would jeopardise a fair trial or the administration of justice.[153]

Prosecutors, as a special category of solicitors, have unique duties and obligations owed to the court.[154] This includes the prosecutor's fundamental role in assisting the court in discovering the truth by presenting all relevant evidence impartially and making adequate submissions of law.[155] They should not present the prosecution's case beyond a full and firm presentation of a case and should not seek to inflame or bias the court against the accused.[156] They must only argue points of law or fact they reasonably believe support a finding of guilt and are obligated to disclose all relevant materials to the opponent promptly unless such disclosure would threaten justice or safety.[157] In the latter case where evidence is not disclosed, they should consider withdrawing the charge or reducing it to a lesser offence.[158] Prosecutors must call all witnesses whose testimony is admissible and necessary for the presentation of the relevant circumstances, unless the opponent gives consent for not calling a witness, or the content of the evidence to be given by the witness has already been covered by an admission or established by other witnesses, or it is believed on reasonable grounds that the evidence is untruthful or unreliable, or the interest of justice would be jeopardised. In this case, they must inform the opponent of any witnesses not

[149] Ibid s 2.24.

[150] Ibid s 2.25.

[151] Ibid s 2.26.

[152] Ibid s 2.27.

[153] Ibid s 2.28.

[154] Ibid s 2.29.

[155] Ibid s 2.29, r 29.1.

[156] Ibid s 2.29, rr 29.2–29.3.

[157] Ibid s 2.29, rr 29.4–29.5.

[158] Ibid s 2.29, r 29.6.

called and the relevant grounds.[159] If prosecutors believe on reasonable grounds that evidence was unlawfully obtained, they must notify the opponent and make available a copy of the material.[160] Communication with the accused must only occur in the presence of their legal representative.[161] They should only inform the court and opponent that the prosecution has evidence regarding a particular aspect of their case on the basis of existing materials.[162] If they had made such assertion and discovered such evidence was not available, they should notify the opponent and the court in a timely manner.[163]

Additionally, prosecutors must correct any error related to sentencing, including those made by the opponent, inform the court the relevant authorities regarding sentence, assist the court to avoid appealable errors on the matter of sentence, and oblige to submit whether a custodial or non-custodial sentence is appropriate in each case.[164]

When acting as a counsel assisting an inquisitorial body (e.g. the Criminal Justice Commission, the Australian Crime Commission, the Australian Securities and Investments Commission, the Australian Competition and Consumer Commission, Royal Commissions, and statutory tribunals and bodies having investigation powers), a solicitor must adhere to the same standards of fairness and impartiality similar to the standard in r 29 as above.[165]

(d) *Relations with Other Persons*

A solicitor also owes ethical duties in dealing with various stakeholders other than their clients and the court in the court proceedings. They must not take unfair advantage of the obvious error of others if to do so would obtain benefits regarding their client which has no supportable foundation in law or fact.[166] Upon receiving materials known or suspected to be confidential, and being aware of the fact that the disclosure was inadvertent, a solicitor should not use the materials unless compelled by law; rather, they should return, destroy, or delete the materials immediately, and should notify the party who disclosed the material the steps taken in preventing the misuse of the material.[167] In the case that the solicitor had read part or all of the material before being aware of its confidential nature, they should not read any further, notify the opposing counsel or other person immediately, and should refrain from using the material unless compelled by law. If they are instructed by a client to read confidential material received in error, they must refuse to do so.[168]

---

[159] Ibid s 2.29, r 29.7.

[160] Ibid s 2.29, r 29.8.

[161] Ibid s 2.29, r 29.9.

[162] Ibid s 2.29, r 29.10.

[163] Ibid s 2.29, r 29.11.

[164] Ibid s 2.29, r 29.12.

[165] Ibid s 2.29, r 29.13.

[166] Ibid s 2.30.

[167] Ibid s 2.31, r 31.1.

[168] Ibid s 2.31, rr 31.2–31.3.

A solicitor should only make allegations against another Australian legal practitioner of unsatisfactory professional misconduct, or professional misconduct, on a bona fide basis and upon belief on reasonable grounds that there had been sufficient evidence supporting such an allegation.[169]

A solicitor must not communicate with a person known to be represented by another practitioner about the subject of representation unless they have obtained prior consent from the other practitioner, or believe urgent circumstances necessitate communication without unfairness to the opposing client, or it is only a communication solely inquiring about representation status, or when the other practitioner has not responded to a notice of intention to communicate after a reasonable time, provided there's a reasonable basis for proceeding.[170]

In communications with other persons, a solicitor must not engage in actions or communications that involve making misleading or intimidating statements that grossly exceed legitimate claims when representing a client. They should not threaten to initiate criminal or disciplinary complaints to coerce the satisfaction of civil claims, nor use tactics beyond legitimate advocacy to embarrass or frustrate others on purpose. The solicitors must not solicit instructions for legal services in a manner that oppresses or harasses individuals who are at a significant disadvantage due to recent trauma, injury, or other circumstances, ensuring that such individuals are treated fairly.[171] If a solicitor instructs a third party on behalf of a client, and they do not intend to accept personal liability for payment of the third party's fee, they should advise the third party in advance.[172]

(e) *Law Practice Management*

A final aspect of the solicitor's ethical obligations falls in their management of the law practice. The principals, or the ones in charge of particular matters, are responsible for various aspects of the legal practice. A solicitor, or principal of a law practice, must ensure that all advertising, marketing, or promotional materials and activities in relation to the solicitor or the law practice are not false, misleading, deceptive, offensive, or prohibited by law. They must avoid creating a false, misleading, or deceptive impression of specialist expertise and should avoid the use the terms "accredited specialist" or similar descriptions in their advertising unless they are accredited by the relevant professional association.[173] A solicitor with designated responsibility for a matter should exercise reasonable supervision over other solicitors, as well as other employees engaged in the legal service in relation to that matter.[174]

If a solicitor or a law practice shares an office with or is affiliated with an entity or business not providing legal services, and a client is receiving services from both the solicitor/law practice and the other entity or business, the solicitor or law practice

[169] Ibid s 2.32.

[170] Ibid s 2.33.

[171] Ibid s 2.34.

[172] Ibid s 2.35.

[173] Ibid s 2.36.

[174] Ibid s 2.37.

should take all reasonable steps to inform the client the nature and terms of the legal services and distinguish it from the non-legal services.[175] They should not share receipts arising from or in connection with the provision of legal service with any disqualified person, or any person who has been found guilty for an indictable offence, or who has a guilty plea accepted in relation to an indictable offence involving dishonest conduct.[176]

A former judicial officer acting as a solicitor should not appear in any court if they were a member of or presided in that court, and any court from which appeals may be made or brought to any court they were a member, within two years after they cease to hold that office, unless otherwise allowed by the court.[177]

More generally, a solicitor has an obligation to not engage in conducts of discrimination, sexual harassment, any other form of harassment, or workplace bullying, in the legal practice and profession.[178] Subject to duties owed to clients, a solicitor should be timely, open, and frank in their dealings with a regulatory authority.[179]

---

175 Ibid s 2.39.

176 Ibid s 2.40.

177 Ibid s 2.38.

178 Ibid s 2.42.

179 Ibid s 2.43.

Chapter 4
A New Era of the Australian Legal Education: In the Context of a Global Trend of New Technology

The modern legal landscape in Australia currently stands at a pivotal juncture, shaped by both challenges and opportunities which continuously demand innovation in the sector. Both the legal education and the legal profession are undergoing a digital transformation with rapid technological advancements such as artificial intelligence and automation redefining traditional legal practices. This technological revolution was accelerated by the impact of the COVID-19 pandemic which propelled law students and legal professionals into remote working and digital collaboration. Additionally, the legal landscape in Australia has felt the pressures of globalisation which demands a broader understanding of the nuances of international laws and legal cultural differences. The legal fraternity in Australia is facing a number of challenges and opportunities at the hands of technological advancements, globalisation, and the effects of the COVID-19 pandemic. The institutional educators in law are expected to navigate these changes to innovatively shape the future of the legal profession and education in Australia.

This chapter aims to address the development of Australian legal education in the context of the global trend of new technology from the following perspectives. Sections 1 and 2 provide the context of the development of legal education in the new era, taking into account the global and cross-cultural elements, and the features arising from the common law/civil law distinctions. On that basis, Section 3 focuses on the changes brought to legal education in recent years in response to technological developments, including the addition of new requirements, examples of the use of technology in the teaching and learning activities, and in particular, the developments and concerns regarding the use of generative AI in law assessments. Section 4 proceeds to discuss legal and interdisciplinary research conducted by legal educators and its contribution to the legal education. Section 5 concludes the chapter by discussing the future of legal education on the basis of the observations and discussions in the previous parts.

S. Zhang et al., *Technology, Legal Education and Legal Profession in China and Australia*, International and Comparative Law in the Asia Pacific,
https://doi.org/10.1007/978-981-96-1639-8_4

4.1 Australian Legal Education in the Global and Cross-Cultural Context

Globalisation has changed the international relations landscape, and as a result law graduates are expected to have acquired the tools to compete in the growing global market for legal services.[1] The far-reaching nature of the modern global legal market creates demand for a new generation of lawyers who appreciate the challenges affiliated with the global economic market.[2] The development of technology has revolutionised business processes and the way people communicate, which has only further propelled globalisation.[3] Consequently, the demand for the exportation of legal services grows.[4] The global shift in the provision of legal services requires practitioners to have sufficient understanding of international markets to undergo this paradigm shift.[5] As a result, legal education providers should take into consideration these international components to ensure that their graduates are equipped to meet the challenges and dimensions of internationalisation and globalisation.[6]

As the global marketplace grows and the Australian legal services market becomes increasingly more cross-national, it becomes inevitable that legal practitioners must be well-versed in the different legal systems of other countries.[7] This increased demand for the legal profession creates flow-down effects on legal education. Graduates are increasingly expected to be working on cross-jurisdictional transactions and matters, and even want to live and work overseas. As such, legal education must respond by ensuring that the curriculum meets these needs but also responds to the global legal market.[8] This is not limited to changing the curriculum to include international law electives; rather, it requires a growth in more international law programs and opportunities to study abroad.[9]

The process of internationalising legal education in Australia began with ILET Committee of the International Legal Services Advisory Council's ("ILSAC") Internationalisation of the Australian Law Degree report ("ILET Report") in 2004.[10] The ILET Committee determined that the impact of globalisation required law schools and legal education to implement strategies to increase the internationalisation of

---

[1] Nirmal and Singh (2018, 30).

[2] Basedow (2014, 6).

[3] Wang (2019, 64, 65).

[4] Law Society of Western Australia (2017, 3).

[5] Nirmal and Singh (n 391) 30.

[6] Ibid.

[7] Chief Justice Robert French, 'The Judiciary in an Age of Global Interdependence' (Speech, International Association for Court Administration Conference, 15 March 2011) <https://www.hcourt.gov.au/assets/publications/speeches/current-justices/frenchcj/frenchcj15mar11.pdf>.

[8] Triggs (2014, 214).

[9] William Van Caenegem, 'Ignoring the Civil Law/Common Law Divide in an Integrated World' in van Caenegem and Hiscock (eds) (n 392) 169.

[10] International Legal Services Advisory Council, *Internationalisation of the Australian Law Degree* (Final Report, June 2004).

legal education and to develop a genuine interest in international legal education.[11] The report concluded that law schools did not view globalisation or the internationalisation of legal education curriculum a priority; rather, they believed that the introduction of international law electives was sufficient preparation of their students for contemporary legal practice.[12] The ILET report made a number of recommendations, including the internationalisation of legal education through the development of international law core legal subjects, and integrating subject areas to ensure students are equipped with the practical skills required to deliver legal services in a modern and global legal system.[13] However, as the legal education sector did not respond to these recommendations enthusiastically, little changes were made in response to this report.[14]

The suggestion to internationalise legal education, while an important concern, has created a tension between the many objectives of legal education.[15] The current Australian core curriculum is heavily focused on substantive domestic law topics like the Priestley 11, creating a challenge for the integration of internationalisation and global law topics within an already quite crowded curriculum.[16] The Priestley 11 accounts for over half of a law degree, and as such it is difficult to make legal education in Australia sufficiently international to meet the global demand for future lawyers.[17] It is unlikely that the Priestley 11 will change, however law schools have a responsibility to ensure that subject offerings for international law topics are made for students who wish to become "global lawyers".[18] Ultimately, despite this tension, it remains crucial that international law be integrated into the core curriculum in the long term to ensure that law graduates are equipped with the required skills to work in diverse global and foreign work environments.[19]

This position was reaffirmed in 2012, when ILSAC in conjunction with the Australian government Office for Learning and Teaching released the *Internationalising the Australian Law Curriculum for Enhanced Global Legal Practice* report.[20]

---

[11] Johnstone and Vignaendra (2003, 3) cited in Lo (2013, 1, 5).

[12] Lo (n 401) 5.

[13] International Legal Services Advisory Council (n 400) 10 cited in Hutchinson (2006, 93, 99).

[14] Michael Coper, 'Internationalisation and Different National Philosophies of Legal Education: Convergence, Divergence and Contestability' in van Caenegem and Hiscock (n 392) 44.

[15] Chief Justice Robert French, 'Internationalising the Australian Law curriculum for enhanced global legal education and practice' (Speech, International Legal Services Advisory Council National Symposium, 16 March 2012), 4–5 <https://www.hcourt.gov.au/assets/publications/speeches/current-justices/frenchcj/frenchcj16mar12.pdf>.

[16] Bobette Wolski, 'Continuing the Internationalisation Debate: Philosophies of Legal Education, Issues in Curriculum Design and Lessons from Skills Integration' in van Caenegem and Hiscock (n 392) 71.

[17] Ibid 89–90.

[18] Ibid 90.

[19] Ibid 90–91.

[20] Office for Learning and Teaching, *Internationalising the Australian Law Curriculum for Enhanced Global Legal Practice* (Final Report, 2013) <https://ltr.edu.au/resources/PP10_1789_Bentley_booklet_2012.pdf>.

This 2012 report reiterated the significant impact that globalisation had on the Australian legal system which required continued efforts to internationalise the law curriculum.[21] The report urges law schools to recognise their role in ensuring that law graduates are prepared to enter legal practice domestically but also internationally.[22] This recommendation requires the law curriculum to ensure that students are receiving a well-rounded domestic education, like the Priestley 11 curriculum, while also developing the practical and intellectual skills required to enter international practice.[23]

This suggests that rather than focusing on amending the Priestley 11 curriculum, law schools should have a greater focus on the development of key legal skills.[24] It is important in the new global legal environment that law students are also trained how to think critically and assess the complexity of legal issues in different legal cultures.[25] In teaching international law, legal education should focus on providing students with an understanding of the underlying principles of the law in different jurisdictions, with a focus on understanding the difference in legal culture and the structure of the law rather than having detailed knowledge on specific rules or legislation in another jurisdiction.[26] Integration of international law into Australia's legal education curriculum does not have to disregard critical and key areas, like those of the Priestley 11; rather, it should facilitate the growth of skills that allow graduates to quickly adapt and acquire the knowledge of a new legal environment.[27]

More recently, in the absence of any national requirements, law schools have integrated international law units into their compulsory curriculum.[28] While there are no formal requirements for knowledge of international law, many law schools have begun incorporating it into their unit offerings as it becomes increasingly more critical for law graduates to have some knowledge of international law for legal practice.[29] This sentiment is common across the 17 law schools who have introduced compulsory international law units. For example, in a survey of the 17 law schools, nearly all their course outlines and subject guides for their international law units of study recognised the importance of international law knowledge for law graduates and prospective lawyers.[30]

There is no clear solution to resolve the tensions created by amending the national legal education curriculum to include international law. The current law school curriculum is already crowded and the addition of international law to the Priestley

---

[21] Ibid 9–10.

[22] Ibid 13.

[23] Ibid.

[24] Hutchinson (n 403) 102.

[25] Van Caenegem and Hiscock (n 392) 171.

[26] Ibid.

[27] Ibid.

[28] Baghoomians (2022, 17).

[29] Ibid.

[30] Ibid 21–2.

11 may simply exacerbate this issue.[31] This addition limits the number of electives students can take, and risks lessening student's interest in pursuing their interest in international law.[32] Additionally it takes away from the purpose of internationalising law curriculum as it becomes a shallow acquisition of substantive law.[33] As explored above, the purpose of internationalising legal education is to allow students to acquire the practical skills required in an increasingly globalised legal services industry. Ultimately, globalisation has had a significant impact on legal education in Australia, however there are a number of issues that are required to be addressed as the system continues to become increasingly internationalised. Growth in the internationalisation of legal education in Australia rests upon addressing these issues in a principled way that recognises the importance of international law in the Australian legal education system.[34]

4.2 Australian Legal Education in the Context of the Common Law and Civil Law Traditions

The traditional divide between common law and civil law systems exists due to profound differences in legal doctrine and culture.[35] However, as globalisation creates an increasingly integrated global legal system, there is increasing growth in international legal education programs that decreases this divide and allows students to experience the differences in educational styles.[36]

The main difference between civil law systems and common law systems is the source of law.[37] Common law countries like the United States of America and Australia rely upon case law where legal principles develop through the judiciary as well as through legislation.[38] Civil law systems operate primarily through legal principles and codified law.[39]

The education system in a civil law tradition jurisdiction focuses on providing students with a theoretical overview of the entire legal system for the jurisdiction.[40] The focus is primarily on legal principles and the framework of the legal system, and how that is translated into statute.[41] Students are not often exposed to specific details

[31] Ibid 33–34.

[32] Lo (n 402) 11.

[33] Ibid 17.

[34] Baghoomians, Crawford and Mowbray (n 418) 35.

[35] William van Caenegem, 'Ignoring the Civil Law/Common Law Divide in an Integrated Legal World' in van Caenegem and Hiscock (n 392) 145.

[36] Ibid 169–70.

[37] Sadi (2018, 165, 170).

[38] Ibid 170–1.

[39] Ibid 171.

[40] Ibid 174.

[41] Ibid.

of case law. This methodology dates back as far as the Roman Empire, and in its essence it teaches students to perceive the law based on the framework for rules.[42]

Common law systems, on the other hand, focus on case law-based reasoning and rule-based learning.[43] Legal education in common law systems has an emphasis on the development of technical skills and knowledge, relying on teaching this knowledge through analysis of precedent.[44]

4.3 Australian Legal Education in the Digital Age

4.3.1 Introduction

The development of technology, and continued innovations in the digital age, is requiring legal education providers to innovate how they deliver their course.[45] Legal professionals are being required to adapt to technological changes, such as automation and digitisation, and as a result law schools are expected to increase the digital literacy of law graduates to ensure that students are adequately prepared for professional practice.[46] This requires law schools not only to innovate the ways in which they deliver content, but also to create opportunities for students to develop and learn the digital literacy skills required for legal practice.

4.3.2 Requirement for Blended Learning

The digital age has not merely impacted the way in which the legal services are delivered, but it has transformed the legal education landscape. Historically the didactic method has been adopted by legal educators, where lecturers are utilised to impart knowledge onto students by academics which is followed up with discussion questions to test students' knowledge in tutorials.[47] In a tutorial setting, the Socratic method of questioning is then utilised to stimulate critical thinking with a focus on fundamental legal concepts, principles, and theories.[48] However, as technology develops, this is no longer the most effective way to teach students the law. Digital literacy and the use of technology is a concern for legal education,

42 Ibid 180.

43 Burridge and Webb (2007, 72, 80).

44 Ibid.

45 Traczykowski and Dale (2023, 260).

46 Ibid.

47 Smith (2020, 209).

48 Blanco (2023, 36, 40).

as well as the broader higher education sector.[49] By utilising technology-driven instruction in legal education, student learning is enhanced by increasing the rate in which students absorb and understand legal concepts while creating an overall more enriched learning environment.[50] The digital age has not only introduced incremental changes to legal education, but it has also fundamentally changed legal education in a way where technology is now inseparable from the educational experience.

Law schools are being challenged to incorporate technology through blended learning. When the Australian Law School Standards were officially adopted in 2020, they challenged law schools to utilise a variety of teaching methods including blending learning.[51] The Standards called for legal education providers to accommodate the increased use of technology in the higher education sector to promote the achievement of the prescribed learning outcomes of the law course.[52] Blended learning is not defined within the Standards, but practically blended learning involves the utilisation of different learning pedagogies and educational tools to achieve educational objectives.[53] As technology develops, this is increasingly looking like a strategic combination of in-person and digital instruction.[54] Additionally, blended learning, or "online" learning, does not simply have to refer to digital classes; rather, it can be the utilisation of technology in both face-to-face and online teaching.[55] Blended learning is more than just recording lectures and making them available online for students to watch; rather, it is the strategic maximisation of the benefits of technology and in-person classes.[56] This requires universities and educators to utilise technology in a way that stimulates student engagement through creative styles of content delivery.[57]

Law schools and educators have the ability to facilitate a more engaged interaction between students, lecturers, and materials through the incorporation of both synchronous and asynchronous digital learning methodologies.[58] As mentioned above, effective blended learning includes more than just recording lectures and making them available for students. Rather, it is more enriching for students if the online materials are supplementary in nature (i.e. supplementary recorded video lectures or online tutorials) which is then followed up in a seminar or tutorial style lesson where the lecturer facilitates discussion on key materials and students engagement in discussion style questions.[59] The blended learning model encourages student engagement by developing a stronger relationship between learning opportunities

[49] Galloway (2017, 1, 3).
[50] Blanco (n 438) 40.
[51] Council of Australian Law Deans (n 15) Standard 2.2.
[52] Ibid Standard 2.2.3.
[53] Houghton (2023, 271, 276).
[54] Ibid.
[55] Corban and Bugden (2018, 1).
[56] Houghton (n 443) 276.
[57] Morton et al. (2016, 36, 40).
[58] Smith (n 437) 212.
[59] Ibid.

pre-class, during-class, and post-class.[60] The learning experience of the students is enriched by this style of blended learning, as they apply learnings from the asynchronous digital materials to problem questions and relate new contexts to existing knowledge.[61]

As such, law schools are challenged to re-imagine the traditional ways of teaching. This especially relates to the Priestley 11 units which historically lend themselves to being taught in a more traditional manner.[62] Law schools are required to shift from a teacher-centred learning model where key legal concepts are taught through lectures and case notes.[63] Academics must draw upon technology, and digital learning methodologies, and reconceptualise how important legal theory is taught to ensure that they do not stifle the development their students as future legal practitioners.[64] This does not mean that students should not be taught underlying legal theory; rather, that technology should be embraced when teaching law.[65]

4.3.3 Digital Literacy of Law Graduates Transitioning to Practice

New technology continues to shape contemporary professional legal practice.[66] The nature of how a legal professional completes work is changing. Legal education must respond to this to ensure students are prepared for contemporary legal practice.[67] As a result, law graduates are required to have a broader skillset that involves the management of automated technology and the ability to practise the law in a virtual setting.[68] It is also strongly recommended by the Law Institute of New South Wales that law students become familiarised with new legal technology.[69] Their inquiry suggests that students should be prepared to utilise technology to service clients in their future legal careers.[70] There is an expectation in the legal profession that the technological developments filter down into law schools, and that law schools adapt and create a range of technology-focused learning opportunities for students.[71] Technology has the potential to change and develop the provision of legal services, and as such

[60] Castan and Hyams (2017, 1, 2).

[61] Smith (n 437) 212.

[62] Galloway (n 439) 25.

[63] Smith (n 437) 215.

[64] Galloway (n 439) 25.

[65] Smith (n 437) 216.

[66] Galloway (n 439) 3.

[67] Ibid.

[68] Smith (n 437) 209.

[69] Law Society of New South Wales Flip Commission of Inquiry (2017).

[70] Ibid.

[71] Smith (n 437) 210.

law schools have a responsibility to incorporate technological developments into the curriculum alongside traditional topics of legislation and legal theory.[72]

Technology utilised in practice is bigger than document management systems and electronic court systems associated with the litigation process.[73] The legal profession is becoming increasingly interdisciplinary, and as such law graduates must be equipped to utilise technology in a variety of legal domains.[74] Law students in the course of their degree will have access to, and will use often, online casebooks, and databases like AUSTLII and JADE for case law, legislation, and journal articles.[75] However, technologies are increasingly integrated into the day-to-day of a legal workplace, and as such law students require a broader digital literacy than the utilisation of online databases for conducting legal research.[76] In particular, graduate lawyers will be expected to deploy automated systems and electronic discovery platforms.

The requirement for digital literacy challenges how law students are taught. For example, as mentioned above, law graduates will be required to utilise technology to complete the discovery process. There is an increase in the use of "e-discovery" technology in civil litigation which challenges how the law of evidence and civil procedure is being taught in law schools.[77] The question becomes whether law schools can continue to require the study of discovery processes without a particular focus on their digital counterparts.[78] The electronic discovery process requires an understanding of its complex computer programs which considers both the operation of the application and the relevant law.[79] This also applies to the utilisation of digital systems during the conveyancing process and how property law is taught.[80] The operation of technology in the legal profession creates expectations of the digital literacy of law graduates, which is not limited to the examples of conveyancing and discovery mentioned above.[81]

It is, however, not as simple as just making an amendment to the required curriculum of law schools to require the integration of digital literacy and technology to law schools. Over the last 30 years, law schools have undergone revolutionary and unprecedented restructuring which has created long-standing tension between the legal profession and legal education providers.[82] While transformation to the legal education system to include technology is fundamental to preparing students for

[72] Ibid 209.

[73] Galloway (n 439) 9.

[74] Ibid 8.

[75] Smith (n 437) 212.

[76] Galloway (n 439) 10.

[77] Ibid.

[78] Ibid.

[79] Ibid 12.

[80] Ibid.

[81] Ibid.

[82] Wang (n 393) 71.

practice, reform to the already crowded curriculum is complicated.[83] There becomes a challenge of balancing priorities: are students taught to think critically and apply critical and ethical reasoning, or should the curriculum provide students with practical and additional skills such as technological understanding?[84]

Despite the above challenges there is a clear need to facilitate the adoption of technology in the delivery of legal education.[85] Core legal topics, like the Priestley Eleven, can remain unchanged but other aspects of the law degree must be transformed to prepare law graduates for legal roles.[86] The fundamental values of legal education, which is built on the basis of critical thinking and ethical decision-making, align with the underlying principles of technology which allows for their reinforcement in the curriculum.[87]

Regardless of whether law students decide to practise law, law schools have a responsibility to ensure that law students understand legal theories but also legal processes and their digital contexts.[88] This not only supports graduation outcomes for students, but also allows future legal practitioners to engage more effectively with their client's, and society's, needs.[89]

4.3.4 Transformation of Law Schools After COVID-19

The COVID-19 pandemic had a substantial health impact on Australians, with almost 6 million confirmed cases and more than 7000 confirmed COVID-19-related deaths between March 2020 and April 2022.[90] While globally the consequences of the pandemic were disastrous, comparatively Australia fared quite well. This does not mean that it did not come with its challenges, including an urgent move to online learning while the country was under orders to stay home and under various lockdowns. COVID-19 forced universities and educators globally to adapt to online methods of delivery. Prior to the pandemic, only eight law schools offered a law degree fully online which meant that many law schools had to quickly adapt to online learning.[91] As mentioned above, only a small portion of law schools offered fully online law courses prior to the pandemic. The remainder of law schools utilised a blended learning or "flipped classroom" model, whereby some teaching materials

[83] Ibid 72.

[84] Ibid.

[85] Ibid 73.

[86] Bullows (n 312) 212.

[87] Wang (n 393) 75.

[88] Galloway (n 439) 25.

[89] Ibid.

[90] Australian Institute of Health and Welfare, *Australia's Health 2022: Data Insights* (Report No 18, 2022) 11.

[91] William van Caenegem and Trish Mundy, *Special Report of Online Legal Education in Australia* (October 28, 2021) 1 <https://ssrn.com/abstract=3951659>.

would be utilised online, and students would then attend a seminar session, or a traditional lecture followed by a tutorial model.[92] Additionally, the pandemic created an environment where law graduates are expected to adapt to hybrid working environments, where they are expected to understand technology and experience supervision and mentoring virtually.[93]

During the pandemic, law schools were forced to adapt and switch teaching methods to online mid-course.[94] Classes moved online, often to live sessions on Zoom (or other video conferencing tools) with supplementary online materials including readings and pre-recorded classes. In-person invigilated examinations became impossible, and assessment methods were changed.[95] Higher education authorities, such as the TEQSA, were accommodating during the pandemic, and supported law schools by allowing them to make any necessary changes to ensure a rapid shift in delivery of classes.[96] TEQSA also released guidelines to ensure that regulatory burdens were reduced and to ensure that the HES Framework was complied with in relation to online delivery of classes.[97]

Concerns also arose during the pandemic about whether law schools were going to remain accredited and if students were going to meet the academic requirements for admission to practice. In correspondence with the University of Melbourne Law School, the Victorian Legal Admissions Board ("VLAB") confirmed that due to the unprecedented nature of the COVID-19 pandemic that online course delivery, including for assessments, that they would work with law schools to ensure continued compliance with the accreditation requirements.[98]

The pandemic forced law schools to adapt and experience with technology and online learning, and as a result there is now almost universal adoption of blended learning methods in Australian law schools.[99] The adoption of blended learning methods predates the pandemic but has been accelerated and adopted due to the transition to online learning during the pandemic.[100] Despite the return to face-to-face learning for most Australian law schools, the challenges faced during the pandemic serve as a reminder of how to improve the utilisation of online learning environments.[101] Law schools had the opportunity to experience with different technology

---

[92] Ibid 10.

[93] Lilley and Do (2002, 22–3).

[94] Nottage (2022, 12).

[95] Ibid.

[96] Caenegem and Mundy (n 481) 5–6.

[97] See Tertiary Education Quality and Standards Agency, 'Reducing Regulatory Burden During COVID-19—Important Update from TEQSA' (Web Page, 26 March 2020) <https://www.teqsa.gov.au/reducing-regulatory-burden-during-covid-19-important-update-teqsa>; Tertiary Education Quality and Standards Agency, 'Online Delivery—Key Considerations for Providers' (Web Page, 8 April 2020) <https://www.teqsa.gov.au/latest-news/publications/online-delivery-key-considerations-providers>.

[98] Nicholson (2022, 215).

[99] Caenegem and Mundy (n 481) 11.

[100] Ibid.

[101] De Maio (2022, 33, 35).

and online learning methods during the pandemic and have continued to use the successful tools and methods. This includes the utilisation of online databases and libraries, which increased during the pandemic.[102] Despite the increase in online research and legal source materials, trends show that the utilisation of physical law libraries as social and academic spaces will continue and are not likely to disappear in favour of online resources.[103]

In addition to the above, some law schools are continuing the integration of online legal education including the practice of online assessment that they utilised during the pandemic.[104] The pandemic resulted in a number of changes being made to the way in which universities conducted assessments, including conducting examinations online. There is some debate about the continued use of online assessment, due to academic integrity and concerns around testing student's abilities.[105]

Following the pandemic online exams have become more common. Not only does it have pedagogical advantages, it also creates a simulated environment that replicates something closer to an environment close to a legal workplace.[106] The pandemic provided an opportunity for law schools to review outdated practices, including outdated forms of assessment like handwritten examinations.[107] During the pandemic some students reported that they were able to focus more closely on the content of their work and that the ability to edit their work increased writing quality.[108] Others reported that the ability to edit their work detracted from their engagement in their writing.[109]

From an academic integrity perspective, the prevalent concerns arise from online services and artificial intelligence that assist students with cheating.[110] This may be resolved by adjusting the weight of an assessment, like a research essay or online examination, where the utilisation of these services may be prevalent to reduce the risk of academic misconduct and artificially generated content.[111] If the weight is moved away from these types of assessments, there is a flexibility created which allows for the introduction of authentic assessments which provide students with the opportunity to apply their skills to an assessment that reflects what they might see in practice.[112]

The pandemic has had a lasting impact on legal education. During the pandemic law schools were forced to transition online and as a result experimented with new technologies and methods of delivery that have remained in practice post-pandemic.

---

102 Caenegem and Mundy (n 481) 12.

103 Ibid.

104 Ibid 21.

105 Ibid 12–14.

106 Ibid 14.

107 Burdon (2022, 1, 3).

108 Steel et al. (2019, 2–4), cited in Caenegem and Mundy (n 481) 14.

109 Ibid.

110 Caenegem and Mundy (n 481)15.

111 Ibid.

112 Burdon (n 497) 35–6.

While blended learning was on the rise pre-pandemic, it is now a permanent feature of many law schools.[113] The pandemic provided law schools with the opportunity to experiment with new technology which has optimised and innovated their blended learning methodologies.[114] Temporary online features, like discussion boards, online quizzes, and participation in online talks and clinics have become permanent fixtures in blended learning, ensuring that online-centred content is dynamic and engaging for students.[115]

4.3.5 Examples of the Use of Technology in Legal Education

There are a number of tools that legal educators can utilise to improve the experience of law students.[116] These tools vary from e-learning tools such as pre-recorded videos, online quizzes, and discussion boards, to internet-based Learning Management Systems where teachers can upload digital content that students can access at any time.[117] The integration of these technologies ensure that legal education reflects the technological growth of the legal profession.[118]

(a) *Learning Management Systems*

The learning management system ("LMS") can host a large variety of resources for legal education including online texts, modules with embedded videos and activities, online quizzes.[119] The LMS system allows academics to create tailor-made modules and pages which incorporate a number of resources for their students.[120] Universities will usually deploy a bespoke version of an LMS like *BlackBoard* (now *Anthology*), *Moodle*, or *Canvas*, which lecturers can utilise to enhance the quality of teaching and increase student engagement.[121] The integration of online materials, like lecture notes, videos, and textbooks that can be freely accessed by students on an LMS system also prepares students for legal practice by improving their general capacity to use these forms of technology.[122]

---

[113] Ibid 25.

[114] Ibid.

[115] Ibid 24.

[116] Wolff and Chan (2016, 4).

[117] Ibid.

[118] Bullows (n 312) 221.

[119] Smith (n 437) 212.

[120] Michael Adams, 'Developments in Australian Curriculum and Teaching Across the Various Law Degrees' (Zhejiang University Guanghua Law School Forum, 28 September 2014) 17.

[121] Ibid.

[122] Bullows (n 312) 211.

(b) *Open Educational Resources*

Open Education Resources ("OERs") are materials and resources that can be utilised at no cost that resides under the public domain or open licence.[123] The use of OERs can enrich a student's experience and improve their engagement with content.[124] Lecturers can utilise OERs to increase the range of materials provided to students in order to demonstrate key legal concepts, and highlight broader protectives and learning styles.[125] In turn, this improves student engagement and expands interactive resources.[126]

(c) *Online Databases*

Online databases, like the Australasian Legal information Institute ("AustLII"), have revolutionised access to legal information.[127] Legal studies are heavily reliant on access to legal information, making databases such as AustLII, as well as JADE, LexisNexis, and Westlaw, which provide students access to case law, journal articles, and legislation at the tips of their fingers extremely beneficial.[128] The ability to navigate such databases will greatly benefit law students as they transition to legal practice and are required to conduct legal research.

(d) *Lecture Recordings—Echo360*

Echo360 is an online media system that can be utilised to record lecturers and embed learning activities for students' access, while allowing teachers to review statistics of student performance.[129] Echo360 allows teachers to record a lecture while screen capturing a PowerPoint or other visual presentation.[130] The program allows teachers to easily edit audio and video clips to then be uploaded online and even embedded into learning modules.[131] Lecture recordings benefit students, especially those who cannot always attend classes.[132] Lecture recordings act as a visual aid in which students can use to supplement their learnings and revise for assessments.[133]

123 Ibid 213.

124 Ibid.

125 Ibid.

126 Ibid.

127 Adams (n 510) 16.

128 Burros (n 312) 212.

129 Wolff and Chan (n 506) 89.

130 Ibid 89–90.

131 Ibid.

132 Draper et al. (2018, 316, 328–9).

133 Ibid 329.

4.3.6 *Innovative Law Subjects and Programs in Relation to Technology and Law*

In addition to the changes and innovations mentioned above, some law schools take further movements towards the combination of law and technology in order to better prepare their graduates for the changes in legal practice. This is reflected in the reforms and innovations in the curriculum.

The following table lists some new law and technology subjects recently offered in Australian law schools.

Institution	Subject	Highlights
University of Sydney	LAWS5218 Law and Technology	This subject examines the regulation of technologies, such as privacy laws and surveillance, AI and its impact on individual rights, etc.
University of Melbourne	LAWS90145 Artificial Intelligence and Law[134] LAWS90248 AI and Justice[135] LAWS90169 Blockchain and Cryptocurrency[136] LAWS90205 Digital Technologies and Labour Law[137] LAWS70362 Information Technology Contracting Law[138] LAWS90110 Regulation of FinTech[139] LAWS90286 Legal AI: Design and Development	These subjects are offered to students enrolled for Specialise Certificate in Law and Technological Innovation (see below)

(continued)

[134] 'Artificial Intelligence and the Law (LAWS90145)', *The University of Melbourne* (Web Page, 3 June 2024) <https://handbook.unimelb.edu.au/2024/subjects/laws90145>.

[135] 'AI and Justice (LAWS90248)', *The University of Melbourne'* (Web Page, 22 May 2024) <https://handbook.unimelb.edu.au/2024/subjects/laws90248>.

[136] 'Blockchain and Cryptocurrency Law (LAWS90169)', *The University mof Melbourne* (Web Page, 8 August 2024) <https://handbook.unimelb.edu.au/2024/subjects/laws90169>.

[137] 'Digital Technology and Labour Law (LAWS90205)', *The University of Melbourne* (Web Page, 11 June 2024) <https://handbook.unimelb.edu.au/2024/subjects/laws90205>.

[138] 'Information Technology Contracting Law (LAWS 70362)', *The University of Melbourne* (Web Page, 25 May 2024) <https://handbook.unimelb.edu.au/2024/subjects/laws70362>.

[139] 'Regulation of FinTech (LAWS90110)', *The University of Melbourne* (Web Page, 11 June 2024) <https://handbook.unimelb.edu.au/2024/subjects/laws90110>.

(continued)

Institution	Subject	Highlights
Australian National University	LAWS4245/LAWS8445 Information Technology Law[140] LAWS8338 Cryptoassets and the Law[141] LAWS8405 Artificial Intelligence, Law and Society[142] LAWS8407 Digital Economies and the Law[143]	Online only; most of the subjects are offered to students enrolled in Graduate Certificate of New Technologies Law (see below)
Monash University	LAW4545 Technology, Design, and Innovation in Legal Services[144]	Students are required to develop a web-based application that solves a legal problem in the context of emerging legal technologies
University of New South Wales	LAWS3346/LAWS8346/JURD7546 Law and Technology: Comparative Perspectives (UNSW/UZH)[145]	This course is offered jointly by University of New South Wales and University of Zurich in Switzerland
University of Technology Sydney	76106 Technology Law, Policy and Ethics 76107 Applied Project in Law, Innovation and Technology	These two subjects are the two Capstones for Major MAJ09443 Legal Futures and Technology[146]
Deakin University	MLL444—Data Law, Privacy and Cybercrime[147]	

(continued)

[140] 'Information Technology Law: LAWS4245', *Australian National University* (Web Page) <https://programsandcourses.anu.edu.au/course/laws4245>; 'Information Technology Law: LAWS8445', *Australian National University* (Web Page) <https://programsandcourses.anu.edu.au/course/LAWS8445>.

[141] 'Cryptoassets and the Law: LAWS8338', *Australian National University* (Web Page) <https://programsandcourses.anu.edu.au/2025/course/LAWS8338>.

[142] 'Artificial Intelligence, Law & Society: LAWS8405', *Australian National University* (Web Page) <https://programsandcourses.anu.edu.au/2025/course/LAWS8405>.

[143] 'Digital Economies and the Law: LAWS8407', *Australian National University* (Web Page <https://programsandcourses.anu.edu.au/2025/course/LAWS8407>.

[144] 'LAW4545: Technology, Design, and Innovation in Legal Services', *Monash University Handbook* (Web Page) <https://handbook.monash.edu/2025/units/LAW4545?year=2025>.

[145] 'Law and Technology: Comparative Perspectives (UNSW/UZH)', *UNSW Handbook* (Web Page) <https://handbook.unsw.edu.au/undergraduate/courses/2025/LAWS3346>.

[146] 'Bachelor of Information Technology Bachelor of Laws', *UTS* (Web Page) <https://www.uts.edu.au/study/find-a-course/bachelor-information-technology-bachelor-laws>.

[147] 'MLL444 Data Law, Privacy and Cybercrime', *Deakin University* (Web Page) <https://www.deakin.edu.au/courses-search/unit.php?unit=MLL444>.

(continued)

Institution	Subject	Highlights
Swinburne University of Technology	LAW20040 Legal Technology and Innovation[148]	
Bond University	LAWS77-556 Information Technology and the Law[149]	
Queensland University of Technology	LLB249 Introduction to Technology Law[150]	
University of Western Australia	Technology Law and Governance[151]	

The following table lists some new law and technology-related courses recently offered in Australian law schools.

Institution	Course	Highlights
Australian National University	Graduate Certificate of New Technologies Law[152]	
University of Melbourne	Specialist Certificate in Law (Digital Law and Technical Innovation)[153]	
University of New South Wales	Master of Laws, with the specialisation option of Media, Intellectual Property & Technology Law[154]	
Monash University	Bachelor of Laws/Bachelor of Information Technology	
University of Technology Sydney	Bachelor of Information Technology, Bachelor of Laws (Combined Degree)[155]	There is a Legal Futures and Technology Major in Bachelor of Laws/Bachelor of Laws Combined Degrees

(continued)

[148] 'Legal Technology and Innovation', *Swinburne University of Technology* (web Page) <https://www.swinburne.edu.au/course/unit/l/law20040/>.

[149] 'LAWS77-556 Information Technology and the Law', *Bond University* (Web Page) <https://bond.edu.au/subject/laws77-556-information-technology-and-law>.

[150] 'LLB249 Introduction to Technology Law', *QUT* (Web Page) <https://www.qut.edu.au/study/unit?unitCode=LLB249>.

[151] The University of Western Australia, 'Technology Law and Governance [LAWS5296]', *Handbook 2024* (Web Page) <https://handbooks.uwa.edu.au/unitdetails?code=LAWS5296>.

[152] 'Graduate Certificate of New Technologies Law', *Australian National University* (Web Page) <https://programsandcourses.anu.edu.au/program/cntl>.

[153] 'Specialist Certificate in Law (Digital Law and Technological Innovation)', *The University of Melbourne* (Web Page) <https://study.unimelb.edu.au/find/courses/graduate/specialist-certificate-in-law-digital-law-and-technological-innovation/>.

[154] 'Media, Intellectual Property & Technology Law', *UNSW* (Web Page) <https://www.unsw.edu.au/law-justice/study/postgraduate/media-intellectual-property-and-technology-law>.

[155] 'Bachelor of Information Technology Bachelor of Laws' (n 536).

(continued)

Institution	Course	Highlights
Queensland University of Technology	Bachelor of Information Technology/Bachelor of Law[156]	
Deakin University	Bachelor of Laws/Bachelor of Cyber Security[157]	This is Australia's only combined laws and cyber security degree
Murdoch University	Bachelor of Laws/Bachelor of Information Technology[158]	
University of Wollongong	Bachelor of Information Technology—Bachelor of Laws[159]	
Bond University	Bachelor of Digital Transformation/Bachelor of Law	

While the above lists are not exhaustive, they demonstrate the broad scope of the interdisciplinary programs offered by Australian law schools in exploring the area of technology and law. The subjects offered by the law schools cover various trending topics, such as the regulation of technology, the legal issues in relation to data collection, privacy and cybersecurity, the legal issues relating to electronic commerce and Fintech, the legal issues in relation to new technologies and their applications such as blockchain, crypto-assets and artificial intelligence, the applicability of technology in legal practice, etc. In addition to the offering of combined bachelor's degrees of law and science and/or technology in many law schools, there are also innovative programs such as new majors, certificate, diploma or specialised master's degree at the post-graduate level, accommodating needs of both law students' need to equip themselves in the changing law market and non-law students' need to obtain a legal perspective.

[156] 'Bachelor of Information Technology/Bachelor of Laws (Honours), *QUT* (Web Page) <https://www.qut.edu.au/courses/bachelor-of-information-technology-bachelor-of-laws-honours>.

[157] 'Bachelor of Laws/Bachelor of Cyber Security', *Deakin University* (Web Page) <https://www.deakin.edu.au/course/bachelor-laws-bachelor-cyber-security>.

[158] 'Bachelor of Laws/Bachelor of Information Technology', *Murdoch University* (Web Page) <https://www.murdoch.edu.au/course/undergraduate/b1398>.

[159] 'Bachelor of Information Technology—Bachelor of Laws', *University of Wollongong Australia* (Web Page) <https://coursefinder.uow.edu.au/information/index.html?course=bachelor-information-technology-bachelor-laws>.

4.3.7 *Generative Artificial Intelligence and the Legal Education*

The use of generative artificial intelligence became a trending phenomenon in early 2020s. It also affects legal education greatly, from impacting the teaching and learning activities and students' ethical responsibilities in studying law, to inspiring the innovation of new designs in the curriculum. Generative AI is a double-edged sword; on the one hand, generative AI greatly improves the efficiency in teaching and learning and brings innovative moves into the field; on the other hand, it gives rise to concerns in relation to the possibility of jeopardising academic integrity of students and ethical standard of future lawyers.

The wide use of generative AI tools, such as ChatGPT and QuillBot, has given rise to concerns that students might utilise these tools to generate work that is of average or even better quality compared to their own work. This is particularly so in the context of text-based written assessments, which are frequently used in law subjects, where the students might rely on generative AI tools to conduct research, summarise and rephrase content, proofread and edit, and put together formal legal writing. In responding to the wide use of generative AI tools, universities have made policies, statements, or guidance, addressing the appropriate way of using them in the completion of assessment tasks. Students are required to understand the benefit and limitation of generative AI tools and to what extent they can use them in various context of learning activities. For example, the Melbourne Centre for the Study of Higher Education requires students using AI in the preparation of their assessment submission to appropriately acknowledge and cite the materials generated from those generative AI tools in accordance with the University's Assessment and Results Policy.[160] This includes, for example, citing and referencing the output from the AI tools as a source in the reference list if the AI tools have been used to paraphrase or quote in the writing including an acknowledgement of how the AI tools have been used in other ways in the process of the completion of the assessment, such as brainstorming, understanding concepts, generating examples, summarising readings, editing, etc.[161] Using materials generated from AI tools as their own outputs would not amount to submissions of their original work. Thus, if someone knowingly having a third party, including AI technologies, involved in the completion of work submitted as their own work as assessment is deliberately cheating and this will amount to academic misconduct.[162] Similarly, Deakin University also provides students with comprehensive guidance on the use of generative AI tools in their study and require students

---

[160] The University of Melbourne, 'Assessment and Results Policy (MPF1326)', *Melbourne Policy Library* (Web Page) <https://policy.unimelb.edu.au/MPF1326/>.

[161] 'Acknowledging AI Tools and Technologies', *The University of Melbourne* (Web Page) <https://students.unimelb.edu.au/academic-skills/resources/academic-integrity/acknowledging-AI-tools-and-technologies>.

[162] 'Statement on the Use of Artificial Intelligence Software in the Preparation of Material for Assessment', *The University of Melbourne* (Web Page, 21 April 2023) <https://academicintegrity.unimelb.edu.au/plagiarism-and-collusion/artificial-intelligence-tools-and-technologies>.

to seek permission from teaching staff for their use. If permission is given, appropriate acknowledgement must be made of the use of AI tools in their assessments.[163] Deakin University also warns students that using content generated from AI tools as a primary source of information is generally unacceptable and should be handled with great caution.[164] The guide provided by the Australian National University ("ANU") states that students should seek guidelines from teaching staff regarding the use of generative AI first, and if they are permitted to do so, use the ANU-supported tool, Copilot Enterprise, with their university account. They should also avoid breaches of academic integrity and verify the accuracy of information supplied by the generative AI.[165] The TEQSA also provides advice for students on the use of generative AI in their study, including that the university or college may restrict or ban the use of generative AI in some parts of their study; and when it is allowed, it should be referenced and acknowledged properly. Using AI in ways inconsistent with an institution's policies and rules might result in academic misconduct.[166]

Further calls for the reform of assessment tasks in response to generative AI are also made in the higher education sector. As Mulder, Baik, and Ryan suggested, it is time for educators to consider whether the existing model of assessments in higher education is still "fit for purpose".[167]While it is proposed that the old-fashioned face-to-face, handwritten, close-book supervised examinations should be relied upon in order to minimise the risk of cheating by using AI tools,[168] Professors Liz Johnson, Helen Partridge, and Philip Dawson pointed out the drawbacks of the old-fashioned approach in the context of a global trend of innovative teaching and learning supported by new technology.[169]

---

[163] 'Acknowledging Your Use', *Deakin University* (Web Page, 4 March 20,204) <https://www.deakin.edu.au/students/study-support/study-resources/artificial-intelligence/acknowledging-your-use>.

[164] Ibid.

[165] 'Guide for Students: Best Practice when Using Generative AI', *Australian National University* (Web Page) <https://www.anu.edu.au/students/academic-skills/academic-integrity/best-practice-principles/guide-for-students-best>.

[166] 'Artificial Intelligence Advice for Students', *Tertiary Education Quality and Standards Agency* (Web Page, 29 July 2024) <https://www.teqsa.gov.au/students/artificial-intelligence-advice-students>.

[167] Raoul Mulder, Chi Baik, Tracii Ryan, 'Rethinking Assessment in Response to AI', (Melbourne Centre for the Study of Higher Education, July 2023) <https://melbourne-cshe.unimelb.edu.au/__data/assets/pdf_file/0004/4712062/Assessment-Guide_Web_Final.pdf>.

[168] Caitlin Cassidy, 'Australian Universities to Return to 'pen and paper' Exams After Students Caught Using AI to Write Essays', *The Guardian* (online, 10 January 2023) <https://www.theguardian.com/australia-news/2023/jan/10/universities-to-return-to-pen-and-paper-exams-after-students-caught-using-ai-to-write-essays>.

[169] Liz Johnson, Helen Partridge and Philip Dawson, '1,300 Years is Long Enough: It's Pen Down for the Exam Hall' (Blog Post, 16 January 2023) <https://blogs.deakin.edu.au/cradle/1300-years-is-long-enough-its-pens-down-for-the-exam-hall/>.

In this regard, the TEQSA published *Assessment Reform for the Age of Artificial Intelligence* in November 2023.[170] It suggests the principles listed below regarding the higher education assessment and AI:

1. "Assessment and learning experiences equip students to participate ethically and actively in a society where AI is ubiquitous";
2. "Forming trustworthy judgements about student learning in a time of AI requires multiple, inclusive and contextualised approaches to assessment".[171]

Based on the principles above, it further proposed that the assessments in higher education in the context of generative AI should "emphasise:

- Appropriate, authentic engagement with AI;
- A systemic approach to program assessment aligned with disciplines/qualifications;
- The process of learning;
- Opportunities for students to work appropriately with each other and AI;
- Security at meaningful points across a program to inform decisions about progression and completion". Needs fn and citation for quotation.

In the light of this, Mulder, Baik, and Ryan proposed following strategies to redesign the assessments to address the problem of AI misuse. The strategies include:[172]

- Shift the emphasis of the tasks from assessing the final product to assessing the student's process of making inquiries and reaching the answer, for example, assess the students' self-reflections or learning journals, or process notebooks, instead of, or in addition to, the final report or essay;
- Incorporate tasks that require students to evaluate and judge other products and outputs. For example, the assessment tasks may require students reviewing and assessing the work of their peers on the basis of their knowledge and skills;
- Design large project-based tasks that can be divided into different steps or phases, and require students to communicate, assess, and reflect on their progress. This can also involve group work and peer review components;
- Diversify the formats and modes of assessments. It is suggested the assessment outputs can be in the format of videos, vlogs, podcasts, poster-presentations, animations, e-Portfolio, in addition to its traditional forms;
- Incorporation of reflections of real world, context-specific assessment, such as specific cases, issues or problems in the local area, or on the basis of the students' personal life experiences;
- Incorporation of in-class and group assessments which requires instant communications and contributions, as well as collaborations among students;

[170] Lodge et al. (2023).

[171] Ibid.

[172] Mulder, Baik and Ryan (n 557).

- Incorporation of oral assessments and interviews. Oral assessment is a good way of testing the student's understanding of the knowledge and application of the knowledge in a conversational context.

While the above responses to generative AI tools are generally made at the university level and are not specific to legal education, they are meaningful in the context of the changes in law schools. For example, some law schools have developed new subjects based on the AI tools. LAWS90286 Legal AI: Design and Development offered by the Melbourne Law School, "steps through how to build Generative AI based programs for legal solutions, giving students an opportunity to put that learning into practice and become leaders in AI within their chosen career area".[173] A similar subject offered by the Monash University Faculty of Law, LAW4545 Technology, Design, and Innovation in Legal Services, also requires students to develop a web-based application for the purpose of resolution of a contemporary legal problem "that meets industrial standards".[174]

4.4 Legal and Interdisciplinary Research That Nurtures Legal Education

While legal research is not directly relevant to the education programs discussed in this book, it is acknowledged that the academic staff in Australian law schools conduct valuable research which nurtures the further development of legal education in this area of law. This includes not only the traditional legal research but also multi-disciplinary and interdisciplinary research with components of both law and technology. To list a few renowned and emerging scholars and their recent research outputs, Professor Lyria Bennet Moses (University of New South Wales) publishes significantly in this area, including her book with Michael Guihot, *Artificial Intelligence, Robots and the Law*[175] as well as various book chapters and journal articles on topics of technology and law.[176] Dr Will Bateman (Australian National University) led various research projects on the regulation of AIs in government decision-making.[177] Dr Paul Burgess (Monash University) published his book *AI and the Rule of Law: The Necessary Evolution of a Concept* in 2024.[178] Dr Ramona Vijeyarasa

[173] The University of Melbourne, 'Legal AI: Design and Development' (LAWS90286), *Handbook* (Web Page, 18 July 2024) <https://handbook.unimelb.edu.au/2024/subjects/laws90286>.

[174] 'Law 4545: Technology, Design, and Innovation in Legal Services' (n 534).

[175] Moses (2021).

[176] See, e.g., Chesterman et al. (2023, 45, 53–4), Lyria Bennett Moses, 'Oversight of Police Intelligence: A Complex Web, But is it Enough?' (2023) 60(2) *Osgoode Hall Law Journal* 291; Moses 2021, 232), Zalnieriute et al. (2021, 91).

[177] 'Law and Technology', *ANU College of Law* (Web Page) <https://law.anu.edu.au/research/law-and-technology>.

[178] Burgess (2024).

(UTS Law School) led a research project on the regulation of AI tools and gender equality which won Women in AI (Law) Award.[179]

Many Australian law schools and practical legal training providers have established research institutions, centres, initiatives, and taskforces in relation to the development of technology and law, and organise events such as conferences, seminars, and webinars on various topics in this area of law. These institutions include, for example, the University of New South Wales Institute for Cyber Security[180] and the University of New South Wales Allens Hub for Technology, Law and Innovation[181]; the Humans Technology Law Centre[182] at the Queensland University of Technology; the University of Western Australia Tech and Policy Lab hosted by the University of Western Australia Law School;[183] and the Monash Data Futures Institute[184] which hosts many law academics and supports many research projects including the perspectives of law, policy, and governance.[185] Deakin Law School's Centre for Law as Protection also includes a research theme that focuses on "protecting people and the environment from technology-based harms", such as those that arise from "the use of automation in government decisions (such as Robodebt), the use of misinformation and disinformation to undermine democracy (particularly during elections), the use of 'deepfakes' and image-based gender violence, pervasive surveillance, and predictive counterterrorism measures that impact a variety of human rights and individual freedoms".[186]

Educational institutions have also established various collaborative projects and institutions with government and industry. The ARC Centre of Excellence for Automated Decision-Making and Society is a collaboration among universities, industry, government, as well as the community. Legal researchers from Australian law schools

---

[179] 'Unbiased AI Could Improve Women's Rights', *UTS* (Web Page) <https://www.uts.edu.au/research-and-teaching/our-research/law-research/snapshots/unbiased-ai-could-improve-womens-rights≥; Vijeyarasa (2023, 114).

[180] 'Welcome to UNSW Institute for Cyber Security', *UNSW Sydney* (Web Page) <https://www.unsw.edu.au/research/ifcyber>.

[181] 'UNSW Allens Hub for Technology, Law & Innovation', *UNSW Sydney* (Web Page) <https://allenshub.unsw.edu.au/>.

[182] 'Humans Technology Law Centre', *Business and Law, Business School QUT* (Web Page) < https://research.qut.edu.au/htlc/>.

[183] 'UWA Tech & Policy Lab', *The University of Western Australia* (Web Page) <https://www.uwa.edu.au/schools/research/uwa-tech-and-policy-lab>.

[184] 'Monash Data Futures Institute', *Monash University* (Web Page) <https://www.monash.edu/data-futures-institute>.

[185] 'Monash Data Futures Institute, 'Flagship Projects in Better Governance and Policy', *Monash University* (Web Page) <https://www.monash.edu/data-futures-institute/research/governance-policy/flagship-projects≥; Monash Data Futures Institute, 'AI and Data Science in Better Governance and Policy, '*Monash University* (Web Page) <https://www.monash.edu/data-futures-institute/research/governance-policy>.

[186] Centre for Law as Protection, 'Protection From Technology-based Harms', *Deakin University* (Web Page) <https://lawasprotection.org.au/stream/protection-from-technology-based-harms/>.

are involved in this multi-disciplinary research framework.[187] The Cyber-Security Cooperative Research Centre is another example representing the participation of educational institutions such as University of New South Wales, the University of Adelaide, Deakin, QUT, Edith Cowan University, Charles Sturt University, the Commonwealth government (Department of Home Affairs), the government of Western Australia, the government of New South Wales, the Australian Federal Police, as well as industrial participants such as CISCO and the National Australia Bank.[188] One of the Centre's research themes is "Law and Policy", which is jointly led by Professor Lyria Bennet Moses (University of New South Wales School of Law, Society and Criminology) and Professor Shiri Krebs (Deakin Law School).[189]

While most of the above-listed movements and outputs in research do not directly relate to the educational aspect of law schools, some of the research projects and institutes offer roles such as research assistants to students. Some even offer scholarships for students who are interested in extending their own research interests in this area.[190] Moreover, the research outputs contribute to the body of knowledge and jurisprudence on various topics relating to technology and law that motivates the evolution of legal education in general.

4.5 The Future of Legal Education in the Context of the Technological Developments

While we have yet to predict how technology will impact higher education in the future, we do know that it is unavoidable that technology will continue to have an impact on legal education.[191] It is certain that technology will influence both the form and modes of delivery of legal education, and also its substance.[192] Higher education is facing unprecedented pressure to innovate and adapt to new technologies, and adapting to these technologies is integral to continue to teach the law effectively.[193] Utilising technology in the classroom recognises that students learn with different styles (for example, some students require visual cues, others need repetition of key concepts and others require problem-based discussions to solidify knowledge) and

---

[187] 'Ground-breaking Research Informs NSW AI Inquiry', *The University of Sydney* (Web Page, 18 March 2024) <https://www.sydney.edu.au/news-opinion/news/2024/03/18/ground-breaking-research-informs-nsw-ai-inquiry.html>.

[188] 'Who We Are', *Cyber Security Cooperative Research Centre* (Web Page) <https://cybersecuritycrc.org.au/who-we-are>.

[189] 'Our Research', *Cyber Security Cooperative Research Centre* (Web Page) <https://cybersecuritycrc.org.au/our-research>.

[190] See, e.g., Monash Data Futures Institute, 'Monash Data Futures Institute PhD Scholarships', *Monash University* (Web Page) <https://www.monash.edu/data-futures-institute/study/phd-scholarship>.

[191] Goldsworthy (2020, 243, 253).

[192] Ibid.

[193] Ibid 257.

the incorporation of new teaching methods through technology accommodates this and broadens access to education.[194]

Law schools have a responsibility to ensure that they respond to technological advancements and, now more than ever, ensure that they are being utilised to frame legal education.[195] This may involve ensuring that law graduates are trained to use artificial intelligence technology as a response to requirements for digital literacy, but also ensuring students understand how to use AI in a manner that is responsible and ethical.[196] Law school is no longer purely a mechanism for teaching future lawyers about the law; prospective lawyers are required to have a broad education which effectively prepares them for the complex reasoning and social intelligence required for successful legal practice.[197]

[194] Williams (2001, 407, 409–10).

[195] Ibid 264.

[196] Traczykowski and Dale (n 435) 262.

[197] Goldsworthy (n 581) 264.

Chapter 5
Technology, Innovation, and the Legal Profession

It is undeniable that technology has had a significant impact on the legal profession and is changing the way in which legal services are delivered. According to the Law Institute of Western Australia, technology has become one of the largest issues that the legal profession is currently facing in Australia.[1] While the impact that technology will have on the profession long term is unknown, those who will thrive in the future will largely be determined by those who adapt effectively to technological changes.[2]

In this chapter, the authors aim to address the development of technology and innovation in the legal market, as well as its impact on the legal profession, in the following manner. Section 5.1 explores the recent technological changes in legal practice. Section 5.2 discusses the changes brought to legal practice in the post-pandemic era. Section 5.3 focuses on the influence of the rapidly developed artificial intelligence tools in the legal context. On the basis of the observations in previous sections, Sects. 5.4 and 5.5 proceed to discuss the benefits and challenges brought to the legal profession by technology and innovations in recent years.

5.1 Technological Change in Legal Practice

As technology continues to develop, its capacity is beginning to surpass that of the traditional solicitor. This requires lawyers to adapt and apply legal knowledge in new modern contexts.[3] The introduction of technology to the legal profession not only improves the efficiency and productivity of the legal profession, but also automates

---

[1] Law Society of Western Australia (n 394) 6.

[2] Ibid.

[3] Bullows (n 312) 258.

S. Zhang et al., *Technology, Legal Education and Legal Profession in China and Australia*, International and Comparative Law in the Asia Pacific,
https://doi.org/10.1007/978-981-96-1639-8_5

routine and standard work and provides deep insights into data that was previously unavailable.[4]

The development of legal technology has roots in artificial intelligence technology developed as early as the 1970s.[5] Researchers at Stanford University focused on developing a computational model and computer programs that were able to perform legal reasoning.[6] As technology developed in the 1980s and 1990s this developed into computer systems that could be used for legal research, that could replicate legal reasoning on simple problems and even developing computational models of how the law operates.[7] In more recent times, the legal profession has seen the introduction of electronic databases and even programs for technology-assisted review of documentation.[8]

The modern lawyer is no longer required to attend the Land Titles Registry in person to search for a title or dictate letters into cassette tapes; rather they have all the technology required to do so from their desk in the form of a computer, mobile phone, or another portable electronic device.[9] As the legal profession in Australia embraces technology, the contemporary legal professional can work from home and utilise practice management software, e-discovery, online databases, and other technology to stay connected with their firm and enhance their role.[10] Other technologies such as *Legal Zoom, LegalVision, Josef*, and *Xakia* have emerged into the market offering solutions to automate and increase the efficiency of legal services.[11]

The COVID-19 pandemic accelerated this adoption of technology in legal practice, with lockdowns forcing lawyers to work from home and the court system forced to switch to online hearings.[12] Common tasks like court filings and electronic signatures transitioned to electronic means.[13] The pandemic also saw increased use of programs like Microsoft Teams and Zoom for conferences and hearings as legal professionals adapted to new ways of servicing clients.[14]

Technology is rapidly changing the legal profession, with modern technology having a massive impact on the profession generally.[15] The legal profession has been required to adapt to new technology and is doing so through the utilisation of technology for electronic file management, cloud computing, virtual law firms,

---

4 Wang (n 393) 66.

5 Michael Legg and Felicity Bell, *Artificial Intelligence and the Legal Profession* (Hart, 2020) 17.

6 Ibid 18.

7 Ibid 18–20.

8 See Medianik (2018), 1503; Legg and Bell (n 592), 35.

9 Kate Galloway, 'Text to Bits: Beyond the Revolution in Law and Lawyering' (2016) https://papers.ssrn.com/sol3/papers.cfm?abstract_id=2879220.

10 Ibid.

11 Hunter (2020), 1202–1203.

12 Lilley and Do (n 483) 23.

13 Dolan and Erwin (2020), 15.

14 Ibid.

15 Wang (n 393) 66.

electronic courts and online dispute resolution, social media, and even artificial intelligence.[16] Technology is changing legal practice, and using it in an effective manner can allow lawyers to focus on more complex and higher order tasks.[17]

To address and further promote the development of technology in the legal context and enhance the legal profession's capacity to adapt to the changes, the College of Law established its own Centre for Legal Innovation,[18] whose "focus is to support legal professionals as they navigate the disruption and new technologies transforming the industry".[19]

5.1.1 Electronic File Management

Electronic File Management refers to software that is designed to automate the creation, storage, use and even the disposal of information and records.[20] As electronic document systems become increasingly more sophisticated with automating filing, automated billing, and increased ability to find documents, more law firms are transitioning away from physical documentation in favour of electronic file management.[21]

One of the main benefits of storing information in an electronic file management system is that it enables documents to be accessed, stored, searched, modified, and copied instantaneously.[22] The creation of documents, including using precedents to draft new documents, becomes more efficient when utilising electronic systems.[23]

5.1.2 Cloud Computing

Cloud computing refers to the delivery of legal services hosted over the internet.[24] This allows for law firms to have on-demand access to data storage as well as

[16] Law Society of Western Australia (n 394) 6.

[17] Ajevski et al. (2023), 357.

[18] 'At the Forefront of Practical Legal Education', *College of Law* (Web Page, 2024) https://www.collaw.edu.au/about/centre-for-legal-innovation.

[19] Ibid.

[20] Law Society of Western Australia (n 394) 7.

[21] Dombosch (2013) 62–3.

[22] Jones (2021) 38–9.

[23] Ibid 39.

[24] Law Society of Western Australia (n 394) 6.

reduce the cost that would ordinarily go towards data storage hardware and software systems.[25] Cloud systems reduce the need for physical filing of documents and physical storage, while also making it simpler to retrieve and access information.[26]

5.1.3 Virtual Law Firms and Alternative Legal Service Providers

Through the application of new and emerging technology, changes are occurring in traditional law firms and creating a new hybrid legal practice environment known as "NewLaw".[27] NewLaw combines the best of traditional legal practice while incorporating elements of technology to deliver online legal services and even fully virtual law firms.[28] Some virtual law firms essentially exist wholly online to provide flexible and low-cost access to legal services.[29]

Alternative legal service arose along with the evolution of technology.[30] The alternative legal service providers ("ALSPs") handled high-demanded fundamental legal services, e.g. document review, discovery and e-discovery, investigation support, litigation support, contract management, intellectual property management, etc.[31] The service might be provided by independent ALSPs, some of which overlaps with the NewLaw firms mentioned above, such as LegalZoom and Axiom. Alternatively, they might be offered by law firm captives or extensions; for example, the leading Australian law firm Herbert Smith Freehills extended its team on the provision of alternative legal services.[32] The Big Four accounting firms now also provide alternative services as Alternative Business Structures. Some services might be provided by legal service outsourcers ("LPOs"), managed service providers and contract and staffing services. It is generally considered that the ALSPs are able to provide specialised expertise and to blend technology-based expertise with legal knowledge for the provision of efficient services.[33]

---

[25] Ibid.

[26] Jones (n 609) 39.

[27] Wang (n 393) 66.

[28] Ibid.

[29] Law Society of Western Australia (n 394) 7.

[30] EY, *Reimagining the Legal Function Report 2019* (2019) 6–10.

[31] 'Paralegals Benefit from the Rise of Alternative Legal Service Provider (ALSP) Companies', *ParalegalEDU.org* (Web Page, 2024). https://www.paralegaledu.org/alternative-legal-service-providers/.

[32] 'Herbert Smith Freehills' World-leading Alternative Legal Services Practice Announced Australian Promotions', *Herbert Smith Freehills* (Web Page, 2024). https://www.herbertsmithfreehills.com/news/2024-01/HSFs-world-leading-Alternative-Legal-Services-practice-announces-Australian-promotions.

[33] Cornelius Grossman, 'Why alternative legal service providers are on the rise' *EY* (Web Page, 18 May 2020). https://www.ey.com/en_es/tax/why-alternative-legal-service-providers-are-on-the-rise

Virtual law firms and ALSPs benefit both lawyers and clients as costs are reduced due to not having overhead costs associated with physical premises, lawyers are encouraged to work flexibly and due to the lack of office waste it is more eco-friendly.[34] With the further development of technology, and in particular, the use of generative AI tools, virtual firms and ALSPs are expected to further increase their influence in the legal market.[35]

5.1.4 *Electronic Courts and Online Dispute Resolution*

As addressed by the Federal Court of Australia's Technology and Court Practice Note,[36] technology is an important tool in assisting with the achievement of quick, inexpensive, and efficient resolution of disputes according to the law by the courts, which are the overarching purpose of the civil practice and procedure.[37] In the meanwhile, the court should deal with the use of technology to prevent the risk of inappropriate use of technology.

As a representation of the use of technology in courts, electronic courts and other digitalised services were being utilised in Australia long before the COVID-19 pandemic.[38] Online courtrooms were used particularly throughout the COVID-19 pandemic as a way to ensure that access to justice continued.[39] Prior to the pandemic supportive technology like audio-visual links were used as a matter of routine.[40] During the pandemic audio-visual links were used to ensure that the courts could keep operating in the interest of continuing access to justice.[41] This technology vastly improved during the pandemic, subsequently the functionality of remote hearings improved too.[42] Online court hearings were conducted across a number of different private sector apps such as *Microsoft Teams*, *Webex*, *LegalZoom*, and *Skype* depending on the jurisdiction.[43] Despite the pandemic being declared over, many

---

[34] Jones (n 609) 49.

[35] Cornelius Grossman, 'Why alternative legal service providers are on the rise' *EY* (Web Page, 18 May 2020). https://www.ey.com/en_au/tax/why-alternative-legal-service-providers-are-on-the-rise. See above.

[36] Federal Court of Australia, *Practice Note GPN-TECH: Technology and the Court*, 25 October 2016. https://www.fedcourt.gov.au/law-and-practice/practice-documents/practice-notes/gpn-tech.

[37] *Federal Court of Australia Act 1976* (Cth) s 37 M.

[38] Law Society of Western Australia (n 394) 9;
Legg and Song (2021), 130.

[39] Ibid 126–7.

[40] Ibid 130.

[41] Ibid 145.

[42] Ibid 148.

[43] Ibid 149.

courts in Australia are continuing to utilise virtual and hybrid hearings over *WebEx* and *Zoom*.[44]

In practice, courts have made detailed instructions on virtual hearings. Taking the Federal Court of Australia as an example, it provides digitalised court services from various perspectives, such as eLodgment which allows the parties to file initial documents and supporting documents electronically[45]; the Commonwealth Courts Portal[46] which provides online access to all case information before the Federal Courts; eCourtoom[47] which allows Judges and Judicial Registrars to manage and hear certain categories of matters, such as ex parte applications for substituted service in bankruptcy proceedings, applications for examination summons, or giving of directions and other orders in General Federal Law matters. It further provides comprehensive guidance on the digitalised services, such as the Technology and Court Practice Note[48] that comprehensively addresses the use of technology in court proceedings, as well specific guidance on the standard for the preparation of documents for electronic lodgement[49] and the handling of online hearings.[50]

Similar instructions and guidance were observed in other courts in States and Territories. For example, the NSW Supreme Court's Practice Note No SC GEN07, which comprehensively addresses the issue of the use of technology in the court, was released early as 2008[51] and, further, Practice Note No SC GEN 15 which provides detailed guidance on the use of audio-visual links in criminal and certain civil proceedings.[52] The Victorian Supreme Court's Practice Note SC Gen 5, which was released on 29 June 2018 also addresses the same matter on the use of technology

---

[44] See 'Digital Litigation at the Court', *Supreme Court of Victoria* (Web Page) https://www.supremecourt.vic.gov.au/going-to-court/virtual-hearings/digital-litigation-resources.

[45] 'eLodgment', *Federal Court of Australia* (Web Page, August 2024) https://www.fedcourt.gov.au/online-services/elodgment.

[46] 'Commonwealth Courts Portal', *Federal Court of Australia* (Web Page, July 2024) https://www.fedcourt.gov.au/online-services/commonwealth-courts-portal.

[47] 'eCourtroom', *Federal Court of Australia* (Web Page, July 2024) https://www.fedcourt.gov.au/online-services/ecourtroom.

[48] Federal Court of Australia (n 623).

[49] 'Preparing Documents for Lodgment', *Federal Court of Australia* (Web Page, July 2024) https://www.fedcourt.gov.au/online-services/preparing-documents-for-the-court.

[50] 'National Practitioners/Litigants Guide to Online Hearings and Microsoft Teams', (Federal Court of Australia) https://www.fedcourt.gov.au/online-services/online-hearings/National-Practitioners-and-Litigants-Guide-V5.pdf.

[51] Supreme Court of New South Wales, *Practice Note No SC GEN 07: Use of Technology* (& September 2008) http://www.lawlink.nsw.gov.au/practice_notes/nswsc_pc.nsf/a15f50afb1aa22a9ca2570ed000a2b08/19ae2d221b09c4fbca257483001d0781?OpenDocument.

[52] Supreme Court of New South Wales, *Practice Note No SC GEN 15: Use of Audio-visual Links in Criminal and Certain Civil Proceedings* (1 January 2009) http://www.lawlink.nsw.gov.au/practice_notes/nswsc_pc.nsf/a15f50afb1aa22a9ca2570ed000a2b08/7bd5e80ccc50a600ca2574fc0080118d?OpenDocument.

in civil litigation.[53] In Section 4.3 the Court has provided several general principles in practice, including that hard copies of documents are to be seen as exceptions rather than the main rule; the capacity to use common technologies should be expected as one of the core skills of lawyers and legal practices, and the failure to use them may be seen as a breach of the overarching obligations of the parties, and should not unfairly increase the costs for other parties; and the outsourcing of technology services is generally accepted. The use of technology should be disclosed to the court at an early stage of the trial.[54] On the basis of the principle, further guidelines are provided to particular aspects of civil litigation, e.g. e-filing, discovery, e-trials.

5.2 The Legal Profession Post-pandemic

COVID-19 forced legal professionals to work from home and adapt to the online environment. The pandemic brought a number of challenges to the legal profession and created substantial change to the modern legal marketplace.[55] According to the Legal Centre for Innovation and College of Law, there are several trends impacting the post-pandemic legal profession, including flexible and remote working arrangements, increased use of technology, and continued innovation in the profession.[56] Similar effects are being felt globally, with similar shifts occurring in the post-pandemic legal market in the United States.[57]

5.2.1 Remote Working

During the pandemic, workers demonstrated that they could work productively in remote and flexible working arrangements.[58] Technology allowed lawyers to demonstrate that flexible work arrangements are possible without losing productivity.[59] As a result, flexible and hybrid working arrangements have become a permanent fixture in many law firms. According to Melbourne Law School Fellow Joel Barolsky, the legal profession has recognised the benefits that flexible working arrangements have, and

---

[53] Supreme Court of Victoria, *Practice Note SC Gen 5: Technology in Civil Litigation* (2 July 2018) https://www.supremecourt.vic.gov.au/sites/default/files/2018-10/gen_5_use_of_technology_first_revision.pdf

[54] Ibid s 4.3.

[55] Jerome Doraisamy, 'How COVID-19 has Changed #auslaw' *Lawyers Weekly* (online, 2020), 7. https://www.lawyersweekly.com.au/pdfs/LW_-_Winter_2020.pdf.

[56] '5 Innovation Trends Defining the Post Pandemic Legal Sector', *College of Law* (Web Page, 18 April 2022) https://mlb.collaw.edu.au/articles/innovation-trends-defining-the-legal-sector.

[57] See Michael Fore and Erin Stevenson, 'The Impact of Covid-19 Pandemic on Overall Well-being of Practicing Lawyers' (2023) *PLOS ONE* 1.

[58] Doraisamy (n 642) 8.

[59] Jones et al. (2021) 4.

firms are adjusting to create a balance between remote working and working in the office.[60] This does not only apply to private practice. For example, Victorian Legal Aid are continuing to operate in hybrid working arrangements that were initiated during the pandemic.[61]

5.2.2 *Increased Technology Use*

The pandemic forced an immediate uptake in the use of digital processes and technology in a matter of weeks.[62] The COVID-19 pandemic became somewhat of a tipping point for the utilisation of technology in legal workplaces.[63] Prior to the pandemic there was little use of remote service delivery in the legal profession or the court system, so when the pandemic hit the profession underwent a major digital transformation in a matter of weeks which would have otherwise taken years.[64] This adoption of technology during the pandemic, while challenging, has seen continued use of that technology post-pandemic. Legal professionals were forced to learn new digital skills and as a result are continuing to utilise these skills post-pandemic. Some of these skills, like digital contract execution through programs like *Adobe Sign* or *DocuSign*, are here to stay. For example, the ability to e-sign documentation on behalf of a corporation was made permanent with the *Corporations Amendment (Meetings and Documents) Act 2022* (Cth).[65]

In other areas, document automation has seen an increase following the pandemic.[66] Utilising technology to automate documents such as transactional documents has seen an increase.[67] While this technology existed prior to the pandemic, it was used increasingly during the pandemic and document automation services have now become a key feature in law firms post-pandemic.[68]

---

[60] Joel Barolsky, 'The Changing Face of the Legal Profession' *Melbourne Law School* (Web Page, 29 October 2020) https://law.unimelb.edu.au/news/MLS/the-changing-face-of-the-legal-profession.

[61] See 'Changes to our Services Due to COVID-19', *Victorian Legal Aid* (Web Page, 1 July 2023) https://www.legalaid.vic.gov.au/changes-our-services-due-covid-19.

[62] Doraisamy (n 642) 7.

[63] Ibid 7.

[64] Brasch (2021), 46.

[65] *Corporations Amendment (Meetings and Documents) Act 2022* (Cth).

[66] McKeith (2021), 36.

[67] Ibid.

[68] Ibid 36–7.

5.2.3 *Legal Jobs in the Digital World*

The COVID-19 pandemic accelerated technological developments, and in turn changed the legal profession.[69] Technological innovation is driving change, and as such future law firms will offer new jobs and alternative career paths for law graduates and lawyers.[70] The role of a lawyer, in addition to the NewLaw alternative career paths, has changed rapidly as a result of the pandemic.[71] The legal profession will continue to grow and change as the profession becomes more digital.

5.3 The Impact of Artificial Intelligence

Artificial intelligence technology is transforming the legal profession. The developments in machine learning and natural language processing are revolutionising the way in which technology is being utilised within the legal profession.[72] This technology is modernising more traditional areas of legal practice, with AI performing tasks like conducting due diligence and even predicting the likely success of a claim.[73]

The full potential of artificial intelligence is unknown, however as the technology becomes increasingly more sophisticated it can outperform humans in tasks such as reviewing legal documents.[74] In one study, when asked to review a non-disclosure agreement, AI outperformed 20 lawyers asked to review the same documents.[75] AI was able to review the documents in 26 s with 94% accuracy, while, on average, the lawyers took 92 min with 84% accuracy.[76] AI, as seen in this example, has the potential to automate routine tasks which increases productivity and allows lawyers to focus on more complex tasks.[77] There is little doubt that artificial intelligence technology will have a major impact on legal practice.[78]

ChatGPT, an AI-based chatbot developed by OpenAI, is an example of an artificial intelligence platform that can be utilised by the legal profession.[79] *ChatGPT* is powered by a language processing algorithm which has the ability to engage with a user and generate a natural language response to their prompt or question.[80] The algorithm is trained through open-source data from the internet prior to September

[69] Ryan et al. (n 292) 373.

[70] Ibid.

[71] Ibid 395.

[72] Benjamin et al. (2018), 107–108.

[73] Wang (n 393) 66.

[74] Ibid.

[75] Ibid.

[76] Ibid.

[77] Ajevski et al. (n 604) 356.

[78] Wang (n 393) 66.

[79] Ajveski et al. (n 604) 356.

[80] Ibid 353.

2021 to learning text patterns and natural language responses in order to engage in conversations and answer questions.[81] As it engages in conversations, the algorithm learns and refines its ability to predict the next sequence of words based on the context provided in the preceding conversation.[82] In its essence, programs like *ChatGPT* have the ability to generate contextually relevant responses based on its dataset to complete various tasks.[83] As such, generative technology like *ChatGPT* has the potential to be valuable tool for legal professionals. This technology has the potential to facilitate the drafting of legal documents, undertaking legal research, and analysing and summarising legal information.[84]

Some law firms have already begun to incorporate similar technology in their practice. For example, global law firms Dentons[85] and Allens Linklaters[86] have released their own versions of this technology. This technology has been introduced to empower lawyers to utilise this technology to automate simple tasks, complete research and even identify legal arguments.[87] Dentons have introduced two generative AI programs, one for conducting research and generating legal content, and a second for analysing multiple legal documents.[88] The data entered into the programs is not used to train the model and is erased after 30 days in an effort to protect confidential information.[89]

AI tools are also used in Technology Assisted Review ("TAR") which is now recognised in Australian legal practice. It is an innovation widely used in the process of e-discovery; a software or application, which is usually based on a trained algorithm, will conduct an automatic review of a large volume of documents to determine the value of the documents. In *McConnell Dowell Constructors (Aust) Pty Ltd v Santam Ltd (No 1)*,[90] the Victorian Supreme Court upheld the use of TAR in this case, commenting that the technology assisted with the just, efficient, timely, and cost-effective resolution under the *Civil Procedure Act 2010* (Vic), and was proportionate to the costs resulted from the dispute resolution process. It further recognised the legitimacy of the TAR in civil proceedings in its practice notes.[91]

---

[81] Ibid.

[82] Ibid.

[83] Ibid.

[84] Ibid 356.

[85] Paul Jarvis, 'Dentons to Launch Client Secure Version of ChatGPT' *Dentons* (Web Page, 1 August 2023). https://www.dentons.com/en/about-dentons/news-events-and-awards/news/2023/august/dentons-to-launch-client-secure-version-of-chatgpt.

[86] Kate Scanlon, 'Allens Launches Enterprise Version of ChatGPT, Airlie' *Allens Linklaters* (Web Page, 18 August 2023) https://www.allens.com.au/insights-news/news/2023/08/allens-launches-enterprise-version-of-chatgpt-airlie/.

[87] Jarvis (n 672).

[88] Ibid.

[89] Ibid.

[90] *McConnell Dowell Constructors (Aust) Pty Ltd v Santam Ltd (No 1)* (2016) 51 VR 421, [18]-[31].

[91] Supreme Court of Victoria (n 640) ss 8.7–8.9.

5.4 Benefits of Technology

5.4.1 New Roles in the Legal Profession

The change in the delivery of legal services has resulted in the creation of a number of new technologies. To keep up with the demands of technology, roles such as legal technologist and legal data analysist/scientist have been created.[92] The above-mentioned virtual law firms and ALSPs have also created new job opportunities for law graduates.[93] These new roles reflect the impact of technology on the sector and demonstrates the need for digital literacy in the legal profession.[94]

5.4.2 Increased Access to Justice

One benefit of utilising technology is that, on a basic level, the introduction of AI tools can assist in decreasing the high cost of legal services and promote access to justice. As AI technology becomes increasingly sophisticated and can complete basic tasks, it can allow firms to produce services at a lower cost.[95] High costs are often a barrier for people when choosing to engage legal services, therefore utilising AI to complete tasks in mere minutes to allow lawyers to focus more closely on the client's needs is often less costly.[96]

Additionally, investments into the advancement of AI technology can further promote access to justice by establishing avenues for vulnerable persons to access legal services. A recent announcement by the New South Wales government exemplifies this commitment.[97] The NSW government has allocated funding through the NSW Innovation Fund Program to various AI technology initiatives aimed at enhancing accessibility to justice for vulnerable individuals.[98] Initiatives being run by Justice Connect, a not-for-profit organisation, in collaboration with the University of Sydney have received a substantial sum to invest in two projects. The first project, run by Justice Connect, seeks to develop a language processing model designed to increase legal literacy of vulnerable persons by making legal resources and services more accessible.[99] The other project, led by the University of Sydney, seeks to leverage AI to create a more equitable assessment model for parents with intellectual

[92] Law Society of Western Australia (n 394) 7.

[93] Ibid s A.3.

[94] Bullows (n 312) 261.

[95] Medianik (n 595) 1506–7.

[96] Bigda (2018), 420.

[97] 'Artificial Intelligence to Help the Most Vulnerable Navigate Justice' (2021) (82) *Law Society Journal* 22, 22.

[98] Ibid.

[99] Ibid.

disabilities who are involved in legal proceedings within the Children's Court.[100] This technology seeks to increase equitable outcomes for people with cognitive disabilities who are statistically more likely to lose their child to statutory care.[101] The impact of these AI advancements is substantial and will increase pathways for the access of justice for vulnerable individuals.

5.5 Challenges to the Legal Profession

While technology is revolutionising the legal profession, its use must be balanced with legal professional responsibility. As technology is introduced to practise, legal professionals must address different challenges from data protection, confidential information, data privacy, to how to ethically interpret automated data.[102]

5.5.1 Challenges to the Legal Profession—Ethical Use of AI

The development of this technology is unpredictable, and it is unclear what artificial intelligence technology is capable of. It is theorised that the technology will become so integrated into the legal profession that failure to utilise technology could result in liability in tort for failure to consult all tools available or for failure to consider predictive information when assessing the viability of a case.[103] It is impossible to consider all of the ethical questions raised by the use of technology in the legal profession, however we are confronted with the question of how large will its ethical impact be, and how can we minimise it.[104]

The wide use of generative AI in legal practice have given rise to serious concerns regarding ethics. It was reported in June 2023 that two US lawyers submitted briefs with legal sources provided by ChatGPT which were later found to be fabricated by this generative AI.[105] This raised concerns on the ethical use of AIs by legal practitioners.

---

[100] Ibid.

[101] Ibid.

[102] Law Society of New South Wales (n308) 41–43. Not sure what this reference is citing to as there have been a few LSNSW citations previously.

[103] Alarie, Niblett and Yoon (n 659) 122.

[104] Bigda (n 683) 419–20.

[105] Dan Milmo, 'Two US Lawyers Fined for Submitting Fake Court Citations from ChatGPT', *The Guardian* (online, 23 June 2023) https://www.theguardian.com/technology/2023/jun/23/two-us-lawyers-fined-submitting-fake-court-citations-chatgpt.

Further, with the assistance of generative AI and other technology-based tools, such as Lawpath,[106] or DoNotPay,[107] the borderline between work generated by the AI and outputs based on logical thinking and independent judgement of a qualified legal professional is no longer clear. It was challenged that the integrity of the legal profession had been compromised due to the substantive work completed by the AI in various areas of law practice. DoNotPay, a US-based technology company, actively sought AI solutions to act as robot lawyers which can replace human lawyers. In February 2023, DoNotPay even proposed to introduce an AI lawyer in a courtroom in the US, requiring the client to wear Airpods in the courtroom to receive information, and then generate instructions and pass them to the client during the trial.[108] This, however, was eventually postponed due to concerns of breaching the court rules and regulations of the legal profession.[109] DoNotPay were even sued against for breaching the current regulatory framework governing the legal profession, which requires the practice of law by qualified lawyers only.[110]

In this regard, the Victorian Supreme Court's *Guidelines for Litigants: Responsible Use of Artificial Intelligence in Litigation*[111] provides principles for use of AI by litigants and judges in court proceedings. The principles bring to the practitioners' attention that they should ensure an accurate understanding of the AI's nature, function, and limitations,[112] and should be aware of the privacy and confidentiality issues in relation to the use of AI tools.[113] The use of AI should be subject to the legal practitioner's fundamental obligations to the court,[114] and should be appropriately disclosed; the use by one party should not indirectly mislead other parties and the courts regarding the nature of work it completed.[115] While encouraging the appropriate use of AI tools to increase the efficiency of civil proceedings (e.g. the use of TAR),[116] the Court took a cautious view on general-purpose AI tools, and suggested that legal practitioners use AI tools based on specialised legal databases.[117] It also acknowledged generative AI tools and Large Language Models ("LLMs") as not a

---

[106] 'About Us', *Lawpath* (Web Page) https://lawpath.com.au/about-us.

[107] 'Your AI Consumer Champion', *DoNot Pay* (Web Page) https://donotpay.com/.

[108] Kristen Niven, 'The Rise of the Robot Lawyer? DoNotPay's Legal AI Faces Several Challenges', *Lexology* (Blog Post, 31 May 2024) https://www.lexology.com/library/detail.aspx?g=fcf42316-ad93-40f5-9e10-c2aecc17cb9a.

[109] Ibid.

[110] Keely McDonough, ''World's first robot lawyer' Hit With Lawsuit for Practising Without a License', *LSJ Online* (16 March 2023) https://lsj.com.au/articles/worlds-first-robot-lawyer-hit-with-lawsuit-for-practising-without-a-license/.

[111] Supreme Court of Victoria, 'Guidelines for Litigants: Responsible Use of Artificial Intelligence in Litigation' (Web Page, May 2024) https://www.supremecourt.vic.gov.au/forms-fees-and-services/forms-templates-and-guidelines/guideline-responsible-use-of-ai-in-litigation.

[112] Ibid [1].

[113] Ibid [2].

[114] Ibid [4].

[115] Ibid [3].

[116] Supreme Court of Victoria (n 640) ss 8.7–8.9.

[117] Supreme Court of Victoria (n 698) [7].

product of reasoning, and the outputs from those tools are not the output of legal research; thus, there is no assumption of the accuracy of the outputs generated by those tools.

5.5.2 Challenges to the Legal Profession—Duty of Competence

As the scope for the use of artificial intelligence and technology grows, so does the potential for significant ethical challenges. Legal professionals owe their clients a fundamental duty to deliver legal services competently.[118] This duty of competence doesn't require perfection from a legal profession: it creates a standard of care whereby legal professionals are qualified, reasonably competent, and careful.[119] This means that where a legal service is delivered and it is supported by the use of technology, legal professionals must ensure that they are reasonably competent in the technology they intend to use.[120] Additionally, having a deep understanding of the law and the ability to exercise judgement and discretion while utilising technology to support a lawyer's job is critical.[121]

Inferences can be drawn from the Professional Conduct Rules which require the ethical use of technology by solicitors and barristers alike, but the current ethical framework does not punish legal practitioners for the abuse of technology or related misconduct. This is an issue that the legal profession is dealing with globally.[122] For example, the American Bar Association made amendments to their Model Rules of Professional Conduct in 2012 to formally insert a technological competence to provide for misconduct and the risks associated with technology use.[123] Rule 1.1 prescribes that lawyers should maintain competence and requisite knowledge for practice including the benefits and risks associated with the use of technology.[124]

This point is also echoed in the Victorian Supreme Court's Guidelines for Litigants: Responsible Use of Artificial Intelligence in Litigation,[125] which reminds practitioners that the use of AI tools "does not relieve the responsible legal practitioner of the need to exercise judgement and professional skill" in reviewing the

[118] See *Legal Profession Uniform Conduct (Solicitors) Rules 2015* (NSW) r 4.1.3; Law Society of New South Wales (n 459) 41.

[119] *Hawkins v Clayton* (1988) 164 CLR 539.

[120] Law Society of New South Wales (n 459?) 41.

[121] Ajevski et al. (n 604) 357.

[122] Ibid.

[123] American Bar Association, *Model Code of Professional Responsibility 1969* (USA), r 1.1. Replaced by the Model Rules of Professional Conduct 1983.

[124] Ibid.

[125] Supreme Court of Victoria (n 698).

final submission to the Court, including that they should not be out-dated, incomplete, inaccurate or erroneous, inapplicable to the current jurisdiction, or biased[126]; and that any practitioner or party should remain responsible for the accuracy of any content they have submitted or relied upon in the trial and cannot use the involvement of AI tools as an excuse for the errors.[127]

5.5.3 Challenges to the Legal Profession—Data Security

The utilisation of technology does not come without concerns for data protection and confidentiality. In order to ensure that technology is being harnessed appropriately, law firms must ensure that they are equipped with digital capabilities to prevent hacking and to ensure that confidential information in the cloud remains confidential.[128] The use of electronic file management and cloud computing, while making access to and use of documents easier, creates a risk that information may be comprised by accidental access by employees or even a cyberattack.[129]

Similar consequences must be considered when information is being stored in blockchain technology, where information is encrypted and stored in "blocks" which then allows the data to be stored across different open-source software globally.[130] Users can then only access the information with an encrypted key on their computer, creating somewhat of a double encryption which is meant to enhance security and prevent hacking.[131] So while blockchain technology appears to better protect information, in terms of storing that information, legal professionals must ensure that when employing this technology that they understand the implications it may create for data protection.[132]

The protection of client confidential information is especially at risk with cloud computing due to the risk of data breaches.[133] Law firms are vulnerable for cyberattack, which has been seen as recently as April 2023 with the HWL Ebsworth hack.[134] This incident resulted in the publishing of confidential information of at

---

126 Ibid [8].

127 Ibid [9].

128 Galloway (n 596) 4.

129 Jones (n 609) 39.

130 Galloway (n 596?) 4.

131 Ibid 5.

132 Ibid.

133 Law Society of Western Australia (n 394) 6.

134 'Cyber Incident', *HWL Ebsworth.* (Web Page, 2023) https://hwlebsworth.com.au/cyber-incident/.

least 65 government departments, insurance companies, major banks, and ASX-listed companies.[135] This demonstrates how devastating and harmful data breaches are in law firms and for legal professionals.

5.5.4 Responsible Use of Technology by Courts and Other Adjudicators

There have also been discussions about whether, and if so, to what extent, technologies, especially the trending general or specialised AI tools, can be utilised by judges and adjudicators in their decision-making process. The Australasian Institute of Judicial Administration provides a comprehensive guide for the use of AI in court decision-making.[136] The guide emphasises that the use of AI tools by adjudicators should be consistent with, and should avoid deviations from, the core values of the court system, i.e. open justice, accountability and independence, impartiality and equality before the law, due process and procedural fairness, accessibility of justice, and efficiency.[137] It discusses various situations where one or more core values of the court system might be facilitated, or alternatively, compromised and the court's obligation to manage the risks of such breaches.[138] In particular, it is doubted that generative AI tools like ChatGPT are an accurate reflection of accurate reasoning or explanation, or rather, is simply generating a predictive text,[139] as evidenced in the US case where fabricated sources and case details were generated.[140] For that reason, the Supreme Court of Victoria suggested that generative AI tools should not be used for decision-making or drafting legal reasoning for the decision because they do not operate on the rationale of reasoning.[141] On that basis, the authors suggested that the use of AI systems proceed with caution, including the establishment of necessary understanding of the nature and limits of each AI system; appointment of technical

[135] Edmund Tadros, 'Scale of HWL Ebsworth Hack Revealed: 2.5 m Files, 65 Agencies' *Australian Financial Review* (online, 20 September 2023) https://www.afr.com/companies/professional-services/scale-of-hwl-ebsworth-hack-revealed-2-5m-files-65-agencies-20230920-p5e64t.

[136] Lyria Bennett Moses et al., *AI Decision-making and the Courts: A Guide for Judges, Tribunal Members and Court Administrators* (Australasian Institute of Judicial Administration, 2023) https://aija.org.au/wp-content/uploads/2023/12/AIJA_AI-DecisionMakingReport_2023update.pdf.

[137] Ibid ch 4.

[138] Ibid.

[139] Ibid 40s 4.1; 59s 4.8.

[140] Benjamin Weiser, 'Here's What Happens When Your Lawyer Uses ChatGPT', *The New York Times* (online, 27 May 2023) https://www.nytimes.com/2023/05/27/nyregion/avianca-airline-lawsuit-chatgpt.html.

[141] Supreme Court of Victoria (n 698) [12].

experts; continuous monitoring and regular evaluation of the AI technology; developments of guides and principles for the use of AI systems in courts; maintenance of transparency and increased public confidence in the application of technology in court setting, etc.[142]

[142] Bennett Moses (n 723) 60–1.

Part II
China

Chapter 6
Overview of Legal Education and the Legal Profession in China

Abstract The historical roots of legal education in China can be traced back to the intellectually vibrant Spring and Autumn period (771—476 BCE) and the subsequent Warring States period (475–221 BCE), marking a golden era in ancient Chinese cultural history.

6.1 Overview of Legal Education in China

The historical roots of legal education in China can be traced back to the intellectually vibrant Spring and Autumn period (771—476 BCE) and the subsequent Warring States period (475–221 BCE), marking a golden era in ancient Chinese cultural history.[1] This time was characterised by the rise of several influential philosophical schools, including Confucianism, Mohism, Daoism, and Legalism, which profoundly shaped Chinese intellectual and cultural discourse. Among these, the interactions and debates, particularly between Confucianism and Legalism, played a pivotal role in the development of diverse and robust legal theories.[2] These foundational debates not only influenced the immediate legal practices of the time but also set the stage for the evolution of legal education in China, providing a rich bedrock of philosophical thought from which later legal principles emerged.[3]

This rich tradition of legal thought found its apex during the Tang Dynasty (618–907 CE) with the establishment of the Tang Code (653 CE) and its Annotations, which was a culmination of legal principles that had been evolving from the Warring States period through the Sui Dynasty (581–618 CE), and became a cornerstone of legal practice and education in China.[4] The Tang Code was revered not only as a definitive legal document within China but also exerted a significant influence on the legal systems of other countries in East Asia, such as Japan, Korea, and Vietnam.[5] This

[1] He and Liu (2024).

[2] He and Liu (2024).

[3] He and Liu (2024).

[4] Zheng (2022).

[5] Zheng (2022).

S. Zhang et al., *Technology, Legal Education and Legal Profession in China and Australia*, International and Comparative Law in the Asia Pacific,
https://doi.org/10.1007/978-981-96-1639-8_6

influence underscores the importance of the Tang Code in shaping what is commonly referred to in both domestic and international legal literature as the traditional Chinese legal system.[6] The reach and impact of the Tang Code illustrate how ancient Chinese legal philosophy and practice set benchmarks that transcended national boundaries and eras, contributing to a shared legal heritage across East Asia.[7]

Despite these significant historical achievements, the nature and purpose of legal education in ancient China were markedly different from modern concepts of legal training and education. Legal education in those times was predominantly an elitist endeavour, aimed at consolidating the power of the ruling classes, rather than promoting justice or the welfare of the general populace.[8] It was often unstandardised and varied, sometimes embodying principles that would be considered contradictory to modern values of justice and equity.[9] For example, while contemporary legal education places a strong emphasis on the principle of proportional justice—arguing that penalties should be commensurate with the severity of the offence to maintain societal order—ancient legal thought often advocated for harsh penalties for even minor transgressions.[10] This was seen as a necessary deterrent to maintain control, as espoused by Legalist thinkers like Han Fei (280–233 BCE), who contended that leniency in punishment would lead to chaos and societal decay.[11]

From a modern perspective, such a punitive approach is often criticised for potentially leading to greater injustices, as it might compel those who commit minor offences, possibly even inadvertently, to undertake more severe criminal actions out of a sense of desperation or fear. These ancient practices, while reflective of the historical and cultural contexts of their times, highlight the evolution and transformation of legal education over centuries. Modern legal education seeks to embody principles of fairness, justice, and humanitarian consideration, viewing individuals as inherently capable of rational thought and deserving of dignified treatment.[12]

Understanding the historical development of legal education in China thus provides a panoramic view of its journey from a tool of power and control to a means of promoting justice and equity. This evolution mirrors a mighty river, enriched by the continuous contributions of philosophical and cultural influences, which meanders through the landscape of history, dynamically adapting and evolving as it flows towards the future. This perspective not only celebrates the progress and achievements of past legal systems but also underscores the ongoing journey of legal education as it strives to meet the needs and challenges of contemporary society.

Professor Jiang Peng from Tsinghua University eloquently articulated the origins of modern legal education in China, stating that the systematic and organised teaching of modern law, which treats law as a distinct academic discipline within modern

[6] Zheng (2022).

[7] Zheng (2022).

[8] Liu (2016).

[9] Liu (2016).

[10] Wang (2024).

[11] Wang (2024).

[12] Zhao (2015).

education, commenced around 1902.[13] His insights were detailed in an influential article titled "The Origins of Modern Legal Education in China" published in the China Law Review.[14]

Over the subsequent century, modern legal education in China has undergone extensive development and transformation, evolving into the robust system we see today. The establishment of the People's Republic of China marked a significant phase in this development. The Central People's Government took decisive steps to uniformly plan and establish key legal institutions across the nation. This wave of establishment included prestigious schools such as Peking University of Political Science and Law, East China University of Political Science and Law, Central South University of Political Science and Law, Southwest University of Political Science and Law, and Northwest University of Political Science and Law.[15] Furthermore, specialised legal departments were set up in comprehensive universities including Renmin University of China, the Northeast People's University, Peking University, and Fudan University.[16] These foundational steps were crucial in laying the groundwork for a structured legal education system in China.[17]

Despite a period characterised by slower development, the initiation of the reform and opening-up policies marked the beginning of a golden era in the expansion of legal education in China. By the early 1980s, the number of institutions offering legal education had increased to over 40 and continued to rise to more than 60 by the mid-1980s.[18] The pivotal decision by the Central Committee, in 1992, to establish a socialist market economy acknowledged that a market economy is fundamentally governed by law, which, in turn, significantly increased the demand for legal professionals.[19] In response, universities and colleges across China swiftly established new law majors, adding over 100 in just a few years, which brought the total to more than 200 institutions offering legal education.[20]

After more than three decades of restoration, reconstruction, reform, and development, coupled with reforms in the higher education system and the popularisation of higher education, the number of universities offering law majors dramatically increased to 389 in just a few years, expanding the total number of institutions with

[13] Peng (2014).

[14] Peng (2014).

[15] "China's Rule of Law Construction." Central People's Government of the People's Republic of China. Accessed April 1, 2024. https://www.gov.cn/zhengce/2008-02/28/content_2615764.htm.

[16] "China's Rule of Law Construction." Central People's Government of the People's Republic of China. Accessed April 1, 2024. https://www.gov.cn/zhengce/2008-02/28/content_2615764.htm.

[17] "China's Rule of Law Construction." Central People's Government of the People's Republic of China. Accessed April 1, 2024. https://www.gov.cn/zhengce/2008-02/28/content_2615764.htm.

[18] Zhang (2023).

[19] Zhang (2023).

[20] Zhang (2023).

a law major to over 600.[21] These institutions now enrol more than 500,000 students, illustrating the vast scale and reach of legal education in contemporary China.[22]

A comprehensive legal education system, primarily focusing on Bachelor's, Master's, and doctoral education in law, has been firmly established.[23] This system effectively combines legal professional education with legal vocational training, is guided by the national macro-direction, primarily executed by law schools in various universities, and plays a crucial role in meeting the needs of building a modern socialist country by effectively supplying the legal talent required for the improvement and development of the country's judicial system, and for advancing the governance of the country according to the law.[24]

However, the rapid advancement of information technology, including the internet, has brought legal education in China to a critical juncture. In February 2023, the General Office of the Communist Party of China Central Committee and the General Office of the State Council issued the "Opinions on Strengthening Legal Education and Theoretical Research in the New Era" (commonly referred to as "Document No 5").[25] The issuance of this document by the two aforementioned offices is a rare and unprecedented event in the history of the development of humanities and social sciences in New China.[26] It highlights the high importance and earnest expectations that the CPC Central Committee and the State Council place on legal education, legal research, and the construction of the law school. Document No 5 also emphasises the critical role of digital technologies in promoting comprehensive progress in legal education and in the overall development of the discipline.[27]

In this context, where legal education faces significant challenges to maintain its integrity while innovating, it is crucial to understand what past experiences are worth summarising, what outdated practices should be discarded, and in what direction future legal education should head and how to proceed.[28] This reflection is essential for ensuring the continued relevance and effectiveness of legal education in meeting contemporary challenges and for guiding its future trajectory in China. This article aims to provide a clear portrayal of the current situation and future prospects of legal education in China, discussing them from several perspectives including an introduction to some leading universities in the field, a systematic exposition of the current state of legal education, and the development and transformation of legal education under the impact of information technology.

---

[21] Zhang (2023).

[22] Zhang (2023).

[23] Fu (2023).

[24] Fu (2023).

[25] "Opinions on Strengthening Legal Education and Legal Theory Research in the New Era." Published on the Central People's Government of the People's Republic of China website, https://www.gov.cn/gongbao/content/2023/content_5745286.htm.

[26] Zhang (2023).

[27] Zhang (2023).

[28] "Opinions on Strengthening Legal Education and Legal Theory Research in the New Era." Published on the Central People's Government of the People's Republic of China website, https://www.gov.cn/gongbao/content/2023/content_5745286.htm.

6.2 Overview of the Legal Profession in China

After receiving a systematic legal education, most law students are likely to pursue careers within the legal sector. It is commonly acknowledged that the strength and respect of the law derive significantly from its effective enforcement.[29] President Xi Jinping has notably stressed the importance of rigorously cultivating a socialist legal workforce that exhibits loyalty to the Party, the State, the people, and the law itself.[30] He underscores that the proper application and enforcement of the law depend not just on institutional frameworks but also on the dedicated efforts of skilled legal professionals.[31]

In China, the pathway to becoming a legal professional involves rigorous screening through a qualification examination process, ensuring that only those adequately prepared are permitted to practise. This examination system for entering the legal profession in China has evolved through several stages, reflecting changes in legal education and professional standards over time.

Initially, from 1986 to 2001, the process was governed by the national unified lawyer qualification examination.[32] This stage set the foundation for standardised assessments of legal knowledge and competencies among aspiring lawyers across the country.[33]

Subsequently, from 2002 to 2017, the examination system transitioned to the national unified judicial examination.[34] This period marked a significant reform in the evaluation process, broadening its scope to include a wider range of legal professions beyond just lawyers. The aim was to create a more comprehensive assessment that reflected the complexities and demands of various legal roles, thereby ensuring a higher standard of legal practice across the board.[35]

Since 2018, the examination has been known as the National Unified Legal Professional Qualification Examination.[36] This current phase continues to adapt

---

[29] See *Decision of the Central Committee of the Communist Party of China on Several Major Issues Concerning the Comprehensive Promotion of the Rule of Law in China*(2014).

[30] See *Decision of the Central Committee of the Communist Party of China on Several Major Issues Concerning the Comprehensive Promotion of the Rule of Law in China*(2014).

[31] Chen, Bingmei. "Research on the Selection and Training of Legal Professionals in China." In: Shanxi Law Society, Henan Law Society, Hubei Law Society, Hunan Law Society, Jiangxi Law Society. *Research on Legal Issues in the Process of New Urbanization—Proceedings of the 10th Central China Legal Forum.* Gaoping City Judicial Bureau Propaganda and Education Department, 2017, p. 14.

[32] Liu et al. (2001).

[33] Wang (2024).

[34] "The National Uniform Judicial Examination will provide a more solid guarantee of human resources for the construction of the rule of law in China", website of the Ministry of Justice of China, https://www.moj.gov.cn/pub/sfbgw/gjsfkssjxw/202103/t20210319_210553.html, accessed on August 21, 2024.

[35] Lian (2021).

[36] "The National Uniform Judicial Examination will provide a more solid guarantee of human resources for the construction of the rule of law in China", website of the Ministry of Justice of

and respond to the evolving needs of the legal system and its professionals. By maintaining a robust and rigorous examination process, China ensures that its legal workforce is well equipped to uphold the law and administer justice effectively, and contributes to the stable and harmonious development of society. This stringent process underscores the country's commitment to fostering a legal environment that is just, efficient, and reflective of socialist values.

In the formative years of China's approach to regulating entry into its legal professions, a decentralised system was initially adopted for the legal profession entry examinations.[37] This meant that, while there were national unified professional qualification examinations for lawyers and notaries, the entry exams for judges and prosecutors were distinctively organised and managed by the court and procuratorate systems, respectively.[38] Such a structure led to a lack of uniformity in the content, question types, and standards across the examinations for different legal roles. As a result, there was considerable disparity in the levels of competency among legal professionals, with some achieving a high standard of legal acumen and others perhaps not meeting the same benchmark.[39] This variance not only affected the quality of legal services provided but also impacted the public's trust in the legal system's capability and integrity.[40]

Learning from the inconsistencies and challenges posed by this fragmented system, China embarked on a significant reform with the introduction of the second phase—a national unified judicial examination system. This system was designed to encompass all legal professions, including judges, prosecutors, lawyers, and notaries.[41] A pivotal change, this phase required passing a comprehensive examination that was standardised across the nation, before any professional could engage in legal work.[42]This exam was meticulously crafted, featuring a unified set of questions derived from the National Judicial Examination Syllabus which was thoughtfully formulated and published by the Ministry of Justice.[43] Conducted in a stringent

China, https://www.moj.gov.cn/pub/sfbgw/gjsfkssjxw/202103/t20210319_210553.html, accessed on August 21, 2024.

[37] See the official WeChat public platform of Democracy and Law Weekly, National Legal Professional Qualification System Develops and Improves in Reform–Interview with Jia Liqun, Director General of the Department of Judicial Examinations, Ministry of Justice, published on September 22, 2017, accessed on August 21, 2024.

[38] See the official WeChat public platform of Democracy and Law Weekly, A Look Back: The Changing Years of China's Legal Profession Admission System, published on July 30, 2018, accessed on August 21, 2024.

[39] Ding (2022).

[40] Ding (2022).

[41] *Measures for the implementation of the National Judicial Examination* (2008), Article 2.

[42] *Measures for the implementation of the National Judicial Examination* (2008), Article 2.

[43] For example, see "Announcement of the Hubei Provincial Department of Justice on the 2024 National Unified Legal Professional Qualification Examination," published on the Ministry of Justice of the People's Republic of China, National Judicial Examination Center website, https://www.moj.gov.cn/pub/sfbgw/jgsz/jgszzsdw/zsdwgjsfkszx/gjsfkszxdt/202406/t20240612_500277.html. Accessed on August 21, 2024.

closed-book format,[44] the examination employed a unified marking system across the country[45] to ensure fairness, justice, and uniformity in the standards of entry into the legal professions. Despite these rigorous standards, the second phase was marked by relatively lenient restrictions on who could take the exam, which diluted its effectiveness as a stringent gatekeeper for the legal profession, somewhat undermining its role in sufficiently vetting candidates' readiness and suitability for legal responsibilities.

Recognising the need for continuous improvement, the third phase of reforms was initiated, building upon the foundation laid by the earlier reforms. This phase introduced more specific educational prerequisites for candidates and widened the eligibility criteria to include a broader range of individuals needing to acquire legal professional qualifications.[46] Such reforms were aimed at elevating the overall standard and quality of legal professionals entering the field, ensuring that only the most capable and well-prepared individuals could practice law. This was crucial in maintaining the integrity of legal services and upholding the rule of law across China.[47]

To this day, the National Unified Legal Professional Qualification Examination system plays a vital role in regulating the entry of new professionals into China's legal sector.[48] This system continuously strives to uphold high standards of legal practice, ensuring that new entrants possess the requisite knowledge and skills to perform effectively in their respective legal roles.[49] However, as society evolves and new challenges emerge in the legal landscape, it has become apparent that the national unified examination system, while robust, has its limitations. The rapid developments in the new era, along with significant changes in socio-economic and technological contexts, have exposed the need for the system to adapt and evolve.[50]

Identifying the current limitations of the National Unified Legal Professional Qualification Examination and exploring how it can better facilitate the interconnection between educational achievements and professional demands is of paramount importance.[51] This exploration holds substantial research value as it can lead to a deeper understanding of the dynamics between legal education and professional practice. Enhancing this connection is crucial for ensuring that legal education remains relevant and that it effectively prepares candidates not only to pass the examination

---

[44] *Measures for the implementation of the National Judicial Examination* (2008), Article 10.

[45] *Measures for the implementation of the National Judicial Examination* (2008), Article 11.

[46] The specific academic requirements can be found in the Article 9 of *Measures for the Implementation of the National Unified Legal Profession Qualification Examination* (2018).

[47] Rukiya and Jin (2023).

[48] "The Deputy Minister of Justice answered reporters' questions on the National Unified Legal Profession Qualification Examination", website of the state council of China, https://www.gov.cn/zhengce/2018-06/09/content_5297394.htm, accessed on August 22, 2024.

[49] "The Deputy Minister of Justice answered reporters' questions on the National Unified Legal Profession Qualification Examination", website of the state council of China, https://www.gov.cn/zhengce/2018-06/09/content_5297394.htm, accessed on August 22, 2024.

[50] Yang (2020).

[51] Gao and Wen (2020).

but also to excel in their professional roles, thereby contributing positively to the legal system and society at large.[52] This ongoing evaluation and adaptation process is essential for maintaining the efficacy and relevance of the Chinese legal profession's entry system in an ever-changing global context.[53]

In China, the legal profession is diverse, encompassing roles such as lawyers, judges, prosecutors, arbitrators, corporate legal advisers, and notaries.[54] These professions, while distinct in their functions and responsibilities, share a common set of prerequisites that ensure a standard level of competency and integrity across the legal system. These common requirements include nationality, political literacy, professional competence, moral character, relevant educational qualifications, successful completion of the necessary examinations, and a requisite amount of work experience.[55] Each of these criteria plays a crucial role in ensuring that the individuals serving in these positions are both capable and trustworthy.[56]

The specific requirements for judges and prosecutors reflect the high stakes of their duties, which often directly affect the outcomes of justice. Both judges and prosecutors are mandated to have Chinese nationality, demonstrating the importance of national allegiance in these high-profile roles.[57] They must exhibit high political and professional competence, ensuring they are capable of navigating complex legal and governmental landscapes. Good moral character is essential to foster trust in their judgements and prosecutorial decisions. Academically, they are required to hold at least a Bachelor's or Master's degree in law, providing a solid foundation of legal knowledge.[58] Additionally, they must pass the National Unified Legal Professional Qualification Examination, a rigorous test that assesses their legal acumen and readiness to uphold the law.[59]

For arbitrators and notaries, the requirements examine work experience, highlighting the practical nature of these roles which often deal with the arbitration of disputes and the authentication of documents in a legal context. Arbitrators, for example, must bring a wealth of experience from either having worked directly in arbitration or having substantial exposure to the legal field as lawyers or judges.[60] A minimum of eight years of relevant experience is required for these roles,[61] ensuring that they have a deep understanding and practical experience in handling complex

52 Gao and Wen (2020).

53 Yang (2022).

54 These legal professions are mentioned in Article 2 of *Measures for the Implementation of the National Unified Legal Profession Qualification Examination* (2018).

55 The professions of lawyers, judges, prosecutors, and arbitrators have specific laws regulating the requirements for their employment, which are described below.

56 Lian (2021).

57 Lan (2012).

58 *Judges Law* (2019), Article 12. *Prosecutors Law* (2019), Article 12.

59 Cao (2019).

60 *Arbitration Law* (2017), Article 13.

61 *Arbitration Law* (2017), Article 13.

cases. Those who have engaged in legal research and teaching with a senior professional title are also eligible, reflecting the value placed on academic contributions to legal practice.[62]

The notary profession demands specific types of work experience to ensure proficiency in handling and certifying legal documents. This includes a requirement of two years of notarial office internship experience or a combination of three years of broader legal professional experience plus an additional year of notarial office internship.[63] If a candidate lacks direct notarial office experience, a substantial ten years of experience in adjudication, prosecution, legal system work, or legal services is necessary.[64] This ensures that notaries are thoroughly familiar with legal processes and documentation standards.[65]

Judges and prosecutors are expected to have engaged in legal work for at least five years, although this requirement can be reduced to four or three years for those who have earned a Master's degree or higher.[66] This reduction acknowledges the advanced understanding and skills that higher education provides, potentially accelerating the readiness of candidates to take on the responsibilities of these critical positions.[67]

Overall, while the foundational requirements across these professions are intended to maintain a high standard of legal practice in China, the specific emphasis on work experience for arbitrators and notaries versus the more academically focused criteria for judges and prosecutors reflects the varied nature of these roles within the legal system.[68] Each set of requirements is designed to ensure that professionals are not only qualified but also specifically prepared for the unique challenges of their respective positions, contributing to the overall effectiveness and integrity of the legal system.

From a comprehensive perspective, the judicial reforms in China, particularly the implementation of the judicial-responsibility system and the initiation of the quota system reform, have significantly enhanced the professional quality of legal practitioners.[69] However, these reforms have also introduced a notable increase in work pressure. The judicial-responsibility system, for example, establishes that judges and prosecutors carry lifelong responsibility for the cases they adjudicate or prosecute.[70] This enduring accountability necessitates that they approach each case with utmost diligence and rigour. Such meticulousness is crucial, as it not only helps to prevent wrongful convictions—thereby upholding the integrity of the justice system—but

---

[62] Li (2017).

[63] *Notarial Law* (2017), Article 18.

[64] *Notarial Law* (2017), Article 19.

[65] Jiang (2018).

[66] *Judges Law* (2019), Article 12. *Prosecutors Law* (2019), Article 12.

[67] Wu (2022).

[68] Shi (2021).

[69] Zeng Lu: "Quality of Judges and Judicial Reform", China Court website, https://www.chinacourt.org/article/detail/2007/12/id/278997.shtml, accessed on August 22, 2024.

[70] *Opinions of the Supreme People's Court on Improving the Judicial Responsibility System of the People's Courts*(2015), Article 25.

also ensures the fair treatment of all parties involved.[71] By fostering a culture of careful consideration and thorough investigation, the judicial-responsibility system plays a vital role in maintaining judicial fairness and enhancing public trust in legal institutions.[72]

The quota system reform, on the other hand, has introduced a set of changes aimed at optimising the allocation and management of judicial resources.[73] Based on a variety of factors, this reform strategically limits the number of active judges and prosecutors to ensure that only the most capable and efficient individuals serve in these high-stake positions.[74] Furthermore, the reform categorises court and procuratorate staff into distinct roles: judges, trial assistants, and judicial administrative personnel in the courts, prosecutors, prosecutorial assistants, and judicial administrative personnel in the procuratorates.[75] This structured division of labour allows for more specialised and focused roles, enhancing the overall functionality and efficiency of the judicial process.[76]

By implementing classified management, the reform has led to what can be described as the specialisation of judicial and prosecutorial staff.[77] This system ensures that each segment of the judiciary and procuratorate is staffed by individuals who are not only highly qualified but also specialised in their respective areas.[78] This specialisation is beneficial for several reasons: it allows for a more in-depth understanding of specific legal areas, promotes a higher standard of case handling, and enhances the speed and accuracy with which legal decisions are made.[79] Consequently, this can lead to a more effective judicial process where cases are handled more efficiently and with greater precision, thereby improving the quality of legal outcomes.[80]

---

[71] "How to Improve the Quality of Judges", website of Higher People's Court of Shanxi Province, www.chinacourt.org/article/detail/2010/08/id/423761.shtml, accessed on August 22, 2024.

[72] Liu (2020).

[73] Sun Fengjuan and Cui Xiaoli: "Post Reform, a Journey of Transformation for the Implementation of Judicial Accountability", website of the Supreme People's Procuratorate of China, https://www.spp.gov.cn/spp/zdgz/202202/t20220222_545202.shtml, accessed April 5, 2024.

[74] Sun Fengjuan and Cui Xiaoli: "Post Reform, a Journey of Transformation for the Implementation of Judicial Accountability", website of the Supreme People's Procuratorate of China, https://www.spp.gov.cn/spp/zdgz/202202/t20220222_545202.shtml, accessed April 5, 2024.

[75] Luo Sha, Huang Jinzhi and Huang Anqi: "Promoting the professionalisation of the judiciary and building the cornerstone of the judicial accountability system," *China Youth Daily Website*, https://zqb.cyol.com/html/2015-07/23/nw.D110000zgqnb_20150723_3-03.htm, accessed April 5, 2024.

[76] Li (2019).

[77] Liu Tao: "Classification and Management of Prosecutorial Personnel: Towards a Scientific Approach to Personnel Management", website of the Supreme People's Procuratorate of China, https://www.spp.gov.cn/spp/zdgz/201906/t20190616_421776.shtml,accessed April 5, 2024.

[78] "Deepening the Reform of Classification and Management of Procuratorial Personnel and Further Promoting the Professionalisation of Procuratorial Assistants", website of People's Procuratorate of Fuping, http://www.sn.jcy.gov.cn/wnsfpx/dwjs/sxzz/202407/t20240730_391094.html, accessed April 5, 2024.

[79] Pan (2019).

[80] Pan (2019).

However, the elevation of judicial and prosecutorial roles to elite status within this structured system also comes with its challenges. The limited number of positions may increase competition among legal professionals, which while driving excellence also significantly amplifies the workload and pressure on each individual.[81] The demand for precision and accountability in their roles means that judges and prosecutors must invest considerable time and effort into each case. This intense focus, necessary to meet the high standards set by the reforms, can lead to increased job stress and the potential for burnout among legal professionals.[82]

Thus, while the judicial-responsibility system and quota system reform have undeniably improved the quality of legal practice in China, they have also intensified the pressures faced by those who work within the system.[83] Managing these pressures while maintaining the high standards of judicial performance and ethical responsibility remains a critical challenge.[84] It is imperative for ongoing reforms to consider not only the efficiency and effectiveness of legal processes but also the well-being and support of the legal professionals entrusted with upholding the law.[85] Balancing these factors is essential for sustaining the improvements made through judicial reforms and ensuring the long-term health of China's legal system.

While the judicial-responsibility system and the quota system reform have introduced significant improvements to the professional quality and efficiency of China's legal system,[86] these changes also present substantial challenges from the perspective of judges and prosecutors. One of the central issues stemming from the reform of the quota system is the reduction in the number of available positions for judges and prosecutors.[87] This contraction occurs at a time when economic growth and an increasing public legal awareness are driving up the volume of cases. As a result, judges and prosecutors find themselves managing a growing caseload each year.[88]

The increasing number of cases, paired with a reduced workforce due to the quota limitations, places an intense pressure on these legal professionals.[89] They are required to handle cases efficiently while also upholding the highest standards of quality in their legal work. Balancing these demands often results in a tension between maintaining thoroughness in case handling and meeting procedural time constraints.

---

[81] Long and Lyu (2022).

[82] Wu (2019).

[83] Long (2016).

[84] Jiang and Lai (2020).

[85] The treatment of legal professions is emphasised in *Opinions on Deepening the Comprehensive Complementary Reform of the Judicial System of the People's Courts—Fifth Five-Year Reform Programme for the People's Courts* (2019).

[86] Zhang (2017).

[87] The number of judges was streamlined from 198,800 to more than 120,000 and the number of prosecutors from 158,000 to 86,000 following the reform of the post system. The data can see in "Video Record of Democracy and the Rule of Law 2017: The Resounding Sound of China's Footsteps under the Rule of Law" on the website of Ministry of Justice of China.

[88] Wang (2022).

[89] Zhang (2019).

This struggle can lead to scenarios where neither efficiency nor quality can be fully achieved, potentially compromising the integrity of the judicial process.[90]

Furthermore, the quota system reform has reshaped the career advancement paths for judicial and prosecutorial staff.[91] The fixed quota on the number of judges and prosecutors means that positions at the top are more limited than ever before, making promotions within these roles more competitive and stringent. This heightened competition can lead to frustration among talented legal professionals, who may feel that their opportunities for advancement are capped. Over time, this situation can result in a talent drain, as skilled individuals might seek better opportunities outside the judiciary or procuratorate, which, in turn, could impact the overall quality and stability of the legal system.[92]

Moreover, as the legal demands continue to escalate with more cases and fewer judges and prosecutors to handle them, these professionals face increasing workloads and stress.[93] This intense work environment not only threatens their personal well-being but also raises concerns about the sustainability of their workload and the potential for judicial errors. The consequent strain could harm the public's perception of judicial credibility and trust in the legal system.

Simultaneously, the legal landscape for lawyers is also becoming more challenging.[94] Following the reforms, the number of lawyers has been consistently rising, fuelling fierce competition within the profession. This competition is further intensified by a growing public awareness and assertion of legal rights, which drives an increase in the demand for legal services. Lawyers, therefore, find themselves under significant pressure to secure clients, deliver results, and maintain a competitive edge in an increasingly saturated market.[95] The combination of expanding caseloads and the public's heightened expectations for rights protection adds another layer of stress, making the practice of law more demanding than ever.[96]

In summary, while the judicial reforms have brought about improvements in the structure and efficiency of China's legal system, they have also introduced complexities that challenge the efficiency, quality, and sustainability of legal practice. Addressing these challenges requires a balanced approach that considers not only the operational efficiencies but also the personal and professional well-being of legal

---

[90] Fang (2023).

[91] Lin Ping: "Qin Qianhong: A Multidimensional View of the Reform of the Judicial Post System" website of The Paper, https://www.thepaper.cn/newsDetail_forward_22162629, accessed August 21, 2024.

[92] Qian and Guo (2021).

[93] Chen Kengping: "A Correct Understanding of the Problem of Overcrowding in the Courts of Justice" Chinese Social Science Net, https://www.cssn.cn/skgz/bwyc/202309/t20230919_5686433.shtml, accessed August 21, 2024.

[94] "Tian Wenchang: China's Lawyer Profession Has Entered a Period of Development and Faces the Sharpest Challenge of Specialisation" The Paper. Accessed August 25, 2024. https://www.thepaper.cn/newsDetail_forward_28523759.

[95] Fan (2017).

[96] Bai (2017).

practitioners.[97] Such considerations are crucial for ensuring that the legal system remains robust, credible, and capable of meeting the evolving needs of society.[98]

The COVID-19 pandemic profoundly affected the legal profession in China, exacerbating work pressures in various dimensions. The pandemic triggered significant market fluctuations and necessitated frequent adjustments to policies, which, in turn, led to a substantial increase in the number of legal disputes.[99] These disputes span a range of issues, from individual conflicts to more complex corporate disagreements.[100]

According to data from Xinhua News Agency, as of February 2022, the legal response to the pandemic was substantial, with prosecution authorities across China handling a large volume of cases linked to pandemic-related activities.[101] Specifically, authorities approved the arrest of 9,377 individuals in 7,047 cases, decided not to arrest 2,528 individuals in 1,584 cases, filed charges against 15,666 individuals in 11,340 cases, and elected not to prosecute 2,393 individuals in 1,437 cases.[102] This surge in legal activity underscores the broad impact of the pandemic on the legal system, stressing the capacity of legal institutions and professionals.[103]

The nature of disputes that arose during the pandemic often revolved around critical areas such as real estate transactions, lease contract disputes, loan contract disputes, and labour disputes. The pandemic introduced unique complexities to these cases, distinguishing them from similar disputes in more typical times.[104] For example, the interpretation and application of laws in the context of pandemic-prevention measures, the need to balance the interests of disputing parties under unusual economic and social conditions, and the adaptation of dispute-resolution methods to accommodate public-health guidelines all required legal professionals to significantly adjust their approaches.[105]

---

[97] Duan (2024).

[98] Duan (2024).

[99] Gao et al. (2020).

[100] Gao et al. (2020).

[101] "Supreme People's Procuratorate: Over 10,000 Epidemic-Related Cases Prosecuted Nationwide Since the Outbreak, Involving Multiple Fields of Crime." Xinhua News, Accessed August 21, 2024. http://www.news.cn/legal/2022-03/31/c_1128520486.htm.

[102] "The Supreme Prosecutor's Office issued the sixteenth batch of typical cases involving the new coronavirus epidemic handled by the national procuratorial organs in accordance with the law:

Strictly on the track of the rule of law and in accordance with the law, the epidemic prevention and control order was strongly maintained." The Supreme People's Procuratorate of China. Accessed August 21, 2024. https://www.spp.gov.cn/spp/xwfbh/wsfbt/202203/t20220331_552924.shtml#1.

[103] "Supreme People's Procuratorate: Over 10,000 Epidemic-Related Cases Prosecuted Nationwide Since the Outbreak, Involving Multiple Fields of Crime." Xinhua News, http://www.news.cn/legal/2022-03/31/c_1128520486.htm.

[104] Li Ping. "A Study of Certain Issues in Cases of Offences Involving the New Crown Epidemic." *Criminal Law Review*, vol. 64, no. 4, pp. 22–38.

[105] Song et al. (2020).

Moreover, the mode of work for legal professionals transformed dramatically. In alignment with pandemic-prevention and control efforts, "remote working" or "contactless office" practices were swiftly adopted.[106] This shift required lawyers, judges, and other legal workers to quickly adapt to, learn, and master new technologies and methods of communication.[107] The challenge for legal professionals was not only to maintain their effectiveness in handling cases remotely but also to ensure that the administration of justice remained authoritative and fair despite the physical distance from traditional court settings.[108]

The need to utilise scientific and technological tools effectively to bridge communication gaps in remote interactions is paramount. Legal professionals must ensure that the use of these tools does not compromise the quality of their work. Instead, they should aim to enhance the efficiency of case management and maintain, if not improve, the thoroughness and fairness for which the legal system is respected.[109] This includes safeguarding confidential communications, ensuring accurate and secure exchange of documents, and conducting virtual hearings and negotiations with the same level of professionalism and diligence as expected in in-person interactions.[110]

Thus, the pandemic has not only increased the workload and complexity of cases but also pushed the legal profession towards a more technologically integrated approach. This rapid adaptation to new working conditions, while necessary, poses ongoing challenges that require continuous learning and adjustments from legal professionals.[111] These changes, while initially disruptive, may eventually lead to long-term improvements in the flexibility and resilience of the legal system.[112]

Historically, the legal profession relied heavily on direct, face-to-face interactions and the management of physical, paper-based documents. This traditional approach defined the modes operand of courts, law offices, and related legal services for centuries. However, over recent decades, the landscape of the legal profession has undergone significant transformations due to the emergence and rapid progression of information technologies such as computers, the internet, big data, and artificial intelligence.[113] These technologies have revolutionised numerous aspects of professional practice across various industries, and the legal field is no exception. The COVID-19 pandemic has further accelerated this technological integration,[114] making the use of

[106] Zhang and Yue (2021).

[107] Zhang and Yue (2021).

[108] Zhou (2017).

[109] "The Evolution of Online Proceedings in China and the Way Forward." China Court website. Accessed August 21, 2024. https://www.chinacourt.org/article/detail/2022/11/id/6997778.shtml.

[110] Wei (2024).

[111] Yang (2022).

[112] Gao et al. (2020).

[113] Hong (2018).

[114] During the epidemic, courts were asked to use Internet technology for online litigation activities. It can be learnt from "Giving Full Play to the Advantages of Internet Justice, Providing Judicial Services and Guarantees for the Integration of Epidemic Prevention and Control and Economic

information technology not just a convenience but a necessity as the circumstances of legal practice have dramatically shifted.

This integration of advanced technologies into the legal industry has yielded numerous positive improvements, fundamentally changing how legal work is conducted and perceived.[115] Firstly, the development of extensive legal resource databases has provided legal professionals with easy access to a vast and diverse range of resources.[116] These digital databases allow for rapid retrieval of case law, statutes, regulations, and other legal texts, which significantly aids in legal research and case preparation.[117] Additionally, the widespread availability of these resources contributes to legislative and judicial transparency, a cornerstone for trust and accountability in legal systems.[118] The public can access legal information more readily, fostering greater understanding and engagement with the legal process.[119]

Secondly, the overall efficiency of legal work has been markedly enhanced through the adoption of online office practices.[120] Digital tools and platforms enable legal professionals to work remotely, saving significant time and costs that were traditionally associated with physical document management and in-person meetings. Furthermore, these tools help overcome geographical and distance limitations, making it possible for legal practitioners to serve clients and collaborate with colleagues from virtually anywhere. The advent of artificial intelligence in the legal field offers additional efficiencies, particularly in automating routine tasks such as document analysis, case prediction, and even some aspects of legal drafting.[121] This automation not only speeds up the workflow but also allows lawyers to focus on more complex, strategic aspects of their work.

Thirdly, the technological evolution within the legal sector has led to the emergence of new legal professions.[122] Roles such as legal technology developers, legal

---

and Social Development—A Review of the Innovative Practices of Internet Justice in the National Courts during the Period of Epidemic Prevention and Control" on the website of The Supreme People's Court of China.

[115] Zhang and Zhao (2024).

[116] Currently, China's domestic legal databases include, but are not limited to, the National Database of Laws and Regulations, Peking University Legal Treasure, WK First, Yuan Dian Zhiqi.

[117] For example, the People's Court Case Database can search for judgements that have been transmitted online; the National Laws and Regulations Database can search for domestic laws and regulations; and many databases can search for both laws and regulations and jurisprudence, e.g. WK first, Peking University Legal Treasure.

[118] Martineau (2020).

[119] "Building and using a database of national laws and regulations to provide authoritative and convenient public legal services to the people." The National People's Congress of China. Accessed August 21, 2024. http://www.npc.gov.cn/npc/c2/c30834/202103/t20210301_310218.html.

[120] "Online Litigation to Enhance Judicial Efficiency (New Essay)"People's Daily Online. Accessed August 21, 2024. http://paper.people.com.cn/rmrb/html/2021-04/16/nw.D110000renmrb_20210416_3-07.htm.

[121] "How Artificial Intelligence Enables Judicial Trials in the Era of AI Explosion—A Synthesis of Views from the Seminar on Judicial Artificial Intelligence and Modernisation of Court Work." The Paper. Accessed August 21, 2024. https://www.thepaper.cn/newsDetail_forward_26708004.

[122] Li (2017).

data analysts, and legal database managers have become crucial as the intersection of law and technology grows ever more integral to the industry.[123] These professionals specialise in developing and managing the technological infrastructure that supports modern legal operations, from database design and maintenance to the application of machine learning algorithms for legal analytics.

Fourthly, the transparency of legal operations has significantly increased due to these technological advancements. On the one hand, this enhanced transparency deepens the public's understanding of legal processes and democratises access to legal information, which strengthens oversight of the judiciary and bolsters judicial credibility.[124] On the other hand, it supports the scientific and democratic nature of legislation. The process of law-making has become more transparent, with laws, regulations, and institutional rules available online from the initial drafting stages through to proposal and final enactment.[125] This openness not only facilitates greater public participation in the legislative process but also ensures that the creation of laws is more accountable, precise, and reflective of the public will.

In conclusion, the integration of information technology into the legal industry has not only transformed traditional practices but also significantly enhanced the accessibility, efficiency, and transparency of legal services.[126] These changes represent a paradigm shift in how legal work is conducted, offering both challenges and opportunities for the legal profession as it continues to evolve in the digital age.

While the integration of information technology into the legal industry has brought about numerous benefits, enhancing accessibility, efficiency, and transparency, it also presents a series of challenges that cannot be overlooked.[127] These challenges highlight some potential negative impacts on the legal profession and its operational dynamics.[128]

Firstly, the automation of many foundational tasks through information technology is reshaping the job landscape within the legal field. Roles such as clerks, paralegals, and lawyer's assistants, traditionally crucial in the management and processing of legal documents, are seeing a shift in demand.[129] As software and applications equipped with artificial intelligence capabilities become capable of

[123] Li (2017).

[124] "Online Litigation Rules for Greater Public Confidence in Online Justice" Intelligent Law Promotion Platform. Accessed August 21, 2024. http://legalinfo.moj.gov.cn/pub/sfbzhfx/sfbzhpfycrp/202108/t20210806_433584.html.

[125] "Creating a New Platform of 'Internet + Public Opinion' to Explore New Ways of Legislating for the People." website of the National People's Congress of China. Accessed August 21, 2024. http://www.npc.gov.cn/npc/c12434/c16114/c16115/201905/t20190521_280622.html.

[126] "Zhou Qiang attended the Science and Technology Frontier Forum on 'Information Technology and Rule of Law Construction', stressing that scientific and technological innovation drives the construction of smart courts and judicial services guarantee scientific and technological innovation." China Court website. Accessed August 21, 2024. https://www.chinacourt.org/article/detail/2021/05/id/6039259.shtml.

[127] Ge (2023).

[128] Ge (2023).

[129] Preston (2017).

performing tasks ranging from document sorting to legal research and preliminary case analysis,[130] the need for human involvement in these areas may decrease. This shift could lead to a gradual reduction in demand for such positions, potentially leading to job displacement or a need for these legal professionals to adapt by acquiring new skills that are complementary to the new technologies.[131]

Secondly, the issue of data compilation and accessibility of legal resource databases poses a significant challenge. While these databases aim to provide comprehensive legal references, their effectiveness is often hindered by incomplete data collection and the lack of integration among various databases.[132] Many legal databases operate in isolation, creating data silos that impede the efficiency of legal research.[133] Legal professionals frequently encounter difficulties in accessing a holistic view of the information due to these silos, which can result in inefficiencies and increase the time spent on legal research.[134] The non-interconnected nature of these databases means that valuable information might remain segmented, reducing the potential for comprehensive analysis and understanding that is critical for effective legal practice.

Finally, the evolution of technology-based evidence in legal proceedings presents its own set of challenges.[135] With the increasing use of electronic materials as forms of evidence, issues concerning the authenticity and security of this evidence have come to the forefront.[136] Electronic evidence, such as emails, text messages, and digital records, must be scrutinised for authenticity, as they can be more easily manipulated or altered compared to traditional paper-based evidence.[137] Moreover, the storage and handling of electronic evidence must involve stringent security measures to prevent unauthorised access and ensure the integrity of the evidence.[138] These factors require legal professionals and judicial organisations to adapt their practices and develop new protocols to effectively manage and verify electronic evidence, ensuring that it meets the legal standards required for admissibility and reliability in court.

---

[130] "How Artificial Intelligence Enables Judicial Trials in the Era of AI Explosion—A Synthesis of Views from the Seminar on Judicial Artificial Intelligence and Modernisation of Court Work." The Paper. Accessed August 21, 2024. https://www.thepaper.cn/newsDetail_forward_26708004.

[131] Zong Bo. "Directions for the Development of Legal Education in the Age of Artificial Intelligence." *Journal of Xidian University (Social Sciences Edition)*, vol. 29, no. 2, pp. 61–67.

[132] Yi and Ma (2017).

[133] Zuo and Wang (2020).

[134] Zuo and Wang (2020).

[135] "Evidence jurisprudence should be kept abreast of scientific and technological developments." The Supreme People's Procuratorate of China. Accessed August 21, 2024. www.spp.gov.cn/llyj/201508/t20150818_103159.shtml.

[136] Wu (2015).

[137] "Analysing Obstacles to the Judicial Application of Electronic Data Evidence and Breaking the Barrier." China Court website. Accessed August 21, 2024. https://www.chinacourt.org/article/detail/2017/11/id/3074519.shtml.

[138] The collection and preservation of electronic evidence is governed by *Several Provisions of the Supreme People's Court on Evidence in Civil Proceedings (Amended 2019)*.

In summary, while information technology undeniably offers significant advantages to the legal profession, its integration also introduces complexities that necessitate careful management and adaptation. Addressing these challenges requires a concerted effort from legal professionals, technology developers, and regulatory bodies to ensure that the benefits of technology do not come at the expense of the core principles of the legal profession, such as equity, accuracy, and the protection of individual rights.

In future, with the further development of information technology, especially with the refinement of artificial intelligence technologies, information technology may have additional impacts on the legal industry.[139] However, what is more crucial is how to respond to and manage these impacts.[140] First, legal professionals should actively adapt to information technology to maintain their competitiveness.[141] Although information technology can replace many repetitive and foundational tasks, a large number of other legal issues still require consideration of factors such as interests, human emotions, and social customs, which only humans can sufficiently manage.[142] Therefore, as long as legal professionals maintain a positive attitude, continuously learn, and strengthen their own advantages, they can avoid being prematurely replaced by information technology.[143] Second, legal professionals need to break down barriers between legal data resources and eliminate information silos. This requires accelerating the opening and sharing of data in the legislative, judicial, and law enforcement processes, streamlining the standards and models for public release of information and data by national authorities, and achieving data interconnection and matching between various agencies. Third, establishing a security system related to electronic evidence to overcome difficulties in this area is important, such as using professional equipment to carefully examine the authenticity of relevant signatures and seals.[144]

The emergence of any new phenomenon brings changes, big or small, to every industry, and the legal industry is no exception. The advent and development of information technology are not the only challenges that the legal industry and legal professionals need to face. As long as they maintain a positive outlook towards all emerging phenomena, make use of them, and stay vigilant, the legal industry and legal professionals can better adapt to the unknown challenges and waves of the future.

---

[139] Sui and Liang (2022).

[140] Sui and Liang (2022).

[141] Tao and Li (2019).

[142] Huang (2020).

[143] Huang (2020).

[144] "Reflections on Improving the Effectiveness of Electronic Evidence." China Court website. Accessed August 21, 2024. https://www.chinacourt.org/article/detail/2013/12/id/1165771.shtml.

Chapter 7
Legal Education in China

7.1 An Introduction to Major Law Schools

In the landscape of modern legal education in China, a distinctive set of institutions, known as the "Five Academies and Four Departments", play a pivotal role. This grouping of premier law academies and departments signifies a cornerstone of legal studies within the country.[1] The term "Five Academies" specifically refers to a collection of institutions that originated as specialised institutes during the mid-twentieth century and have since evolved into comprehensive universities with a strong emphasis on politics and law.[2] These include the Beijing Institute of Political Science and Law, now known as China University of Political Science and Law; the Southwest Institute of Political Science and Law, now Southwest University of Political Science and Law; the Northwest Institute of Political Science and Law, now Northwest University of Political Science and Law; the Central South Institute of Political Science and Law, now Zhongnan University of Economics and Law; and the East China Institute of Political Science and Law, now East China University of Political Science and Law.

The transformation of these institutes into multidisciplinary universities specialising in legal and political education underscores their critical role in shaping the legal minds tasked with navigating the complexities of Chinese and international law.[3] Each of these institutions has expanded its academic offerings beyond their traditional focus, integrating a broader curriculum that includes economics, management, and the humanities, reflecting the interdisciplinary nature of modern legal challenges.[4]

---

[1] Wang (2022).

[2] Wang (2022).

[3] Wang (2022).

[4] Wang (2022).

S. Zhang et al., *Technology, Legal Education and Legal Profession in China and Australia*, International and Comparative Law in the Asia Pacific,
https://doi.org/10.1007/978-981-96-1639-8_7

The "Four Departments", on the other hand, include the law school at Peking University, now Peking University Law School; the law school at Renmin University of China, now Renmin University of China Law School; the law school at Jilin University, now Jilin University Law School; and the law school at Wuhan University, now Wuhan University Law School. These departments have been elevated to the status of Law Schools and are regarded as heavyweight faculties within their respective universities, their upgrade from departments to full-fledged law schools marks a significant elevation in their academic and professional stature, further enhancing their capacity to contribute to the legal profession both nationally and internationally.[5]

It is important to note that the designations "academy" and "department" used here are customary expressions rather than official terminologies currently used by these universities for their law programs.[6] This nomenclature traces back to educational reforms in the late Qing Dynasty (1644–1911/12CE), a period marked by significant institutional experimentation and the establishment of modern educational systems. Initially referred to as "schools" or "learning halls" prior to the abolition of the imperial examination system, these institutions were pivotal in transitioning China towards modern specialist training.[7]

With the founding of the Republic of China in 1949, further adjustments were made. "Schools" were transformed into "academies", and "departments" were organised under these academies or as independent entities capable of establishing "groups" as needed.[8] This evolution continued into New China, where the terminology and structure were retained but with significant ideological shifts.[9] The earlier "Law Schools" were renamed to "Institutes of Political Science and Law", emphasising the primacy of political science over law in alignment with the political orientations of the time.[10] These institutes were tasked explicitly with cultivating legal and political cadres dedicated to upholding and protecting the people's democratic government, reflecting a strategic alignment with governmental priorities.[11]

The regional distribution and management system of these legal education institutions were meticulously planned to ensure a balanced geographical spread across the country, addressing the previous concentration of such institutions in eastern China.[12] Managed by political and legal departments, this arrangement has become a foundational model for training legal professionals in China, profoundly influencing the trajectory of the development of legal education in the country.[13]

In contemporary contexts, such as the college entrance examination and postgraduate entrance examinations, the "Five Academies and Four Departments" attract a

---

[5] Wang (2022).

[6] Wang (2022).

[7] Wang (2022).

[8] He (2018).

[9] He (2018).

[10] He (2018).

[11] He (2018).

[12] Xu (2017).

[13] Xu (2017).

high number of applicants, underscoring their prestige and importance as renowned institutions in the fields of humanities and social sciences. Here, a brief introduction to these universities will follow, highlighting their unique contributions and standing within both the national and international academic communities.

7.1.1 China University of Political Science and Law

China University of Political Science and Law (CUPL) stands out as a key university in China's 211 Project, primarily recognised for its excellence in legal studies while also offering comprehensive programs in political science, economics, management, literature, history, philosophy, education, science, and engineering.[14] This institution is part of prestigious initiatives such as the 985 Project Advantageous Discipline Innovation Platform, the 2011 Plan, and the 111 Plan, all of which which aimed to promote innovation and attract global expertise in academic disciplines, solidifying CUPL's position as a "Double First Class" university under the direct oversight of the Ministry of Education of China.[15]

Established in 1952, CUPL was founded on the intellectual legacy and facilities of four major universities—Peking University, Tsinghua University, Yenching University, and Fu Jen Catholic University.[16] Mr Qian Duansheng, a celebrated legal scholar, politician, social activist, and advocate for democracy, served as the university's first dean.[17] His leadership helped shape the university's early direction and set a standard of excellence that continues to this day.[18]

Widely acclaimed as "the premier academic institution for legal education in China" and a central pillar in the field of humanities and social sciences, CUPL has been instrumental in shaping the landscape of legal education in the nation.[19] It has played a critical role in training legal and governance personnel, deeply influencing nearly all legislative processes in the country since its establishment.[20] The university is a leader in the innovation of legal education, the evolution of legal theory, and the modernisation of rule of law concepts, significantly impacting these fields both nationally and internationally.[21]

---

[14] See the official website of China University of Political Science and Law, https://www.cupl.edu.cn/xxgk/xxjj1.htm, accessed May 1, 2024.

[15] See footnote 14.

[16] See footnote 14.

[17] See footnote 14.

[18] See footnote 14.

[19] See footnote 14.

[20] See footnote 14.

[21] See footnote 14.

CUPL also stands as a beacon of academic diplomacy, representing China in the global arena through scholarly exchanges and cultural dialogues on law and governance.[22] These interactions not only enrich the university's academic environment but also enhance China's cultural and intellectual footprint worldwide, emphasising CUPL's pivotal role in the advancement of legal studies and its contribution to the global academic community.[23]

CUPL boasts an impressive array of academic credentials, with 39 doctoral degree authorisation points, 77 master's degree authorisation points, 11 professional master's degree authorisation points, and four post-doctoral research stations.[24] The university offers first-level doctoral degree programs in Law, Political Science, Marxist Theory, and Theoretical Economics.[25] Additionally, it provides first-level master's degree programs in Philosophy, Applied Economics, Sociology, Psychology, Foreign Languages and Literatures, Journalism and Communication, Chinese History, Business Administration, and Public Administration.[26] Notably, Law is recognised as a national key discipline at the first-level, while Political Science is distinguished as a first-level key discipline by the city of Beijing. The field of Evidence Science has been included in Beijing's list for the construction of high-level disciplines in universities.[27]

The university currently serves a diverse student body of 18,442, including 9,630 mainland undergraduate students, 8053 mainland graduate students, and 759 students from Hong Kong, Macau, Taiwan, and international backgrounds.[28] The faculty includes 1058 full-time members, among whom 718 hold senior academic titles.[29] There are 320 doctoral supervisors and 884 master's supervisors, with an impressive 87.7% of the faculty holding doctoral degrees.[30] The university operates across two campuses located in Haidian District's Xueyuan Road and Changping District's Fuxue Road.[31]

In the field of legal education, the university has established multiple specialised colleges including the School of Law; School of Civil, Commercial, and Economic Law; School of International Law; School of Criminal Justice; Sino-European School of Law; and the School of Juris Master.[32] Law, as a first-level national key discipline, has achieved the highest ranking of A+ in the Ministry of Education's discipline assessment, reflecting its prominence and excellence in legal education.[33]

---

22 See footnote 14.

23 See footnote 14.

24 See footnote 14.

25 See footnote 14.

26 See footnote 14.

27 See footnote 14.

28 See footnote 14.

29 See footnote 14.

30 See footnote 14.

31 See footnote 14.

32 See footnote 14.

33 See footnote 14.

Since entering the new era, CUPL has further expanded its academic horizon by establishing the Xi Jinping Institute of Jurisprudence, a dedicated research institution for studying the legal thought of Xi Jinping.[34] Among its many specialised facilities, the university boasts one Ministry of Education Philosophy and Social Sciences Experimental Laboratory dedicated to data and legal governance research.[35] Additionally, it houses high-profile entities such as a national-level think tank development unit and a national human rights education and training base (Human Rights Research Institute).[36]

Furthermore, the university hosts two Ministry of Education Key Research Bases in Humanities and Social Sciences, specifically focused on litigation law (Litigation Law Research Institute) and legal history (Legal History Research Institute), alongside one key laboratory (Evidence Science Research Institute).[37] Other significant research centres include the Beijing Philosophy and Social Sciences Research Base, the Ministry of Education's Youth Legal Education Base, the Ministry of Education's Teacher Legal Education Research Center, and the Beijing Legal Education Research Base (Institute of Rule of Law Government).[38]

The university is directly connected to the Ministry of Education's National Committee for the Collation and Study of Ancient Texts through its Institute for the Collation and Study of Legal Texts.[39] It also hosts a base for the study of Xi Jinping's Thoughts on Socialism with Chinese Characteristics for a New Era under the Beijing Municipal Government at CUPL, along with the Beijing Universities Collaborative Innovation Center for Theoretical Research on Chinese Socialism.[40]

In partnership with the Supreme People's Procuratorate and other national and provincial-level government bodies, CUPL has co-established 16 high-level research bases. Moreover, the university supports a diverse array of research institutions including the Comparative Law Research Institute, the Law and Economics Research Institute, and the Institute for Globalisation and Global Issues, totalling nine traditional research institutions and eight innovative research entities.[41]

CUPL is fully committed to implementing an international development strategy, continuously enhancing the global standards of its educational offerings.[42] Each year, the university sends over a thousand students and faculty abroad through various collaborative exchange programs and invites hundreds of foreign experts for short and long-term teaching stints, gradually establishing a framework for cultivating international talent.[43] The university has established cooperative and exchange relationships

[34] See footnote 14.

[35] See footnote 14.

[36] See footnote 14.

[37] See footnote 14.

[38] See footnote 14.

[39] See footnote 14.

[40] See footnote 14.

[41] See footnote 14.

[42] See footnote 14.

[43] See footnote 14.

with 297 renowned universities, research institutions, and international organisations across 58 countries and regions, joining international groups such as the Global Law School Alliance, the Eurasia-Pacific Alliance, the Association of Universities of China and Central and Eastern European Countries, the Asian Society of Law, and initiating the Mainland China-Hong Kong-Macau Law Education Alliance.[44]

The China–Europe School of Law at CUPL is the largest cooperative project in legal education between the Chinese government and the European Union.[45] The university also collaborates with Washington University in St Louis, USA, to offer a dual master's degree program in International Law, creating a high-level platform for Sino-American legal education.[46] Furthermore, CUPL has established three overseas Confucius Institutes in the United Kingdom, Romania, and Barbados.[47]

CUPL regularly organises the "World Jurist Forum", which not only promotes Chinese legal culture abroad but also significantly enhances the university's international competitiveness, influence, and collaborative capabilities.[48]

7.1.2 Southwest University of Political Science and Law

Southwest University of Political Science and Law (SWUPL) is one of the earliest higher education institutions for political and legal studies established in New China.[49] Following the reform and opening up, it was designated by the State Council as one of the first key universities nationwide.[50] It is jointly managed by the Ministry of Education and the Chongqing Municipal People's Government.[51] The university is among the first batch of national bases for the excellent legal-talent education program, a designated institution for training international students under the Chinese Government Scholarship Program, and a participant in the Central and Western Universities Capacity Building Project.[52]

The precursor to the university was the Southwest People's Revolutionary University, founded in 1950 with Marshal Liu Bocheng as its president.[53] In 1953, based on the Department of Political Science and Law of the Southwest People's Revolutionary University, the Southwest College of Political Science and Law was established, with the name inscribed by Mr Guo Moruo. In 1995, with the approval of the former State

---

[44] See footnote 14.

[45] See footnote 14.

[46] See footnote 14.

[47] See footnote 14.

[48] See footnote 14.

[49] See the official website of Southwest University of Political Science and Law, https://www.swupl.edu.cn/xxgkn/xxjj/index.htm, accessed May 1, 2024.

[50] See footnote 49.

[51] See footnote 49.

[52] See footnote 49.

[53] See footnote 49.

Education Commission, it was renamed Southwest University of Political Science and Law.[54]

Over more than 70 years of dedicated and diligent development, SWUPL has steadfastly adhered to its motto of "broad learning, steadfast practice, profound virtue, and respect for the law".[55] It has embraced the educational philosophy of "establishing the school through teaching, revitalising the school through talent, strengthening the school through research, and governing the school by law".[56] This philosophy has crystallised into the distinct "SWUPL spirit", characterised by a commitment to "caring for the world, striving ceaselessly for self-improvement, fostering harmony, and pursuing rigour and pragmatism".[57] The university has developed a multidisciplinary synergy centred on legal studies but also encompassing philosophy, economics, literature, management, and engineering, offering a multi-tiered and diverse training system from undergraduate to doctoral and post-doctoral levels, including continuing education and international student programs.[58]

The university is qualified to enrol students through various special admissions programs, including recommended students, high-level athletes, students from classes for Tibetans and Uyghurs from mainland China, joint admissions for students from Hong Kong, Macau, Taiwan, and overseas Chinese, as well as direct admissions for students from Hong Kong and Macau without examinations, and recommended students from Taiwan.[59]

In its more than 70 years of operation, SWUPL has trained over 300,000 professionals of various levels for the nation, making it one of the largest contributors to the country's legal workforce.[60] Among its alumni are one member of the 20th Central Politburo of the Chinese Communist Party; seven members, alternate members, and Discipline Inspection Committee members of the 20th Central Committee of the Chinese Communist Party; and over a hundred who have held provincial or ministerial-level leadership positions. Nearly 60 SWUPL graduates have held or currently hold the positions of Chief Justice or senior judges and prosecutors at the national level.[61]

SWUPL currently operates across three campuses: the Shapingba Campus, the Yubei Campus, and the Baosheng Lake Campus, collectively covering an area of over 3000 mou (approximately 200 hectares).[62] The Yubei Campus serves as the primary centre for undergraduate and graduate education, the Shapingba Campus is dedicated

[54] See footnote 49.

[55] See footnote 49.

[56] See the official website of Southwest University of Political Science and Law, https://www.swupl.edu.cn/xxgkn/bswh/xx/index.htm, accessed May 1, 2024.

[57] See footnote 56.

[58] See the official website of Southwest University of Political Science and Law, https://www.swupl.edu.cn/xxgkn/xxjj/index.htm, accessed May 1, 2024.

[59] See footnote 58.

[60] See footnote 58.

[61] See footnote 58.

[62] See footnote 58.

to continuing education and cadre training, and the Baosheng Lake Campus focuses on research and innovation activities.[63]

The university has a total enrolment of over 25,000 students and employs more than 2000 staff members, including over 600 faculty members with senior professional technical positions.[64] In the realm of legal education, the university features a Law School and several specialised colleges, including the College of Civil and Commercial Law (which also encompasses the Intellectual Property Institute), the College of Economic Law (Ecological Law Institute), the Administrative Law College (Discipline Inspection and Supervision College), the International Law College, the Artificial Intelligence Law College (Applied Law College), the Criminal Investigation College, and the National Security College.[65] In the Ministry of Education's academic evaluation, law as a first-level discipline has been ranked within the top tier, category A.[66]

In 2018, in the first national professional degree-level assessment, the Juris Master (JM) degree program of SWUPL was awarded an A-grade, placing it alongside prestigious institutions such as Tsinghua University and CUPL.[67]

SWUPL hosts a variety of prestigious research platforms and development projects, reflecting its standing as a centre of academic excellence and innovation.[68] These include a national high-end think tank development unit, which is co-established with the State Council's Office of Press and Publicity and the Ministry of Education, and is also a founding member of the Ministry of Education's alliance of high-end university think tanks. Additionally, the university features a national-level research base for foreign-related legal studies, a Ministry of Education Engineering Research Center development project, a provincial and ministerial collaborative innovation centre, a Ministry of Education country and regional studies centre, and an international governance research base for cyberspace.[69]

Collaborative research bases have been jointly established with top national bodies such as the Supreme People's Court, the Supreme People's Procuratorate, the Ministry of Culture and Tourism, and the National Audit Office.[70] The university is also involved in 44 research platforms including a provincial and ministerial "2011" Collaborative Innovation Center, key research bases in humanities and social sciences, a new-type think tank in Chongqing, a science popularisation base in Chongqing, and a humanities and social sciences popularisation base in Chongqing.[71]

---

[63] See footnote 58.

[64] See footnote 58.

[65] See footnote 58.

[66] See footnote 58.

[67] See footnote 58.

[68] See footnote 58.

[69] See footnote 58.

[70] See footnote 58.

[71] See footnote 58.

The Judicial Appraisal Center at the university is the only national-level forensic institution in the central and western regions of China.[72]

From 2018 to the present, the university has secured a total of 1660 provincial and ministerial-level and higher vertical research projects, including 45 major national projects and 84 annual projects funded by the National Social Science Fund of China in the field of law, ranking it among the leading universities in the nation in this respect.[73]

SWUPL consistently pursues an open education strategy, having established exchange and cooperation relations with over 190 universities and institutions in nearly 40 countries and regions, and launched more than 130 student exchange programs.[74] The university has been selected for the Ministry of Education's "Outstanding Undergraduate International Exchange Program" and the "National Project for Sending Graduate Students to High-Level Universities Abroad". It is also recognised as a Chongqing Internationalised Featured University and is part of the "Ba-Yu Overseas Talent Introduction Plan".[75]

The university collaborates with well-known universities in the United States, Russia, Canada, Japan, Australia, Belgium, Israel, and other countries to offer over 20 short-term academic-course projects for international students coming to China.[76] Notably, it hosts two Sino-foreign cooperative education projects: the Coventry University Law Undergraduate Program from the UK and the Case Western Reserve University Master of Laws Program from the United States, making it the only institution in the western region of China to offer a dual-degree program in legal studies through international cooperation.[77]

The education for international students at SWUPL covers bachelor's, master's, and doctoral levels.[78] The university has introduced a range of "Study at SWUPL" brand programs, including the ASEAN Talents PhD Program, the "Chinese Law" all-English master's program, and the Sino-Cambodian overseas cooperative undergraduate "2 + 2" program.[79]

7.1.3 East China University of Political Science and Law

East China University of Political Science and Law (ECUPL) is one of the earliest higher education institutions for political and legal studies established in New

[72] See footnote 58.

[73] See footnote 58.

[74] See footnote 58.

[75] See footnote 58.

[76] See footnote 58.

[77] See footnote 58.

[78] See footnote 58.

[79] See footnote 58.

China.[80] In June 1952, with the approval of the East China Military and Political Committee, the law, political science, and social science departments from nine universities—St John's University, Fudan University, Nanjing University, Soochow University, Xiamen University, Hujiang University, Anhui University, Shanghai College, and Aurora University—were merged to establish the East China Institute of Political Science and Law at the former site of St John's University.[81] In 1958, the institution was incorporated into the Shanghai Academy of Social Sciences; it was reestablished in 1963 and began enrolling students the following year.[82] The university ceased admissions in 1966 and was dissolved in 1972; however, it was reestablished for the second time, in March 1979, following approval by the State Council.[83] In March 2007, with the approval of the Ministry of Education, the institution was renamed East China University of Political Science and Law.[84] The university is managed by the city of Shanghai. The current Party Secretary is Professor Guo Weilu, and the President is Professor Ye Qing.[85]

Over the years, ECUPL has adhered to the motto "Commitment to practice and knowledge, reverence for virtue and law" and has promoted the spirit of "rising through adversity, striving amidst peril, and excelling in glory".[86] The university has developed into a distinctively multidisciplinary institution with a focus on law, incorporating economics, management, literature, and engineering. It is renowned as the "Pearl of the Orient in Legal Education".[87]

ECUPL currently operates across three campuses located in the Songjiang, Changning, and Putuo districts, covering a total area of over 750,000 square metres.[88] The university is home to 19 schools (departments) and more than 180 research institutions. It employs over 1300 faculty and staff, with 57% holding senior academic titles. The student body comprises more than 18,000 individuals.[89]

The university is authorised to award doctoral and master's degrees in first-level disciplines of Law and Public Administration, as well as master's degrees in the areas of Applied Economics, Political Science, Marxist Theory, Sociology, Foreign Language and Literature, and Journalism and Communication.[90] It also holds the right to confer professional master's degrees in fields such as Law, Public

---

[80] See the official website of East China University of Political Science and Law, https://www.ecupl.edu.cn, accessed May 1, 2024.

[81] See footnote 80.

[82] See footnote 80.

[83] See footnote 80.

[84] See footnote 80.

[85] See footnote 80.

[86] See the website of the Publicity Department of the Party Committee of East China University of Political Science and Law, https://xcb.ecupl.edu.cn/3146/list.htm, accessed May 1, 2024.

[87] See footnote 86.

[88] See the official website of East China University of Political Science and Law, https://www.ecupl.edu.cn, accessed May 1, 2024.

[89] See footnote 88.

[90] See footnote 88.

Management, Finance, Social Work, Translation, Journalism and Communication, and Accounting.[91]

Furthermore, ECUPL has established 24 second-level doctoral disciplines and 52 second-level master's disciplines across 26 undergraduate programs. Additionally, the university hosts two post-doctoral research stations in Law and Public Management, further enhancing its academic and research capabilities.[92]

In the realm of legal education, ECUPL has been recognised as one of the Ministry of Education's first batch of bases for the education and training of outstanding legal talent.[93] It also serves as a base for the cultivation of excellent legal talent and outstanding talent in Journalism and Communication in Shanghai.[94] Moreover, the university places a strong emphasis on international exchange and cooperation.[95] As of September 2023, it has established partnerships with 191 universities and institutions across 46 countries and regions, as well as with nine international and regional organisations, including the World Intellectual Property Organisation, the Asian Society of Law, and the European Law Firms Alliance, signing a total of 404 agreements.[96]

The university also hosts Sino-foreign cooperative education projects approved by the Ministry of Education.[97] In 2012, it was granted the qualification to accept international students under Chinese government scholarships; by 2014, it became one of the first six universities nationwide to receive the "Chinese Government Scholarship for Outstanding International Students Coming to China".[98]

Looking forward, ECUPL will continue to champion its educational tradition that places teaching at its core, prioritises faculty excellence, and centres on student development.[99] The university is committed to a philosophy of openness, inclusivity, and innovation in its operations.[100] It aims to reinforce its development strategy which emphasises educational excellence, academic advancement, and talent cultivation.[101] The focus will be on establishing a top-tier law program while promoting an integrated approach across multiple disciplines.[102]

Guided by Xi Jinping's Thoughts on Socialism with Chinese Characteristics for the New Era, the university is devoted to the foundational mission of moral and intellectual education.[103] It seeks to deepen higher education reforms, unlock new

---

[91] See footnote 88.

[92] See footnote 88.

[93] See footnote 88.

[94] See footnote 88.

[95] See footnote 88.

[96] See footnote 88.

[97] See footnote 88.

[98] See footnote 88.

[99] See footnote 88.

[100] See footnote 88.

[101] See footnote 88.

[102] See footnote 88.

[103] See footnote 88.

productive capacities, and pursue high-quality development.[104] The goal is to establish ECUPL as a world-class institution distinguished by its Chinese characteristics, striving to make significant contributions to national development, people's well-being, and the advancement of human civilisation.[105]

7.1.4 Zhongnan University of Economics and Law

Zhongnan University of Economics and Law is a key national university directly under the Ministry of Education and is prominently featured in national development programs such as the 211 Project and the 985 Project Advantageous Discipline Innovation Platform.[106] It is also designated as a "Double First-Class" university, co-established by the Ministry of Education, the Ministry of Finance, and the Hubei Provincial Government.[107] The university originated in 1948 founded by the Central Plains Bureau of the Communist Party of China, with Deng Xiaoping as its first secretary and Chen Yi, the second secretary, serving as the head of the preparatory committee for Zhongyuan University.[108]

During the national higher education adjustment period, the university integrated high-quality finance, economics, and legal educational resources from universities across six central and southern provinces, including Henan University, Zhonghua University, Sun Yat-sen University, Hunan University, Guangxi University, and Nanchang University.[109] Based on the faculties of finance and law from Zhongyuan University, in May 1953, the Central South Institute of Finance and the Central South Institute of Law were established.[110] In September 1958, these institutions merged with the Central South Law Cadre School and the law school of Wuhan University to form Hubei University.[111]

In December 1971, Hubei University was renamed Hubei College of Finance and Economics; in January 1978, it was renamed again to Hubei Institute of Finance and Economics, becoming one of the first institutions to resume undergraduate and graduate admissions after the Cultural Revolution; in December 1984, based on the law school of the Hubei Institute of Finance and Economics, the Central South Institute of Law was reestablished; in September 1985, the Hubei Institute of Finance and Economics was renamed Central South University of Finance and Economics.[112]

[104] See footnote 88.

[105] See footnote 88.

[106] See the official website of Zhongnan University of Economics and Law, https://www.zuel.edu.cn/about/, accessed May 1, 2024.

[107] See footnote 106.

[108] See footnote 106.

[109] See footnote 106.

[110] See footnote 106.

[111] See footnote 106.

[112] See footnote 106.

On 26 May 2000, Central South University of Finance and Economics, and Central South Institute of Law merged to form the new Zhongnan University of Economics and Law, which now boasts a history of over 70 years.[113]

Zhongnan University of Economics and Law currently operates across two campuses. The Nanhu Campus is located by the picturesque South Lake, while the Shouyi Campus sits beneath the historic Yellow Crane Tower.[114] The university hosts over 20,000 full-time undergraduate students, more than 8600 master's students, over 1200 doctoral students, and more than 500 international students. Additionally, there are over 17,000 continuing education students.[115]

The university employs more than 2500 staff members, including over 1500 full-time faculty members.[116] Among the teaching staff, there are over 370 professors, 580 associate professors, and 240 doctoral supervisors.[117] The university offers 60 undergraduate majors, 30 of which are recognised as national first-class undergraduate programs.[118] It also provides 25 national first-class undergraduate courses, three national demonstration courses in ideological and political education, 17 first-level discipline master's degree authorisation points, 18 professional master's degree programs, seven first-level discipline doctoral degree authorisation points, and seven post-doctoral research stations.[119]

Since 2000, the university has developed over 400 integrated professional courses, establishing one of the largest systems of integrated courses in economics, law, and management in China. It has received one first-place national award for teaching achievements, six second-place awards, and has received recognition for advanced contributions to national textbook construction.[120] Additionally, the university has secured four national-level New Liberal Arts research and reform projects and five New Engineering research and practice projects.[121] It has been recognised with three national experimental teaching demonstration centres, one national virtual simulation experimental teaching centre, and two national virtual teaching and research offices.[122] The Ministry of Education has designated it as one of the first bases for the "Outstanding Legal Talent Education" program.[123] Over the past decade, the university has won three national gold awards and ten silver awards in the "Internet +", "Challenge Cup", and "Creative Youth" innovation and entrepreneurship competitions.[124]

---

[113] See footnote 106.

[114] See footnote 106.

[115] See footnote 106.

[116] See footnote 106.

[117] See footnote 106.

[118] See footnote 106.

[119] See footnote 106.

[120] See footnote 106.

[121] See footnote 106.

[122] See footnote 106.

[123] See footnote 106.

[124] See footnote 106.

In the field of legal education, Zhongnan University of Economics and Law hosts a variety of academic units including the Law School, which comprises departments like Theoretical Law, Constitutional and Administrative Law, Procedural Law, Civil and Commercial Law, Economic Law, International Law, International Economic Law, and a Legal Experiment Teaching Center.[125] Additionally, the university has established the Criminal Justice College, Juris Master Education Center, National Governance College, and the College of Law and Economics.[126]

The university has developed an academic structure that harmonises and integrates major fields such as economics, law, and management with other disciplines including philosophy, education, literature, history, science, engineering, arts, and interdisciplinary studies, encompassing a total of 11 academic categories.[127] Currently, it maintains four national key disciplines and one national key (cultivating) discipline.[128] The law discipline has been selected for the national "Double First-Class" initiative.[129] In 2018, its Intellectual Property Center was approved as a national innovation and talent-introduction base under the 111 Plan; in January 2022, the law discipline was selected again in the second round for top-tier discipline development.[130] The Law and Economics Discipline Group Construction Plan[131] was also approved by the Ministry of Education.

Furthermore, as one of the founding members, the university established the "Lige Alliance" among national universities with legal and political programs, spearheading the creation of several industry-specific academic-development alliances.[132] These include the First-Class Discipline Construction Alliance in Finance and Economics, the International Criminal Justice Alliance, and the Guangdong-Hong Kong-Macao Greater Bay Area Intellectual Property Law Alliance, each reflecting the unique industry characteristics and fostering specialised academic collaboration.[133]

Simultaneously, Zhongnan University of Economics and Law actively promotes both domestic and international academic exchanges and collaborations: it has established cooperative relationships with over 100 universities and research institutions across more than 20 countries and regions.[134] The university has been approved for several prestigious projects, including the Ministry of Education's first batch of High-Level International Talent Training Innovation and Practice Projects and the

[125] See footnote 106.

[126] See footnote 106.

[127] See footnote 106.

[128] See footnote 106.

[129] See footnote 106.

[130] See footnote 106.

[131] See the website of the School of Law and Economics at Zhongnan University of Economics and Law, http://zyxy.zuel.edu.cn/8066/list.htm, accessed May 1, 2024.

[132] See the official website of Zhongnan University of Economics and Law, https://www.zuel.edu.cn/about/, accessed May 1, 2024.

[133] See footnote 132.

[134] See footnote 132.

Foreign-related Rule of Law Talent Collaborative Training Innovation Base (Cultivation).[135] Additionally, it has been involved in the Ministry of Science and Technology's High-end Foreign Experts Introduction Plan and the Foreign Young Talents Plan, both of which are key national projects for attracting international expertise.[136] The university is also part of the China Scholarship Council's Innovative Talent International Cooperation Training Project, the International Organisation Reserve Talent Project, and the Country and Regional Studies Talent Support Plan Project.[137] It was selected as one of the first pilot universities for the University International Organisation Faculty Study Abroad Program.[138]

The university has signed cooperation agreements with more than 30 universities and institutions, including Pennsylvania State University in the USA, the University of Leeds in the UK, Saarland University in Germany, the Sapienza University of Rome in Italy, the University of Montreal in Canada, Bond University in Australia, and the International Institute for the Unification of Private Law (UNIDROIT).[139] In 2017, the Sino-Italian Law Studies Center and the China Law Library were established at Sapienza University of Rome. In 2019, in collaboration with the same institution, the Sino-Italian Institute was established, and the European Studies: Comparative Law and European Law master's degree program was approved by the Ministry of Education.[140]

7.1.5 Northwest University of Political Science and Law

Northwest University of Political Science and Law is located in Xi'an, a city renowned for its rich historical and cultural heritage.[141] It is a multidisciplinary university with a distinctive focus on law, supported and complemented by disciplines such as philosophy, economics, management, and literature.[142] The university serves as a national base for the training of legal talents and is a key centre for legal education, legal research, and humanities and social sciences research in the Northwest region.[143] It is also recognised as a high-level university for key construction in Shaanxi Province and is part of elite educational alliances including the National

[135] See footnote 132.

[136] See footnote 132.

[137] See footnote 132.

[138] See footnote 132.

[139] See footnote 132.

[140] See footnote 132.

[141] See the official website of Northwest University of Political Science and Law, https://www.nwupl.edu.cn/hjgk/hjjg/66293.htm, accessed May 1, 2024.

[142] See footnote 141.

[143] See footnote 141.

Higher Education Lige Alliance for law and the Chang'an Alliance of high-level universities with distinctive characteristics in Xi'an.[144]

The university's origins trace back to 1937, when the Chinese Communist Party founded the Shaanbei Public School in Yan'an.[145] It has evolved through various phases, including Yan'an University, Northwest People's Revolutionary University, Northwest Cadre School of Political Science and Law, and the Northwest Branch of the Central Political and Legal Cadre School.[146] In 1958, the entire law school of Northwest University was transferred to establish the Xi'an College of Political Science and Law, which was later renamed the Northwest College of Political Science and Law and ultimately became Northwest University of Political Science and Law.[147]

Since its inception, the university has been deeply rooted in the western region, fostering the venerable Yan'an tradition of "political steadfastness, seeking truth from facts, innovation, and hard work".[148] It has established the motto of "rigorous, pragmatic, civilised, and just"[149] and crystallised an educational philosophy that emphasises "belief in the rule of law, a Chinese standpoint, an international perspective, and a populist ethos".[150] Over the years, it has trained more than 180,000 high-quality professionals who are both morally upright and legally proficient.[151]

Northwest University of Political Science and Law currently has over 12,000 undergraduate students, more than 3900 full-time master's students, and around 130 doctoral students. Moreover, the university employs over 1000 full-time faculty members, among whom more than 50 have been recognised in various national and provincial talent programs.[152] Additionally, over 40 faculty members have been honoured with distinctions such as the State Council Special Allowance, recognised nationally as exemplary teachers in ethics, national model teachers, national outstanding teachers, and in Shaanxi Province as role models in teaching ethics and outstanding teachers.[153]

In the realm of legal education, the university comprises several specialised academic units including the College of Jurisprudence, College of Juris Master, College of Administrative Law (Discipline Inspection and Supervision College), College of Criminal Law, College of Civil and Commercial Law, College of

---

[144] See footnote 141.

[145] See footnote 141.

[146] See footnote 141.

[147] See footnote 141.

[148] See the official website of Northwest University of Political Science and Law, https://www.nwupl.edu.cn/hjgk/dhjs/62331.htm, accessed May 1, 2024.

[149] See the official website of Northwest University of Political Science and Law, https://www.nwupl.edu.cn/hjgk/dhjs/62330.htm, accessed May 1, 2024.

[150] See the official website of Northwest University of Political Science and Law, https://www.nwupl.edu.cn/hjgk/hjjg/66293.htm, accessed May 1, 2024.

[151] See footnote 150.

[152] See footnote 150.

[153] See footnote 150.

Economic Law (Intellectual Property College), and the College of International Law.[154] The university began enrolling master's students in 1979 and was authorised, in 2012, to offer a first-level discipline in Law under the Doctoral Program Serving National Special Needs; in 2014, it was approved to establish a post-doctoral research station in law.[155] The university was also among the first to undertake the national Juris Master degree program for professional degrees in foreign-related lawyering and arbitration.[156]

Currently, the university has seven first-level discipline master's degree authorisation points, 42 second-level discipline master's degree authorisation points, nine interdisciplinary master's degree authorisation points, and nine professional master's degree authorisation points.[157] In 2018, it was designated by Shaanxi Province as a university for the construction of first-class disciplines domestically, with the Law discipline being approved as a first-class discipline; in 2023, it was selected as a Shaanxi Province "Double First-Class" cultivation university, and its Law discipline was approved as a cultivation discipline.[158] The Law program has also been recognised as a national first-class undergraduate major construction site.[159]

Northwest University of Political Science and Law places significant emphasis on the modern development of legal education. It is among the first batch of universities to implement the national Outstanding Legal Talent Education and Training Program, undertaking all three types of outstanding legal-talent-training tasks.[160] The Law Talent Training Model Innovation Experimental Zone at the university is recognised as a national-level innovation experimental zone.[161] The university's Law Experimental and Training Center is among the first batch of national-level experimental teaching demonstration centres, supplemented by two provincial-level experimental teaching demonstration centres and three provincial-level virtual simulation experimental teaching centres.[162] Additionally, there are two basic experimental centres on campus: the Computer Experiment Center and the Language Experiment Center.[163]

The university employs a mentorship system for undergraduate students and places a strong focus on the development of extracurricular systems, establishing a continuous, year-round, and high-level extracurricular activities system that is segmented and categorised to enhance the comprehensive development of students.[164]

---

[154] See footnote 150.

[155] See footnote 150.

[156] See footnote 150.

[157] See footnote 150.

[158] See footnote 150.

[159] See footnote 150.

[160] See footnote 150.

[161] See footnote 150.

[162] See footnote 150.

[163] See footnote 150.

[164] See footnote 150.

Northwest University of Political Science and Law actively implements an international development strategy, having established partnerships with over 80 universities and institutions in nearly 20 countries and regions.[165] The university is vigorously advancing the internationalisation of talent cultivation, faculty development, and scientific research, actively engaging in education for international students at the bachelor's, master's, and doctoral levels.[166] The university proactively integrates into the Belt and Road Initiative, serving as a founding member of the Shanghai Cooperation Organisation University of Law Alliance, and is a member of both the Silk Road University Alliance and the Belt and Road Language and Culture University Alliance.[167] It hosts the Chang'an and Rome Belt and Road Legal and Cultural Dialogue series of international academic seminars, conducts civil servant training for Belt and Road countries, and organises the Chinese Bridge Legal Study Camp for Central Asian students, aiming to become a hub for innovative legal studies and cultural exchange along the Silk Road.[168]

The university actively creates platforms for the international development of its students and faculty, implementing the Overseas Faculty Training Program and conducting over 80 joint talent-training programs with domestic and international partners.[169] Approved by the Ministry of Education as a High-Level International Talent Training Innovation Practice Base and an International Organisational Legal Talent Training Project, the university attracts high-quality educational resources from abroad, establishes overseas internship bases, and continuously enhances the level of internationalisation in talent training and its capability to compete on the international stage.[170]

7.1.6 Peking University Law School

The Law School of Peking University was established on 26 June 1999, evolving from the Department of Law, which was the cradle of modern legal education in China and boasts the longest history in the field of modern legal education in the country.[171] Since the establishment of a law program at the Imperial University of Peking in 1904, the Law School has adhered to its mission of serving the nation through legal education and upholding justice.[172] It continues to craft profound scholarly works within the iconic red buildings of the campus and engrave significant academic

[165] See footnote 150.

[166] See footnote 150.

[167] See footnote 150.

[168] See footnote 150.

[169] See footnote 150.

[170] See footnote 150.

[171] See the official website of the Law School of Peking University, https://www.law.pku.edu.cn/sjb/xygk/xyjj/index.htm, accessed May 1, 2024.

[172] See footnote 171.

contributions in Yan Garden.[173] The school is dedicated to fostering a deep commitment to scholarship and the pursuit of excellence, enhancing the "soft power" of its cultural influence to improve the "hard quality" of its education.[174] It strives to mould faculty, students, and alumni who embody the spirit of China, and engage in mainstream academic dialogues worldwide, preserving the shared spiritual home of generations of Peking University's legal community and perpetuating the spirit of rule of law indefinitely.[175]

Since the reform and opening up, and particularly since the entry of Chinese socialism into a new era, the Law School of Peking University has achieved significant accomplishments in various areas including the cultivation of top innovative talents, construction of high-quality faculty teams, scientific research and academic innovation, service to societal progress, the inheritance and innovation of excellent culture, and international exchanges and cooperation.[176] The school has consistently led the way among law schools nationwide.[177]

The Law School boasts a nationally recognised first-level key discipline in law, with a comprehensive and fully equipped range of specialised areas, each of which rank at the top of China's legal education and research sector, and it is home to many renowned scholars who are well-respected both domestically and internationally, along with a core group of young and middle-aged teaching and research leaders.[178] Each year, it recruits, trains, and develops a large number of exceptional legal talent who possess firm ideals and beliefs, strong patriotic sentiments, and a solid foundation in law.[179] The consistent and remarkable achievements in the school's reforms and development have laid a solid foundation for steadily advancing its Double First-Class construction and securing a position among the top-tier global law schools.[180]

Peking University Law School offers first-class teaching and research facilities, including the Kaiyuan Teaching and Administration Building, the Chenming Research Building, the Guoshuang Courtyard (a traditional Siheyuan), and the Law Pillar Plaza to support its educational and research activities.[181] In recent years, the Law School has made significant strides in internationalisation, establishing close ties with nearly a hundred of the world's top law schools and setting up joint research institutions with numerous prestigious law schools in Europe and America.[182]

In 2013, Peking University Law School was ranked first among the mainland Chinese law schools in the renowned QS World University Rankings for higher

[173] See footnote 171.

[174] See footnote 171.

[175] See footnote 171.

[176] See footnote 171.

[177] See footnote 171.

[178] See footnote 171.

[179] See footnote 171.

[180] See footnote 171.

[181] See footnote 171.

[182] See footnote 171.

education.[183] From 2015 to 2017, it consistently placed in the top 20 globally, remained the top-ranked law school in mainland China and among the top three in Asia.[184] In the latest 2024 QS World University Rankings, the Law School was ranked 31st worldwide.[185]

Peking University Law School is home to four national key disciplines: Jurisprudence, Constitutional and Administrative Law, Economic Law, and Criminal Law.[186] In 1988, during the first selection of national key disciplines, Peking University's Jurisprudence and International Law were designated as two national key disciplines; by 2001, Jurisprudence, Constitutional, and Administrative Law, Economic Law, and Criminal Law at Peking University were recognised as national key disciplines; in 2007, the Law program at Peking University was elevated to a national first-level key discipline.[187]

The theoretical law discipline at Peking University Law School is one of the earliest disciplines in China to establish both master's and doctoral programs.[188] The school has long held a leading position nationally in teaching and research strength in legal theory.[189] The doctoral program in legal theory includes specialisations in jurisprudence, legislative science, sociology of law, law and economics, and comparative law, while the master's program includes specialisations in jurisprudence, legislative science, sociology of law, law and economics, comparative law, and judicial system, among others.[190]

Eminent scholars such as Chen Shouyi and Shen Zongling from the older generation, along with middle-aged and young academic leaders like Zhu Suli and Zhou Wangsheng, have kept Peking University at the forefront of legal theory research in China.[191] The jurisprudence discipline primarily engages in theoretical research, teaching, and talent development, while also providing research and consultancy services to the national government and various relevant departments.[192] Tailoring its focus to China's national conditions and the developmental needs of the country's rule of law, the discipline fully leverages its academic strengths.[193] It closely follows both domestic and international developments in legal theory, maintains an open and broad academic perspective, emphasises the connection between theory and

[183] See footnote 171.

[184] See footnote 171.

[185] See QS World University Rankings by Subject: Law & Legal Studies 2024, https://www.qschina.cn/en/university-rankings/university-subject-rankings/2024/law-legal-studies, accessed August 29, 2024.

[186] See the official website of the Law School of Peking University, https://www.law.pku.edu.cn/sjb/xygk/xyjj/index.htm, accessed May 1, 2024.

[187] See footnote 186.

[188] See footnote 186.

[189] See footnote 186.

[190] See footnote 186.

[191] See footnote 186.

[192] See footnote 186.

[193] See footnote 186.

practice, focuses on empirical research, and strives to address significant theoretical legal issues during China's social transformation.[194] This approach has significantly advanced research and teaching in legal theory, resulting in a number of internationally recognised research achievements and training a cadre of professionals who link theory with practice.[195]

The Constitutional and Administrative Law discipline at Peking University Law School has a history of 50 years, with master's programs initiated in 1978, initially recruiting master's students in research directions such as Chinese Constitution and Foreign Constitutions.[196] Subsequently, new specialisations in Administrative Law, Administrative Litigation Law, and the study of the Basic Laws of Hong Kong and Macau were added.[197] In 1989, doctoral programs were established, enrolling PhD students in Chinese Constitution, Foreign Constitutions, Administrative Law, Administrative Litigation Law, Foreign Administrative Law, and Basic Laws of Hong Kong and Macau.[198] Professors such as Xiao Weiyun, Luo Haocai, and Jiang Mingan are leading scholars in China's field of constitutional and administrative law.[199]

The Constitutional and Administrative Law discipline has a solid historical foundation and leverages its strength in basic theoretical research while actively exploring new areas. Theories and areas such as Balance Theory, Soft Law and Public Governance, Public Participation, Quasi-Governmental Organisations, Legitimacy of Public Administration, New Administrative Law, and Education Administrative Law have garnered widespread attention and significant impact domestically.[200] Additionally, the discipline has been involved in drafting, proving, or consulting on numerous laws, regulations, and rules.[201]

Peking University Law School was the first in the country to establish undergraduate and master's programs in Economic Law, with the doctoral program established in 1996.[202] The Economic Law discipline at Peking University boasts a strong faculty, including renowned senior scholars like Yang Zixin and prominent mid-career scholars such as Wu Zhipan, Zhang Shouwen, and Liu Jianwen.[203] The discipline has maintained a leading position in China in areas like economic law theory, fiscal and tax law, financial law, and competition law.[204]

---

194 See footnote 186.

195 See footnote 186.

196 See footnote 186.

197 See footnote 186.

198 See footnote 186.

199 See footnote 186.

200 See footnote 186.

201 See footnote 186.

202 See footnote 186.

203 See footnote 186.

204 See footnote 186.

The Economic Law discipline progresses steadily along the goals of institutionalisation, standardisation, and maintaining a "domestically leading, internationally first-class" level of scientific development.[205] This includes areas like discipline construction, research innovation, talent acquisition, student training, academic exchange, and infrastructure development.[206] Characterised by leading practices, substantial depth, and inclusiveness, the Economic Law discipline at Peking University not only consolidates its leading position domestically but also strives to achieve prominence in global economic law studies, already becoming a key centre for economic law research in China.[207]

The Criminal Law discipline at Peking University Law School hosts one of China's earliest master's programs in Criminal Law, which began enrolling master's degree students specialising in criminal law since 1978; doctoral students have been admitted since 1991.[208] The faculty includes a strong lineup of both veteran criminal law scholars, such as Chu Huai, Zhang Wen, Liu Shoufen, and younger professors, like Chen Xingliang, who have made significant contributions to the development of criminal law theory in China, the training of advanced criminal legal talent, and the improvement of legislation.[209]

Peking University's Criminal Law discipline holds a leading position nationally in criminal law theory, criminal policy, and criminology.[210] The doctoral program in Criminal Law includes research directions in Chinese Criminal Law, Foreign Criminal Law, and Criminology.[211] The master's program offers specialisations in Chinese Criminal Law, Foreign Criminal Law, Criminal Policy, Criminology, and Criminal Execution Law (including Prison Law).[212]

The discipline has consistently adhered to the important guiding principle of integration within criminal justice under the leadership of scholars like Yang Chunxi and Chu Huai, it has strengthened the internal integration of its various sub-disciplines and broken down barriers between Criminal Law, Criminal Procedure Law, and other criminal legal disciplines, thereby broadening and deepening its academic perspective and theoretical scope in Criminal Law.[213] The discipline has conducted highly effective theoretical research in the field of Chinese Criminal Law, achieving prominent outcomes and earning a high reputation within the national criminal law

[205] See footnote 186.

[206] See footnote 186.

[207] See footnote 186.

[208] See footnote 186.

[209] See footnote 186.

[210] See footnote 186.

[211] See footnote 186.

[212] See footnote 186.

[213] See footnote 186.

community.[214] In terms of empirical research in Criminal Law, the Peking University's criminal law case database, and studies on relational criminology, have developed distinct and unique features, increasingly expanding the university's influence within the field of criminal law.[215]

In addition to the four key national disciplines mentioned, Peking University Law School also boasts strong teaching and research capabilities in International Law, Civil and Commercial Law, Procedural Law, Legal History, and Environmental Law.[216] In recent years, the school has further enhanced its faculty by recruiting new talents and retaining post-doctoral researchers, achieving outstanding results in both teaching and research, thereby laying a solid foundation for establishing a world-class law school.[217]

Peking University Law School also houses more than 30 research institutes, including the Economic Law Research Institute, International Law Research Institute, International Economic Law Research Institute, Labour Law and Social Security Law Research Institute, Criminal Law Theory Research Institute, World Trade Organisation Law Research Center, Tax Law Research Center, Financial Law Research Center, Human Rights and Humanitarian Law Research Center, and the Legal Information Center.[218] These institutes organise numerous professional academic activities annually and provide many opportunities for academic exchange and discussions for graduate students, significantly contributing to the overall academic atmosphere of the Law School.[219]

7.1.7 Renmin University of China Law School

The law school of Renmin University of China was established in 1950, making it the first formal institution of higher legal education founded after the establishment of New China.[220] It is hailed as the "mother machine" of legal education in China and the "cradle of jurists", becoming a leading centre in legal education, a platform for gathering outstanding domestic legal talents, and a conduit for international legal exchanges.[221] The law school incorporated Chaoyang University, which was founded in 1912 and was renowned as "China's finest law school" at the time.[222] In the history of modern legal education in China, it enjoyed the reputation of being the "Northern

[214] See footnote 186.

[215] See footnote 186.

[216] See footnote 186.

[217] See footnote 186.

[218] See footnote 186.

[219] See footnote 186.

[220] See the official website of the Law School of Renmin University of China, http://www.law.ruc.edu.cn/home/gk/?id=44401, accessed May 1, 2024.

[221] See footnote 220.

[222] See footnote 220.

Chaoyang, Southern Soochow", and was famously praised as "Without Chaoyang, no courtroom could be established".[223]

In 1998, it was the first among national universities to be awarded the National May Day Labor Medal; in the Ministry of Education's national assessments of first-level disciplines conducted in 2004, 2009, 2012, 2017, and 2022, it consistently ranked first or received an A + rating; in 2018, it was rated A + in the Ministry of Education's first national evaluation of professional degree levels.[224] It was among the first group selected for the World-Class Universities and First-Class Disciplines initiative by the national government, in 2017, and was selected again in the new round of the Double First-Class initiative in 2022.[225] In 2019, it was designated a National First-Class Undergraduate Major Construction Site and identified as a Key Construction First-Class Major among Beijing's universities.[226]

Renmin University Law School boasts one national key first-level discipline (Law), four national key second-level disciplines, and one undergraduate major (Law).[227] It also has one professional master's degree point in Law and was among the first batch of institutions nationally authorised to grant doctoral degrees in Law.[228] The doctoral and master's programs cover all secondary disciplines, and it hosts the first national post-doctoral research station in Law.[229] The school has won the first prize in the National Teaching Achievement Awards in higher education four times, in 2005, 2014, 2018, and 2022. In 2021, it was honoured as the only "National Advanced Collective in Textbook Construction" among law schools nationwide in the first such awarding.[230]

Since its inception, in 1950, Renmin Law School has graduated over 20,000 students and trained over 300,000 participants including trainees, continuing education students, judges, prosecutors, lawyers, university professors, and civil servants, and among its alumni, are distinguished legal figures such as Xiao Yang, former Chief Justice, and Zhang Jun, former Chief Prosecutor, who are prominent leaders in the Republic's legal system construction.[231] Currently, the school has over 2200 registered students, primarily graduate students, with undergraduates making up about a quarter of the student body.[232]

Renmin University Law School hosts 70 research centres (institutes and institutes), including the Civil and Commercial Law Science Research Center and the Criminal Law Science Research Center, both recognised as Ministry of Education Humanities and Social Sciences research bases, it also features national-level bases

---

223 See footnote 220.

224 See footnote 220.

225 See footnote 220.

226 See footnote 220.

227 See footnote 220.

228 See footnote 220.

229 See footnote 220.

230 See footnote 220.

231 See footnote 220.

232 See footnote 220.

such as the Human Rights Education and Training Base and the Foreign-Related Rule of Law Research Base.[233] Additionally, the school has established several specialised institutes such as the Future Rule of Law Institute, Intellectual Property Institute, Lawyer Institute, Asia–Pacific Law Institute, Collaborative Innovation Center for Food Safety Governance, Institute for the Prevention and Resolution of International Commercial Disputes, and the Urban Social Governance Research Institute.[234] It hosts ten research bases established in collaboration with national authorities like the Central Comprehensive Rule of Law Office, the Supreme People's Court, the Supreme People's Procuratorate, and the State Administration for Market Regulation, furthermore, the school is equipped with a 985 Project national key innovation base and a comprehensive legal experimental and practical teaching centre.[235]

Renmin University Law School possesses a robust faculty with a well-structured team of educators that includes both internationally renowned senior legal scholars and a large number of influential middle-aged and young legal scholars in the national legal community and related disciplines.[236] As of April 2024, the faculty includes 98 full-time teachers, comprising 59 professors and 33 associate professors.[237] Professor Gao Mingxuan, the sole representative from the legal community, has been honoured with the national title of "People's Educator" and the "Most Beautiful Struggler" award; professor Xu Chongde, as the sole representative from the academic legal community at universities, received the "Reform Pioneer" honour and is acclaimed as an "Active Promoter of the Construction of the Socialist Legal System with Chinese Characteristics".[238]

Thirty-seven experts have been selected as chief experts or main members of the "Marxism Theory Research and Construction Project" team, the highest number among law schools nationwide.[239] Sixteen faculty members have participated in the "Republic Forum", serving as speakers for collective studies of the Political Bureau of the CPC Central Committee or legal lectures for the Standing Committee of the National People's Congress; 17 have been selected as "Yangtze River Scholars" by the Ministry of Education, with nine professors giving 13 legal lectures to the Political Bureau of the CPC Central Committee and the Standing Committee of the National People's Congress over the years; nine faculty members have been honoured in the "Top Ten Outstanding Young Jurists" by the China Law Society.[240] Both of the UNESCO Chairs in legal studies in China are held at this institution.

In the national assessments of first-level disciplines formally announced by the Ministry of Education in 2004, 2009, 2012, and 2017, Renmin University Law

[233] See footnote 220.

[234] See footnote 220.

[235] See footnote 220.

[236] See footnote 220.

[237] See footnote 220.

[238] See footnote 220.

[239] See footnote 220.

[240] See the website of the China Law Society, https://www.chinalaw.org.cn, accessed May 1, 2024.

School consistently ranked first among all law schools in China and has begun to be recognised among the world's elite law schools.[241]

Renmin University Law School consistently emphasises its role as a think tank and advisory group for national legal construction, participating in the drafting and revision of major laws including the Constitution of New China and nearly all significant legislation since the reform and opening up.[242] The school has been deeply involved in major national legislative projects such as the compilation of the Civil Code, providing theoretical assurance and intellectual support to promote the comprehensive rule of law in China.[243]

The Law School actively expands exchanges and collaborations with law schools overseas, establishing platforms for legal education exchanges and cooperation such as the World Top 100 Law Schools Deans Forum, China-US Law Schools Deans Forum, China–Europe Law Schools Deans Joint Meeting, Asian Law Schools Deans Forum, China-Australia Law Schools Deans Forum, China-Africa Law Schools Deans Forum, and the China-Latin America Rule of Law Dialogue; these platforms contribute significantly to promoting the international exchange and cooperation of Chinese legal education.[244]

The law library at the Law School currently holds over 300,000 volumes, including more than 200,000 Chinese legal books, over 60,000 foreign legal books, more than 400 types of Chinese legal journals totalling over 30,000 volumes, and over 120 types of foreign legal journals totalling more than 3000 volumes, along with over 3000 types of electronic legal journals.[245] The school hosts and manages several national core academic journals, including *Jurists*, *Human Rights*, *Renmin Law Review*, *Law and Social Sciences*, *Case Study Research*, *Economic Law Review*, *Chaoyang Law Review*, and *Chinese Colleges Academic Digest—Law*, and operates nationally renowned websites such as the China Civil and Commercial Law Network.[246]

Guided by Xi Jinping's Thought on Socialism with Chinese Characteristics for the New Era, the Law School diligently implements Xi Jinping's Thought on the Rule of Law and fully carries out the requirements of the directives issued by the General Office of the Communist Party of China Central Committee and the General Office of the State Council on strengthening legal education and theoretical research in law in the new era.[247] Addressing the major strategic needs of the nation and serving the comprehensive practice of governing the country according to law, the school is accelerating the development of an independent Chinese legal knowledge system.[248] It is

[241] See the official website of the Law School of Renmin University of China, http://www.law.ruc.edu.cn/home/gk/?id=44401, accessed May 1, 2024.

[242] See footnote 241.

[243] See footnote 241.

[244] See footnote 241.

[245] See footnote 241.

[246] See footnote 241.

[247] See footnote 241.

[248] See footnote 241.

deeply advancing the construction of a legal discipline system, academic system, and discourse system that reflect Chinese characteristics, contemporary relevance, and practical features.[249] The school is innovating its talent-training systems and mechanisms, optimising pathways for cultivating talent, and striving to become a pinnacle of legal research and legal-talent training, and it is dedicated to forging a distinctive path towards building a world-class institution with Chinese characteristics.[250]

7.1.8 Wuhan University Law School

The legal education at Wuhan University originated from the Hubei School of Law and Politics, established in 1908; when the National Wuhan University was founded in 1928, the Law School became an integral part of it.[251] Wang Shijie and Zhou Gengsheng, renowned legal scholars and presidents of Wuhan University, once served as deans of the Law School.[252] In 1979, Wuhan University reinstated the Department of Law and rebuilt the Law School in 1986.[253] The school has been led by several distinguished legal scholars, including Professor Han Depei, a well-known legal scholar; Professor Ma Kechang, a renowned criminal law expert; Professor Ma Junju, a notable civil and commercial law expert; Professor Yu Jinsong, a prominent international law expert; as well as Professor Zeng Lingliang and Professor Xiao Yongping, who have both served as heads of the department and deans of the school.[254]

The Law School boasts a comprehensive and distinct range of disciplines, forming a complete system for talent cultivation.[255] It was among the first in the nation to be authorised to confer doctoral degrees in first-level disciplines of law, with both doctoral and master's programs covering all secondary disciplines.[256] It currently offers two undergraduate programs, ten master's degree authorisation points, 12 doctoral degree authorisation points in second-level law disciplines, two national key disciplines, a nationally supported discipline for development, and a professional master's degree point in law.[257] Approved by the State Council, it also established one of the first post-doctoral mobility stations in law (including all doctoral disciplines),

---

249 See footnote 241.

250 See footnote 241.

251 See the official website of the Law School of Wuhan University, https://law.whu.edu.cn/xygk/lsyjj.htm, accessed May 1, 2024.

252 See footnote 251.

253 See footnote 251.

254 See footnote 251.

255 See footnote 251.

256 See footnote 251.

257 See footnote 251.

and offers an International Law and Chinese Law master's program for international students.[258]

Since its reestablishment in 1979, the school has graduated nearly 20,000 students and trained over 300,000 individuals in various capacities including trainees, continuing education students, judges, prosecutors, lawyers, university professors, and civil servants.[259] A large number of graduates have become outstanding talents in the construction of the rule of law in the Republic.[260] Currently, there are over 2500 students enrolled, including more than 1100 undergraduates, approximately 1400 master's students, over 400 doctoral students, and about 80 international students.[261]

The Law School has a robust array of academic institutions and research platforms; it currently hosts 34 research institutes, including a 985 Project national key innovation base, two Ministry of Education humanities and social sciences research bases, one national high-end think tank (among the first batch), two Ministry of Education 2011 Collaborative Innovation Centers, one national human rights education and training base, one national research base for international governance in cyberspace, one Supreme People's Court judicial theory research base for environmental and resource cases, and one Supreme People's Procuratorate administrative prosecution research base.[262] The school also publishes several academic journals, including *Legal Studies Review*,[263] *Wuhan University International Law Review*,[264] *Chinese Journal of International Law*,[265] *Chinese Journal of Environmental Law*,[266] *Climate Law*,[267] and *Environmental Law Review*.[268]

The Law School has a strong and well-structured faculty, comprising both internationally renowned senior legal scholars and a significant number of influential middle-aged and young legal scholars within the national legal community and related disciplines.[269] Currently, there are 118 full-time faculty members, including 56 professors, 47 associate professors, and 62 doctoral advisers.[270] This team is led by

---

[258] See footnote 251.

[259] See footnote 251.

[260] See footnote 251.

[261] See footnote 251.

[262] See footnote 251.

[263] See the website of *Law Review*, https://fxpl.cbpt.cnki.net, accessed May 1, 2024.

[264] See the website of the Editorial Office of *Wuhan University International Law Review*, http://ilr.whu.edu.cn, accessed May 1, 2024.

[265] See the website of Academy of Humanities and Social Sciences of Wuhan University, https://ahss.whu.edu.cn/info/1006/1079.htm, accessed May 1, 2024.

[266] See the website of Academy of Humanities and Social Sciences of Wuhan University, https://ssroff.whu.edu.cn/info/1165/2486.htm, accessed May 1, 2024.

[267] See the official website of the Law School of Wuhan University, https://law.whu.edu.cn/info/1054/5302.htm, accessed May 1, 2024.

[268] See the official website of the Law School of Wuhan University, https://law.whu.edu.cn/info/1054/1042.htm, accessed May 1, 2024.

[269] See the official website of the Law School of Wuhan University, https://law.whu.edu.cn/xygk/lsyjj.htm, accessed May 1, 2024.

[270] See footnote 269.

senior professors in humanities and social sciences, and national-level distinguished teaching professors, complemented by innovative teams of young researchers.[271]

The Law School is highly active in international exchanges. It has established extensive and deep cooperative relationships with world-renowned universities such as Université Paris XI and Université de Lille II in France; the University of Göttingen, Philipps University of Marburg, and Saarland University in Germany; Ghent University in Belgium; Erasmus University Rotterdam in the Netherlands; Northeastern University and the University of California, Davis in the United States; the University of Leeds and the University of Sheffield in the United Kingdom; and the University of Melbourne in Australia.[272]

The Law School is well-equipped with comprehensive facilities. The Law Building has a usable area of over 25,000 square metres, including a law library spanning more than 5000 square metres, a 500-square-metre mock courtroom and mock arbitration court, and a 200-square-metre law laboratory.[273] There are also nine multimedia classrooms that can accommodate 130–160 people each, and an electronic information reading room.[274] The Law School's library boasts a rich collection of legal documents with strong academic and professional emphasis, particularly renowned for its collection of original international law publications in Western languages, original criminal law publications in Japanese, legal publications from Hong Kong and Taiwan, and environmental law literature, earning a distinguished reputation within the industry.[275]

After a century of development, especially since the reform and opening up, generations of Luojia legal professionals have diligently worked towards the construction of a socialist rule of law, cultivating outstanding legal talent and making significant contributions to the revitalisation and prosperity of legal studies.[276] In 2017, Wuhan University's Law discipline was successfully selected for inclusion in the national World-Class Universities and First-Class Disciplines initiative.[277] It has consistently ranked among the top in domestic assessments of law schools.[278] According to the 2024 QS World Rankings for Law Schools, Wuhan University's Law discipline was ranked between 50 and 100th globally, reflecting its high international reputation and influence. It has become one of the most influential law schools in China, and is acclaimed as the "ace force on Luojia Mountain".[279]

[271] See footnote 269.

[272] See footnote 269.

[273] See footnote 269.

[274] See footnote 269.

[275] See footnote 269.

[276] See footnote 269.

[277] See footnote 269.

[278] See footnote 269.

[279] See QS World University Rankings by Subject: Law & Legal Studies 2024, https://www.qschina.cn/en/university-rankings/university-subject-rankings/2024/law-legal-studies, accessed August 29, 2024.

7.1.9 Jilin University Law School

Legal education and research at Jilin University began in 1948 and was established and developed by the Communist Party of China as an institution for training legal talent; during the difficult decade of the Cultural Revolution (1966–1976), higher education across the country was severely impacted, and the discipline of law nearly came to a halt.[280] Thanks to the perseverance and efforts of the leaders and teachers of the law school at Jilin University, legal research and talent training were preserved, making it one of the only two legal education units in the country that were not abolished at that time.[281]

Since the reform and opening up, legal education and research at Jilin University entered a period of rapid development. In 1988, with the approval of the former State Education Commission, Jilin University's Department of Law was transformed into the Law School.[282] After more than 70 years of development and improvement, Jilin University's Law School has become a stronghold of legal research in China, an important base for the training of legal talent, a crucial think tank for the construction of a law-governed China, and a key institution for the inheritance and exchange of legal civilisation.[283]

Jilin University Law School places a high priority on the cultivation and structural optimisation of its faculty, forming a highly qualified and well-educated teaching team with comprehensive disciplinary expertise. Currently, the school has 109 full-time faculty members, including 58 professors, 29 associate professors, and 22 lecturers.[284] With an average age below 45, the faculty is academically profound, highly innovative, and possesses strong research capabilities.[285] The senior professors set academic standards and maintain the scholarly tradition of the Law School; middle-aged faculty have achieved academically, and support continuity and progress, forming the backbone of the institution; and the young faculty, diligent and discerning, symbolise the future development of the Law School.[286]

Prominent legal scholars at the school include Professor Zhang Wenxian, a renowned legal scholar and educator, director of the Academic Committee of the China Law Society, and a senior professor of philosophy and social sciences at Jilin University; professor Fang Shaokun, a national-level distinguished teacher and leader in philosophy and social sciences under the Ten Thousand Talents Program, a recognised cultural expert by the Ministry of Propaganda and part of the "Four Batches" talent program, and a specially appointed professor under the Ministry of Education's significant talent project; professor Cai Lidong, an expert under the national Millions

[280] See the official website of the Law School of Jilin University, http://law.jlu.edu.cn/xygk1/xyjj.htm, accessed May 1, 2024.

[281] See footnote 280.

[282] See footnote 280.

[283] See footnote 280.

[284] See footnote 280.

[285] See footnote 280.

[286] See footnote 280.

of Talents Project, a leader in philosophy and social sciences under the Ten Thousand Talents Program, and a young scholar under the Ministry of Education's significant talent plan; professor He Zhipeng, one of the national Top Ten Outstanding Young Jurists, a leader in philosophy and social sciences under the Ten Thousand Talents Program, recognised as a cultural expert by the Ministry of Propaganda and part of the "Four Batches" talent program, and a young scholar under the Ministry of Education's significant talent project.[287]

The Law School boasts a member of the State Council Degree Committee, a member of the State Council Academic Evaluation Group, a member of the Ministry of Education's Social Science Committee, two national distinguished teachers, a chair of the Ministry of Education's Law Teaching Guidance Committee, a vice-chair of the Ministry of Education's Higher Education Law Professional Teaching Guidance Committee, a member of the Ministry of Education's Social Science Committee on Academic Integrity, three leaders in philosophy and social sciences under the Ten Thousand Talents Program, three cultural experts under the "Four Batches" talent program, a mid-career expert with national outstanding contributions, two specially appointed professors under the Ministry of Education's significant talent project, three young project leaders under the Ministry of Education's significant talent plan, a young top-notch talent under the Ten Thousand Talents Program, a chief expert (convener) of the Central Marxism Theory Research and Construction Project, two chief experts of major projects under the Ministry of Education's philosophy and social sciences, 12 chief experts of major projects under the National Social Science Fund, two chief experts of major research projects under the Ministry of Education, seven outstanding talents of the New (Interdisciplinary) Century, two national candidates of the New Century Millions of Talents Project, two of the national Top Ten Outstanding Young Jurists (two nomination awards), eight Changbai Mountain Scholars (Changbai Mountain Talent Project) of Jilin Province, 22 Kuang Yaming Scholars of Jilin University, and five Dingxin Scholars of Jilin University.[288]

As an important base for legal education in China, Jilin University's Law School consistently prioritises moral education as its fundamental mission.[289] Guided by the Party and the State's directives on the cultivation of legal talent, the program aims to nurture outstanding legal professionals with a solid foundation, broad knowledge, and strong capabilities.[290] It shifts from passive to active education and from exam-oriented to quality education. At the core of its strategy is the development of the Legal Engineering Training Center, using the "Four-Three" realms of legal-talent development as a foundation to establish a "Knowledge Transfer + Skill Training + Wisdom Development" 3.0 version of the legal-talent cultivation system.[291]

The Law School places a high emphasis on teaching quality, adopting various measures to encourage faculty to offer new courses, update teaching content, research

[287] See footnote 280.

[288] See footnote 280.

[289] See footnote 280.

[290] See footnote 280.

[291] See footnote 280.

teaching methods, and enhance teaching appeal.[292] To optimise students' knowledge structure, stimulate learning motivation, and foster interest, Jilin Law School has expanded the range of elective courses, encouraging interdisciplinary and cross-specialty course selection.[293] To increase the rate at which senior faculty teach undergraduate courses, the school has implemented a responsibility system for senior faculty teaching; additionally, college leaders serve as undergraduate class advisers, and outstanding young teachers act as college student mentors, providing targeted guidance in their specialties.[294]

Under the leadership of Professor Zhang Wenxian, Jilin University's Law School has developed interconnected and organically combined pathways for training undergraduates, master's students (including Juris Master and Master of Laws students), and doctoral students. Professor Zhang Wenxian's teaching reforms have consecutively won four national-level teaching achievement awards, and the legal theory teaching team was recognised as a national-level teaching team in 2008.[295]

The Law School houses the Jilin University Key Research Base for Textbook Construction, and faculty actively participate in the writing of key textbooks for the Marxism Theory Research and Construction Project.[296] Professor Zhang Wenxian serves as the chief expert for the Marxism Project key textbooks, "An Introduction to Xi Jinping's Thoughts on Rule of Law" and "Jurisprudence"[297] The second edition of "Jurisprudence", edited by Professor Zhang Wenxian, won the first National Textbook First Prize, and the courses in Jurisprudence and Commercial Law have been recognised as national-level excellent courses.[298] The law program is designated as a national-level first-class undergraduate major, and both the courses in Jurisprudence (Part I) and International Law are national-level first-class undergraduate courses.[299] For more than 70 years, Jilin University's Law School has cultivated a large number of distinguished alumni for the nation.[300]

Jilin University's Law School adheres to the guiding principle of "deepening jurisprudence and embracing technology"[301] for scientific research, consistently following the purpose of establishing the school on academic foundations. Adhering to a serious and pragmatic approach to scholarship, the discipline has produced abundant research achievements, it has carried out significant theoretical and practical research projects such as the Basic Categories of Law, The Spirit of Modern

[292] See footnote 280.
[293] See footnote 280.
[294] See footnote 280.
[295] See footnote 280.
[296] See footnote 280.
[297] See footnote 280.
[298] See footnote 280.
[299] See footnote 280.
[300] See footnote 280.
[301] See the website of the Ministry of Justice of the People's Republic of China, https://www.moj.gov.cn/pub/sfbgw/gwxw/xwyw/szywszxx/202101/t20210122_147366.html, accessed May 1, 2024.

Law, Knowledge Economy and Legal System Innovation, The Theoretical System of Socialist Legal Theory with Chinese Characteristics, Research on Emerging Rights, Theories of Human Rights with Chinese Characteristics, Digital Rule of Law, and Xi Jinping's Thoughts on Rule of Law.[302] These projects propose using Xi Jinping's Thoughts on Rule of Law as a guide to reconstruct the theoretical system of Chinese legal studies with "rights and duties as the basic categories", to drive innovation in China's legal system with "the spirit of modern law" at its core, to shift the paradigm of contemporary Chinese legal philosophy with "rights-based orientation", and to build an autonomous Chinese legal knowledge system centred on "jurisprudence and rights-based orientation".[303]

Since 2017, faculty members have published more than 20 articles in the top three journals, undertaken over 300 research projects, published nearly 500 papers in CSSCI journals, authored more than 90 academic books, and received over 30 research awards at the provincial and ministerial level or above, enhancing the reputation of Jilin University's Law research.[304] The active research environment and growing academic influence of Jilin University's Law School are evident through the hosting of over 350 events, including lectures by contemporary legal scholars, emerging legal scholar tea talks, and lectures by renowned international scholars.[305]

The Basic Categories of Law Seminar, held in 1988, marked the formal establishment of the "rights-based orientation" idea, and since then, this concept has guided the development of rule of law and legal studies in China for 30 years, forming the legal endorsement for the overall direction of China's reform and opening-up policies.[306]

Since 2015, Jilin University's Law School has been at the forefront in China in advancing the academic direction of summarising and synthesising the ideological concepts of rule of law in the new era. It pioneered the study of Xi Jinping's Thoughts on Rule of Law, not only driving iterative upgrades in Jilin University's legal research but also initiating a new journey to construct an autonomous Chinese legal knowledge system under the guidance of Xi Jinping's Thoughts on Rule of Law, thereby exploring new realms in Chinese legal studies.[307] In 2020, the Human Rights Research Center at Jilin University was selected as a national-level base for human rights education and training, aligning with major national strategic needs.[308] It continually contributes to a deep interpretation of China's path to human rights development, systematically enhancing Chinese human rights theories, shaping and

[302] See the official website of the Law School of Jilin University, http://law.jlu.edu.cn/xygk1/xyjj.htm, accessed May 1, 2024.

[303] See footnote 302.

[304] See footnote 302.

[305] See footnote 302.

[306] See footnote 302.

[307] See footnote 302.

[308] See footnote 302.

improving the discourse on human rights in China, and enhancing the quality of international exchanges on human rights civilisation.[309]

Building on the solid foundation laid by pioneers like Gao Shusen, Jilin University's foreign-related legal research has gained momentum.[310] In 2022, Jilin University's Institute for Foreign-Related Rule of Law was designated as a national-level research base for foreign-related rule of law, providing a new platform for ambitious plans in foreign-related legal research and talent cultivation; in the new era, the construction of first-class law disciplines at Jilin University deeply summarises the manifestations and characteristics of Chinese-style modernisation, with the core task of constructing a discipline system for socialist law with Chinese characteristics.[311] It focuses on four major directions: the theory of socialist law with Chinese characteristics, contemporary Chinese political and legal civilisation, the theory and practice of socialist judiciary with Chinese characteristics, and modern technology with the development of Chinese law. It is committed to providing Jilin University's solutions for China's rule of law and contributing Chinese wisdom to the global rule of law.[312]

Jilin University's Law School boasts a comprehensive academic system and is authorised to confer doctoral degrees in the first-level discipline of law, it has ten doctoral programs in various fields including Theoretical Jurisprudence, Legal History, Constitutional and Administrative Law, Criminal Law, Civil and Commercial Law, Procedural Law, Economic Law, International Law, Intellectual Property Law, and Human Rights, along with two additional self-established doctoral programs in Legal Political Science and Legal Economics.[313] At the secondary discipline level, it offers 11 master's programs in Law and two professional Master of Laws degrees, covering fields such as Theoretical Jurisprudence, Legal History, Constitutional and Administrative Law, Criminal Law, Civil and Commercial Law, Procedural Law, Economic Law, Environmental and Resource Protection Law, International Law, Intellectual Property Law, and Human Rights.[314]

Theoretical Jurisprudence and Criminal Law are recognised as national key disciplines, with Civil and Commercial Law designated as a provincial key discipline; other disciplines such as Procedural Law, Constitutional and Administrative Law, Economic Law, Legal History, and International Law also considered potential-rich and distinctive strengths of the school.[315] The professional degree of Master of Laws at Jilin University is among the first group of eight institutions nationwide authorised to offer such education.[316] In line with the important directives of General Secretary Xi Jinping on strengthening the training of foreign-related legal professionals,

[309] See footnote 302.

[310] See footnote 302.

[311] See footnote 302.

[312] See footnote 302.

[313] See footnote 302.

[314] See footnote 302.

[315] See footnote 302.

[316] See footnote 302.

Jilin University's Law School has been selected to implement the "Master of Laws (Foreign Lawyer)" and "Master of Laws (International Arbitration)" programs.[317] It received an A-level rating in the nation's first professional degree-level evaluation, ranking among the top of all 109 evaluated institutions.[318]

Jilin University's Law School places great emphasis on conducting a variety of international and domestic academic exchanges and collaborations, having hosted a series of internationally and domestically significant academic conferences and seminars that have progressively deepened the internationalisation of its education.[319] Jilin University's Law School was one of the first five Chinese Law schools selected for exchange during US President Clinton's visit to China in 1998, and is a member of the joint meeting of deans from famous Chinese and American law schools, actively participating and hosting the first and the last American law workshops.[320]

Embracing a comprehensive international development strategy, Jilin Law actively engages in regional exchanges in Northeast Asia.[321] The China Law Society's Northeast Asia Legal Research Center, Northeast Asia Advanced Legal Talent Training Base, and China-Russia Law Research Center are all based at Jilin University Law School.[322] Additionally, the school is actively integrating into international and regional academic organisations, currently being a member of the Asian Law Institute (ASLI) and a founding member of the Asian Law Schools Association (ALSA).[323] Building on its solid multi-level substantive exchanges with law schools in Northeast Asia, such as Japan, South Korea, and regions like Taiwan, Hong Kong, and Macau, the school is actively advancing substantial exchanges and cooperation with law schools in the UK, USA, and the EU.[324] Currently, the school has established academic partnerships with over 20 renowned universities and research institutions, creating personalised international cooperation projects for students, including short-term visits, exchange programs, and dual-degree programs.[325]

Each year, dozens of faculty members participate in lectures and academic conferences abroad or online, and the school invites numerous international scholars and practitioners for academic exchanges.[326] Professor John from Touro University in the USA, Professor Du Ming from Durham University in the UK, and Professor Alexander from Saint Petersburg State University in Russia have been appointed as visiting professors at Jilin University; professor Xu Ting from the University of Essex in the UK and Professor Xi Chao from the Chinese University of Hong Kong

[317] See footnote 302.
[318] See footnote 302.
[319] See footnote 302.
[320] See footnote 302.
[321] See footnote 302.
[322] See footnote 302.
[323] See footnote 302.
[324] See footnote 302.
[325] See footnote 302.
[326] See footnote 302.

have been appointed as Changbai Mountain Distinguished Scholars at the school.[327] The Law School has established a bilingual teaching team and actively conducts bilingual education, fostering a rich international atmosphere through hosting, and participating in activities like summer camps.[328]

Teachers in the Law discipline at Jilin University actively participate in major national legislative processes, providing valuable suggestions and advice for the drafting and revision of significant laws such as the Constitution, Criminal Law, General Principles of Civil Law, and the Civil Code.[329] In December 2011, the Law School established a legal aid station that provides legal services to the community, serving as an important vehicle for faculty and students to fulfil their social responsibilities, and as a crucial platform for defending the rights of socially vulnerable groups.[330]

The Law School is home to more than ten important research institutions. Among these, the Judicial Civilisation Collaborative Innovation Center is a national 2011 Plan Collaborative Innovation Center.[331] The Theoretical Jurisprudence Research Center is a key research base in humanities and social sciences, designated by the Ministry of Education.[332] The Crime Governance Research Center and the Judicial Data Application Research Center were selected, in December 2019, for inclusion in the China Think Tank Index (CTTI).[333] Additionally, the Law School also boasts significant research entities such as the Xi Jinping Thought on Rule of Law Research Center (Comprehensive Rule of Law Research Center) and the Jilin University Property Law Research Center.[334]

Jilin University's Law School places a strong emphasis on improving teaching and research conditions, striving to establish a nationally leading legal education and research base.[335] The Jilin University Law Library, Theoretical Jurisprudence Research Center Library, and the Law Alumni Library have amassed a rich collection of legal literature in both Chinese and foreign languages.[336] The Law School has invested significant funds to establish technologically advanced and top-quality facilities such as simulated courtrooms and multimedia classrooms, creating excellent conditions for experiments and teaching.[337] In 2006, the Chinese Theoretical Jurisprudence Research Information Network was ranked among the top ten academic websites by national universities.[338]

---

327 See footnote 302.

328 See footnote 302.

329 See footnote 302.

330 See footnote 302.

331 See footnote 302.

332 See footnote 302.

333 See footnote 302.

334 See footnote 302.

335 See footnote 302.

336 See footnote 302.

337 See footnote 302.

338 See footnote 302.

Currently, the Law School hosts the *Contemporary Legal Studies* journal, and the Theoretical Jurisprudence Research Center manages the *Legal System and Social Development* magazine, both of which are recognised as CSSCI source journals in the Chinese social sciences.[339] Moreover, the Theoretical Jurisprudence Research Center publishes a series of publications including *Collected Essays on Jurisprudence*, *Jurisprudence in Life*, *The Rhythm of Legal Thought*, and *Departmental Law Philosophy*.[340] These publications provide a platform for teachers and students to publish outstanding academic papers.

7.2 The Structure of Academic Degrees and Graduation Requirements

China places a high priority on legal education, reflecting its commitment to fostering a rule-of-law society, and this commitment is underscored by the establishment of stringent and well-defined requirements for legal education programs across the country.[341] The National Standards for Teaching Quality of Law Disciplines (2021 Edition) (hereafter referred to as the Standards) plays a crucial role in setting these benchmarks.[342]These Standards, along with various training programs formulated by universities, provide a clear framework for how higher education institutions in China should structure degree programs in legal education and define the graduation requirements for different levels of degrees.

In China, legal education at higher education institutions begins at the undergraduate level, and the system is structured to provide a comprehensive and systematic legal education through three progressive degrees: bachelor's, master's, and doctoral degrees.[343] Each level is designed to build on the previous one, ensuring a depth of knowledge and expertise that is appropriate for various roles within the legal profession.

Bachelor's Degree in Law: This initial degree lays the foundational knowledge of law, introducing students to key concepts, legal principles, and the workings of the legal system. Undergraduate programs are typically structured to provide a broad overview of law, combined with critical-thinking and analytical-skills training, preparing students for further study or entry-level positions in various legal contexts.[344]

---

[339] See footnote 302.

[340] See footnote 302.

[341] Wang Ping. "The Rule of Law Helps to Write the Answer Sheet for the Era of a Strong Educational Nation." *China National People's Congress Magazine*, no. 15 (2024). Accessed August 30, 2024. http://www.npc.gov.cn/c2/c30834/202408/t20240827_438847.html.

[342] Reference the Ministry of Education of the People's Republic of China website: "http://www.moe.gov.cn/srcsite/A08/s7056/202106/t20210602_535109.html," accessed on May 10, 2024.

[343] See "the Standards".

[344] Xie (2023).

Master's Degree in Law: The master's program deepens the legal knowledge acquired at the undergraduate level, and often allows for specialisation in areas such as commercial law, international law, environmental law, or human rights law, among others.[345] Master's degrees are designed to enhance professional skills, such as legal research, writing, and analysis, essential for higher-level professional practice or academic pursuits.[346]

Doctoral Degree in Law: The doctoral programs are intended for those who wish to pursue careers in legal research or academia, these programs focus on original research, culminating in a dissertation that contributes new insights to the field of law.[347] Doctoral candidates are expected to engage deeply with their chosen topics, demonstrating comprehensive knowledge and thought leadership in their area of specialisation.[348]

The Standards serve as a guide to ensure that each degree program meets higher educational quality benchmarks and is aligned with the national objectives for legal education.[349] These Standards emphasise not only the acquisition of legal knowledge but also the development of professional ethics, critical thinking, and practical skills, and they ensure that graduates are well-prepared to contribute to the legal profession and uphold the rule of law effectively.[350]

Moreover, the graduation requirements set forth in these Standards are rigorously designed to ensure that students not only understand legal theories but can also apply this knowledge practically in legal settings.[351] This approach aims to create a competent, ethical, and knowledgeable legal workforce capable of addressing both the current and future needs of society.[352]

Overall, the structured approach to legal education in China, from the bachelor's level to doctoral studies (see Table 7.1), reflects a comprehensive strategy to develop a robust legal system supported by well-trained legal professionals. This educational framework is pivotal in supporting China's broader goals of enhancing legal expertise and promoting justice and fairness in society through the diligent application of the law.

Firstly, the structure and degree requirements for legal education at the undergraduate level in China are meticulously outlined in Section 4.1 of the Standards.[353] These regulations provide a clear framework for universities, specifying that the basic duration of study for law-related majors should be four years. The Standards establish a uniform timeline that aligns with international norms for undergraduate

345 Ying (2023).
346 Ying (2023).
347 Deng (2023).
348 Deng (2023).
349 See "the Standards".
350 See "the Standards".
351 Zhan and Jin (2022).
352 Zhan and Jin (2022).
353 See "the Standards".

Table 7.1 The structure of professional degrees in law in mainland China[354]

	Degree	Abbreviation	Common duration of study	Brief description
Undergraduate Education	Bachelor of Laws	LL.B	4 years full time	Basic Undergraduate Degree in Law
Master's Education	Juris Master (Law Undergraduate)	J.M	2 years (and above) full time	Designed for undergraduate law graduates, the curriculum focuses on the content of judicial examinations and judicial practice
	Juris Master (Non-Law Undergraduate)	J.M	2 years (and above) full time	Designed for undergraduate graduates from non-law majors, the curriculum focuses on the content of judicial examinations and judicial practice
	Master of Laws	LL.M	2 years (and above) full time	Master of Laws graduate degree, emphasising the learning of theoretical knowledge and the cultivation of academic abilities
Doctoral Education	Doctor of Laws	LL.D	3 years (and above) full time	Doctoral Degree in Law

legal education, ensuring students receive a comprehensive education that spans the breadth of legal disciplines.[355]

However, recognising the diversity in student needs and educational goals, the Standards also permit universities to adopt a flexible education system.[356] This flexibility allows institutions to accommodate students who may require a shorter or longer duration to complete their studies, with the stipulation that the duration must not be less than three years and not more than six years.[357] This provision ensures that all students, regardless of their individual circumstances, have adequate time to fulfil the rigorous requirements of their law degree while also providing the opportunity to accelerate or extend their studies according to their personal or professional needs.

To qualify for graduation, students must complete the prescribed courses and credit requirements of their law majors. They must also pass the assessments associated with their courses, which are designed to rigorously test their knowledge and understanding of the law. This ensures that all graduates possess a solid foundation

354 The content in the table is compiled based on the training programs of several university law schools and is for reference only.

355 See "the Standards".

356 See "the Standards".

357 See "the Standards".

in legal principles and are well-prepared for the practical challenges they will face in the legal profession.

Upon successfully meeting these criteria, students are eligible to receive a Bachelor of Laws degree. This degree signifies that they have not only met the academic standards set forth by their university but also possess the skills and knowledge necessary to embark on a career in law nationwide.[358] The awarding of this degree is contingent upon students demonstrating their proficiency in a range of legal subjects, reflecting the comprehensive nature of legal education as outlined by the Standards.[359]

This structured approach to the undergraduate legal education in China is critical for maintaining high educational quality and ensuring that all law graduates are capable of contributing effectively to the legal profession.[360] It underscores the commitment of Chinese legal education institutions to uphold rigorous academic standards while also providing the flexibility necessary to accommodate a diverse student population. This balance between standardisation and adaptability is a hallmark of China's legal education system, ensuring it remains robust and responsive to the needs of both students and the broader legal community.[361]

Regarding graduate legal education in China, the framework is meticulously structured into two distinct stages: the master's and the doctoral. Each of these stages is tailored to meet the different educational needs and career aspirations of students, ensuring a comprehensive and specialised legal training.

The Master's stage of legal education is subdivided into two primary pathways: Master of Law (LL.M) and Master of Legal Studies (MLS).[362] Each pathway serves different academic and professional objectives, beginning right from the entrance examination, which varies in content focus, to the training methodologies employed thereafter.[363]

The Master of Legal Studies is designed predominantly for students who wish to gain a deep understanding of legal theories with a supplementary focus on practical skills.[364] This program adopts a mentorship system where each student is assigned a mentor—either a professor or an associate professor—who provides continuous guidance throughout their studies.[365] This close mentor-student relationship facilitates a thorough exploration of legal knowledge, primarily focusing on legal theory and supplemented by practical teaching to ensure a well-rounded educational experience.[366]

---

358 Li (2024).

359 Li (2024).

360 Lü (2020).

361 Lü (2020).

362 Qiu and Wang (2023).

363 Qiu and Wang (2023).

364 Wu (2017).

365 Wu (2017).

366 Wu (2017).

Conversely, the Master of Law program is often structured around a "dual mentor" system or a teaching-team system.[367] This approach emphasises "practical application" of knowledge, whereby the curriculum is designed to prioritise practical legal training alongside theoretical learning.[368] The dual-mentor or team-teaching approach enriches the learning experience by providing students with multiple perspectives and a broader range of expertise, which is particularly beneficial in handling complex legal issues.[369]

Since 2009, the Master of Law pathway has been further refined into two categories based on the undergraduate degree obtained by students: Master of Law (Legal Studies) and Master of Law (Non-Legal Studies).[370] The former typically extends over two years, although some universities may offer specific specialisations that require up to three years of study.[371] The latter, aimed at students from non-legal undergraduate backgrounds, generally spans three years, ensuring that students acquire the necessary legal acumen to transition into legal careers.[372]

The doctoral stage in legal education is designed to cultivate high-level legal scholars and practitioners, and the standard duration for doctoral programs is set at a minimum of three years.[373] However, due to rigorous graduation qualification requirements, which include the completion of a substantial original thesis and often additional coursework and examinations, the actual duration tends to extend to four years or more.[374] This extended period allows doctoral candidates to undertake deep, meaningful research that contributes significantly to the field of law, under the guidance of experienced faculty members.[375]

The structured approach to both master's and doctoral studies in legal education in China reflects a commitment to developing a pool of highly skilled legal professionals who are equipped to meet the demands of both the national and international legal systems. Through this detailed and systematic educational pathway, China aims to foster legal experts who are not only well-versed in legal theory but also adept in practical applications, thereby enhancing the overall quality and effectiveness of the legal profession.

In China, the academic journey of a law student is rigorously structured to ensure a comprehensive legal education, characterised by a clear framework for credit accumulation and course completion. To qualify for graduation, law students must not only complete their studies within the designated timeframe but also meet specific credit requirements set by the university.

---

[367] Zong (2023).

[368] Zong (2023).

[369] Zong (2023).

[370] See "Introduction to the Graduate Program in Law (Jurisprudence)," New Oriental Online. Accessed August 30, 2024. https://news.koolearn.com/kaopei/kysx/145421/.

[371] Chen and Jie (2020).

[372] Chen and Jie (2020).

[373] Deng (2023).

[374] Deng (2023).

[375] Deng (2023).

Universities in China typically establish a total credit requirement that encapsulates the entirety of a student's academic work across various categories. These credits are divided into different modules that include core courses, which are essential for a deep understanding of law; public compulsory courses, which provide a broad educational foundation; elective professional courses, which allow students to specialise in areas of interest within law; general elective courses, which offer broader knowledge outside the core curriculum; and practical courses, which are crucial for applying theoretical knowledge in real-world settings.

Each institution may define these categories slightly differently, reflecting their unique educational philosophies and the specific demands of their law programs. Students are required to fulfil the credit requirements for each of these modules in addition to achieving the overall credit total needed for graduation.

The process for earning credits in Chinese universities is meticulously defined. It is generally based on the successful completion of courses over a semester. Students earn credits by independently choosing courses that align with their academic and professional goals, actively participating in and attending classes, completing various assignments and tasks assigned by their instructors, and passing the assessments associated with each course. The assessment formats can vary but are designed to comprehensively evaluate the students' grasp of the material.

Credits are awarded based on achievement in these courses, with a passing grade—typically 60% of the total possible score or higher—being sufficient to earn the designated credits for that course. It is important to note that, while achieving a score at or above the "passing line" guarantees credits, the actual score or grade has no bearing on the number of credits received. Instead, variations in scores or grades primarily affect the student's Grade Point Average (GPA) or weighted average score. These metrics are used to gauge a student's overall academic performance and capabilities but do not directly impact the credit requirements for graduation, serving instead as indicators of a student's comprehensive abilities.[376]

Furthermore, the assignment of credits is generally correlated with the number of course hours, reflecting the relative importance and depth of each course. Typically, courses that are more central to the major and involve more comprehensive study, will require more hours and, consequently, offer more credits upon successful completion. This system ensures that students dedicate appropriate time and effort to the most critical aspects of their legal education, aligning academic workload with educational priorities and career objectives in the field of law.[377]

In China, the academic journey of a law student is meticulously structured not only to ensure the accumulation of necessary course credits but also to complete significant research milestones.[378] Credits are one of the core elements determining eligibility for graduation, but the requirement to write and successfully defend a thesis is equally critical. This component of the educational process varies by academic

[376] Yan and Wu (2015).

[377] Yan and Wu (2015).

[378] Yang (2021).

level, with expectations for the length, depth, and rigour of the defence increasing progressively from undergraduate to doctoral studies.

At every educational stage, the writing of a thesis and its defence are mandatory, and directly reflected as an independent credit requirement.[379] For undergraduates, the thesis may be a less extensive research project designed to introduce students to legal research methodologies; at the master's level, the thesis becomes more complex, requiring a deeper analytical approach and often involving original research that contributes new insights to the field; for doctoral students, the thesis is expected to be a substantial work of scholarship that makes a significant contribution to the existing body of legal knowledge.[380]

Beyond thesis requirements, law students in China are often expected to engage in further scholarly activities, which may include the publication of academic papers. At the undergraduate level, students might be required to complete annual papers depending on the specific curriculum set by their university; for master's students, there is typically a requirement for the publication of one to two academic papers, which helps develop their skills in writing and research further; doctoral students face more stringent requirements, generally needing to publish a certain number of papers in core academic journals.[381] These publications serve as a quantitative measure of a student's academic output and provide concrete evidence of their ability to comprehend and apply legal knowledge in a scholarly context.[382]

Moreover, some universities in China enhance their legal education programs by integrating additional requirements, such as extracurricular internships and moral education, and these elements are designed to foster a well-rounded legal education, emphasising not only academic excellence but also practical experience and ethical conduct.[383] Like thesis and publication requirements, these components are often structured as independent credit requirements, ensuring that they are recognised as integral parts of the educational journey of a law student.[384]

Overall, the comprehensive approach to legal education in China—encompassing rigorous coursework, extensive research and writing, publication, and practical experience—aims to produce highly qualified legal professionals. These requirements are crafted not only to challenge students and foster academic growth but also to prepare them effectively for the demands and responsibilities of legal careers, ensuring they contribute meaningfully to the legal profession and society.

---

379 Sun (2024).
380 Sun (2024).
381 Fu (2012).
382 Fu (2012).
383 Yang (2021).
384 Yang (2021).

7.3 Curriculum Settings for Undergraduate Legal Education

Before delving into the specific curriculum settings for legal education in Chinese universities, it is crucial to grasp the underlying rationale for such academic structures. The primary aim of establishing legal education courses in universities is detailed in Sections 4.2–4.4 of the Standards, which outline distinct requirements concerning the knowledge,[385] abilities,[386] and qualities[387] that students are expected to develop. These sections emphasise the necessity for a well-rounded legal education that equips students not only with extensive legal knowledge but also with the practical skills and ethical sensibilities required for the legal profession.

To meet these comprehensive educational objectives, Section 5 of the Standards specifies the curriculum requirements for legal education majors. It states that the curriculum should include both theoretical and practical teaching components.[388] The theoretical teaching aspect of the curriculum encompasses ideological and political theory courses, general education courses, and professional courses.[389] These are designed to provide students with a strong foundation in legal principles and the broader socio-political context within which the law operates.[390]

The practical teaching aspect of the curriculum is equally critical. It includes laboratory and practical-training courses, professional internships, social practice opportunities, and the completion of a graduation thesis.[391] This blend of activities is intended to bridge the gap between theoretical knowledge and real-world application, ensuring that students gain hands-on experience and develop their ability to apply legal theories in practical settings.[392]

---

[385] "Acquire foundational knowledge in both the humanities and social sciences, as well as the natural sciences. Develop a solid grasp of the fundamental knowledge and basic theories within one's field of study, thereby forming a well-rounded and comprehensive knowledge structure".

[386] "Possess the ability to independently acquire and update relevant knowledge in their field of study; demonstrate the skills to integrate and apply professional theories and knowledge in a flexible manner to practical work; have the capability to conduct scientific research and engage in innovative entrepreneurial practices using creative thinking methods; and possess a high level of proficiency in computer operation and foreign languages".

[387] "Love the motherland, support socialism, and uphold the leadership of the Communist Party of China. Master the theoretical system of socialism with Chinese characteristics and firmly establish a correct worldview, outlook on life, and values. Acquire the thinking and research methods specific to legal studies, and possess a good foundation in both humanities and scientific literacy. Develop strong moral character, a well-rounded professional personality, and a strong sense of identification with the legal profession, coupled with a sense of responsibility and mission to serve the construction of a socialist rule of law state. Maintain a healthy mind and body".

[388] See "the Standards".

[389] See "the Standards".

[390] See "the Standards".

[391] Ye (2021).

[392] Ye (2021).

Furthermore, the Standards stipulate that the total credits for a legal education program generally should not exceed 160 credits, with at least 15% of these credits dedicated to practical teaching.[393] This allocation underscores the importance of experiential learning in the formation of competent legal professionals.[394] The emphasis on practical teaching credits ensures that students engage significantly in activities that enhance their practical skills, from internships that expose them to the workings of the legal system to social practices that deepen their understanding of the law's impact on society.[395]

This structured approach to curriculum design in Chinese legal education seeks to create a balanced educational experience that fosters a comprehensive understanding of the law, cultivates critical thinking and analytical skills, and promotes ethical practices.[396] By integrating both theoretical and practical elements, the curriculum aims to prepare students to meet the challenges of the legal profession effectively, and to contribute positively to the advancement of justice and rule of law within society.[397]

The theoretical teaching courses in Chinese legal education are systematically categorised into three primary groups: ideological and political theory courses, general education courses, and professional courses, and this structured approach ensures a comprehensive educational experience, tailored to imbue students with a deep understanding of legal principles, societal contexts, and the political landscape influencing the law.[398]

The ideological and political theory courses have a well-defined system and curriculum, reflecting the emphasis on integrating political education with legal studies, and this integration is pivotal in shaping students' perspectives on the rule of law within the context of China's socio-political framework.[399] General education courses, in contrast, are arranged with more flexibility, allowing teaching staff from various institutions to tailor these courses to provide a diverse and broad educational experience, and this flexibility helps to foster a well-rounded academic environment that encourages critical thinking and broad knowledge.[400]

The focus here, however, is primarily on the professional courses, which are crucial for providing specialised legal training. The core curriculum for legal studies within Chinese universities adopts a "1 + 10 + X" classification setting model.[401] In this model, "1" refers to the course "An Introduction to Xi Jinping's Thoughts on the Rule of Law", which underscores the contemporary political and legal philosophies

---

[393] See "the Standards".

[394] Dai et al. (2021).

[395] Dai et al. (2021).

[396] Liu and Xin (2023).

[397] Liu and Xin (2023).

[398] Zhang and He (2023).

[399] Lei and Yang (2023).

[400] Lei and Yang (2023).

[401] Refer to the Ministry of Education of the People's Republic of China website, http://www.moe.gov.cn/srcsite/A08/s7056/202106/t20210602_535109.html, accessed May 10, 2024.

guiding China's legal system; the "10" in the model represents the ten mandatory professional courses that law students are required to complete.[402] These courses form the backbone of legal education and include Jurisprudence, Constitutional Law, History of Chinese Law, Criminal Law, Civil Law, Criminal Procedure Law, Civil Procedure Law, Administrative Law and Administrative Procedure Law, International Law, and Legal Professional Ethics.[403] Each of these courses is designed to ensure that students gain a robust and thorough grounding in key legal disciplines.

The "X" in the model refers to other mandatory professional courses that institutions may offer based on their unique educational characteristics.[404] These courses, which include areas such as Economic Law, Intellectual Property Law, Commercial Law, Private International Law, International Economic Law, Environmental and Resource Law, Labour and Social Security Law, Evidence Law, and Financial and Tax Law, are tailored to the institution's specialties and student interests, with a requirement that no fewer than five such courses are offered.[405] This flexibility allows universities to adapt their curriculums to evolving legal challenges and opportunities, thus maintaining the relevance and rigour of their legal education programs.

Furthermore, elective professional courses are designed to logically extend and continue from the mandatory professional courses, forming course modules or course groups from which students can choose.[406] This elective system enables majors to independently set up their elective professional course system, promoting a customised educational path for each student.[407] Additionally, the development of interdisciplinary, cross-major emerging courses, and innovation and entrepreneurship courses is encouraged to foster creativity, adaptability, and comprehensive problem-solving abilities among students.[408]

This detailed curriculum structure ensures that law students in China not only receive a thorough grounding in core legal concepts but are also able to specialise and adapt to the specific needs and challenges of the legal profession, preparing them effectively for diverse career paths in law.

In the comprehensive legal education system of China, practical courses play a crucial role, effectively bridging the gap between theoretical knowledge and real-world application, these courses are intricately designed to enhance the practical skills of law students, ensuring they are well-prepared for the demands of legal professions.[409]

Practical teaching involves integrating hands-on methods into the traditional theoretical education framework, including reforming teaching methodologies to focus

---

[402] See footnote 401.

[403] See footnote 401.

[404] See footnote 401.

[405] See footnote 401.

[406] Liang (2019).

[407] Liang (2019).

[408] Liang (2019).

[409] Wang and Ma (2023).

more on case-based teaching.[410] This approach helps students better understand how legal principles apply in real scenarios, developing their critical-thinking and problem-solving skills which are essential for the practice of law.[411]

The component involving laboratories and training typically utilises facilities such as mock courts,[412] legal clinics,[413] professional laboratories, training bases, and off-campus internship bases. These resources allow universities to establish specialised laboratory and training courses that cater to the practical needs of legal education. Furthermore, professional internships, and innovation and entrepreneurship education are organised in the later stages of the program to provide students with hands-on experience in professional settings. According to the Standards, this segment requires a detailed syllabus that outlines teaching objectives, basic requirements, main content, and hours allocation for professional internships.[414] The duration of these internships is mandated to be no less than ten weeks, providing students sufficient time to engage deeply with the practical aspects of their education.[415]

Social practice is usually facilitated by the school, which provides students with macro-level direction and methodological suggestions. Students typically form practice teams, design the process, and implement it independently, fostering a sense of initiative and responsibility as they apply theoretical knowledge to solve practical problems in real-world contexts.[416] Upon completion, students must submit activity materials and written reports to the college, which are used to assess their performance and understanding of the practical applications of their studies.[417]

The graduation thesis or project serves as a capstone for students, requiring them to undertake significant research or a practical project that showcases their cumulative learning.[418] This critical component not only serves as the culmination of the students' academic efforts but also as a demonstration of their ability to conduct in-depth legal research or execute a substantial legal project.[419]

Collectively, these components ensure that law students in China are not only proficient in legal theories but are also adept at applying these theories in practical settings. This holistic approach prepares them for successful careers in the legal field, equipped with both the knowledge and skills necessary to navigate complex legal challenges.

This paper takes the comprehensive training program for undergraduate law students of the 2020 cohort at Zhongnan University of Economics and Law as an

[410] Wang and Ma (2023).
[411] Wang and Ma (2023).
[412] Lü et al. (2024).
[413] Yang (2023).
[414] See "the Standards".
[415] See "the Standards".
[416] Dai (2023).
[417] Dai (2023).
[418] Ma (2023).
[419] Ma (2023).

example for further explanation (see Table 7.2).[420] It is evident that, under the current Chinese legal education system, universities demonstrate characteristics of making detailed adjustments based on the Standards, combined with their own features and resource advantages, to meet students' professional quality improvement and diverse development needs.

The thesis or project component is a pivotal aspect of a law student's journey towards graduation, intricately tied to their ability to synthesise, analyse, and apply the knowledge they have gained throughout their course of study.[421] While the thesis primarily relates to students' qualification for graduation, additional form requirements provide a framework for its execution, ensuring that the final output not only reflects comprehensive legal understanding but also adheres to high academic and ethical standards.[422]

According to the Standards, graduate theses or projects in legal studies can take various forms, including academic papers, case analyses, graduation projects, and research reports.[423] This variety allows students to choose a format that best suits their skills, academic interests, and career aspirations. Students are encouraged to select thesis topics that are problem-oriented, prompting students to engage with current challenges and issues within the legal landscape, and this approach ensures that the work they produce is relevant and contributes meaningful insights into existing legal debates or issues.[424]

Students are encouraged to write their theses or projects under the close guidance of their instructors, integrating their academic pursuits with practical experience gained through social practice.[425] This integration is designed to enrich their academic work with real-world relevance, particularly by addressing contemporary and challenging issues in the socio-economic environment.[426] By combining personal interests with practical application, students can produce work that is not only academically rigorous but also of practical value in the broader context of legal practice and policy.[427]

The content of the thesis or project should comprehensively utilise the theoretical and professional knowledge that students have acquired during their studies, and this ensures that the outcomes of their research are grounded in solid legal theory while being informed by practical application and realities.[428] Adherence to academic

420 The content in the table is compiled based on the student training program of the School of Law at Zhongnan University of Economics and Law and is for reference only.

421 Zhang (2019).

422 Zhang (2019).

423 See "the Standards".

424 See "the Standards".

425 Dong and Liu (2024).

426 Dong and Liu (2024).

427 Dong and Liu (2024).

428 Wang et al. (2018).

Table 7.2 Training program for the class of 2020 in Law

Training segments/course categories		Credit	Type	Credit	Remark
Classroom teaching	Common required course	43	Required	27	
			Optional	16	
	Professional platform course	52	Required	38	
			Optional	8	
			Interdisciplinary	6	
	Professional courses	36	Required	24	Requirements for No Specific Direction: 24
					Requirements for Civil and Commercial Law: 22
					Requirements for Foreign-related Rule of Law: 24
					Requirements for Government Rule of Law: 21
					Requirements for Criminal Law: 24
			Optional	12	Requirements for No Specific Direction: 12
					Requirements for Civil and Commercial Law: 14
					Requirements for Foreign-related Rule of Law: 12
					Requirements for Government Rule of Law: 15
					Requirements for Criminal Law: 12
Quality-oriented education		16	Required	10	
			Optional	6	
Practical teaching		19	Required	19	Including four Extracurricular Credits
Total credits		166			
In-class credits		156			

(continued)

Table 7.2 (continued)

Course categories	Course title	Hours	Type	Credit	Remark
General Education	Ideology, Morality and Rule of Law	40	Required	2.5	
	Outline of Chinese Modern History	40		2.5	
	Introduction to the Basic Principles of Marxism	40		2.5	
	Introduction to Mao Zedong Thought and the Theoretical System of Socialism with Chinese Characteristics	72		4.5	Course divided into two semesters
	Situation and Policy	64		2	Course divided into eight semesters
	English	112		7	Course divided into two semesters
	Introduction to Data Analysis	32		2	
	Fundamentals of Artificial Intelligence and Data Processing	32		2	
	Military Theory	32		2	
	Total Credits for Required General Education Courses			27	
	Patriotism	96	Optional	6	
	International View	64		4	
	Cultural Inheritance	64		4	
	Scientific Literacy	32		2	
	Total Credits for Optional General Education Courses			16	
Professional Platform Course	Nomology	64	Required	4	
	General Introduction to Civil Law	40		3	
	Constitutional Jurisprudence	54		4	
	Legal Professional Ethics	32		2	

(continued)

Table 7.2 (continued)

Course categories	Course title	Hours	Type	Credit	Remark
	Criminal Jurisprudence (1)	54		4	
	Legal History of China	64		4	Need to finish Nomology first
	General Introduction to the Law of Debt	54		4	Need to finish General introduction to civil law first
	Criminal Jurisprudence (2)	40		3	
	Law of Criminal Procedure	54		4	Need to finish Nomology and Criminal jurisprudence (1) first
	International Law (Bilingual)	54		4	Need to finish Nomology first
	General Introduction to Xi Jinping Thought on the Rule of Law	32		2	
	Total Credits for Required Professional Platform Course			38	
	Total Credits for Optional Professional Platform Course			8	There is a wide variety of courses, which will not be elaborated here
Professional Courses (No Specific Direction) *The Specific Course Arrangements Vary Slightly According To Different Directions	Law of Civil Procedure	54	Required	4	Need to finish Nomology and General introduction to the law of debt first
	Administrative Law and Administrative Procedure Law	54		4	

(continued)

Table 7.2 (continued)

Course categories	Course title	Hours	Type	Credit	Remark
	Economic Jurisprudence	40		3	Need to finish Nomology, General Introduction to the Law of Debt and Constitutional Jurisprudence first
	Jurisprudence of Business	40		3	Need to finish Nomology and General Introduction to the Law of Debt first
	Private International Law (Bilingual)	32		2	Need to finish Nomology and General Introduction to the Law of Debt first
	International Economic Law (Bilingual)	32		2	
	Environmental Jurisprudence	32		2	Need to finish Nomology, General Introduction to the Law of Debt and Economic Jurisprudence first
	Evidence Jurisprudence	32		2	
	Real Right Jurisprudence	32		2	Need to finish Nomology first
	Total Credits for Required Professional Course			24	
	Total Credits for Optional Professional Course			12	
Concentrated Practical Teaching Session	The Practice of Ideological and Political Theory Course	32	Required	2	
	Social practice			2	

(continued)

Table 7.2 (continued)

Course categories	Course title	Hours	Type	Credit	Remark
	Military training			2	
	Term paper			2	
	Graduation Field Work			4	
	Graduation Thesis			4	
	Legal Practice (Divided By Directions)	48	Optional*	3	*Choose one practical course to study within the optional range
	Total Credits for Practical Teaching Session			19	
Quality-Oriented Education	Public Physical Education	64	Required	2	Course divided into two semesters
	Special Education of Physical Education	64		2	Course divided into two semesters
	College Students' Mental Health Course	32		2	
	Academic Research Innovation			1	
	Innovation and Entrepreneurship Education Practice			2	
	Labour Education and Experience			1	
	Total Credits for Required Quality-Oriented Education			10	
	Aesthetic Education Courses and Practice	32	Optional	2	
	Personal Physical and Professional Development	64		4	
	Total Credits for Optional Quality-Oriented Education			6	

ethics and standards in the writing process is paramount, safeguarding the integrity of the academic work and the credibility of the student's research.[429]

To support students in these endeavours, each discipline is required to appoint thesis or project advisers for undergraduate students, and these advisers should be

[429] Wang et al. (2018).

faculty members with at least the rank of lecturer in their respective disciplines, ensuring that they possess the necessary academic proficiency and experience to guide students effectively.[430] Additionally, professionals from related practical fields may also be appointed to provide joint guidance, offering students insights from alternative fields and bridging the gap between theoretical knowledge and practical application.[431]

Advisers are expected to provide stringent guidance and oversight at all stages of the thesis or project preparation, from topic selection and proposal development to the final writing stages.[432] This structured guidance helps to maintain rigorous academic standards and supports students in achieving a high level of scholarly work.

While this framework outlines the setup for undergraduate legal education, the approach to thesis and project work at the graduate level tends to be more specialised and can vary significantly across different law schools and centres for legal education. Graduate-level projects typically focus more intensively on the student's major field of study and involve a greater degree of autonomous planning, reflecting the advanced nature of the study and the specific requirements of each academic institution.[433] This level of specialisation allows for a deeper exploration of complex legal issues and fosters a more nuanced understanding of specific areas of law.

7.4 Higher Levels of Legal Education

Due to the complex and expansive nature of legal education, which encompasses a broad array of primary and secondary disciplines, an undergraduate degree often does not suffice for those aiming to become high-level legal professionals, especially for those interested in pursuing theoretical research in legal fields.[434] Consequently, further education becomes a crucial step for these individuals after completing their undergraduate studies. This is particularly vital for those who wish to delve deeper into the theoretical aspects of law, where ongoing education can significantly enhance their understanding and expertise.

For graduates who have completed their undergraduate legal education and are looking to further their studies, there are generally three main pathways to consider for advancing their legal education at higher levels. The most common route is to take graduate admission exams to enter master's programs within domestic universities. Another option is to access direct entry pathways that some undergraduate institutions offer for continuing master's studies in related disciplines, allowing a smoother transition for students from undergraduate to graduate studies.

[430] Sun et al. (2024).

[431] Sun et al. (2024).

[432] Sun et al. (2024).

[433] Zhao and Gao (2024).

[434] Wang et al. (2024).

This first path is overwhelmingly popular among undergraduates. Data from a *China Youth Online* article reveals compelling statistics: "Nearly 90 per cent of college students have considered postgraduate studies, about 70 per cent had this idea before university, and nearly 60 per cent would not choose to switch majors for postgraduate studies".[435] These figures indicate a strong preference among students to continue their education within the same field, underscoring the perceived value of specialised, continuous academic pursuit in law.

These educational trajectories underscore the dedication and commitment required to excel in the legal field, highlighting the importance of advanced studies for those aspiring to higher levels of expertise and specialisation in law. For many, this commitment to further education is driven by the desire to gain deeper insights and to make meaningful contributions to the field of law, whether in practice, academia, or research. Thus, for those committed to advancing their legal knowledge, pursuing master's or doctoral studies becomes an essential step towards achieving their professional and academic goals.

The benefits of continuing studies at domestic universities in China, particularly for a Master's in Law, are multifaceted and significant. Firstly, the financial aspect is considerably advantageous as the tuition and living expenses at domestic institutions are generally more affordable compared to the costs associated with studying abroad. This affordability reduces the financial strain on students and their families, making higher education more accessible.[436]

Secondly, pursuing further legal education within China allows students to maintain a consistent and coherent understanding of the legal system that is unique to the country. The legal frameworks across the world differ greatly due to variations in the political, cultural, and historical contexts. China's socialist legal system, with its distinct characteristics, both theoretically and practically, is quite different from those found in other countries. For students aiming to contribute to legal development within China, continuing their education domestically provides an unrivalled depth of relevance and contextual understanding that is crucial for effective practice and innovation in the Chinese legal environment.

Moreover, degrees from domestic universities are highly recognised within China's job market. Graduates who study locally face almost no restrictions in employment opportunities compared to those who study abroad, making this a secure career path.[437] Furthermore, the study of law as a social science benefits greatly from its robust networks. Pursuing further education in domestic universities allows students to leverage existing relationships with mentors, classmates, and other professional contacts. These networks are invaluable for resource sharing, information exchange, and creating a supportive learning environment, which are essential for building a successful legal career.[438]

---

[435] Refer to China Youth Network, https://t.m.youth.cn/transfer/toutiao/url/edu.youth.cn/jysx/jyxw/202010/t20201019_12535624.htm, accessed May 3, 2024.

[436] Yang and Zuo (2017).

[437] Li et al. (2022).

[438] Li et al. (2022).

However, there are challenges associated with this path due to the growing demand for higher education. The competition for postgraduate positions is fierce, as reflected by the increasing number of postgraduate exam takers and the rising cut-off scores for law majors. In 2022, the number of students taking postgraduate exams reached 4.57 million, marking a significant increase from the previous year.[439] This surge is indicative of a broader trend where individuals are seeking more than just an undergraduate degree, driven by a heightened thirst for knowledge and the challenging economic conditions exacerbated by the global COVID-19 pandemic. The pandemic has not only slowed economic growth but also impacted job prospects for graduates, prompting many to continue their studies as a way to mitigate the uncertain job market.[440] Additionally, changes in international travel policies diverted some students from studying abroad to pursuing their education domestically.[441]

This scenario prompts a critical re-evaluation of the current legal education system in China, raising questions about whether the primary goal of education is still focused on knowledge acquisition or if, for some, it has become a strategic delay from entering a challenging job market. This situation underscores the need for ongoing adjustments and enhancements in legal education to ensure it meets the evolving needs of students and the broader societal and economic landscapes.

The remaining two paths involve applying to universities in Hong Kong, Macau, Taiwan, or abroad where master's programs in law are offered. First, it is important to understand how law degrees are structured not only in mainland China but also in the regions of Hong Kong, Macau, Taiwan, and other countries (such as the UK and the United States, for example), as shown in Table 7.3.

Legal education in the United States holds a unique position in the global landscape because it typically does not offer a bachelor's degree in law; instead, it commences at the master's level with degrees such as the Juris Doctor (J.D.), which is considered the primary law degree necessary for practicing law in the United States.[442] This structure places higher demands on students, who must already possess an undergraduate degree before commencing their legal studies, thus contributing to a more selective and arguably elitist form of education.[443] Additionally, the structuring of law degrees varies significantly across different countries, with degrees like the LL.M. (Master of Laws), LL.D. (Doctor of Laws), and J.D. (Juris Doctor) enjoying high international recognition.[444]

For students considering their options for legal studies, studying abroad presents a distinct set of advantages and focuses. One common benefit of pursuing legal education outside one's home country is the alleviation of competitive pressures due to the entrance examination. Unlike systems that rely heavily on the grades of the

[439] Refer to the Ministry of Education of the People's Republic of China website, http://www.moe.gov.cn/fbh/live/2021/53908/mtbd/202112/t20211223_589603.html, accessed May 4, 2024.

[440] Mao and Zeng (2022).

[441] Lin (2024).

[442] Guo et al. (2020).

[443] Guo et al. (2020).

[444] Guo et al. (2020).

Table 7.3 The mode of setting law degrees

Degree	Abbreviation	General length of schooling
The mode of setting law degrees in Taiwan, China[445]		
Bachelor of Laws	LL.B	Four or five years full-time
Master of Laws	LL.M	Two years (and above) full-time
Doctor of Laws	LL.D	Four years (and above) full-time
The mode of setting law degrees in Hong Kong, China[446]		
Bachelor of Laws	LL.B	Four years full-time or five years part-time
Juris Doctor	J.D	Two years full-time or three and a half years part-time
Master of Laws	LL.M	One-year full-time or two years part-time
Master of Common Law	M.C.L	One-year full-time or two years part-time
Master of Philosophy	M.Phil	Two years full-time or three years part-time
Doctor of Judicial Science	S.J.D./J.S.D	Three or four years full-time or four and a half years or six years part-time
Doctor of Philosophy	Ph.D	Four years full-time or five and a half years part-time
The mode of setting law degrees in UK[447]		
Bachelor of Laws	LL.B	Three years full-time
Bachelor of Arts	B.A	Three years full-time
Bachelor of Civil Law	B.C.L	One-year full-time
Magister Juris	M.Jur	One-year full-time
Master of Studies	M. St	One or two years full-time or two years (and above) part-time
Master of Laws	LL.M	One-year full-time
Master of Philosophy	M.Phil	One-year full-time or two years part-time
Doctor of Philosophy	Ph.D	Two years to four years full-time or three years (and above) part-time
The mode of setting law degrees in the USA[448]		
Juris Doctor	J.D	Three years full-time
Master of Laws	LL.M	One-year full-time
Doctor of Laws	LL.D	Three years (and above) full-time

[445] Refer to the College of Law at National Taiwan University website, https://www.law.ntu.edu.tw/#gsc.tab=0, accessed May 4, 2024.

[446] Refer to the Faculty of Law at the University of Hong Kong website, https://www.law.hku.hk, accessed May 4, 2024.

[447] Refer to the University of Oxford Faculty of Law website, https://www.law.ox.ac.uk, accessed May 4, 2024.

[448] Refer to the Harvard Law School website, https://hls.harvard.edu, accessed May 4, 2024.

examination, the application process for studying abroad tends to apply a holistic evaluation of a candidate's accumulated knowledge and comprehensive skills over time. This method allows for a more nuanced assessment of a student's capabilities and offers candidates more time to prepare their applications thoughtfully, reducing the risk of their educational trajectory being derailed by one poor exam performance.

Moreover, the duration required to complete law degrees abroad, particularly for an LL.M., is generally shorter compared to the lengthy periods often required by universities in mainland China.[449] In many international institutions, students can complete an LL.M. program within one to two years, enabling them to expediently transition to the next stages of their academic or professional lives.[450] This efficiency not only accelerates their career progression but also represents a significant time-saving advantage, allowing students to attain their educational and career goals swiftly.

This streamlined approach to legal education, offered by universities outside of mainland China, is especially attractive to students looking to specialise quickly and enter the legal profession in an international context.[451] It underscores the broader appeal of global legal education pathways that cater to a diverse student body, aiming to equip them with the necessary legal expertise and qualifications in a more accessible and time-efficient manner.[452]

Discussing the distinct advantages of studying in regions like Hong Kong, Macau, or Taiwan, versus studying abroad, provides a clear illustration of how geopolitical and cultural contexts can shape educational experiences. The former option—studying in Hong Kong, Macau, or Taiwan—draws particular benefits from the "One Country, Two Systems" policy, which fosters closer integration with mainland China while maintaining unique administrative and legal frameworks. These regions are often viewed as gateways between East and West, blending multiple cultures and ideologies. This multicultural environment provides students with a range of diverse learning approaches and professional perspectives, enriching their educational experience without causing any misalignment with the legal system or ongoing judicial reforms in mainland China.

In recent years, the appeal of studying in Hong Kong, Macau, or Taiwan has noticeably increased among mainland Chinese students. The 2022/23 academic year saw significant enrolment numbers with 31,000 students in taught master's programs and 13,300 in research-based master's and PhD programs in Hong Kong alone.[453] Presently, 15 universities in Hong Kong welcome students from mainland China

449 Xu (2010).

450 Xu (2010).

451 Guo (2013).

452 Guo (2013).

453 Refer to the website of the Liaison Office of the Central People's Government in the Macao Special Administrative Region, http://www.zlb.gov.cn/2023-09/26/c_1212276004.htm, accessed May 5, 2024.

at the undergraduate level and above. Graduates from these programs are eligible for degree certification by the Ministry of Education's Service Center for Scholarly Exchange, ensuring that their qualifications are recognised as on par with those of returnees from abroad. This recognition affirms the quality and compatibility of their education with mainland China's legal and professional standards, making this option increasingly popular for students seeking advanced degrees close to home, yet still within a globally resonant educational framework.[454]

On the other hand, opting to study abroad offers a completely different set of advantages. International study destinations are renowned for their mature, comprehensive education systems, which provide a diverse and rigorous legal education.[455] Students who choose to study abroad benefit from exposure to a variety of legal traditions and practices, often different from the socialist legal system with Chinese characteristics. This exposure is invaluable for students who aim to work in international law or in contexts that require a broad understanding of various legal systems. The education abroad is targeted and challenging, designed to push students to develop critical thinking and adaptability, skills that are crucial for navigating the complexities of global legal environments.[456]

Both educational paths—whether closer integration through studying in Hong Kong, Macau, or Taiwan, or broadening one's horizons by studying abroad—offer unique advantages that cater to the diverse aspirations of students. These choices reflect the students' strategic decisions based on their career goals, personal circumstances, and the specific legal landscapes they wish to engage with in their professional lives.

While considering the educational pathways of studying in Hong Kong, Macau, Taiwan, or abroad, it is crucial to address the potential inconveniences and challenges associated with these options. One of the primary concerns is the significant increase in study costs, which include tuition fees and living expenses.[457] These costs are considerably higher than those of studying within mainland China. Even focusing solely on tuition, the increase is substantial. When currency exchange rates and different price levels in these regions are factored in, the cost disparity compared to mainland China becomes even more pronounced. For many students from middle- and low-income families, these expenses could represent a significant, if not prohibitive, financial burden.

Additionally, there is the issue of misalignment or disconnection in the legal education systems.[458] Apart from Macau, where the legal education still adheres to the civil law tradition similar to that of mainland China, many regions and countries

[454] Yu and Wen (2007).

[455] Li and Sun (2018).

[456] Li and Sun (2018).

[457] Yu and Wen (2007).

[458] Yu and Wen (2007).

adopt the common law system or other unique legal frameworks. These systems can differ significantly from the socialist legal system with Chinese characteristics, which is predominantly based on the civil law tradition. This discrepancy poses a considerable challenge for students from mainland China who pursue their legal studies in these regions or countries.[459] After completing undergraduate studies in mainland China, these students often require a significant amount of time to acclimate to new legal content and methodologies. This adjustment phase can be both time-consuming and demanding.

Moreover, upon returning to mainland China, the legal knowledge and qualifications acquired abroad may not seamlessly align with the requirements of the mainland legal profession. This misalignment can lead to difficulties in job searches where local employers may not fully recognise or value a degree from a foreign or even a regional institution outside mainland China.[460] This could result in personal and professional maladaptation, where the graduates might find it challenging to apply their acquired skills effectively within the mainland's legal context or struggle to secure employment in their field of study.[461]

These challenges underscore the need for prospective law students to carefully consider their educational and career goals against the backdrop of financial constraints and the specific legal system they intend to practice in. While international exposure and education can offer broadened perspectives and a competitive edge in some contexts, they also come with hurdles that require careful planning and consideration to overcome (Table 7.4).

Regardless of the chosen method or destination for further studies, the ambitions of law students to gain professional knowledge and attain higher levels of education should be both respected and encouraged. Law can be likened to "a boundless ocean of learning", where the relentless pursuit of fairness and justice brings us closer to the truth and embodies the true spirit of legal education. This journey towards understanding and implementing justice is central to the development of competent and ethical legal professionals who can effectively contribute to society.

In recent years, the field of law has faced its challenges, notably being labelled as a "red card" major in some regions due to perceived employment difficulties.[462] This label suggests a high level of risk associated with the pursuit of a law degree, given the competitive job market and the substantial investment of time and resources required for legal studies. Such challenges have compelled some graduates to reconsider their career paths and, in some cases, to abandon their pursuit of law altogether. However, it is crucial to recall the adage that "success depends on human effort". The obstacles and experiences faced today should act as motivators rather than deterrents, encouraging both students and educational institutions to adapt and overcome.

---

459 Yu and Wen (2007).

460 Lin et al. (2023).

461 Lin et al. (2023).

462 See "Understanding the 2020 China College Graduate Employment Report at a Glance," Guangming Online, published July 9, 2020. Accessed September 4, 2024.

Table 7.4 Reference for Law Master's tuition fees by region

University	Location	Tuition per year (converted to RMB)
China University of Political Science and Law[463]	Beijing, China	J.M.: 8000 RMB LL.M.: 15,000 RMB
East China University of Political Science and Law[464]	Shanghai, China	J.M.: 8000 RMB LL.M. (Law Undergraduate): 22,500 RMB LL.M. (Non-Law Undergraduate): 18,000 RMB
Wuhan University[465]	Wuhan, China	J.M.: 8000 RMB LL.M.: 13,000 RMB
University of Hong Kong[466]	Hong Kong, China	LL.M.: about 160,000–200,000 RMB
City University of Hong Kong[467]	Hong Kong, China	LL.M.: about 160,000–200,000 RMB
University of Macau[468]	Macau, China	LL.M.: about 80,000 RMB
Yale University[469]	USA	LL.M.: about 500,000 RMB
Stanford University[470]	USA	LL.M.: about 510,000 RMB
Harvard University[471]	USA	LL.M.: about 450,000 RMB
University of Cambridge[472]	UK	LL.M.: about 280,000 RMB

[463] Refer to the Graduate School website of China University of Political Science and Law, http://yjsy.cupl.edu.cn/info/1035/8881.htm, accessed May 5, 2024.

[464] Refer to the Graduate School website of East China University of Political Science and Law, https://gs.ecupl.edu.cn/2023/0920/c13332a204082/page.htm, accessed May 5, 2024.

[465] Refer to the Graduate School website of Wuhan University, https://gs.whu.edu.cn/info/1252/11209.htm, accessed May 5, 2024.

[466] Refer to the website of the Faculty of Law at the University of Hong Kong, https://www.law.hku.hk/prospective-students/tuition-fees, accessed May 5, 2024.

[467] Refer to the website of the Faculty of Law at the City University of Hong Kong https://www.cityu.edu.hk/fo/htm/degree_fees.htm, accessed May 5, 2024.

[468] Refer to the website of University of Macau, https://grs.um.edu.mo/wp-content/uploads/Tuition-Fees-for-Postgraduate-Programmes-AY-24-25-Chi.pdf, accessed May 5, 2024.

[469] This data is derived from information provided by several international students and official information from related schools. For details, see the website of Yale University, https://www.yale.edu, accessed May 5, 2024.

[470] This data is derived from information provided by several international students and official information from related schools. For details, see the website of Stanford University, https://studentservices.stanford.edu/tuition-rates/2023-2024-graduate-and-professional-tuition-rates#LawSchool, accessed May 5, 2024.

[471] This data is derived from information provided by several international students and official information from related schools. For details, see the website of Harvard University, https://www.gse.harvard.edu/admissions-and-aid/tuition-and-costs, accessed May 5, 2024.

[472] This data is derived from information provided by several international students and official information from related schools. For details, see the website of University of Cambridge, https://www.postgraduate.study.cam.ac.uk/finance/fees, accessed May 5, 2024.

Past experiences in the field of law should not be seen as stumbling blocks but rather as stepping stones to achieving greater goals. The essence of education, particularly legal education, is to "cultivate character and develop talents".[473] It aims not just to fill students with knowledge but to shape individuals who can think critically, act ethically, and contribute meaningfully to society.[474]

Perhaps by setting aside purely utilitarian motives, where education is seen merely as a means to secure employment, both students and educators can engage more deeply with the core purposes of legal education. This approach allows for a richer understanding of the law's role in society and fosters a more profound appreciation of the responsibilities that come with legal expertise. Embracing this perspective could rejuvenate the perception of legal education and inspire a new generation of lawyers committed to the principles of justice and equity, equipped to tackle the legal challenges of the future.

473 Chen and Jie (2020).

474 Chen and Jie (2020).

Chapter 8
The Legal Profession in China

As the wheels of time turn, the evolution of legal education in China marches on, adapting to the shifting demands of society and the legal profession. At its core, the quintessential aim of all educational endeavours is to nurture talent and to furnish society with a robust supply of well-trained, skilled individuals ready to contribute to various sectors. Legal professionals, after their thorough academic training, join the broader legal community where they serve in various capacities. The spectrum of legal professions is broad, encompassing roles such as lawyers, judges, prosecutors, arbitrators, corporate legal counsel, and notaries. Each of these professions plays a vital role in the functioning of the legal system and justice administration. Despite the diversity of roles within the legal field, there are universally applicable entry standards that all candidates must meet to ensure competence and integrity in the profession. Furthermore, each specific role comes with its own set of distinct requirements and qualifications that reflect the unique challenges, duties, and responsibilities associated with it. These prerequisites are designed to ensure that every legal professional is not only competent in the theoretical aspects of the law but is also equipped to handle the practical demands of their specific legal role.

8.1 The National Legal Professional Qualification Exam in China

Today, as China fully embraces an era governed by a comprehensive rule of law, the commitment to cultivating a high-quality legal workforce, characterised by both integrity and skill, remains a pivotal endeavour in advancing this comprehensive

S. Zhang et al., *Technology, Legal Education and Legal Profession in China and Australia*, International and Comparative Law in the Asia Pacific,
https://doi.org/10.1007/978-981-96-1639-8_8

legal governance.[1] The legal sector demands that its practitioners not only possess specialised professional knowledge but also exhibit high overall quality. A critical milestone for entering this profession is successfully passing the legal professional qualification exam.

Since the pivotal year of 1986, China has embarked on a structured journey with its legal professional qualification exams, evolving through three distinct phases that have been crucial in shaping the legal landscape. First, from 1986 to 2001, there was the National Unified Bar Exam (referred to as the Bar Exam).[2] Then the National Unified Judicial Exam, from 2002 to 2017 (referred to as the Judicial Exam), was developed which further refined the assessment and qualification process.[3] Since 2018, the examination process has been consolidated under the National Unified Legal Professional Qualification Exam (referred to as the Legal Exam).[4] This structured evolution of the examinations has been instrumental in not only ensuring the competence of new entrants into the legal field but also in elevating the overall standards and quality of the legal workforce. This rigorous examination framework underpins the integrity and capability of the legal profession, ensuring that it keeps pace with the demands of governance by law.[5]

8.1.1 Bar Examination Period

During this specific era, China embraced a diversified and decentralised approach for entry examinations across various legal professions, including roles such as judges, prosecutors, lawyers, and notaries.[6] This comprehensive system was characterised by not only the general Bar Exam but also distinct evaluations tailored to specific legal roles. These specialised exams were administratively orchestrated by different national bodies: the Supreme People's Court was responsible for organising exams for aspiring entry-level judges and their assistants,[7] the Supreme People's Procuratorate

---

[1] "Adherence to Building a Highly Qualified Rule of Law Workforce of Both Virtue and Talent." The National People's Congress of China. Accessed May 5, 2024. http://www.npc.gov.cn/npc/c2/c30834/202103/t20210322_310820.html.

[2] On 12 April 1986, the Ministry of Justice of China issued *the Circular on the National Unified Examination for the Qualification of Lawyers.*

[3] *The Measures for the Implementation of the National Judicial Examination (for Trial Implementation)* came into force on 1 January 2002.

[4] On 28 April 2018, the Ministry of Justice of China issued *the Measures for the Implementation of the National Unified Legal Vocational Qualification Examination.*

[5] Zhang (2022).

[6] See the official WeChat public platform of Democracy and Law Weekly, National Legal Professional Qualification System Develops and Improves in Reform—Interview with Jia Liqun, Director General of the Department of Judicial Examinations, Ministry of Justice, published on September 22, 2017, accessed on August 21, 2024.

[7] Interim Measures of the Supreme People's Court for the Examination of Junior Trial Attorneys and Assistant Trial Attorneys (1999), Article 2.

handled the examinations for entry-level prosecutors and assistant prosecutors,[8] and the Ministry of Justice oversaw the certification process for notaries.[9] This array of exams formed the backbone of what came to be known as China's decentralised system for the entry into legal professions.

The inception of this examination system for legal professionals can be traced back to significant regulatory developments. In 1980, a pivotal moment occurred with the issuance of the "Interim Regulations of the People's Republic of China on Lawyers".[10] Specifically, Article 8 of the regulations made it clear that acquiring lawyer qualifications was contingent upon passing a designated assessment.[11] Furthermore, Article 9 expanded on this by stipulating that, in order to be officially recognised as a lawyer, one must successfully pass an assessment sanctioned by the justice departments of provinces, autonomous regions, or municipalities; obtain a lawyer's certificate; and register with the Ministry of Justice of the People's Republic of China.[12] This regulatory framework established a preliminary yet clear pathway for the acquisition of lawyer qualifications through formal assessments.

However, due to the absence of specific guidelines on the assessment processes and China's nascent experience in this domain, the Ministry of Justice initially refrained from conducting a nationwide examination immediately after the regulations were enacted. Consequently, this led to the emergence of localised testing practices tailored to the contexts of various regions. A notable development occurred, in 1984, when Jiangxi Province pioneered a unified provincial examination for lawyer qualifications.[13] This initiative was soon taken up in Beijing and several other regions, and they began conducting their own lawyer qualification exams by 1985.[14]

In 1986, leveraging the accumulated experiences from various regional practices, and aiming to establish uniform entry standards for lawyers across the country

---

[8] Provisional Measures for the Examination of Junior Prosecutors and Assistant Prosecutors (1995), Article 5.

[9] There is no written method of administering the notary public examination, but the Ministry of Justice has issued a circular relating to the examination, Circular of the Ministry of Justice on the Holding of the 1992 Unified National Qualification Examination for Notaries Public (1992).

[10] This regulation became invalid on January 1, 1997.

[11] "Article 8: Those who uphold the Constitution of the People's Republic of China and meet the following conditions may apply for a lawyer's practice certificate:

(1) Possess lawyer qualifications;

(2) Complete a one-year internship at a law firm;

(3) Have good conduct."

[12] "Article 9: To qualify as a lawyer, a person must be examined and approved by the justice department (bureau) of a province, autonomous region or municipality directly under the Central Government, and a lawyer's certificate must be issued and reported to the Ministry of Justice of the People's Republic of China for the record. If the Ministry of Justice finds that the approval has been improperly granted, it shall notify the department (bureau) of justice to re-examine the case".

[13] See the official WeChat public platform of Jiangxi Provincial Judicial Administration, *Focus: In 40 years, the number of lawyers in the province has grown from hundreds to 6100,* published on October 26, 2018, accessed on May 6, 2024.

[14] "Chronicle of 30 Years of the Beijing Lawyer Profession". Beijing Lawyers Association. Accessed on May 6, 2024. https://www.beijinglawyers.org.cn/cac/1575879081010.htm.

while enhancing the overall quality of legal professionals, the Ministry of Justice promulgated the "Notice on the National Unified Examination for Lawyer Qualifications". Consequently, on September 27–28 of the same year, China conducted its inaugural national unified examination for lawyer qualifications.[15] The statistics from this event indicated that while 29,000 individuals registered to take the exam, only 1134 succeeded in passing and thereby obtained the requisite lawyer qualifications.[16] Initially, this examination was exclusively available to those already engaged in legal practice, either full- or part-time, as well as those involved in legal research and teaching who fulfilled the necessary criteria to practice law.[17]

In a strategic move to broaden the base of qualified legal professionals, the 1988 bar exam marked a pivotal transition by opening up to the general public, extending beyond the previously specified groups.[18] At this juncture, the format and content of the bar exam were still under development, lacking standardised guidelines. The examination predominantly covered key areas of law including constitutional law, civil law, criminal law, and various procedural laws.[19] The Ministry of Justice continued this initiative by organising subsequent national bar exams in 1990 and 1992.[20]

A significant policy change occurred in 1993 when, with the endorsement of the State Council, the Ministry of Justice resolved to conduct the national bar exam on an annual basis. In a further expansion of inclusivity, the 1994 "Notice on Organizing Residents of Hong Kong, Macau, and Taiwan to Participate in This Year's National Bar Exam" was issued, allowing residents from these regions to partake in the examination for the first time.[21] The inclusion of a foreign language component in the bar exam, in 1996, marked another notable development, although this component was phased out after four years.[22]

To establish a more standardised, open, fair, and just system for the bar examination, the Ministry of Justice introduced the "Interim Regulations on the Lawyer Qualification Examination"[23] in 1993, followed by the more comprehensive "Regulations on the Lawyer Qualification Examination"[24] in 2001. These regulations effectively consolidated and revised the earlier interim regulations and their implementation measures. They delineated specific details regarding registration timelines,

---

[15] Li and Li (2008).

[16] See the official WeChat public platform of the Ministry of Justice of the People's Republic of China, *The Legal Profession's "Threshold Examination" Selects Talent and Witnesses China's Rule of Law Progress*, published on July 22, 2019, accessed on May 6, 2024.

[17] Gao and Wen (2020).

[18] Gao and Wen (2020).

[19] Du (2022).

[20] Du (2022).

[21] "Preparations for the National Lawyer Qualification Examination in 1994 Are Complete." *People's Mediation*, no. 07, 1994, pp. 26–27.

[22] Liu et al. (2001).

[23] This interim regulation has been abolished.

[24] See the website of the Central People's Government of the People's Republic of China, https://www.gov.cn/gongbao/content/2001/content_60691.htm, accessed on May 6, 2024.

entry prerequisites, examination room conduct, and the nature of the exam questions. According to these directives, the bar exam encompassed a broad spectrum of legal subjects, including but not limited to Constitution, Basic Theories of Law, Administrative Law, and International Law, along with procedural and specialised areas such as Criminal Procedure Law and International Economic Law,[25] thereby reflecting the comprehensive scope intended to evaluate the candidates' legal knowledge and application skills. The examination format includes four papers, featuring a variety of question types such as multiple-choice, case analysis, short-answer, and essay questions.

From 1986 to 2001, during which time China held 12 national unified examinations for lawyer qualifications, approximately 140,000 individuals successfully passed and obtained their licences to practice law.[26]

Concurrently, the profession of notaries also required passing a national qualification examination to standardise and elevate professional standards. The first such national unified examination for notary qualifications was initiated by the Ministry of Justice in 1992.[27] From that year until 2002, four such examinations were systematically organised.[28] These exams were meticulously structured, featuring a unified review syllabus, uniformly prepared examination questions, standardised scoring methods, and a consistent passing threshold across the nation.[29] Individuals who succeeded in these rigorous examinations were awarded a "Notary Qualification Examination Certificate", which was issued by their local justice department, yet produced uniformly by the Ministry of Justice.[30]

In contrast, entry into the judicial branches, such as the courts and the procuratorates, did not necessitate a national unified examination during this period. Instead, these roles were filled through recruitment processes that were independently managed by the judicial and procuratoriial systems. Specifically, the *Judges Law 1995* articulates, in Article 12, that the selection of initial judges and assistant judges should be executed through public examinations and rigorous evaluations, focusing on selecting candidates who excel both in integrity and capability.[31] These candidates were proposed and appointed through formal procedures established by

---

[25] *Regulations on the Lawyer Qualification Examination* (Order No. 61 of the Ministry of Justice, now repealed), Article 16.

[26] See the official WeChat public platform of Shanxi Legal Daily, "Following the 'Legal Exam Road'" published on June 13, 2024, accessed on May 6, 2024.

[27] The Ministry of Justice of China issued *Circular of the Ministry of Justice on the Holding of the 1992 Unified National Qualification Examination for Notaries Public* in 1991.

[28] See the official WeChat public platform of Democracy and Law Weekly, A Look Back: The Changing Years of China's Legal Profession Admission System, published on July 30, 2018, accessed on August 21, 2024.

[29] Circular of the Ministry of Justice on the Holding of the 1992 Unified National Qualification Examination for Notaries Public (1991), Article 1.

[30] Circular of the Ministry of Justice on the Holding of the 1992 Unified National Qualification Examination for Notaries Public (1991), Article 1.

[31] Judges Law (1995), Article 12.

the People's Congress.[32] Similarly, the recruitment of prosecutors is governed by the *Prosecutors Law 1995*. This legislation includes provisions, in Articles 12 and 13, emphasising a stringent selection process for prosecutors. It mandates that aspiring prosecutors undergo a thorough assessment of their qualifications to ensure that only those with the requisite legal expertise and moral integrity were appointed to uphold justice.[33]

Based on the specific legislative provisions set forth earlier, the judicial and prosecutorial systems in China undertook the establishment of examination systems tailored for the recruitment and advancement of entry-level judges and prosecutors. In pursuit of this goal, the court system administered a series of four examinations during the years 1995, 1997, 1998, and 1999.[34] Similarly, the procuratorial system, paralleling this schedule, also organised its set of examinations in the years 1995, 1996, 1998, and 1999.[35] These examinations were specifically designed for internal staff members of the respective systems, aiming to standardise and elevate the qualifications within these critical legal professions.

Each of these examinations included four papers, carefully structured to assess a variety of competencies through both objective and subjective questions.[36] The objective components comprised multiple-choice questions, true/false assessments, and error-correction tasks, designed to evaluate the foundational legal knowledge and quick analytical skills of the candidates.[37] The subjective components, on the other hand, included short-answer questions, material analysis, case analysis, and document-writing tasks.[38] These sections were intended to test the candidates' deeper understanding of legal concepts, their ability to apply this knowledge in practical scenarios, and their proficiency in constructing coherent legal documents.

The examinations for judges covered a somewhat different range of topics compared to the standard bar exams, notably omitting subjects such as international law and private international law, which were less relevant to their everyday judicial functions. Conversely, the focus of the prosecutors' examinations was significantly narrower, primarily centring on criminal law.[39] This focus reflected the primary role of prosecutors in the legal system, underscoring the need for profound knowledge in criminal proceedings, while less emphasis was placed on civil and economic law.[40]

[32] Judges Law (1995), Article 11.

[33] Prosecutors Law (1995), Article 12, Article 13.

[34] See the official WeChat public platform of Democracy and Law Weekly, A Look Back: The Changing Years of China's Legal Profession Admission System, published on July 30, 2018, accessed on August 21, 2024.

[35] See the official WeChat public platform of Democracy and Law Weekly, A Look Back: The Changing Years of China's Legal Profession Admission System, published on July 30, 2018, accessed on August 21, 2024.

[36] Gao and Wen (2020).

[37] Gao and Wen (2020).

[38] Gao and Wen (2020).

[39] Du (2002).

[40] Du (2002).

8.1.2 Judicial Examination Period

As analysed above, the access mode for the bar exam during specific periods for some legal professions did not fundamentally ensure the quality of legal practitioners, nor did it fully guarantee the fairness and justice of the assessment processes. This situation was problematic, as the integrity and reliability of legal professionals are crucial for the effective administration of justice. Additionally, the varied and fragmented nature of the examination systems in place at the time led to significant resource wastage among departments, as each department might have duplicated efforts or operated in isolation without leveraging shared resources or standardised procedures. This inefficiency not only increased costs but also slowed the process towards achieving homogeneity among the legal professions, which is vital for maintaining consistent standards of legal practice across the country.[41] Therefore, establishing a unified judicial examination was deemed necessary.

In July 2000, during the pivotal 16th meeting of the 9th Standing Committee of the National People's Congress, the draft amendments to the *Judges Law 1995* and *Prosecutors Law 1995* were thoroughly reviewed for the first time.[42] During this session, some committee members strongly advocated for the creation of a national unified judicial examination system, highlighting the need for a standardised approach to qualifying legal professionals across the country.[43]

Subsequently, on 30 June 2001, at the 22nd meeting of the 9th National People's Congress, these laws were revisited. After extensive discussions, amendments were made to both laws, introducing a crucial provision that mandated the State to implement a unified judicial system for entry-level judges, entry-level prosecutors, and those qualifying as lawyers.[44] It was stipulated that the Administrative Department of Justice of the State Council would collaborate closely with the Supreme People's Court and the Supreme People's Procuratorate to jointly formulate the implementation measures for this judicial examination.[45] This system was to be administered by the judicial administrative organs of the State Council, ensuring a coordinated and centralised approach to the examination process.

On 31 October of the same year, the Ministry of Justice, in conjunction with the Supreme People's Court and the Supreme People's Procuratorate, officially issued

---

[41] Ding (2008).

[42] "Summary of the Sixteenth Meeting of the Standing Committee of the Ninth National People's Congress." The National People's Congress of China. Accessed May 5, 2024. http://www.npc.gov.cn/zgrdw/npc/cwhhy/content_9521.htm.

[43] "On the Construction of China's Judicial Examination System." China Court website. Accessed May 5, 2024. https://www.chinacourt.org/article/detail/2005/10/id/183011.shtml.

[44] "Summary of the Twenty-second Meeting of the Standing Committee of the Ninth National People's Congress." The National People's Congress of China. Accessed May 5, 2024. http://www.npc.gov.cn/zgrdw/npc/cwhhy/content_141977.htm.

[45] "Summary of the Twenty-second Meeting of the Standing Committee of the Ninth National People's Congress." The National People's Congress of China. Accessed May 5, 2024. http://www.npc.gov.cn/zgrdw/npc/cwhhy/content_141977.htm.

the Interim Measures for the Implementation of the National Judicial Examination.[46] These measures provided the detailed framework and guidelines necessary for conducting the unified examination. Shortly thereafter, on 13 November, the Ministry of Justice announced via a formal notice that the recruitment of notaries would also be included under this unified examination framework, thus expanding its scope.[47] Finally, the comprehensive establishment of the national unified judicial examination system was solidified on 29 December, when the 25th meeting of the 9th Standing Committee of the National People's Congress passed an amendment to the *Lawyers Law 1995*, as proposed by the State Council.[48] This amendment explicitly stated that qualification as a legal professional must be obtained through passing the national unified judicial examination.

With the establishment of this unified system, China set a new standard for the legal profession, ensuring that entry-level judges, prosecutors, notaries, and legal professionals would be preferentially selected from among those who had successfully obtained qualification certificates through this rigorous and comprehensive national examination. This initiative marked a significant reform aimed at standardising the qualifications of legal professionals across the nation, thereby enhancing the effectiveness, fairness, and integrity of the judicial system.

According to the regulations governing the judicial examination in the People's Republic of China, this critical assessment is conducted annually. The specific date for the examination is publicly announced three months prior to its occurrence, ensuring that all prospective applicants have adequate time to prepare and arrange their schedules accordingly.[49] This approach underscores the transparent and organised nature of the examination process, which is integral to maintaining a high standard of fairness and accessibility for all participants.

Applicants who wish to sit the judicial examination must fulfil several stringent criteria to be considered eligible. They must be citizens of the People's Republic of China and demonstrate their support for the Constitution of the People's Republic of China. Additionally, they must possess the right to vote and be elected, indicating their active participation and standing in civic life. Full civil capacity is another prerequisite, ensuring that the applicants have the legal ability to engage in civil

[46] "A Brief Introduction to the National Judicial Examination System." China Court website. Accessed May 5, 2024. https://www.chinacourt.org/article/detail/2003/01/id/32842.shtml.

[47] Circular of the Ministry of Justice on the Recruitment of Notaries from among those who have passed the State Judicial Examination (2001).

[48] "Summary of the Twenty-fifth Meeting of the Standing Committee of the Ninth National People's Congress." The National People's Congress of China. Accessed May 5, 2024. http://www.npc.gov.cn/zgrdw/npc/cwhhy/content_282874.htm.

[49] See Article 7 of the 'Implementation Measures for the National Judicial Examination,' published on the website of the National Judicial Examination Center, Ministry of Justice, accessed on May 6, 2024.

conduct without any restrictions.[50] Importantly, the regulations stipulate that applicants must meet specific educational and professional qualifications as outlined in the *Judges Law 2011*, *Prosecutors Law 2001*, and *Lawyers Law 2001*, and they must also exhibit good moral character, which is essential for upholding the ethics and integrity required in the judicial profession.[51]

Elaborating on the "educational and professional qualifications" required, the regulations, as per the *Judges Law 2011*, *Prosecutors Law 2001*, and *Lawyers Law 2001*, specify that applicants must first possess at least a bachelor's degree in law from a recognised higher education institution.[52] Alternatively, they can hold a bachelor's degree in another major, provided they have acquired sufficient legal professional knowledge to competently fulfil the responsibilities of the role.[53] Additionally, in recognition of varying regional educational opportunities and resources, the Ministry of Justice, in consultation with the Supreme People's Court and the Supreme People's Procuratorate, has established principles and opinions that allow for some flexibility in these educational requirements. Specifically, in regions where it is exceptionally challenging to meet the standard educational prerequisites, the regulations permit the relaxation of these requirements to an associate degree in law from a higher education institution.[54] This relaxation is allowed for a designated period, acknowledging the disparities in educational access and aiming to promote inclusivity while maintaining the professional standards essential for the legal system.

To ensure the utmost fairness and impartiality in the evaluation of prospective legal professionals, the judicial examination employs a rigorous and uniform set of questions, which are derived from the National Judicial Examination Syllabus.[55] This syllabus is meticulously formulated and published by the Ministry of Justice to guarantee that all candidates are tested under equitable conditions.[56] The examination is conducted as a closed-book exam, which means that candidates are not permitted to refer to any external materials during the test.[57] Additionally, a uniform national marking scheme is applied to ensure that the assessment of candidates' responses is

---

[50] See Article 15 of the 'Implementation Measures for the National Judicial Examination,' published on the website of the National Judicial Examination Center, Ministry of Justice, accessed on May 6, 2024.

[51] See Article 9 of the 'Judges Law' (2011), Article 10 of the 'Procurators Law' (2001), and Article 6 of the 'Lawyers Law' (2001).

[52] See Article 9 of the 'Judges Law' (2011), Article 10 of the 'Procurators Law' (2001), and Article 6 of the 'Lawyers Law' (2001).

[53] See Article 9 of the 'Judges Law' (2011), Article 10 of the 'Procurators Law' (2001), and Article 6 of the 'Lawyers Law' (2001).

[54] See Article 9 of the 'Judges Law' (2011), Article 10 of the 'Procurators Law' (2001), and Article 6 of the 'Lawyers Law' (2001).

[55] See Article 8 of the 'Measures for the Implementation of the National Judicial Examination (Trial)' (2001).

[56] See Article 8 of the 'Measures for the Implementation of the National Judicial Examination (Trial)' (2001).

[57] See Article 9 of the 'Measures for the Implementation of the National Judicial Examination (Trial)' (2001).

consistent across the board, thereby upholding the integrity and standardisation of the examination process.[58]

The judicial examination is primarily designed to evaluate the candidates' legal knowledge and their practical capabilities in the legal professions. The content of the exam is comprehensive, covering areas such as theoretical jurisprudence, which delves into the philosophical and conceptual foundations of law; applied jurisprudence, focusing on the application of legal theories to real-world situations; current legal regulations, ensuring candidates are up-to-date with the latest laws and statutes; legal practice, which tests the practical skills necessary for the daily workings of legal professions; and legal professional ethics, which assesses the candidates' understanding of ethical standards in the legal field.[59]

Candidates are required to complete four papers during the examination: three objective papers that include various types of questions such as multiple choice, true/false, and fill-in-the-blanks, and one paper dedicated to case analysis.[60] This structure is intended to test a broad spectrum of skills from basic recall of facts to complex analytical abilities. The examination spans two days, demanding a high level of endurance and comprehensive preparation from each participant.[61]

In the initial years following the establishment of the judicial examination, specifically in 2002 and 2003, each paper was scored out of a maximum of 100 points.[62] However, from 2004, the Ministry of Justice adjusted the scoring system, increasing the maximum points for each paper to 150.[63] Consequently, the passing mark was also raised from the original 240 points to 360 points. This change was introduced to better reflect the depth and breadth of understanding required from candidates, aligning the scoring with the heightened expectations and standards of legal expertise expected from future legal practitioners.

By the year 2017, the Ministry of Justice in China had successfully organised and implemented a total of 16 annual judicial examinations since the system's inception. This rigorous process saw a significant increase in participation over the years, with the number of candidates rising substantially from 360,000 in the inaugural 2002 examination, to an impressive 646,000 by 2017.[64] This growth not only reflects the

[58] See Article 10 of the 'Measures for the Implementation of the National Judicial Examination (Trial)' (2001).

[59] The content of the examination subjects is fixed every year, as can be seen from the examination circulars issued by the Ministry of Justice of China every year.

[60] The specific types of questions for each examination are known from the examination circulars issued annually by the Ministry of Justice.

[61] The duration of the examination is fixed every year, and the exact date is known from the examination circular issued by the Ministry of Justice every year.

[62] See 'Circular of the Ministry of Justice on the Preparation of the National Judicial Examination in 2002' (2001), and 'Circular of the Ministry of Justice on the Preparation of the National Judicial Examination in 2003' (2002).

[63] See 'Circular of the Ministry of Justice on the Preparation of the National Judicial Examination in 2004' (2003).

[64] Refer to the Ministry of Justice of the People's Republic of China website, https://www.moj.gov.cn, accessed May 8, 2024.

rising interest and demand for legal careers in China but also highlights the expanding accessibility and recognition of the judicial examination as a crucial gateway for aspiring legal professionals.

Among the vast pool of candidates who successfully passed the examination over these years, nearly half found themselves engaged in various key legal professions.[65] This included roles such as judges, who are essential for the fair and effective administration of justice; prosecutors, who play a critical role in upholding the law and public order; lawyers, who provide necessary legal representation and advice to the public; and notaries, who ensure the legality and authenticity of documents.[66] The successful integration of these individuals into such pivotal positions demonstrates the examination's effectiveness in qualifying competent and ethical legal professionals who are prepared to contribute significantly to the judicial system.

8.1.3 Legal Examination Period

The Fourth Plenary Session of the 18th Central Committee of the Communist Party of China, held at a critical juncture in the country's legal reform trajectory, proposed a significant enhancement to the existing judicial examination framework.[67] This proposal was aimed at "improving the National Unified Legal Professional Qualification Examination system", and it set the stage for substantial reforms that would reshape the way legal professionals are qualified in China. This initiative underscored the Party's commitment to strengthening the rule of law by ensuring a high calibre of practitioners across the legal system.

In response to this directive from the Plenary Session, in December 2015, the General Office of the Communist Party of China along with the General Office of the State Council took a decisive step forward by issuing the "Opinions on Improving the National Unified Legal Professional Qualification System".[68] This pivotal document proposed a significant adjustment: transforming the existing judicial examination into a broader, more inclusive National Unified Legal Professional Qualification

---

[65] See the official WeChat public platform of Ministry of Justice of China, Responsible comrade of the Ministry of Justice answered reporters' questions on the Measures for the Implementation of the National Unified Legal Profession Qualification Examination, published on April 29, 2018, accessed on accessed May 8, 2024.

[66] See the official WeChat public platform of Ministry of Justice of China, Responsible comrade of the Ministry of Justice answered reporters' questions on the Measures for the Implementation of the National Unified Legal Profession Qualification Examination, published on April 29, 2018, accessed on accessed May 8, 2024.

[67] Decision of the Central Committee of the Communist Party of China on Several Major Issues Concerning the Comprehensive Promotion of the Rule of Law in China (2014).

[68] Refer to the Central Government Portal of the People's Republic of China website, https://www.gov.cn/xinwen/2015-12/20/content_5025966.htm, accessed May 10, 2024.

Examination.[69] This change was designed to streamline the qualification process and ensure a standardised assessment mechanism across all legal professions, thereby enhancing the integrity, accessibility, and quality of legal services nationwide.

After extensive planning, consultations, and preparatory work that spanned more than three years, the Ministry of Justice achieved a major milestone. In April 2018, it published the "Implementation Measures for the National Unified Legal Professional Qualification Examination"[70] (hereinafter referred to as the Measures). These Measures detailed the operational aspects, scope, and procedures of the revamped examination system, marking the official commencement of a new era in the legal examination framework. This updated system was not merely a procedural update but represented a foundational shift towards a more integrated and unified approach to assessing and certifying legal professionals in China.

In June 2018, a significant step was taken by the Ministry of Justice with the release of the "2018 National Unified Legal Professional Qualification Examination Announcement".[71] The examination was structured to comprehensively assess the aptitude and knowledge of prospective legal professionals through both objective and subjective components, ensuring a balanced evaluation of theoretical knowledge and practical application.[72]

The objective part of the examination was scheduled to take place over the course of a single day, divided into two sessions—morning and afternoon.[73] Each session was designed to challenge the candidates with 100 multiple-choice questions,[74] allowing them to demonstrate their quick reasoning and knowledge under time constraints. The objective papers were each allotted a duration of 180 min and were capped at a maximum score of 150 points,[75] reflecting the depth and complexity of the questions posed.

In addition to the core subjects traditionally covered in the previous judicial examination—such as constitutional law, civil law, criminal law, and procedural law—the 2018 examination syllabus introduced new areas of focus.[76] Notably, environmental

---

[69] See the Opinions on Improving the National Unified Legal Professional Qualification System (2015).

[70] Refer to the Central Government Portal of the People's Republic of China website, https://www.gov.cn/gongbao/content/2018/content_5341398.htm, accessed May 10, 2024.

[71] Refer to the Ministry of Justice of the People's Republic of China website, https://new.moj.gov.cn/pub/sfbgw/jgsz/jgszzsdw/zsdwgjsfkszx/gjsfksgatzq/201806/t20180608_172270.html, accessed May 10, 2024.

[72] See the Article 8 of Measures for the Implementation of the National Unified Legal Profession Qualification Examination (2018).

[73] The timetable for the examination can be found in the annual examination bulletin of the Ministry of Justice of China.

[74] The type of questions on the exam can be found in the annual examination bulletin of the Ministry of Justice of China.

[75] The time limit for the examination can be found in the annual examination bulletin of the Ministry of Justice of China.

[76] See Announcement of the Ministry of Justice No. 181—Announcement of the 2018 National Unified Legal Profession Qualification Examination (2018).

resource law and intellectual property law were added to the curriculum,[77] signifying a response to the evolving legal landscape and the increasing importance of these areas in global and national contexts. This expansion in the syllabus was indicative of the examination's aim to equip legal professionals with a broader range of knowledge to address contemporary legal challenges effectively.

The subjective part of the examination remained largely consistent with the format of the previous judicial examination, designed to test candidates' abilities to analyse complex legal materials and articulate their arguments effectively.[78] This part of the exam required deep analytical skills, and the ability to construct well-founded responses based on scenarios and case studies similar to those they would encounter in professional practice.

By 2019, the structure of the National Unified Legal Professional Qualification Examination had evolved through several refinements, culminating in a relatively stable pattern that is currently utilised. This structured approach to the examination is deliberately designed to assess the comprehensive capabilities of candidates in a phased manner, ensuring that only the most proficient individuals progress through each stage of the assessment.

The examination is meticulously divided into two distinct stages.[79] The first stage consists of objective questions, which candidates must pass in order to advance to the second stage.[80] This progression criteria ensures that those who reach the subjective portion of the examination have demonstrated a requisite level of knowledge and aptitude in applying legal principles in a structured format. The objective questions are administered via a computer-based testing format, adhering to a closed-book policy.[81] This format is intended to evaluate candidates' immediate recall and understanding of legal facts and principles without the aid of external materials, thereby testing the candidates' foundational legal knowledge under controlled conditions.

Upon successful completion of the objective questions, candidates are allowed to proceed to the second stage, which involves answering subjective questions. This part of the examination allows for a deeper evaluation of the candidates' analytical skills and their ability to apply legal knowledge to complex scenarios. Unlike the objective section, during the subjective questions examination, candidates are permitted to access electronic versions of legal statutes within the answering system. This adjustment reflects the real-world conditions under which legal professionals operate, where access to legal resources is essential for thorough analysis and decision-making.

---

[77] See Announcement of the Ministry of Justice No. 181—Announcement of the 2018 National Unified Legal Profession Qualification Examination (2018).

[78] The exams in both periods contain case study questions, legal writing questions, and expository questions.

[79] See Announcement of the Ministry of Justice No. 4—Announcement of the 2024 National Unified Legal Profession Qualification Examination (2024).

[80] See Announcement of the Ministry of Justice No. 4—Announcement of the 2024 National Unified Legal Profession Qualification Examination (2024).

[81] See Announcement of the Ministry of Justice No. 4—Announcement of the 2024 National Unified Legal Profession Qualification Examination (2024).

Furthermore, recognising the diverse needs of all candidates, the examination system is designed with inclusivity in mind. Candidates who face challenges in using computers due to physical impairments or age-related reasons have the option to request the use of paper and pencil to complete the subjective questions.[82] This accommodation ensures that all candidates, regardless of their proficiency with technology, are provided with a fair opportunity to demonstrate their legal acumen.

This dual-stage, computer-based examination format, with accommodations for accessing legal statutes and alternative answering methods, has established a rigorous yet fair assessment process.

The objective examination consists of two papers.[83] Each paper contains 100 questions, both valued at 150 points each.[84] Single-choice questions account for 50 questions at one point each, while multiple-choice and indefinite-choice questions account for 50 questions at two points each, bringing the total possible score for both papers to 300 points.[85] Paper One specifically examines legal ideology, jurisprudence, the Constitution, Chinese legal history, international law, the judicial system, and legal professional ethics, criminal law, criminal procedure law, administrative law, and administrative litigation law; Paper Two examines civil law, intellectual property law, commercial law, economic law, environmental and resource law, labour and social security law, private international law, international economic law, and civil procedure law.[86] The passing score for the objective questions is valid within the year of the examination and the following examination year.[87]

The subjective examination consists of one paper, including case analysis, legal document drafting, and essay questions, with a total score of 180 points.[88] It specifically assesses legal ideology, jurisprudence, the Constitution, criminal law, criminal procedure law, civil law, commercial law, civil procedure law (including arbitration system), administrative law and administrative litigation law, judicial system, and legal professional ethics.[89] In the subjective examination, optional questions are provided, allowing candidates to choose between commercial law and administrative law and administrative litigation law.

---

[82] See Announcement of the Ministry of Justice No. 4—Announcement of the 2024 National Unified Legal Profession Qualification Examination (2024).

[83] Measures for the Implementation of the National Unified Legal Profession Qualification Examination (2018), Article 13.

[84] See Announcement of the Ministry of Justice No. 4—Announcement of the 2024 National Unified Legal Profession Qualification Examination (2024).

[85] See Announcement of the Ministry of Justice No. 4—Announcement of the 2024 National Unified Legal Profession Qualification Examination (2024).

[86] See Announcement of the Ministry of Justice No. 4—Announcement of the 2024 National Unified Legal Profession Qualification Examination (2024).

[87] Measures for the Implementation of the National Unified Legal Profession Qualification Examination (2018), Article 13.

[88] See Announcement of the Ministry of Justice No. 4—Announcement of the 2024 National Unified Legal Profession Qualification Examination (2024).

[89] See Announcement of the Ministry of Justice No. 4—Announcement of the 2024 National Unified Legal Profession Qualification Examination (2024).

Compared to the previous judicial examinations, the current legal examination has three major changes.

One of the most notable changes is the expansion in the range of personnel required to obtain legal professional qualifications. Previously, the examination was primarily targeted at four specific categories of legal professionals: judges, prosecutors, lawyers, and notaries.[90] However, under the current framework, as detailed in Article 2 of the "Implementation Measures for the National Unified Legal Professional Qualification Examination", the scope has been significantly widened to nine categories. This expansion now encompasses individuals serving as legal arbitrators and civil servants who are engaged initially in reviewing administrative penalty decisions, administrative reconsiderations, administrative adjudications, and providing legal consultations.[91] This broadening of the scope is intended to encapsulate a more extensive array of legal functions and responsibilities, ensuring that a greater diversity of key legal roles are staffed by individuals who have met rigorous qualification standards.

Secondly, there has been a substantive elevation in the entry requirements for candidates wishing to register for the exam. During the period when the judicial examination was in place, the registration requirements were comparatively lenient. Individuals possessing associate degrees or non-full-time undergraduate degrees could participate under certain conditions, allowing a broader range of candidates to enter the legal profession.[92] In contrast, the new legal examination has tightened these prerequisites, now requiring candidates to possess at least a full-time ordinary higher education undergraduate degree and a bachelor's degree or higher.[93] Additionally, candidates holding a Bachelor of Laws, Master of Laws, or higher law degrees are eligible to participate in the examination without needing any work experience.[94] In contrast, those without such degrees must have at least three years of legal work experience to qualify for registration. This shift underscores a move towards enhancing the academic and professional standards among new entrants to the legal field, aiming to raise the calibre of practice and expertise within the profession.[95]

---

[90] See Measures for the Implementation of the National Unified Legal Profession Qualification Examination (2018), Article 2.

[91] "Article 2: The National Unified Legal Profession Qualification Examination is a national examination organised to select qualified legal professionals.

Those assuming the positions of junior judges, junior prosecutors, applying for lawyer or notary public practice, or serving as legal arbitrators for the first time, as well as civil servants engaging in administrative penalty decision review, administrative reconsideration, administrative adjudication, or legal advisory roles for the first time, must pass the National Unified Legal Profession Qualification Examination to obtain legal professional qualifications.

Except as otherwise provided by laws or administrative regulations."

[92] See Measures for the Implementation of the National Judicial Examination (Trial) (2001), Article 13.

[93] See Measures for the Implementation of the National Unified Legal Profession Qualification Examination (2018), Article 9.

[94] See Measures for the Implementation of the National Unified Legal Profession Qualification Examination (2018), Article 9.

[95] Zhang (2022).

Lastly, the format of the examination itself has undergone a transformation. Previously, the judicial examination comprised four papers—including three objective papers and one case analysis paper—conducted over two consecutive days.[96] The legal examination has adapted this format by increasing the proportion of case analysis questions, reflecting a shift towards evaluating candidates' practical and analytical skills more heavily. Furthermore, the examination has been divided into two distinct stages: objective and subjective, allowing for a more nuanced assessment of candidates' knowledge and application skills in legal contexts.[97]

These changes collectively represent a significant evolution in the approach to qualifying legal professionals in China, aiming to enhance the legal system's integrity, capability, and responsiveness to contemporary legal challenges.

Since its establishment, the National Unified Legal Professional Qualification Examination has been administered six times, witnessing a steady increase in participant numbers over the years.[98] Initially, in 2018, the examination attracted 473,000 candidates, a significant turnout that highlighted the demand for legal qualifications.[99] This number slightly decreased in 2019 to 470,000 participants but rebounded strongly in 2020 to 545,000 candidates, indicating sustained interest in legal careers despite various external challenges.[100]

The trend continued upwards in 2021, with an impressive 718,000 individuals registering for the exam,[101] showcasing a growing recognition of the legal profession's value and the increasing appeal of a legal career in China's evolving job market. Over these years, the pass rates also demonstrated considerable growth: starting with 120,000 successful candidates in 2018,[102] increasing to 129,000 in 2019,[103] then to 162,000 in 2020,[104] and reaching 169,000 in 2021.[105] These figures reflect not only

---

96 Gao and Wen (2020).

97 See Measures for the Implementation of the National Unified Legal Profession Qualification Examination (2018), Article 13.

98 The national unified legal professional qualification examination is held every year and there has been six years since 2018.

99 Refer to the Ministry of Justice of the People's Republic of China website, https://www.moj.gov.cn/pub/sfbgw/qmyfzg/fzgzzffz/fzzfndbg/202104/t20210401_351314.htm, accessed May 10, 2024.

100 Refer to the Ministry of Justice of the People's Republic of China website, https://www.moj.gov.cn, accessed May 10, 2024.

101 Refer to the Ministry of Justice of the People's Republic of China website, https://www.moj.gov.cn/pub/sfbgw/gwxw/xwyw/202203/t20220330_451784.htm, accessed May 10, 2024.

102 Refer to the Ministry of Justice of the People's Republic of China website, https://www.moj.gov.cn/pub/sfbgw/qmyfzg/fzgzzffz/fzzfndbg/202104/t20210401_351314.htm, accessed May 10, 2024.

103 Refer to the Ministry of Justice of the People's Republic of China website, https://www.moj.gov.cn/pub/sfbgw/qmyfzg/fzgzzffz/fzzfndbg/202003/t20200323_351313.htm, accessed May 10, 2024.

104 Refer to the Ministry of Justice of the People's Republic of China website, https://www.moj.gov.cn/pub/sfbgw/qmyfzg/fzgzzffz/fzzfndbg/202103/t20210326_351312.html, accessed May 10, 2024.

105 Refer to the Ministry of Justice of the People's Republic of China website, https://www.moj.gov.cn/pub/sfbgw/gwxw/xwyw/202203/t20220330_451784.htm, accessed May 10, 2024.

the expanding pool of candidates but also the rigorous standards maintained by the examination process.[106]

8.2 The Lawyer Profession

With the reform of the national judicial examination into the National Unified Legal Professional Qualification Examination, a profound impact has been made on the access to legal professions. Lawyers, as one of the most representative professions, have also taken on a new role in today's rule of law system. "Strive to let the people feel fairness and justice in every judicial case",[107] is a demand put forward at the National Central Conference on Comprehensively Governing the Country According to Law. The involvement of lawyers in each judicial case helps make fairness and justice more tangible and accessible.

8.2.1 Job Description

A lawyer is a professionally qualified individual who, after legally obtaining a lawyer's practice certificate through appropriate channels, is appointed or designated to offer a variety of legal services to clients.[108] As an essential member of the legal services team, a lawyer's role is multifaceted and extends to various areas of law. They are engaged, not only in accepting commissions to act as legal advisers, agents, or defenders, but also in representing clients across diverse litigation cases, engaging in mediation and arbitration processes, providing a breadth of non-litigation legal services, and skilfully drafting legal documents tailored to client needs.[109]

When functioning as a legal adviser, a lawyer's responsibilities are comprehensive. They are expected to provide well-grounded opinions on legal issues in accordance with the agreements made with their clients.[110] This involves drafting and meticulously reviewing legal documents to ensure they meet legal standards and serve the client's interests.[111]

---

[106] Data are referenced from the *Ministry of Justice Annual Reports on the Construction of the Rule of Law Government* for the years 2018, 2019, 2020, 2021, and 2022. The *Ministry of Justice 2023 Annual Report on the Construction of the Rule of Law Government* did not mention data related to the 2022 legal examination.

[107] "Xi Jinping: Strive to make people feel fairness and justice in every judicial case." People's Daily Online. Accessed May 10, 2024. http://politics.people.com.cn/n/2013/0224/c70731-20581921.html.

[108] *Lawyers Law* (Amended 2017), Article 2.

[109] *Lawyers Law* (Amended 2017), Article 28.

[110] Zhao (2005).

[111] Zhao (2005).

Additionally, lawyers represent clients in various legal proceedings, including litigation, mediation, or arbitration, effectively navigating the complexities of each forum to advocate for their client's position.[112] They are tasked with managing any other legal matters that clients entrust to them, which requires a broad understanding of legal principles and the ability to apply them in practical scenarios.

In the role of a defender, a lawyer adopts a slightly different set of responsibilities. They must gather, present materials, and articulate opinions that advocate for the innocence of their client, or argue for a reduction or exemption from criminal responsibility.[113] This advocacy is based on a careful analysis of the facts and a sound interpretation of the law, aiming to ensure the fairest possible outcome for the client under the legal system.[114]

In summary, regardless of the type of services a lawyer provides, they should always protect the lawful rights and interests of their clients or principals.[115]

8.2.2 Professional Requirements

To guarantee that lawyers deliver high-quality legal services, they are held to rigorous standards that are established by a combination of legal norms, the broader industry ecosystem, and specific regulations imposed by law firms. These standards are designed to foster professionalism, ethical conduct, and competence among lawyers. Legal norms provide a foundational framework that outlines the ethical and professional behaviour expected of lawyers. The industry ecosystem, which includes bar associations and legal professional bodies, also plays a crucial role in maintaining high standards within the legal profession. Additionally, specific regulations set forth by individual law firms further tailor these standards to fit particular organisational contexts and specialisations. Together, these layers of standards and regulations ensure that lawyers are well-equipped to handle legal matters effectively and ethically, providing their clients with services that are not only competent but also delivered with the highest degree of professionalism.

8.2.2.1 Legal Requirements

To become a lawyer and engage in related activities, one must obtain a lawyer's practice licence.[116] Individuals who do not have a lawyer's practice certificate are not allowed to provide legal services under the name of a lawyer; unless otherwise specified by law, they are also not permitted to engage in litigation representation

[112] *Lawyers Law* (Amended 2017), no. 30.

[113] Chen (1994).

[114] Chen (1994).

[115] Zhou and Liu (2008).

[116] *Lawyers Law* (Amended 2017), Article 13.

or defence.[117] Applying for a lawyer's licence requires meeting certain conditions, as stipulated in China's "Lawyers Law" and "Measures for the Administration of Lawyer Practice": First, applicants for lawyer practice must possess good political integrity and support the Constitution of the People's Republic of China.[118] Second, applicants must pass the National Unified Legal Professional Qualification Exam to obtain legal professional qualifications.[119] Prior to the implementation of the National Unified Legal Professional Qualification Exam, an applicant who had obtained a National Unified Judicial Examination Certificate or Lawyer Qualification Certificate had the same capacity as provided by a National Unified Legal Professional Qualification Certificate. Third, applicants must complete a one-year internship at a law firm.[120] Fourth, applicants must possess good personal character.[121] In summary, individuals applying for a lawyer's licence should possess good political integrity, robust legal knowledge, and appropriate moral character. After completing a year of internship activities organised by the Bar Association as required, and passing the Bar Association's assessment, they can become practising lawyers. In addition to meeting the above conditions, applicants for a lawyer's licence must also have full civil capacity; must not have been subjected to criminal punishment, other than for negligence; and must not have been dismissed from public office or had their lawyer or notary licences revoked.[122] Additionally, practising lawyers must not hold the status of civil servants.[123] Personnel engaged in legal education and research at higher education institutions and scientific research institutions, who meet the above conditions and with the consent of their respective institutions, may apply for part-time legal practice in accordance with legal procedures.[124]

During their professional practice, lawyers are obligated to adhere strictly to the Constitution and laws, embodying the ethics and discipline integral to the legal profession.[125] They must conduct their practice in a manner that is legal, honest, and thoroughly professional, holding themselves to the highest standards of integrity and fairness.[126] Lawyers are expected to anchor their work in factual evidence, using the law as their guiding criterion, and must be open to scrutiny and supervision from the State, society, and their clients, ensuring transparency and accountability in all their legal dealings.[127]

---

[117] *Lawyers Law* (Amended 2017), Article 13.
[118] *Lawyers Law* (Amended 2017), Article 5.
[119] *Lawyers Law* (Amended 2017), Article 5.
[120] *Lawyers Law* (Amended 2017), Article 5.
[121] *Lawyers Law* (Amended 2017), Article 5.
[122] *Lawyers Law* (Amended 2017), Article 7.
[123] *Lawyers Law* (Amended 2017), Article 11.
[124] *Lawyers Law* (Amended 2017), Article 12.
[125] *Lawyers Law* (Amended 2017), Article 3.
[126] *Lawyers Law* (Amended 2017), Article 3.
[127] *Lawyers Law* (Amended 2017), Article 3.

Firstly, lawyers are strictly prohibited from engaging in any activities that could potentially violate the lawful rights and interests of their clients or that could undermine the integrity of the judicial process.[128] Upholding judicial fairness and justice is paramount, and any actions contrary to these principles are unacceptable. Lawyers must avoid exploiting their role to seek undue benefits for their clients. This includes not accepting any form of remuneration or benefits from the opposing parties,[129] as such actions could compromise the lawyer's objectivity and the trust placed in them.

Secondly, it is critical for lawyers to refrain from any form of collusion that could harm their clients' interests.[130] Malicious collusion with opposing parties or third parties is expressly forbidden, as it undermines the legal and ethical standards expected of legal practitioners.

Thirdly, lawyers are also required to adhere to strict regulations concerning interactions with judges, prosecutors, arbitrators, and other relevant personnel involved in the legal process.[131] Engaging in unauthorised meetings or communications with such individuals could lead to conflicts of interest and could compromise the fairness of the legal proceedings.

8.2.2.2 Industry Requirements

The All-China Lawyers Association, commonly referred to as the National Lawyers Association, serves as a pivotal national self-regulatory organisation for the legal profession in China.[132] This association plays a critical role in managing and overseeing the professional conduct and standards within the legal community. As part of its mandate, the National Lawyers Association is instrumental in legally administering various aspects of the legal profession, ensuring that practises and behaviours align with established legal norms and ethical standards.

Given that lawyers in China are required to complete a one-year internship at a law firm prior to applying for a practice licence,[133] this period is not only a preparatory stage but also a critical juncture that significantly shapes the capabilities and professional demeanour of future lawyers. Interns are, in many ways, the burgeoning reserve force of the legal profession, and their training, conduct, and professional development during this phase are crucial to the overall health and future prospects of the legal industry.

Recognising the importance of this formative stage, the National Lawyers Association has put forth a series of industry rules and norms specifically designed to guide both interns aspiring to practise law and those already practising. These regulations

[128] See *Lawyers Law* (Amended 2017), Article 40.

[129] *Lawyers Law* (Amended 2017), Article 40.

[130] *Lawyers Law* (Amended 2017), Article 40.

[131] *Lawyers Law* (Amended 2017), Article 40.

[132] Refer to All China Lawyers Association website, https://www.acla.org.cn/, Accessed on June 1, 2024.

[133] *Lawyers Law* (Amended 2017), Article 5.

are meticulously crafted to refine the entry system into the lawyer industry and to ensure a standardised approach to the training and professional growth of interns.

This structured approach helps maintain the integrity of the legal profession by ensuring that new entrants are not only well-prepared in terms of knowledge and skills, but are also aligned with the ethical and professional standards expected of practising lawyers. By establishing and enforcing these rules and norms, the National Lawyers Association plays a crucial role in safeguarding the quality and reputation of the legal profession, fostering a legal environment that is competent, ethical, and capable of upholding justice effectively.

Unlike the broader stipulations in the *Lawyers Law*, the "Management Rules for Interns Applying for Lawyer Practise"[134] outline the criteria for "good conduct" in more specific terms. The rules detail several conditions under which applicants are deemed not to meet the "good conduct" requirement. These include having received criminal penalties for intentional crimes; having been dismissed from public office; and having been dismissed by State organisations or public institutions for violations of laws or discipline.[135] Additionally, those who have been subjected to party disciplinary actions involving removal from party positions or higher, those whose lawyer or notary practice certificates have been revoked, and those who have had other professional qualifications revoked or practice certificates suspended due to legal or regulatory violations also fail to meet the standard.[136] Furthermore, applicants who have been administratively detained for violating public security; identified as subjects of joint-credit punishment for serious, dishonest behaviours and included in the national credit information sharing platform; or those who have been punished with a prohibition on reapplying for an internship, with the penalty period yet unexpired, are disqualified.[137] Additionally, applicants who have engaged in other behaviours that result in a severe adverse social impact are considered not to meet the "good conduct" criteria. However, exceptions are made for certain circumstances—they may still qualify if the third, fourth, sixth, seventh, and tenth conditions occurred before the applicant turned 18 years of age, or more than three years prior to the internship registration and the applicant has shown genuine corrective behaviour.[138] In such cases, the applicant must submit a written commitment and relevant proof materials.[139] These submissions are then reviewed and potentially approved by a special committee established by the Lawyers Association, thereby allowing the applicant to proceed with the internship registration.[140]

The Code of Conduct for Lawyer Practice (Trial Implementation) establishes a comprehensive framework that governs the professional behaviour of lawyers,

---

[134] The document was amended at the nineteenth meeting of the Executive Council of the Ninth China Law Society in 2021.

[135] Management Rules for Interns Applying for Lawyer Practice (2021), Article 6.

[136] Management Rules for Interns Applying for Lawyer Practice (2021), Article 6.

[137] Management Rules for Interns Applying for Lawyer Practice (2021), Article 6.

[138] Management Rules for Interns Applying for Lawyer Practice (2021), Article 6.

[139] Management Rules for Interns Applying for Lawyer Practice (2021), Article 6.

[140] Management Rules for Interns Applying for Lawyer Practice (2021), Article 6.

outlining standards for their conduct in various aspects of their practice. This code addresses key areas including basic behaviour norms, business promotion activities, and involvement in litigation or arbitration processes. It also clarifies the ethical boundaries concerning the relationships between lawyers and their clients, or other parties involved in legal proceedings.

Firstly, a critical aspect defined by the code is the agency relationship between lawyers and their clients, where it stipulates clear guidelines to prevent any misconduct.[141] It explicitly prohibits lawyers from making false promises to clients, which could mislead or misinform them about the prospects of their legal matters.[142] Secondly, the code forbids lawyers from profiting illegally from the interests of their clients, ensuring that all financial dealings are conducted transparently and ethically.[143] Thirdly, there is a strict requirement for the safekeeping of client property, mandating that lawyers must handle client assets and documents with the utmost care and responsibility, safeguarding them against loss, damage, or misuse.[144]

The code also explicitly emphasises the importance of mutual respect and cooperation among lawyers.[145] It encourages a professional environment where lawyers work collaboratively and supportively, avoiding any forms of improper competition which could undermine the integrity of the legal profession. Such competition is expressly prohibited, promoting a culture of fair and ethical professional practices.

Furthermore, the Code of Conduct extends to cover the relationships between lawyers and their respective law firms or bar associations.[146] Lawyers are expected to adhere to the norms and rules set by the Bar Association, which governs the overall legal profession.[147] These associations play a pivotal role in the continuous professional development of lawyers by organising mandatory training sessions and assessments that lawyers must participate in and complete.[148] In addition to training provided by bar associations, lawyers are also subject to education, management, and supervision by the law firms to which they belong.[149] Law firms are responsible for enforcing the code's stipulations within their operations, ensuring that their lawyers, not only comply with external regulations, but also adhere to internal standards and practices.

141 Code of Conduct for the Practice of Lawyers (Trial) (2018), Chapter 4.

142 Code of Conduct for the Practice of Lawyers (Trial) (2018), Chapter 4, Section 2.

143 Code of Conduct for the Practice of Lawyers (Trial) (2018), Chapter 4, Section 3.

144 Code of Conduct for the Practice of Lawyers (Trial) (2018), Chapter 4, Section 5.

145 Code of Conduct for the Practice of Lawyers (Trial) (2018), Article 73.

146 Code of Conduct for the Practice of Lawyers (Trial) (2018), Chapter 6, Chapter 7 and Chapter 8.

147 Code of Conduct for the Practice of Lawyers (Trial) (2018), Article 98.

148 Code of Conduct for the Practice of Lawyers (Trial) (2018), Article 99.

149 Code of Conduct for the Practice of Lawyers (Trial) (2018), Article 86.

8.2.2.3 Job Requirements

In the realm of legal practice, aside from adhering to legal statutes and industry norms, law firms hold distinct expectations for lawyers who specialise in various fields. These expectations largely hinge on the respective law firms' interpretations and approaches to legal work. Consequently, there are diverse requirements concerning the amount of work experience and depth of knowledge that attorneys must possess in different practice areas. Nevertheless, despite these differences, there tends to be a significant degree of uniformity in the core qualifications and capabilities that law firms generally require from their legal practitioners.

As seen in Table 8.1, the common requirements for lawyers at some well-known domestic law firms are as follows. First, lawyers should have attended and graduated from well-known law schools domestically or internationally, with most positions requiring a master's degree or higher. However, for lawyers engaged in intellectual-property-related services, there is a demand for additional qualifications in life sciences, computer science, communications, electrical engineering, mechanical engineering, or other relevant fields at the master's level or higher. Second, lawyers need to have solid legal knowledge, pass the National Unified Legal Professional Qualification Exam, or possess a lawyer's professional qualification certificate, and have a sufficient understanding and knowledge reserve in their field of practice. Third, lawyers should have strong English-language skills in listening, speaking, reading, and writing to meet the needs of international business. Fourth, it is preferable for lawyers to have two to three years of work experience in a specific area of practice, with higher requirements for lead lawyers or senior lawyers in terms of experience. Fifth, lawyers should have good communication skills, learning ability, and team-collaboration skills, and specific positions may also require leadership abilities, client-management skills, and business acumen. Sixth, it is beneficial for lawyers to have good physical health, resilience, and the ability to adapt to a fast-paced work environment and high work pressure.

8.2.3 Industry Status

Lawyers are one of the most common career choices for graduates with a degree in law. According to statistics released by China's Ministry of Justice, as of the end of 2022, there were over 651,600 practising lawyers and more than 38,600 law firms nationwide.[150] There were over 13,000 grassroots legal service institutions and over 56,000 grassroots legal service workers.[151] Compared to 2021, the number of

---

150 Zhang Liqing: "Statistical Analysis of Lawyers and Grassroots Legal Services Work in 2022," on *Ministry of Justice Website*, Accessed April 5, 2024. http://www.moj.gov.cn/pub/sfbgw/zwxxgk/fdzdgknr/fdzdgknrtjxx/202306/t20230614_480740.html.

151 Zhang Liqing: "Statistical Analysis of Lawyers and Grassroots Legal Services Work in 2022," on *Ministry of Justice Website*, Accessed April 5, 2024. http://www.moj.gov.cn/pub/sfbgw/zwxxgk/fdzdgknr/fdzdgknrtjxx/202306/t20230614_480740.html.

Table 8.1 Job requirements at well-known law firms

Law firm	Position	Requirements
Beijing King & Wood Law Firm[152]	Lawyer (Capital Markets)	1. Graduated from a well-known domestic or international law school, with a master's degree or higher 2. Passed the legal qualification exam; those with a lawyer's practice certificate will be given priority 3. Able to work in both Chinese and English (with good English speaking and writing skills) 4. At least two years of experience working as a lawyer in the domestic capital market sector at a law firm 5. Passionate about the capital market, hardworking, and able to withstand high work pressure
	Lawyer (Cross-border Dispute)	1. Master's degree or higher in law or a related field from a well-known domestic or international law school, with a background in Chinese law, understanding of Anglo-American law, and an undergraduate degree in law 2. Solid legal foundation, passed the unified Chinese Legal Professional Qualification Exam, and obtained a lawyer's practice licence 3. At least two to three years of experience in litigation and arbitration at a top-tier law firm 4. Possesses good logical and analytical abilities, communication skills, a strong team spirit, and a sense of service 5. Strong English-language skills, proficient in using English for communication and drafting legal documents
Beijing Junhe Law Firm[153]	Leading Counsel (IP Litigation)	1. Graduated from a well-known domestic or international law school with a master's degree or higher in law, or holds a master's degree or higher in related fields such as life sciences, computer science, communications, electrical engineering, or mechanical engineering, along with a legal background 2. Holds a Chinese lawyer's practice licence, with overseas patent agent qualifications or experience in intellectual property 3. Excellent bilingual (Chinese and English) expression and writing skills, capable of direct and barrier-free communication with international clients 4. Preference given to candidates with three to six years of practical experience in intellectual property projects 5. Possesses corresponding leadership abilities, client-management skills, and business acumen

(continued)

[152] Refer to the King & Wood Law Firm website, https://www.kwm.com/cn/zh/home.html, accessed May 15, 2024.

[153] Refer to the JunHe Law Firm website, https://www.junhe.com, accessed May 15, 2024.

Table 8.1 (continued)

Law firm	Position	Requirements
	Lawyer (Asset Restructuring)	1. Graduates from well-known domestic or international law schools with a master's degree or higher will be given priority 2. Have passed the National Unified Legal Professional Qualification Exam 3. Possess good communication skills and the ability to work well in a team 4. Able to adapt to a fast-paced work environment
Beijing Zhonglun Law Firm[154]	Lawyer (Anti-trust and Competition Law)	1. Graduates from renowned domestic or international law schools with a master's degree or higher, candidates with a dual-degree background preferred 2. Interested in working in the field of anti-trust law 3. Strong English skills, candidates with an international educational background preferred 4. Good communication, learning, and team-collaboration abilities 5. Physically healthy, resilient, able to endure hardships, and withstand high work pressure
	Lawyer (Cybersecurity and Data Protection)	1. Graduated from a renowned domestic or international law school with a master's degree or higher 2. More than two years of work experience in a relevant business area at a well-known law firm 3. Passed the Chinese National Unified Legal Professional Qualification Exam 4. Fluent in English listening, speaking, reading, and writing; candidates with international educational backgrounds are preferred 5. Have a good understanding of cutting-edge technologies such as the internet, big data, and AI 6. Familiar with privacy protection laws, both domestically and internationally, such as the EU GDPR 7. Candidates with information security management certifications or CIPP credentials are preferred

practising lawyers in 2022 increased by 76,800, a rise of more than 13%.[155] There were 23 provinces with more than 10,000 lawyers and eight provinces with more than 30,000 lawyers, namely Guangdong, Beijing, Jiangsu, Shanghai, Shandong, Zhejiang, Sichuan, and Henan—the latter entering the "30,000+" category for the

[154] Refer to the Zhong Lun Law Firm website, https://www.zhonglun.com, accessed May 15, 2024.

[155] The number of practicing lawyers in 2021 was about 574,800. This data can be known from "Statistical Analysis of the Work of Lawyers and Grassroots Legal Services for the Year 2021" on *Ministry of Justice Website.*

first time.[156] Over 2,100 new law firms were established nationwide; more than 500 law firms now employ over 100 lawyers each, representing a growth of over 20%.[157]

As of the end of 2022, there were over 504,700 full-time lawyers, accounting for 77.46% of the total legal profession; over 14,300 part-time lawyers, making up 2.19%; over 95,900 public service lawyers, representing 14.73%; over 29,900 corporate lawyers, accounting for 4.6%; and over 1500 military lawyers, representing 0.23%.[158] Looking at the age structure, there were over 107,900 lawyers under the age of 30, accounting for 16.56%; over 419,500 lawyers between 30 and 50 years old, accounting for 64.39%; over 106,300 lawyers between 50 and 65 years old, accounting for 16.32%; and over 17,700 lawyers aged 65 and above, accounting for 2.73%.[159] In terms of education level, there were over 466,900 lawyers with an undergraduate degree, accounting for 71.66%; over 130,400 with a master's degree, accounting for 20.01%; and over 7800 with a doctoral degree, accounting for 1.21%.[160] There were over 46,400 lawyers with less than an undergraduate degree, representing 7.12%. There were 8727 lawyers who had received education abroad and obtained degrees, accounting for 1.34%.[161]

On the one hand, the aforementioned data suggest that the legal profession does not impose stringent educational and age requirements; rather, success in this field is largely contingent upon an individual's capabilities and competence. This flexibility allows a diverse range of candidates to pursue a career in law, thereby democratising access to the profession. On the other hand, the legal profession is characterised by its considerable growth potential and the lucrative salary prospects that it offers, making it a typical career path where high investment leads to high returns. This aspect is particularly attractive and motivates many to endure the rigorous demands of legal education and training.

During the initial stages of their careers, particularly during the internship phase, lawyers may receive relatively modest earnings. However, upon successful completion of this period and subsequent admission to the bar, their salaries can experience a substantial increase—often doubling or rising significantly. This potential for a sharp

[156] Zhang Liqing: "Statistical Analysis of Lawyers and Grassroots Legal Services Work in 2022," on *Ministry of Justice Website*, Accessed April 5, 2024. http://www.moj.gov.cn/pub/sfbgw/zwxxgk/fdzdgknr/fdzdgknrtjxx/202306/t20230614_480740.html.

[157] See People's Daily Online, http://society.people.com.cn/n1/2023/0614/c1008-40013434.html, accessed April 5, 2024.

[158] Zhang Liqing: "Statistical Analysis of Lawyers and Grassroots Legal Services Work in 2022," on *Ministry of Justice Website*, Accessed April 5, 2024. http://www.moj.gov.cn/pub/sfbgw/zwxxgk/fdzdgknr/fdzdgknrtjxx/202306/t20230614_480740.html.

[159] Zhang Liqing: "Statistical Analysis of Lawyers and Grassroots Legal Services Work in 2022," on *Ministry of Justice Website*, Accessed April 5, 2024. http://www.moj.gov.cn/pub/sfbgw/zwxxgk/fdzdgknr/fdzdgknrtjxx/202306/t20230614_480740.html.

[160] Zhang Liqing: "Statistical Analysis of Lawyers and Grassroots Legal Services Work in 2022," on *Ministry of Justice Website*, Accessed April 5, 2024. http://www.moj.gov.cn/pub/sfbgw/zwxxgk/fdzdgknr/fdzdgknrtjxx/202306/t20230614_480740.html.

[161] Zhang Liqing: "Statistical Analysis of Lawyers and Grassroots Legal Services Work in 2022," on *Ministry of Justice Website*, Accessed April 5, 2024. http://www.moj.gov.cn/pub/sfbgw/zwxxgk/fdzdgknr/fdzdgknrtjxx/202306/t20230614_480740.html.

increase in income upon qualification is a compelling incentive for many. The allure of these benefits is reflected in the steady growth in the number of practising lawyers across the nation.[162] This continuous increase underscores the sustained appeal of the legal profession among graduates.

Moreover, the expanding number of legal professionals not only enhances the availability and accessibility of legal services to society, but also intensifies the competition within the field itself. In response to this competitive environment, lawyers are compelled to continually advance their knowledge and refine their skills. This pursuit of professional development is essential not only for individual success but also for the provision of superior-quality legal services to the public. As the legal landscape evolves, maintaining a competitive edge and adapting to new legal challenges are crucial for long-term success and contribution to the broader societal good.

8.3 Courts and Judges

In the comprehensive construction of a socialist modernised nation on the path of rule of law, the People's Courts are important participants, active promoters, and firm defenders. Judges, who are involved in the adjudication and execution activities of the People's Courts, are a crucial force in advancing justice for the people and a fair judiciary, and are also an essential part of the legal-talent pool. The quality of judges effects the high-quality development of the People's Courts and the progress of the judiciary in upholding social fairness and justice.

8.3.1 Court Structure

The establishment of the People's Courts in China is clearly stipulated by law. According to the Constitution and the Organic Law of the People's Courts, the People's Courts in China are divided into the Supreme People's Court, local people's courts at various levels, and specialised courts.[163] Local people's courts include the High People's Courts, Intermediate People's Courts, and Primary People's Courts. Specialised People's Courts include Military Courts, Maritime Courts, Intellectual Property Courts, Financial Courts, and others.[164]

The Supreme People's Court supervises the judicial work of local people's courts at all levels, serving as the highest judicial body in the country and the appellate

---

[162] As of 2021, 2020, and 2019, the number of practicing lawyers nationwide was 574,800, 522,000, and 473,000, respectively. Data sourced from the *Ministry of Justice Annual Statistical Analysis of Lawyers and Grassroots Legal Services Work* published each year.

[163] *Constitution*, Article 129; *Organic Law of the People's Courts (amended 2018)*, Article 12.

[164] *Organic Law of the People's Courts (amended 2018)*, Article 13, 15.

court for the High People's Courts. The cases it handles include: (i) first-instance cases under its jurisdiction as stipulated by law or deemed by it to fall under its jurisdiction; (ii) appeals and protests against judgements and rulings of the High People's Courts; (iii) appeals and protests initiated in accordance with the provisions of the Standing Committee of the National People's Congress; (iv) retrial cases initiated under judicial supervision procedures; and (v) death penalty cases submitted for approval by the High People's Courts.[165] Currently, the Supreme People's Court has established six circuit courts as branches of the Supreme Court to handle relevant cases within their respective circuits. The judgements and rulings of the circuit courts are the judgements and rulings of the Supreme People's Court.[166]

Local people's courts at all levels in China are primarily established in correspondence with administrative divisions. High People's Courts include provincial High People's Courts, autonomous region High People's Courts, and municipal High People's Courts in directly administered cities.[167] Intermediate People's Courts are generally established in provinces, cities under the jurisdiction of autonomous regions, directly administered cities, and autonomous prefectures, with some also set up regionally within provinces and autonomous regions.[168] Primary People's Courts are located in counties, autonomous counties, cities not divided into districts, and districted cities.[169] Depending on the area, population, and caseload, Primary People's Courts may establish several people's tribunals and necessary specialised courts based on judicial needs.[170] Intermediate People's Courts and Primary People's Courts with fewer judicial positions may establish comprehensive tribunals or no tribunals at all.[171]

In addition to being established according to administrative divisions, some local courts are also set across administrative boundaries. The Third Intermediate People's Court of Shanghai is China's first cross-administrative division people's court, established in 2014.[172] In the four centrally administered municipalities of Beijing, Tianjin, Shanghai, and Chongqing, there are High People's Courts, Intermediate People's Courts, and Primary People's Courts within the city. High People's Courts and Primary People's Courts correspond to specific administrative regions, while Intermediate People's Courts in directly administered cities do not correspond to specific administrative regions, thus they may also be considered as set across administrative divisions. Moreover, local people's courts at all levels may also be established in specific areas, such as economic and technological development zones, high-tech

[165] *Organic Law of the People's Courts (amended 2018)*, Article 16.

[166] See *Provisions of the Supreme People's Court on Several Issues Concerning the Hearing of Cases by Circuit Courts* (amended 2016).

[167] *Organic Law of the People's Courts (amended 2018)*, Article 20.

[168] *Organic Law of the People's Courts (amended 2018)*, Article 22.

[169] *Organic Law of the People's Courts (amended 2018)*, Article 24.

[170] *Organic Law of the People's Courts (amended 2018)*, Article 26.

[171] *Organic Law of the People's Courts (amended 2018)*, Article 27.

[172] Refer to the website of The Third Intermediate People's Court of Shanghai, Accessed April 5, http://www.shszfy.gov.cn/detail.jhtml?id=10007119.

development zones.[173] The names of courts in these specific areas are not uniform, but they often include the name of the specific area, such as the People's Court of the Wuhan Economic and Technological Development Zone.

Specialised People's Courts are established by the State according to the Constitution, laws, and decisions of the Standing Committee of the National People's Congress, specifically tasked with jurisdiction over certain types of cases.[174] Maritime courts handle litigation brought by parties involved in maritime tort disputes, maritime commercial contract disputes, and other maritime disputes as stipulated by law.[175] Intellectual Property Courts have jurisdiction over first-instance cases related to intellectual property within the districts under their city's jurisdiction, as well as appeals against civil and administrative judgements, and rulings on intellectual property made by the Primary People's Courts in the city where the Intellectual Property Court is located.[176] Among them, the Intellectual Property Court in Guangzhou exercises cross-regional jurisdiction over certain relevant cases within Guangdong Province.[177] The Intellectual Property Court in Beijing also has jurisdiction over first-instance administrative cases involving challenges to administrative actions related to the authorisation and confirmation of intellectual property rights, which are made by departments of the State Council.[178] Financial courts have jurisdiction over financial, civil, and commercial cases, and financial disputes within a specific jurisdiction.[179] The organisational structure, powers, appointment, and dismissal of judges for specialised People's Courts are stipulated by the Standing Committee of the National People's Congress.[180] The established Maritime Courts, Intellectual Property Courts, and Financial Courts are equivalent in status and trial level to Intermediate People's Courts. Except for Maritime Courts, which only handle first-instance cases, both Intellectual Property Courts and Financial Courts have functions for first-instance trials and appellate trials.

[173] "Whither Specialised Courts - An Inquiry into the Establishment of a Jurisdictional System Appropriately Separated from Administrative Districts". China Court website, Accessed April 5. https://www.chinacourt.org/article/detail/2016/12/id/2501461.shtml.

[174] He (2022).

[175] *Maritime Procedure Law*, Article 4.

[176] *Supreme People's Court Provisions on the Jurisdiction of Cases by the Intellectual Property Courts in Beijing, Shanghai, and Guangzhou* (Legal Interpretation [2020] No. 19), Article 1.

[177] *Supreme People's Court Provisions on the Jurisdiction of Cases by the Intellectual Property Courts in Beijing, Shanghai, and Guangzhou* (Legal Interpretation [2020] No. 19), Article 2, Article 6.

[178] *Supreme People's Court Provisions on the Jurisdiction of Cases by the Intellectual Property Courts in Beijing, Shanghai, and Guangzhou* (Legal Interpretation [2020] No. 19), Article 5.

[179] See *Provisions of the Supreme People's Court on the Jurisdiction of Cases in the Beijing Financial Court* (2021).

[180] *Organic Law of the People's Courts (amended 2018)*, Article 15.

According to statistics from *Chinese Judicial Studies* edited by Zhou Yuhua and published in June 2015, "There are 32 High People's Courts, 409 Intermediate People's Courts, and 3117 Primary People's Courts in the inland areas of the country".[181]

8.3.2 *Professional Requirements*

Achieving judicial fairness is heavily reliant on both the personal attributes and the professional performance of judges. These judicial officers, who embody and exercise the State's judicial power, operate strictly within the framework of the law. This esteemed group includes various key positions such as the Presidents, Vice-Presidents, members of the Judicial Committee, chiefs and deputy chiefs of divisions, and judges at all tiers of the judicial system.[182] Specifically, this encompasses judges from the Supreme People's Court, local people's courts at various levels—from provincial to municipal—and specialised courts that focus on particular areas of law.[183]

Judges within this system are systematically categorised into 12 distinct ranks.[184] Judges' grades are determined on the basis of their moral and aptitude performance, operational level, trial performance, and years of service.[185] Judges are promoted by a combination of scheduled promotions and merit-based promotions, and judges in front-line casework positions, who are particularly outstanding or whose work requires them to do so, may be specially selected for promotion.[186]

Judges carry a significant responsibility for the cases they oversee within their designated jurisdictions.[187] This includes their active participation in collegial panels, where they are tasked with adjudicating a wide range of proceedings, including criminal, civil, and administrative cases. Obviously, they are involved in more specialised legal matters such as State compensation cases.[188] Their responsibilities also extend to handling international legal issues such as extradition and judicial assistance in accordance with established laws.[189] Furthermore, judges fulfil other legally specified duties that contribute to the administration of justice.

By exercising their judicial power, judges play a critical role in bridging the gaps between factual circumstances and legal norms, and between these norms and broader societal values. This vital function enhances the public's understanding and

[181] Zhou Yuhua: *Chinese Judicial Studies*, Law Press, 2015 edition.

[182] *Judges Law (Amended 2019)*, Article 2.

[183] *Judges Law (Amended 2019)*, Article 2.

[184] *Judges Law (Amended 2019)*, Article 26.

[185] *Judges Law (Amended 2019)*, Article 28.

[186] *Judges Law (Amended 2019)*, Article 28.

[187] *Judges Law (Amended 2019)*, Article 8.

[188] *Judges Law (Amended 2019)*, Article 8.

[189] *Judges Law (Amended 2019)*, Article 8.

appreciation of the law, fostering a deeper respect and trust in the legal system. Through their diligent application of the law, judges uphold its authority and integrity, thereby contributing significantly to achieving judicial fairness.

8.3.2.1 Eligibility Criteria

Beyond what has already been mentioned, the following is a more detailed examination of the qualifications for becoming a judge from various perspectives. From a legal standpoint, the *Judges Law* stipulates a series of requirements for serving as a judge.[190] First, one must possess Chinese nationality to serve as a judge in China.[191] Second, judges must exhibit good political qualities, support the Constitution of the People's Republic of China, and uphold the leadership of the Communist Party of China and the socialist system.[192] In the current era, these requirements have been heightened compared to the past, where the demand was only to "support the Constitution of the People's Republic of China", but now it also requires judges to "uphold the leadership of the Communist Party of China and the socialist system".[193] Third, judges must possess good professional competence and moral character.[194] The most recent revision of the *Judges Law* specifically emphasises "morality" in describing "conduct", indicating that judges should also maintain high moral standards. Fourth, judges must be physically capable of performing their duties effectively.[195] Only with a healthy physique and good condition can judges exercise their judicial power effectively. Fifth, judges must meet the specified educational qualifications.[196] Judges should have at least an undergraduate degree in law from a recognised university and have obtained at least a bachelor's degree. For those with an undergraduate degree in a non-law field, they must have obtained a Master of Laws, Master of Legal Studies, or higher degree and must also possess legal knowledge.[197] In regions where it is genuinely difficult to meet these educational requirements, with approval from the Supreme People's Court and within a certain time frame, the educational qualifications for becoming a judge can be relaxed to a university undergraduate degree.[198] Sixth, judges are required to have at least five years of legal

---

[190] *Judges Law (Amended 2019)*, Article 12.

[191] *Judges Law (Amended 2019)*, Article 12.

[192] *Judges Law (Amended 2019)*, Article 12.

[193] In 1995, 2001, and 2017, Article 9, Section 3 of the *Judges Law* stated, "Support the Constitution of the People's Republic of China." In 2019, Article 12, Section 3 of the *Judges Law* was revised to state, "Support the Constitution of the People's Republic of China, support the leadership of the Communist Party of China, and the socialist system."

[194] *Judges Law (Amended 2019)*, Article 12.

[195] *Judges Law (Amended 2019)*, Article 12.

[196] *Judges Law (Amended 2019)*, Article 12.

[197] *Judges Law (Amended 2019)*, Article 12.

[198] *Judges Law (Amended 2019)*, Article 12.

experience.[199] However, for those who have obtained a Master of Laws, Master of Legal Studies, or a doctoral degree in law, the required years of legal experience may be reduced to four and three years, respectively.[200] Seventh, entry-level judges must pass the National Unified Legal Professional Qualification Exam to obtain their legal professional qualifications.[201]

Even when all the requisite qualifications are fulfilled, certain individuals remain disqualified from serving as judges due to their previous legal and professional history. This includes those who have faced criminal penalties, have been dismissed from any public office, or have experienced revocation of their licences as lawyers or notary publics.[202] Additionally, individuals who have been expelled from positions on arbitration committees, among other similar disqualifications, are also barred from holding judicial positions.[203] These criteria ensure that only those with unblemished professional records and high ethical standards are eligible to enforce and interpret the law.

To maintain judicial impartiality and prevent conflicts of interest, judges are strictly prohibited from holding any positions in for-profit organisations.[204] They are also not allowed to engage in activities as arbitrators or notary publics.[205] These restrictions are designed to ensure that judges remain fully dedicated to their judicial duties and that their decisions are not influenced by any external business interests or personal financial gains.

Entry-level judges undergo a rigorous selection process, ensuring that only candidates who demonstrate the highest levels of moral integrity and professional competence are appointed.[206] This process specifically targets individuals who meet the stringent qualifications required to hold a judicial position. Typically, the selection procedure is divided into three distinct rounds, each designed to evaluate different aspects of a candidate's abilities and knowledge.[207]

The first round consists of a comprehensive written examination where candidates are tested on their understanding of legal theory and their proficiency in drafting legal documents.[208] This test is crucial for assessing the foundational legal knowledge and technical skills essential for a career in the judiciary. Following the written exam, the

---

[199] *Judges Law (Amended 2019)*, Article 12.

[200] *Judges Law (Amended 2019)*, Article 12.

[201] *Judges Law (Amended 2019)*, Article 12.

[202] *Judges Law (Amended 2019)*, Article 13.

[203] *Judges Law (Amended 2019)*, Article 13.

[204] *Judges Law (Amended 2019)*, Article 22.

[205] *Judges Law (Amended 2019)*, Article 22.

[206] *Judges Law (Amended 2019)*, Article 14.

[207] "Reflections on Improving the System of Selection of Judges." China Court website, Accessed April 5. https://www.chinacourt.org/article/detail/2020/11/id/5577005.shtml.

[208] *Provisional Measures for the Public Selection of Candidates for Appointment as Judges and Prosecutors at the Early Stage of Their Career* (2008), Article 13.

second round involves a courtroom interview.[209] In this stage, candidates participate in simulated court sessions where their capability to effectively manage a trial is scrutinised. This round is also particularly important as it evaluates the candidates' practical skills in a courtroom setting, including their familiarity with trial procedures and their ability to apply legal knowledge in a dynamic environment. The final hurdle in the selection process is the third round, which involves a direct interview with a selection committee organised by the provincial high court.[210] During this interview, candidates must demonstrate their suitability for the role of a judge through their responses to various scenarios and questions posed by the committee. This round is designed to assess the candidates' critical thinking, ethical reasoning, and overall readiness to assume the responsibilities of a judge.

Successfully passing all three rounds of examinations and assessments qualifies an individual to officially become a judge. This comprehensive selection process ensures that only the most qualified, capable, and ethically sound candidates are chosen to uphold the law and administer justice.

Junior judges usually serve in the Basic People's Courts, but may also serve in people's courts above the basic level.[211] Judges of higher courts are generally selected gradually; judges of the Supreme People's Court and the Higher People's Court may be selected from the lower two levels of courts. Judges wishing to be selected to a higher court must have worked for a certain number of years in a lower court and have work experience relevant to the position.

Furthermore, according to the specific requirements and needs of the judiciary, people's courts have the authority to publicly select judges from a pool of professionals already engaged in the legal field, including lawyers, legal scholars, and researchers.[212] This selection process is designed to enrich the judiciary with diverse experiences and deep expertise.

Lawyers who wish to participate in these public selections are required to have a minimum of five years of practical experience in the field. They must also demonstrate a track record of extensive legal practice and are expected to have maintained a good professional reputation throughout their careers. Additionally, legal scholars and researchers interested in joining the judiciary must hold at least a mid-level professional title. They should have been actively involved in legal teaching or research for more than five years.[213] Additionally, these candidates must show exceptional research capabilities and have significant achievements in their fields.

---

[209] *Provisional Measures for the Public Selection of Candidates for Appointment as Judges and Prosecutors at the Early Stage of Their Career* (2008), Article 16.

[210] *Provisional Measures for the Public Selection of Candidates for Appointment as Judges and Prosecutors at the Early Stage of Their Career* (2008), Article 17.

[211] *Provisional Measures for the Public Selection of Candidates for Appointment as Judges and Prosecutors at the Early Stage of Their Career* (2008), Article 7.

[212] *Provisional Measures for the Public Selection of Candidates for Appointment as Judges and Prosecutors at the Early Stage of Their Career* (2008), Article 7.

[213] *Judges Law (Amended 2019)*, Article 15.

By incorporating lawyers and academics with substantial experience and proven competence, the judiciary aims to enhance the depth and quality of legal interpretation and judgements within the courts, ensuring that justice is both informed and impartial.

8.3.2.2 Education and Training

Education and training for judges represent a groundbreaking, essential, and strategic initiative that is fundamental to the development of a high-quality judiciary system. This educational endeavour is not merely an enhancement of their professional capabilities but is pivotal in ensuring that judges are equipped with the latest legal knowledge, ethical standards, and judicial skills necessary to meet the evolving demands of justice administration.

Judges possess both the legal right and the obligation to participate in such training programs.[214] This dual aspect underscores the importance of continuous professional development in the judicial profession.

The content of judicial education and training focuses on political capabilities, professional ethics, and judicial-skills enhancement, with an emphasis on overall quality improvement, aiming to comprehensively enhance the qualifications and capabilities of judges. Judge training is divided into pre-service training, induction training, promotion training, and in-service training, with different training programs implemented for different groups.[215] Pre-service training targets entry-level judges, focusing on developing their practical trial skills and enhancing their judicial capabilities, with a duration of one year.[216] Newly appointed court presidents and vice-presidents must undergo induction training focused on improving their leadership and management capabilities within the court, with training lasting no less than half a month.[217] For promotion to senior judge, individuals must undergo advanced training to enhance their comprehensive judicial abilities in both theory and practice, with a duration of one month.[218] In-service training, unlike the other three types, is an ongoing process that focuses on improving legal theoretical knowledge and judicial capabilities.[219] Judges are required to participate throughout their tenure, with a minimum of 12 days of training annually.[220]

Individuals who are candidates for entry-level judicial positions, as well as those seeking promotion to senior judicial ranks, are required to participate in the aforementioned training programs. This structured training is essential, as it equips them with the necessary skills and knowledge to perform their duties effectively. Before these candidates can assume their new roles or advance to higher positions within

[214] *Regulations on the Education and Training of Judges* (2020), Article 10.

[215] *Regulations on the Education and Training of Judges* (2020), Article 16.

[216] *Regulations on the Education and Training of Judges* (2020), Article 17.

[217] *Regulations on the Education and Training of Judges* (2020), Article 18.

[218] *Regulations on the Education and Training of Judges* (2020), Article 19.

[219] *Regulations on the Education and Training of Judges* (2020), Article 20.

[220] *Regulations on the Education and Training of Judges* (2020), Article 20.

the judiciary, they must not only complete the requisite training but also successfully pass rigorous assessments designed to evaluate their comprehension and application of legal principles.[221]

Upon successfully completing these evaluations, candidates receive official completion certificates.[222] These certificates serve as formal recognition of their achievement in both pre-service training for incoming judges and promotional training for existing judges seeking advancement.

8.3.2.3 Professional Assessment

Merely providing education and training is insufficient to ensure the quality of judicial work performed by judges. In China, there is also a formal assessment process for judges. The content of this assessment generally encompasses the areas covered by education and training, and serves as a bridge between the two. The assessment of judges is based fundamentally on their job responsibilities and tasks, utilising a standardised evaluation system that comprehensively assesses their virtues, abilities, diligence, achievements, and integrity, with a focus on political qualities and judicial performance.[223]

In terms of "virtue", judges are rigorously assessed on their depth of study and implementation of Xi Jinping's Thought on Socialism with Chinese Characteristics for a New Era, their adherence to the leadership of the Communist Party over judicial work, their commitment to the path of socialist rule of law in China, and their enhancement of political acumen, understanding, and execution.[224] They are also evaluated on their compliance with political disciplines and rules, their proactive resistance to opposing ideologies such as Western constitutional democracy, judicial independence, and separation of powers, as well as their commitment to socialist core values, adherence to professional judicial ethics, and observance of public, family, and personal morals.[225]

For "ability", the assessment focuses on legal expertise and professional capacity, particularly the ability to apply legal policies, the level of judicial business handling, understanding of legal theory, and research in judicial practice, as well as capabilities in risk prevention, public relations, application of technology, and guiding public opinion.[226]

---

221 *Regulations on the Education and Training of Judges* (2020), Article 48.

222 *Regulations on the Education and Training of Judges* (2020), Article 48.

223 Wang (2019).

224 See *Guidelines of the Supreme People's Court on Strengthening and Improving the Assessment of Judges* (2021).

225 See *Guidelines of the Supreme People's Court on Strengthening and Improving the Assessment of Judges* (2021).

226 See *Guidelines of the Supreme People's Court on Strengthening and Improving the Assessment of Judges* (2021).

The "diligence" category of the assessment concentrates on judges' mental state and work style, specifically examining their dedication to duty, compliance with work discipline, commitment to their positions, diligence, willingness to accept responsibility, and readiness to serve.[227]

For "achievements", evaluations primarily consider case handling performance and other work achievements, with case performance indicators focusing on the quantity, quality, efficiency, and effectiveness of case handling.[228]

The "integrity" assessment revolves around maintaining judicial integrity and self-discipline, particularly adherence to anti-corruption regulations, implementation of the Central Government's eight-point guidelines, and adherence to regulations designed to prevent judicial interference.[229]

Judges undergo a comprehensive evaluation process that includes both continuous and annual assessments, employing a methodology that combines quantitative scoring as the primary measure and qualitative scoring as a secondary measure.[230]

Continuous assessments are systematically categorised into four distinct grades: excellent, good, average, and poor. This grading system allows for a nuanced understanding of a judge's ongoing performance and areas for improvement. Similarly, the results of the annual assessments are classified into four levels: outstanding, competent, basically competent, and incompetent.[231] This yearly evaluation provides a broader overview of a judge's capabilities and achievements over the longer term.

The outcomes derived from these rigorous assessments are instrumental in making critical decisions regarding the professional lives of judges. These decisions include judicial promotions to higher ranks, demotions to lower positions, removal from judicial duties for those found incompetent, and the allocation of performance bonuses. Such assessments play an essential role in guiding, regulating, and motivating judges to adhere to the highest standards of legal practice, ensuring they execute their duties lawfully, justly, and efficiently.[232]

From the above, it is clear that China not only sets a series of requirements for the judicial profession at the entry stage but also establishes continuous education and training phases, and professional assessment phases. This ongoing process encourages judges to remain true to their original aspirations, be strict with themselves, and keep their mission in mind.

[227] See *Guidelines of the Supreme People's Court on Strengthening and Improving the Assessment of Judges* (2021).

[228] See *Guidelines of the Supreme People's Court on Strengthening and Improving the Assessment of Judges* (2021).

[229] See *Guidelines of the Supreme People's Court on Strengthening and Improving the Assessment of Judges* (2021).

[230] *Guiding Opinions on Strengthening and Improving the Assessment of Judges*, Article 15.

[231] *Guiding Opinions on Strengthening and Improving the Assessment of Judges*, Article 16.

[232] "Value Construction and Completion of the Judges' Performance Evaluation System." Tianjin Court Website, Accessed on April 20, https://tjfy.tjcourt.gov.cn/article/detail/2017/07/id/2918705.shtml.

8.3.3 Industry Status

At present, the judicial profession provides a significant level of stability in several key areas, including the nature of job responsibilities, the work environment, and financial compensation.[233] This stability not only enhances job security but also offers judges expedited opportunities for local residency in the regions where they are employed, facilitating smoother transitions and greater community integration for those relocating for their roles.[234] When compared with other civil service positions at similar levels, those occupying judicial roles, primarily within the court system, typically receive a relatively higher salary. This financial advantage reflects the high value placed on the critical functions they perform within the legal system, further adding to the attractiveness of pursuing a career in this field. Importantly, for students who have studied law, embarking on a career as a judge not only aligns perfectly with their academic background but also offers a high degree of job satisfaction. The role allows them to directly apply their knowledge and skills in real-world scenarios, contributing to the administration of justice. This alignment, combined with the inherent prestige associated with being part of the judiciary, contributes significantly to their professional fulfilment and pride in their work, making it a highly sought-after career path for law graduates.[235]

However, the disadvantages cannot be overlooked. First, the job involves significant pressure. As of March 2023, there were over 120,000 quota judges nationwide.[236] In the same year, the Supreme People's Court handled 21,081 cases and concluded 17,855 cases, representing increases of 54.6% and 29.5% respectively compared to the previous year; local courts at all levels handled approximately 45.574 million cases, with 45.268 million cases concluded or enforced, marking increases of 15.6% and 13.4%, respectively.[237] The average number of cases handled per judge rose from 242 in 2022 to 357 in 2023.[238] Although there is no official data to support the number of cases handled by quota judges in grassroots courts for 2023, in 2022, the average number of cases concluded per judge at this level reached 274. Among them, grassroots courts in nine provinces (regions, municipalities) had an average

---

[233] Wu and Wu (2015).

[234] Wu and Wu (2015).

[235] "Myths and Thoughts on Legal Career Paths—On Law Students' Career Choices and Development Planning." The Paper. Accessed on *April 20, 2024.* https://www.thepaper.cn/newsDetail_forward_25937824.

[236] Refer to *the Report on the Work of the Supreme People's Court at the First Session of the Fourteenth National People's Congress* (2023).

[237] Supreme People's Court: "Work Report of the Supreme People's Court—Delivered on March 8, 2024 at the Second Session of the Fourteenth National People's Congress." the official website of the Supreme People's Court. Accessed on April 5, 2024. https://www.court.gov.cn/zixun/xiangqing/427412.html.

[238] *Supreme People's Court: "Work Report of the Supreme People's Court—Delivered on March 8, 2024 at the Second Session of the Fourteenth National People's Congress." the official website of the Supreme People's Court. Accessed on April 5, 2024.* https://www.court.gov.cn/zixun/xiangqing/427412.html.

caseload exceeding 300 cases per judge, with the highest exceeding 400 cases.[239] Based on the aforementioned data, it is highly probable that the figures for 2023 will show a significant increase from the previous year. This indicates that the number of cases handled by judges each year is continuously rising over time, and correspondingly, the workload and pressure on judges are also increasing. Secondly, the rate of salary growth is slow, and compared to professions like lawyers, which have higher salary ceilings, the income disparity among different professionals might become more pronounced as they gain more experience. Thirdly, the difficulty and length of time required for promotion are substantial; the high standards required of professionals in this field mean that only those with solid qualifications, a positive mindset, and strong capabilities can stand out.[240] This characteristic is also true for other public service roles related to legal studies, such as prosecutors.

In addition to the inherent disadvantages of the judicial profession, the Supreme People's Court's 2023 work report highlights several ongoing issues and challenges directly related to judicial work, which require active engagement from judges.[241] First, there is a gap in deeply understanding and effectively implementing Xi Jinping's legal governance ideology.[242] Second, the awareness and capability to strengthen source governance needs to be enhanced, and there needs to be a stronger initiative and willingness to form a governance synergy under the leadership of the Party committee.[243] Third, there are still numerous issues with the implementation of the judicial management system, and the comprehensive supporting reforms of the judicial system need further deepening and advancement.[244] Fourth, there are weaknesses in the comprehensive and strict management and governance of the judiciary, with profound lessons from the disciplinary and legal violations of some judicial personnel, hence, rectifying conduct, enforcing discipline, and fighting corruption must continue to be intensified.[245] Fifth, the shortage of specialised judicial personnel in specific fields needs to be acknowledged and addressed.[246]

---

[239] Refer to the data mentioned by Liao Xiangyang, Director of the Trial Management Office of the Supreme People's Court, during the fifth full-media live interview session held on March 10, 2023, to explain the "Work Report of the Supreme People's Court".

[240] "Public Selection: Cracking the Judge Promotion Puzzle." China Court Website. Accessed on April 20, 2024. https://www.chinacourt.org/article/detail/2014/03/id/1262251.shtml.

[241] Refer to *the Report on the Work of the Supreme People's Court at the First Session of the Fourteenth National People's Congress* (2023).

[242] Refer to *the Report on the Work of the Supreme People's Court at the First Session of the Fourteenth National People's Congress* (2023).

[243] Refer to *the Report on the Work of the Supreme People's Court at the First Session of the Fourteenth National People's Congress* (2023).

[244] Refer to *the Report on the Work of the Supreme People's Court at the First Session of the Fourteenth National People's Congress* (2023).

[245] Refer to *the Report on the Work of the Supreme People's Court at the First Session of the Fourteenth National People's Congress* (2023).

[246] *Supreme People's Court: See "Work Report of the Supreme People's Court — Presented on March 8, 2024, at the Second Session of the Fourteenth National People's Congress," available on the official website of the Supreme People's Court,* https://www.court.gov.cn/zixun/xiangqing/427412.html, *accessed on April 5, 2024.*

Given the distinctive nature of the judicial profession, and the myriad challenges it presents, it is imperative for judges to remain current with evolving legal practices, and continually refine their skills and capabilities in judicial practice. This entails a dedicated focus on fostering their political integrity and moral character, attributes that are essential for maintaining the trust and respect of the public they serve.[247] While it is crucial for judges to ensure that they administer justice with both efficacy and efficiency, they must also pay attention to their personal well-being.[248] Maintaining both physical and mental health is vital, as the demands of their role can often lead to significant stress. Learning effective strategies to mitigate work-related stress is essential for judges to sustain their performance over the long term and avoid burnout.

8.4 The Procuratorate and Procurators

After decades of methodical development, China's procuratorial system achieved substantial progress under the resolute and unwavering leadership of the Communist Party. Throughout this period, the system was not immune to setbacks; indeed, it encountered various challenges and obstacles. However, these difficulties were meticulously and systematically addressed, and resolved sequentially, showcasing the system's resilience and commitment to continuous improvement. Now, entering a new stage of development, under the strong leadership of the Party Central Committee with Comrade Xi Jinping at its core, and guided by Xi Jinping's Thought on Rule of Law, various aspects of procuratorial work have seen new developments,[249] primarily reflected in the establishment of procuratorates and the appointment of procurators.

8.4.1 Establishment of Procuratorates

In China, the People's Procuratorate serves as the national legal supervision agency.[250] Through the exercise of procuratorial powers, the People's Procuratorate prosecutes crimes; safeguards national security and social order; protects the legitimate rights and interests of individuals and organisations; upholds national interests and public interests; ensures correct implementation of laws; maintains social fairness and justice; upholds the unity, dignity, and authority of the legal system;

[247] "The Three Qualities and Competences of Judges." Luoyang City Luolong District People's Court. Accessed on April 20, 2024. https://lyllqfy.hncourt.gov.cn/public/detail.php?id=728.

[248] "For the Good Health of Judges." China Court Website. Accessed on April 20, 2024. https://www.chinacourt.org/article/detail/2002/07/id/8709.shtml.

[249] Sun Qian, "The Development Process and Original Mission of the People's Procuratorate," accessed April 5, 2024, Supreme People's Procuratorate of the People's Republic of China website, https://www.spp.gov.cn/spp/zdgz/202201/t20220113_541583.shtml.

[250] *Organic Law of the People's Procuratorates* (revised in 2018), Article 2.

and guarantees the smooth progress of the construction of socialism with Chinese characteristics.[251]

In order to better exercise their powers and ensure the People's Procuratorate performs its duties in accordance with the law, China has made systematic arrangements for the establishment of procuratorates, with the main provisions outlined in the *Organic Law of the People's Procuratorates of the People's Republic of China* (hereinafter referred to as the *Procuratorate Organic Law*).[252] According to the *Procuratorate Organic Law*, procuratorates in China are categorised into three main types: the Supreme People's Procuratorate, local procuratorates at various levels, and specialised procuratorates.[253] Among them, the local procuratorates can be further divided into three tiers: provincial-level procuratorates, procuratorates at prefecture-level cities, and grassroots procuratorates.[254] The establishment, organisation, powers, and appointment and removal of procurators in specialised procuratorates are subject to regulations by the Standing Committee of the National People's Congress.[255]

Within the procuratorate system, the Supreme People's Procuratorate serves as the highest procuratorial authority. It is responsible for leading the work of the local procuratorates and specialised procuratorates. Additionally, higher-level procuratorates oversee the work of lower-level procuratorates. The Supreme People's Procuratorate is accountable to the National People's Congress and its Standing Committee,[256] while local procuratorates at various levels are accountable to the State organisations that create them, and to higher-level procuratorates.[257]

In addition to the regular, regional procuratorates, Chinese law also makes special provisions for the establishment of procuratorates in the Xinjiang Production and Construction Corps. According to the provisions of the *Procuratorate Organic Law*, the organisation, jurisdiction, and appointment and removal of procurators in the procuratorates established in the Xinjiang Production and Construction Corps is conducted in accordance with the relevant provisions of the Standing Committee of the National People's Congress.[258] Moreover, the *Procuratorate Organic Law* also stipulates that procuratorates may establish special agencies as needed. Firstly, with the approval of the Supreme People's Procuratorate and relevant departments at the provincial level, and upon submission to and approval by the Standing Committee of the People's Congress at the corresponding level, provincial and municipal procuratorates may establish procuratorates in specific areas within their jurisdiction as

[251] *Organic Law of the People's Procuratorates* (revised in 2018), Article 2.
[252] *Organic Law of the People's Procuratorates* (revised in 2018), Article 1.
[253] *Organic Law of the People's Procuratorates* (revised in 2018), Article 12.
[254] *Organic Law of the People's Procuratorates* (revised in 2018), Article 13.
[255] *Organic Law of the People's Procuratorates* (revised in 2018), Article 2.
[256] *Constitution* (amended in 2018), Article 137.
[257] *Constitution* (amended in 2018), Article 138.
[258] *Organic Law of the People's Procuratorates* (revised in 2018), Article 14.

dispatched agencies to meet the needs of procuratorial work.[259] Secondly, procuratorates may establish procuratorial offices in prisons, detention centres, and other places as needed for procuratorial work, exercising some of the powers of the procuratorate that dispatched them, and may also conduct inspections in the aforementioned places.[260] However, although procuratorates may establish procuratorial offices as needed for procuratorial work, they must also be subject to certain limitations. According to the *Procuratorate Organic Law*, the establishment of procuratorial offices by provincial-level procuratorates requires the approval of the Supreme People's Procuratorate and relevant departments at the provincial level.[261] The establishment of procuratorial offices by municipal and grassroots procuratorates requires the approval of the provincial-level procuratorate and relevant departments at the provincial level.[262] Furthermore, procuratorates may establish necessary functional departments according to the needs of procuratorial work. In municipal and grassroots procuratorates, where the number of posted procurators is relatively small, comprehensive functional departments may be established.[263] Finally, procuratorates may establish necessary auxiliary procuratorial and administrative management institutions as required by their work.[264]

8.4.2 Requirements for Prosecutors

Before explaining the professional requirements of prosecutors, it is essential to clarify what constitutes a prosecutor, so as to make a clear distinction between the professional requirements of prosecutors and those of other procuratorial personnel. According to the provisions of the *People's Republic of China Prosecutor Law* (hereinafter referred to as the *Prosecutor Law*), prosecutors are procuratorial personnel who exercise State prosecutorial power in accordance with the law, including the procurators-general, deputy procurators-general, members of procuratorial committees, and procurators of specialised procuratorates such as the Supreme People's Procuratorate, local procuratorates at all levels, and military procuratorates.[265] Prosecutors in this context do not include auxiliary procuratorial personnel or judicial administrative personnel. Auxiliary procuratorial personnel refers to individuals responsible for case reception, evidence collection, drafting legal documents, and other auxiliary tasks, while judicial administrative personnel are responsible for administrative management, logistical support, and other related tasks. In the process of handling judicial cases, prosecutors play the primary role in case handling, while

[259] *Organic Law of the People's Procuratorates* (revised in 2018), Article 16.
[260] *Organic Law of the People's Procuratorates* (revised in 2018), Article 17.
[261] *Organic Law of the People's Procuratorates* (revised in 2018), Article 17.
[262] *Organic Law of the People's Procuratorates* (revised in 2018), Article 17.
[263] *Organic Law of the People's Procuratorates* (revised in 2018), Article 18.
[264] *Organic Law of the People's Procuratorates* (revised in 2018), Article 19.
[265] *Prosecutors Law* (revised in 2019), Article 2.

auxiliary procuratorial personnel and judicial administrative personnel respectively play supporting and service roles to facilitate case proceedings.[266]

In China, serving as a prosecutor requires meeting certain criteria. According to the provisions of the *Procuratorate Organisation Law*, prosecutors are selected from individuals who have obtained legal professional qualifications and meet other conditions specified by law.[267] The provision indicates that serving as a prosecutor requires two conditions: first, obtaining legal professional qualifications, and second, meeting other conditions specified by law.[268] The legal professional qualification system evolved from the Unified National Judicial Examination during the judicial system reform, which has been elaborated upon in the earlier sections. The other conditions specified by law mainly refer to the specific requirements for prosecutors' appointment as stipulated in the *Prosecutors Law*.[269] According to the *Prosecutors Law*, there are seven conditions for serving as a prosecutor in China: First, being a citizen of the People's Republic of China; second, upholding the Constitution of the People's Republic of China, and supporting the leadership of the Communist Party of China and the socialist system; third, having good political, professional, and moral qualities; fourth, having the physical conditions necessary for performing duties normally; fifth, (i) holding a bachelor's degree or higher in law from a regular institution of higher education, or (ii) holding a non-law undergraduate degree or higher from a regular institution of higher education and obtaining a master's degree or higher in law, or (iii) holding a non-law undergraduate degree or higher from a regular institution of higher education and obtaining another corresponding degree while possessing legal professional knowledge; sixth, having engaged in legal work for at least five years, or for those who have obtained a master's degree in law or jurisprudence, or a doctoral degree in law, their years of legal work experience may be reduced to four years or three years respectively; seventh, newly appointed prosecutors must pass the National Unified Legal Professional Qualification Examination to obtain legal professional qualifications.[270] The *Prosecutors Law* also stipulates that, in areas where achieving the academic qualifications poses difficulties, upon review and determination by the Supreme People's Procuratorate, the educational requirements for serving as a prosecutor may be relaxed to graduation from a regular undergraduate institution within a certain period.[271] The above-mentioned conditions are positive requirements for serving as a prosecutor, and in addition to these, one must also meet the negative requirements stipulated in the *Prosecutors Law*, which specify circumstances under which one may not serve as a prosecutor. According to the *Prosecutors Law*, the following categories of individuals are disqualified from serving as prosecutors: those who have been criminally punished; those who have

[266] He (2017).

[267] *Organic Law of the People's Procuratorates* (revised in 2018), Article 42.

[268] *Prosecutors Law* (revised in 2019), Article 12.

[269] Liu Tao, "The Composition, Appointment and Removal Procedures, and Qualifications for Office in the Procuratorate," *Procuratorial Daily*, June 13, 2019, edition 3.

[270] *Prosecutors Law* (revised in 2019), Article 12.

[271] *Prosecutors Law* (revised in 2019), Article 12.

been dismissed from public office; those whose lawyer's or notary's practice certificates have been revoked, or who have been removed from an arbitration committee; and those who meet other circumstances as prescribed by law.[272]

In addition to the basic qualifications for appointment, the *Prosecutors Law* and the Provisions on the Oath of Office for Prosecutors of the People's Republic of China (Trial) (hereinafter referred to as the Oath Provisions) further elaborate on the requirements for appointment. According to the *Prosecutors Law*, the selection of newly appointed prosecutors is conducted through examinations and assessments, based on the criteria of both moral integrity and competence, selecting the best candidates from those meeting the requirements for prosecutors.[273] The specific selection methods are outlined in the "Interim Measures for the Open Selection of Candidates for Initial Appointment of Judges and Prosecutors" issued by the Organisation Department of the Central Committee of the Communist Party of China, the Supreme People's Court, and the Supreme People's Procuratorate. The Procurator-General of the People's Procuratorate must possess expertise in legal matters and have professional experience in the legal profession. Vice Procurators-General and members of procuratorial committees are selected from among prosecutors, judges, or other individuals meeting the qualifications for prosecutors.[274] The Oath Provisions stipulate that, upon assuming the position of a prosecutor for the first time or upon each subsequent promotion, one should solemnly pledge loyalty to the State, love for the people, respect for the law, dedication to duties, and willingly accept supervision, by publicly declaring an oath.[275]

In addition to conventional selection methods, the *Prosecutors Law* also stipulates that procuratorates may openly select prosecutors from professionals in the legal field, such as lawyers, legal academics, and researchers, based on the needs of prosecutorial work.[276] However, in the selection process of these individuals, besides meeting the conditions for appointment as prosecutors, participating lawyers must have practical experience of no less than five years, with extensive professional experience and a good reputation. Similarly, legal academics and researchers, participating in open selection must hold at least a mid-level professional title, have engaged in teaching or research for more than five years, and demonstrate outstanding research abilities and corresponding research achievements.[277]

In summary, in China, becoming a prosecutor requires meeting a series of conditions. It is through these layers of screening criteria that the country is able to select prosecutors with excellent skills and qualities, thereby contributing to the cultivation of high-quality talent for the rule of law and governance.

---

272 *Prosecutors Law* (revised in 2019), Article 13.

273 *Prosecutors Law* (revised in 2019), Article 14.

274 *Prosecutors Law* (revised in 2019), Article 14.

275 *Regulations on the Oath of Prosecutors of the People's Republic of China (Provisional)*, Article 2.

276 *Prosecutors Law* (revised in 2019), Article 15.

277 *Prosecutors Law* (revised in 2019), Article 15.

8.4.3 *Industry Status*

In recent years, China has taken proactive steps to enhance the performance and efficiency of its procuratorial organisations, as part of a broader commitment to advancing the rule of law. This drive towards judicial reform has manifested in several significant policy changes aimed at optimising the operations within the judicial system and ensuring greater adherence to legal principles.

One of the most notable reforms has been the transfer of the authority for investigating duty-related crimes from procuratorial organisations to newly established supervisory commissions. This move is designed to specialise the functions of judicial and supervisory bodies, thereby increasing the focus and effectiveness of investigations into official misconduct. By segregating duties that were traditionally managed within a single institution, these reforms aim to reduce conflicts of interest and enhance the integrity of legal proceedings. Additionally, China has established a system of judicial accountability which seeks to hold judges and prosecutors more accountable for their work. This system is intended to improve transparency in legal proceedings and ensure that decisions are made fairly and justly. The accountability measures are a key component in fostering a culture of responsibility among judicial personnel, which is critical for maintaining public trust in the legal system. Another major aspect of the judicial reforms is the reforming of the quota system for prosecutors. This initiative aims to standardise the number of cases each prosecutor handles, thereby ensuring that each case receives adequate attention and resources. By optimising caseloads, the reform seeks to improve the quality of legal proceedings and reduce the risk of errors or oversights.

These reforms collectively represent a substantial shift in how procuratorial and judicial activities are conducted in China. The establishment of supervisory commissions, the integration of arrest and prosecution powers under these new bodies, the implementation of judicial accountability measures, and the adjustments to the quota system for prosecutors are all designed to create a more robust, efficient, and transparent judicial system. Such changes are undoubtedly having a profound impact on the structure and functioning of procuratorates and prosecutors, aligning them more closely with international standards of justice and efficiency. These initiatives not only enhance the operational capabilities of the legal system but also reinforce the commitment to upholding and advancing the rule of law in China.

8.4.3.1 Impact of the Establishment of Supervisory Commissions on Procuratorates

The recent reform of the supervisory system, which has involved transferring the authority for investigating duty-related crimes from procuratorial organisations to supervisory commissions, has had deep and lasting effects on the structure and functioning of procuratorates and prosecutors. This change has brought about significant transformations, impacting both the practical and theoretical aspects of legal supervision.

On the one hand, separating investigatory and prosecutorial powers has led to certain shifts within the procuratorial organisations themselves. Most notably, there has been a reduction in the substantive deterrent power traditionally held by these organisations. Their ability to directly supervise and investigate duty-related offences has been diminished, which, in turn, has necessitated adjustments in their approach to legal oversight.

However, the benefits of this restructuring are considerable and manifold. Prior to this reform, procuratorates were tasked with both the investigation and prosecution of duty-related crimes, placing them in the precarious position of having to self-examine and self-monitor. This dual role often led to inherent contradictions within the system and raised concerns regarding procedural fairness. Operating under the principle that "no one shall act as a judge in their own case", procuratorial organisations, before the reforms, found themselves in a situation where they were essentially acting as judges in cases where they were also the investigators.[278] This overlap of roles could potentially compromise the integrity of legal proceedings and raise questions about the legitimacy of the outcomes.

Transferring the investigative powers to supervisory commissions addresses these concerns effectively by removing the inherent conflict of interest, thus enabling procuratorial organisations to place greater focus on impartiality in legal supervision. This shift was not only a strategic realignment but also a move towards enhancing the credibility and authority of these organisations in the public eye. By exercising their supervisory rights from a more neutral standpoint, procuratorates can now engage more effectively in upholding the law without the burden of potential biases that come with dual roles.

Moreover, the reform of the supervisory system facilitated a broader re-evaluation and restructuring of the legal supervision framework within procuratorates. This reorganisation has led to the development of what is now known as the "four major procuratorates" system, which encompasses criminal, civil, administrative, and public-interest litigation supervisions. Each segment focuses on specific areas of legal supervision, aiming to strengthen the overall mechanism of judicial oversight. This framework emphasises enhancing the capacities in criminal prosecution, improving civil litigation procedures, solidifying administrative legal actions, and ensuring the effective management of public-interest litigation cases.[279]

In conclusion, while the reform of the supervisory system has indeed presented certain challenges to procuratorial organisations, it has also provided a significant opportunity for these bodies to realign with their foundational judicial review roles.

---

[278] Zhang (2018).

[279] Dai Jia, "Striving at the Forefront of the Tide: The Five Years of Prosecutorial Reform in the New Era," accessed April 5, 2024, Supreme People's Procuratorate of the People's Republic of China website, https://www.spp.gov.cn/spp/2023qglh/202303/t20230305_606354.shtml.

The separation of investigatory and prosecutorial functions allows for a more focused and reasonable exercise of legal supervisory powers, aligning procuratorial practices more closely with the principles of fairness and justice.

8.4.3.2 The Integration of Investigation and Prosecution and Its Impact on the Procuratorate

The concept of "integration of investigation and prosecution", as defined in Article 8 of the "Criminal Procedure Rules of the People's Procuratorates",[280] highlights a pivotal organisational strategy whereby all phases of a criminal case—examination, arrest, prosecution, court representation, case supervision, investigation oversight, and trial oversight—are managed by the same procurator or a dedicated team of procurators. This approach is a cornerstone in the ongoing evolution of legal frameworks in the new era, representing a profound shift towards greater procedural efficiency and reform within the institutional structures of procuratorates.

This integrative model was designed to enhance the coherence and consistency of handling criminal cases, ensuring that the entire process from initial investigation to final prosecution is streamlined and managed under a unified command. This alignment not only improves procedural efficiency but also ensures a higher level of accuracy and integrity in legal proceedings, reducing the likelihood of errors that might occur when multiple departments handle different stages of the same case.

The significance of this integration was further underscored by Procurator-General Zhang Jun during a press conference, on 3 January 2019, organised by the State Council Information Office. He discussed the reforms of the internal institutions of the Supreme People's Procuratorate and the comprehensive execution of its legal supervision functions. Zhang Jun elaborated on the historical context and the rationale behind adopting this integrated approach, noting that, before the year 2000, a model of separation between investigation and prosecution was prevalent. This model was initially valued for its internal checks and balances, designed to prevent the progression of investigative errors into wrongful prosecutions. However, it became apparent that this separation was also causing inefficiencies and challenges in terms of substantive internal supervision, as each transition from investigation to prosecution involved a handover that could lead to informational losses and procedural delays.[281]

This realisation led to a significant restructuring within procuratorates. By integrating the roles of investigators and prosecutors within the same departments, the reform aimed to address these inefficiencies and enhance the overall effectiveness of the legal process. This integration not only streamlined the procedural steps but also facilitated a more cohesive and coordinated approach to case handling. Consequently, this structural change has had a direct impact on the internal architecture of procuratorial bodies. The merging of the investigative oversight department with the

---

[280] *Criminal Procedure Rules of the People's Procuratorates*, Article 8.

[281] Meng (2019).

prosecution department simplified the internal organisational structure to a considerable extent, thereby enabling a more focused and unified execution of legal supervision responsibilities. This consolidation helps in minimising bureaucratic complexities and enhances the ability of the procuratorial staff to perform their duties more effectively and with greater accountability.

Thus, the integration of investigation and prosecution is not merely a procedural update; it is a strategic overhaul that significantly refines the operations of procuratorates, enhancing both their functional efficiency and institutional effectiveness in the broader context of legal and judicial reform.

8.4.3.3 The Impact of Judicial Accountability System on Prosecutors

The "judicial accountability system" holds a pivotal position in the ongoing reforms of the judicial system, and significantly influences the roles and responsibilities of prosecutors. This system has brought about considerable changes in the way judicial activities are conducted, ensuring that those involved in the administration of justice, including judges and prosecutors, are held accountable for their actions.

On 24 March 2015, during an influential collective study session of the Political Bureau of the CPC Central Committee, General Secretary Xi Jinping made a compelling case for deepening the reform of the judicial system and enhancing judicial fairness. He metaphorically referred to grasping the "bull's nose" of the judicial accountability system to underscore its critical importance. General Secretary Xi emphasised the necessity of bolstering supervision, and imposing strict constraints on the conduct of judges and prosecutors. He advocated for a multifaceted oversight mechanism encompassing legal, social, and public opinion supervision over judicial power. His directive was clear: to ensure that those in judicial positions perform their duties with a deep sense of public duty, and maintain a demeanour that is both honest and transparent, while operating strictly within the established legal framework.[282] These remarks set the tone for a more accountable and transparent judicial process. Following these directives, the Supreme People's Procuratorate acted by issuing the "Several Opinions on Improving the Judicial Responsibility System of People's Procuratorates".[283] This document lays down explicit guidelines for delineating the responsibilities and authority of prosecutorial staff, and for instituting robust measures for accountability, determination, and enforcement.[284] By clarifying these elements, the system aims to mitigate the risks of judicial errors and enhance the integrity of prosecutorial decisions, significantly diminishing the likelihood of miscarriages of justice.

---

[282] Yu, Xiangling. 'Firmly Grasping the Bull's Nose of the Judicial Accountability System.' *Procuratorial Daily*, July 3, 2015. For details, see the website of the Supreme People's Procuratorate of the People's Republic of China, https://www.spp.gov.cn/llyj/201507/t20150703_100715.shtml.

[283] See the website of the Supreme People's Procuratorate of the People's Republic of China, https://www.spp.gov.cn/zdgz/201509/t20150929_105342.shtml, accessed April 5, 2024.

[284] Jiang (2016).

In practice, the judicial accountability system has indeed shown tangible results. By making prosecutors more circumspect in their handling of cases, it has reduced instances of judicial error. Nevertheless, while the system has brought about positive changes, such as heightened diligence in case processing, it has also introduced challenges. The burden of lifelong accountability for wrongful convictions has introduced a degree of caution that occasionally impedes the effective and confident handling of cases. Some prosecutors, wary of the long-term repercussions of an erroneous decision, might exhibit excessive caution, which can sometimes result in a reluctance to prosecute cases with less than absolute certainty, leading to a higher incidence of acquittals or decisions not to prosecute due to insufficient evidence.[285]

Undoubtedly, the judicial accountability system has shifted the focus from merely driving case efficiency to enhancing the quality of case handling. This transformation is instrumental in improving the overall standard of legal construction within the country. It is a shift that fosters a more meticulous and quality-focused judicial process. However, it is equally important to address the challenges introduced by this system. These include the potential for overly cautious decision-making and the implications it has for the flow of justice. Addressing these issues requires proactive and thoughtful measures to balance accountability with effective judicial practice, ensuring that the system enhances, rather than inhibits, the delivery of justice.

8.4.3.4 The Impact of Quota System Reform on Prosecutors

The concept of a quota typically signifies a cap or restriction on the number of individuals that can occupy certain positions or roles within an organisation. In the context of the judiciary, the term "judicial quota system" refers to a specific framework used to determine the number of judicial officers, such as judges and prosecutors, that are permitted within a judicial entity like courts and procuratorates. This system is based on various criteria, including the volume of cases handled, the population under jurisdiction, and the level of economic development within the region.[286] This system is designed to optimise the allocation of judicial resources, ensuring that personnel are appropriately distributed according to the needs and demands of the population they serve.

Within procuratorial organisations, the "prosecutor quota system" applies a similar principle but is tailored specifically for the management of prosecutorial staff. It categorises personnel into distinct groups—prosecutors, prosecutorial assistants, and judicial administrative personnel—and applies a classification management approach. This system serves multiple purposes but primarily aims to rectify the mismatch between the title of prosecutor and the actual engagement in case-related

[285] Zhang (2023).

[286] Researcher from the Center for the Development of Rule of Law and Judicial Reform at Zhongnan University of Economics and Law, "The Staffing System Contributes to the Professionalization, Career Specialization, and Elitism in the Judiciary," accessed April 5, 2024, Supreme People's Procuratorate of the People's Republic of China website, https://www.spp.gov.cn/spp/ztk/dfld/2015dfld/dfld93/ywtt/201512/t20151211_109216.shtml.

duties.[287] It seeks to ensure that those who bear the prosecutor's title are directly involved in the substantive legal processes and are not sidelined by non-case-related administrative tasks.

The implementation of this quota system has led to significant strides towards the professionalisation of the prosecutorial roles, markedly enhancing the efficiency and quality of legal proceedings by ensuring that qualified, specialised personnel handle the intricacies of case management. Nonetheless, despite these advantages, the system is not without its flaws. A critical issue is the uniform application of quotas across various regions and levels, which has led to a palpable shortage of prosecutorial staff at more grassroots levels of the judiciary. This shortage is exacerbated by the rigid quota limits, which also foster a sense of uncertainty and insecurity among non-quota personnel about their chances of entering into the quota ranks. Such conditions have precipitated a notable drain of talent within the procuratorates, as potential candidates may seek alternative career paths outside the quota system.

This talent drain poses a substantial challenge, especially for prosecutors who are already operating under the quota system at the grassroots level. These prosecutors often face overwhelming caseloads, which can impair their ability to deliver justice efficiently and effectively. The situation calls for a thoughtful reassessment and potential recalibration of the quota system to better accommodate the dynamic needs of the judiciary, ensuring that it can continue to serve the public effectively while also fostering a supportive environment for its legal staff.

8.5 Arbitration Institutions and Arbitrators

Arbitration, often referred to as "public judgment", serves as a critical, alternative legal pathway for the resolution of economic disputes outside the traditional court litigation system. This method involves the disputing parties voluntarily agreeing to submit their conflict to a pre-selected arbitration institution, based on an arbitration agreement that is established either before or after the dispute has arisen. The fundamental principle of arbitration is that both parties commit to adhere to the arbitration award, which is the final decision made by the arbitrators, as their method of resolving the dispute.[288] This system not only provides a binding resolution but also offers a streamlined process that tends to be faster and more cost-effective than going through court proceedings.

With the acceleration of global economic activities and the increasing complexity of commercial relationships, the incidence of various types of disputes has also risen. Traditional court litigation, with its often lengthy and cumbersome procedures,

[287] Zhang (2023).

[288] Researcher from the Center for the Development of Rule of Law and Judicial Reform at Zhongnan University of Economics and Law, "The Staffing System Contributes to the Professionalization, Career Specialization, and Elitism in the Judiciary," accessed April 5, 2024, Supreme People's Procuratorate of the People's Republic of China website, https://www.spp.gov.cn/spp/ztk/dfld/2015dfld/dfld93/ywtt/201512/t20151211_109216.shtml.

struggles to keep pace with the demand for swift and efficient resolution of these conflicts. In this context, arbitration has emerged as an increasingly popular choice among businesses and individuals seeking a quicker resolution.[289] Its advantages are particularly pronounced in international business transactions, where arbitration is often favoured due to its global enforceability and the neutrality it offers compared to domestic courts.[290]

In response to the growing reliance on arbitration, a multitude of arbitration institutions have been established across the nation. These institutions are staffed by seasoned professionals who bring specialised knowledge and experience to the arbitration process.[291] The arbitrators are typically chosen for their expertise in specific fields relevant to the disputes they are tasked with resolving, ensuring that all parties involved receive the most informed and fair judgement. The proliferation of these institutions across the country reflects the trust and reliance placed in the arbitration process as an effective and impartial means to adjudicate disputes.

Moreover, the flexibility offered by arbitration, in terms of procedural rules and the choice of arbitrators, makes it an attractive option for parties seeking more control over how their dispute is handled.[292] This aspect of arbitration is particularly appealing to those who wish to keep their legal matters private and away from the public eye, as arbitration proceedings are generally confidential.[293]

In conclusion, as the economic landscape continues to evolve and as disputes become more frequent and complex, arbitration stands out as a vital mechanism for dispute resolution. Its capacity to provide effective, efficient, and equitable resolutions, without the formalities and delays often associated with court litigation, makes it a cornerstone of modern legal practice, indispensable for meeting the contemporary needs of rapid dispute resolution.

8.5.1 Establishment of Arbitration Committees

There are significant differences in the establishment of arbitration committees compared to courts and procuratorates, which can be seen from the legal provisions regarding the establishment of arbitration committees, courts, and procuratorates. In terms of geographical location, arbitration committees can be established in municipalities directly under the Central Government, cities where the people's governments of provinces and autonomous regions are located, and other prefecture-level cities as needed, without the need for hierarchical establishment according to administrative divisions like courts and procuratorates.[294] Furthermore, unlike judicial institutions,

---

[289] Cheng (2004).

[290] Cheng (2004).

[291] Generally, arbitrators are required to have extensive experience in the practice of law.

[292] Deng (2001).

[293] Deng (2001).

[294] *Arbitration Law* (revised in 2017), Article 10.

arbitration committees are not subject to hierarchical jurisdiction or territorial jurisdiction. In terms of establishment procedures, arbitration committees are organised in a unified manner by the relevant departments of the people's governments and chambers of commerce in municipalities directly under the Central Government; cities where the people's governments of provinces and autonomous regions are located; and should be registered with the judicial administrative departments of provinces, autonomous regions, and municipalities directly under the Central Government.[295] Nevertheless, arbitration committees are independent of administrative authorities, and there is no subordinate relationship between them and administrative agencies. There are also no hierarchical relationships between arbitration committees.[296] In addition to the above requirements, the establishment of an arbitration committee should also meet a series of conditions. These conditions include having its own name, domicile, and articles of association, possessing necessary assets, having constituent members, and appointing arbitrators.[297] Additionally, according to the *Arbitration Law of the People's Republic of China* (hereinafter referred to as the *Arbitration Law*), the articles of association of an arbitration committee should be formulated in accordance with the *Arbitration Law*.[298] In terms of the composition of the arbitration committee personnel, according to the laws of China, an arbitration committee should consist of one director, two to four deputy directors, and seven to 11 members.[299] The director, deputy directors, and members of the arbitration committee should be experts in law, economics, and trade, and have practical work experience. Additionally, among the composition of personnel in the arbitration committee, experts in law, economics, and trade should not be less than two-thirds of the total committee.[300]

8.5.2 Arbitrator Professional Requirements

In terms of the professional requirements for arbitrators, these can be divided into basic requirements and specific requirements. Basic requirements refer to the essential conditions that all arbitrators must meet according to the *Arbitration Law*, while specific requirements are additional criteria set by the arbitration committee based on its particular circumstances.

According to the *Arbitration Law*, arbitrators must meet the following basic conditions: firstly, they must be individuals known for their fairness and integrity.[301] Secondly, to serve as an arbitrator in China, one must meet one of the following

[295] *Arbitration Law* (revised in 2017), Article 10.
[296] *Arbitration Law* (revised in 2017), Article 14.
[297] *Arbitration Law* (revised in 2017), Article 11.
[298] *Arbitration Law* (revised in 2017), Article 11.
[299] *Arbitration Law* (revised in 2017), Article 12.
[300] *Arbitration Law* (revised in 2017), Article 12.
[301] *Arbitration Law* (revised in 2017), Article 13.

conditions: (i) passing the National Unified Legal Professional Qualification Examination and having eight years of experience in arbitration work; (ii) working as a lawyer for eight years; (iii) serving as a judge for eight years; (iv) engaging in legal research or teaching with a senior professional title; or (v) having expertise in law, and engaging in professional work such as economics and trade with a senior professional title or equivalent professional level.[302] Only when meeting the above conditions can relevant individuals meet the basic requirements for serving as arbitrators.

Although the *Arbitration Law* stipulates requirements for serving as arbitrators, these are just the basic conditions. In China, besides meeting the aforementioned criteria, individuals must also fulfil higher and more specific requirements, as outlined by arbitration commissions across the country when appointing arbitrators. For instance, the Shanghai International Economic and Trade Arbitration Commission specifies, in its recruitment announcement, that applicants must not only meet the conditions stipulated in Article 13 of the *Arbitration Law* but also be under the age of 68, and have no criminal record or misconduct that could independently challenge their ability to serve as arbitrators.[303] Similarly, the China International Economic and Trade Arbitration Commission states, in its arbitrator recruitment notice that, in addition to meeting the basic requirements specified in the *Arbitration Law*, Chinese arbitrators must also meet the following conditions: firstly, they must uphold the Commission's Charter and be willing to abide by its Arbitration Rules and Arbitrator Code of Conduct; secondly, they must be proficient in a foreign language that can be used as a working language, although this requirement may be relaxed for some prominent individuals; thirdly, they must be able to ensure availability for arbitration proceedings; and fourthly, they must meet any additional conditions stipulated by the arbitration commission.[304] For foreign arbitrators, the China International Economic and Trade Arbitration Commission does not require them to meet the conditions specified in Article 13 of the *Arbitration Law*, but the other requirements are essentially the same as those for Chinese arbitrators.[305] Additionally, the commission specifies that the qualifications for arbitrators from the Hong Kong, Macau, and Taiwan regions should follow the criteria for foreign arbitrators.[306]

[302] *Arbitration Law* (revised in 2017), Article 13.

[303] Refer to the official website of the Shanghai International Economic and Trade Arbitration Commission, https://www.shiac.org/pc/SHIAC?moduleCode=to_arbitrator. Accessed on April 20, 2024.

[304] Refer to the official website of the China International Economic and Trade Arbitration Commission states, https://www.cietacodr.org. Accessed on April 23, 2024.

[305] Refer to the official website of the China International Economic and Trade Arbitration Commission states, https://www.cietacodr.org. Accessed on April 23, 2024.

[306] Refer to the official website of the China International Economic and Trade Arbitration Commission states, https://www.cietacodr.org. Accessed on April 23, 2024.

8.5.3 Industry Status

Traditionally, when discussing the legal industry, the focus typically gravitates towards the more visible roles such as judges, prosecutors, and lawyers. These professions are often the most prominently recognised within the judicial system, receiving considerable attention in both education and media portrayals. In contrast, other legal professions, such as notaries and arbitrators, tend to be less highlighted and somewhat marginalised in public discourse. This discrepancy is also reflected in the legislative arena, where laws and regulations pertaining to the judiciary have historically been given priority. Legislative bodies and other pertinent governmental departments have continually revised and updated judicial laws to ensure they remain relevant and effective in addressing new legal challenges as they arise.

However, with the continuous growth and evolution of China's market economy, there has been a noticeable shift in the methods preferred for dispute resolution. Arbitration, in particular, has emerged as a favoured choice due to its cost-effectiveness and efficiency.[307] This method of settling disputes outside traditional courtrooms has gradually gained popularity among businesses and individuals alike, largely because it provides a faster resolution compared to the often protracted processes observed in conventional litigation.[308]

Moreover, the role of various media platforms has been instrumental in enhancing the visibility and understanding of arbitration. Through consistent promotion and coverage, these platforms have played a crucial role in shifting arbitration from a peripheral option to a mainstream method of dispute resolution. As more people become aware of its benefits, the demand for and reliance on arbitration continue to grow.

Simultaneously, there has been a concerted effort to strengthen the legal framework surrounding arbitration. This includes both the formulation and refinement of specific rules related to the practice of arbitration, thereby making the arbitration system more robust and comprehensive. Presently, China boasts a relatively well-established system for arbitration, underscored by the amended *Arbitration Law* and various rules that have been autonomously formulated by arbitration institutions themselves.

As a result of these enhancements, the number of arbitration institutions has seen a significant increase, as has the volume of cases being handled through this method. This uptrend not only reflects the growing acceptance and trust in arbitration as a reliable and impartial means of resolving disputes, but also signifies its integral role in the modern legal landscape of China. The establishment of more dedicated arbitration institutions is indicative of the system's maturation and its ability to adapt to the needs of a dynamic, economic environment, further solidifying its position as a critical component of the legal framework designed to support economic development and maintain social harmony.

[307] Xie (2013).

[308] Cheng (2004).

As of 2022, Chinese arbitration institutions were still showing a trend of development and growth. Despite the impact of the COVID-19 pandemic, the number of cases handled in arbitration has steadily increased. Geographically, the Guangdong-Hong Kong-Macao Greater Bay Area, Beijing, and Shanghai remain the major centres for arbitration in China, with an absolute advantage in the number of cases. In 2022, the overall dispute amount of newly accepted arbitration cases in the Greater Bay Area and Beijing exceeded 200 billion yuan each.[309] This is closely related to the important position of these cities as the economic centres of the country. In terms of the internationalisation of case acceptance, Chinese arbitration institutions have also made further progress. In recent years, influenced by the economic environment, there have been significant changes in the arbitration field, with major cases involving claim amounts exceeding 100 million yuan, 1 billion yuan, and even cases with greater claim amounts becoming increasingly common.[310] While acknowledging the positive developments in the arbitration industry, the challenges must also be addressed. For example, arbitrators' decisions may be influenced by conflicts of interest, leading to unfair rulings. Additionally, lack of expertise and experience among arbitrators can result in unjust outcomes, undermining the credibility of arbitration institutions. Consequently, some arbitration committees may experience a decline in public trust.

8.6 Other Legal Professions

In addition to the more traditionally recognised legal professions, such as judges, prosecutors, and lawyers, China's legal landscape encompasses a diverse array of other legal roles, each playing a critical function within the broader judicial and regulatory framework. These roles include corporate legal counsel, notaries, supervisory officials, administrative law enforcement personnel, and many others. Each of these professions is crucial in its own right, catering to specific aspects of legal and regulatory compliance and governance.

Corporate legal counsels, for example, serve as vital advisers in the business sector, providing companies with crucial legal guidance to navigate the complexities of commercial law, ensuring compliance, and mitigating risks. Notaries play an essential role in the authentication of documents and agreements, ensuring their legality and enforceability. Supervisory officials are tasked with overseeing various aspects of legal compliance and governance within public and private entities, ensuring that laws and regulations are adhered to. Administrative law enforcement personnel are responsible for the implementation and enforcement of laws at the administrative

---

[309] "2022 China Arbitration Institutions Development Data: Case Amount (Trillions / Five Hundred Billion / Hundred Billion) and Others," accessed April 5, 2024, Arbitration Network website, http://www.china-arbitration.com/index/news/detail/id/2153.html.

[310] "2022 China Arbitration Institutions Development Data: Case Amount (Trillions / Five Hundred Billion / Hundred Billion) and Others," accessed April 5, 2024, Arbitration Network website, http://www.china-arbitration.com/index/news/detail/id/2153.html.

level, dealing directly with violations of regulations that do not necessarily warrant criminal prosecution.

Each of these professions is supported by a distinct organisational structure that defines its operations and hierarchies. These structures are designed to ensure that each professional can perform their duties effectively and efficiently, within a framework that supports their specific needs and responsibilities. Furthermore, these roles come with professional requirements that may include specific educational qualifications, training, and certification, which are essential for maintaining the high standards expected within the field.

Over time, as society evolves and new challenges emerge, the roles and requirements of these legal professions also undergo significant changes. This evolution is necessary to keep pace with developments in the legal landscape, technological advancements, changes in business practices, and shifts in public policy. As these changes occur, the organisational structures and professional standards of these roles are continually reviewed and updated to ensure they remain relevant and effective in meeting the needs of society and the economy.

This dynamic and responsive approach to the development of legal professions ensures that China's legal system remains robust, adaptable, and equipped to handle the complexities of a rapidly changing world. The ongoing improvement and adaptation of these roles are essential for ensuring justice, maintaining legal order, and supporting economic and social development.

8.6.1 Corporate Legal Affairs

Corporate legal affairs refer to the specialised personnel who manage and oversee legal functions within a company. In China, it is common for large enterprises to have dedicated departments tasked with handling corporate legal matters, whereas small and medium-sized enterprises may not have such departments but often employ one or several legal officers to manage legal responsibilities. The role of corporate legal affairs is crucial in the daily operations and strategic management of companies. Their primary duties include drafting, reviewing, and formulating contracts and other legal documents; handling litigation and arbitration cases to protect the company's legal rights; developing and enhancing company policies and management systems; providing legal opinions and guidance to support business operations and strategic decision-making; offering legal training to personnel from various departments; and conducting thorough legal compliance audits.[311]

As an essential internal function, the position of corporate legal affairs demands a high level of professionalism and expertise. When hiring, companies typically seek candidates with specific attributes and qualifications. Essential requirements often include a solid understanding of company and contract law,[312] attention to detail, a

[311] Zheng (2021).

[312] Tao (2019).

strong sense of responsibility, the ability to handle stress, effective communication skills, logical thinking, and team collaboration. Proficiency in various office software is also expected. Additionally, many firms require candidates to possess at least a bachelor's degree, though a master's degree may be preferable. They may also need to have passed the National Unified Legal Professional Qualification Examination, be well-versed in legal regulations pertinent to the company's primary business activities, and have relevant experience either in corporate legal roles or with law firms.

Moreover, given the varied nature of businesses, some companies may seek candidates with specialised knowledge that aligns with their specific industry focus. For instance, companies in the new energy sector might look for legal officers familiar with the regulations and challenges of that industry, while software development companies might prioritise candidates with a strong background in intellectual property law.

Salary levels within corporate legal affairs vary significantly and are typically influenced by the size, scale, and sector of the company rather than the volume or complexity of the daily tasks performed. Generally, legal personnel in larger companies, or in industries with significant capital flow, tend to receive higher remuneration, although this can fluctuate based on overall industry conditions.

The role of a corporate legal officer offers several advantages, including the opportunity to acquire deep insights into the industry in which the company operates and its related sectors. This position requires a profound understanding of specific legal areas, and interacting with various industry stakeholders provides valuable experience and networking opportunities that can be beneficial for future career advancements. Many law graduates view positions in corporate legal affairs as an effective "springboard" into the professional world.

However, there are also notable challenges associated with this role. The work can often be monotonous and repetitive, and there is typically little opportunity to gain experience in more dynamic legal practices such as litigation and trial work. This is largely due to most companies' preference for stable business operations and their aversion to legal risks, which limits the scope for corporate legal officers to expand their practice into other areas of law. Such constraints can affect the long-term career growth and diversity of experience for legal professionals within corporate settings.[313]

8.6.2 Notaries

According to the stipulations set forth in the *Notary Law* of China, notarisation is defined as a critical legal process conducted by designated notary institutions.[314] This vital activity involves the verification and certification of the authenticity and

[313] Wang (2021).

[314] *Notary Law (Amended 2017)*, Article 2.

legality of various civil legal acts, important factual events, and documents.[315] This certification is undertaken upon the request of natural persons, legal entities, or other organisations, and must be carried out strictly following the procedures that are prescribed by law.[316] This ensures that all notarised documents and acts conform to the highest standards of legal rigour, thereby providing a reliable basis for their acceptance in legal and civil proceedings.

Within these notary institutions, the role of notaries is central and multifaceted. Notaries are highly trained professionals who are tasked with executing the notarial activities in accordance with the specific provisions outlined in the *Notary Law*.[317] Their responsibilities are profound, as they ensure that the documents and acts they notarise are both authentic and compliant with the relevant legal frameworks, thus playing a pivotal role in the legal validation process.

As with other specialised legal professions, the position of a notary comes with a set of stringent professional requirements. These requirements are designed to ensure that those who take on this role are thoroughly prepared to handle the responsibilities it entails. In China, the *Notary Law* stipulates the following conditions for serving as a notary: (i) being a citizen of the People's Republic of China; (ii) aged between 25 and 65 years old; (iii) being upright, law-abiding, and of good conduct; (iv) obtaining the legal professional qualification through the National Unified Legal Professional Qualification Examination; and (v) interning in a notary institution for more than two years, or having more than three years of experience in other legal professions and interning in a notary institution for more than one year, and passing the assessment.[318] Additionally, individuals engaged in legal teaching or research; holding senior professional titles; having a bachelor's degree or above; having ten years of experience in adjudication, prosecution, legal work, or legal services as a civil servant or lawyer; and have left their original position, may also serve as notaries if they pass the assessment.[319] Furthermore, the *Notary Law* specifies four situations in which individuals cannot serve as notaries: those without or with limited capacity for civil conduct, those who have been criminally punished for intentional crimes or negligent crimes in their duties, those who have been dismissed from public office, and those whose notary or lawyer practising certificates have been revoked.[320]

As society progresses, there is a marked increase in the public's understanding and awareness of legal issues, which naturally leads to a greater need for notarisation services. This heightened awareness and need have spurred a corresponding rise in both the demand for notaries and the expectations for their professional qualifications.

In response to these changing dynamics, notary institutions must evolve and adapt to meet these new challenges. It is essential for these institutions to focus more intently on the practical aspects of notarial work during their training programs.

---

[315] *Notary Law (Amended 2017)*, Article 2.

[316] *Notary Law (Amended 2017)*, Article 2.

[317] *Notary Law (Amended 2017)*, Article 16.

[318] *Notary Law (Amended 2017)*, Article 18.

[319] *Notary Law (Amended 2017)*, Article 19.

[320] *Notary Law (Amended 2017)*, Article 20.

By doing so, they can ensure that notaries are well-prepared to meet the complex demands of their roles.[321]

Furthermore, notary institutions should enhance the rigour of their assessments of notaries' daily work. Strengthening these evaluations helps maintain high standards of professional practice and ensures that notaries are performing their duties with the utmost competency and integrity. This proactive approach in training and evaluation is crucial for notary institutions to continue fulfilling their role effectively in the face of growing public demand for notarial services.

8.6.3 Supervisors

Since the comprehensive launch of the supervision system reform in 2018, China's supervision system has entered a new stage of development. Therefore, in 2021, the State promulgated the *Supervisor Law* to better regulate the behaviour of supervisors.[322] According to the relevant provisions of the *Supervisor Law*, serving as a supervisor in China requires meeting a series of conditions, including being a citizen of the People's Republic of China; being loyal to the Constitution, adhering to the leadership of the Communist Party of China and the socialist system; possessing good political quality, moral integrity, and a clean work style; being familiar with laws, regulations, and policies; and having professional knowledge and abilities to perform supervisory, investigative, and disposal duties; having physical and psychological qualities necessary for the normal performance of duties; having a bachelor's degree or above from a higher education institution; and meeting other conditions specified by law.[323] However, unlike the strict educational requirements in the *Judges Law* and *Procurators Law*, the *Supervisor Law* makes special arrangements for supervisory personnel who were already working but did not meet the educational requirements.[324] It stipulates that such individuals should undergo training and assessment, and the specific training and assessment methods are formulated by the National Supervisory Commission.[325] In other words, the State has made flexible arrangements for the appointment of supervisors to realistically meet the need.

While making the above provisions, the *Supervisor Law* also specifies circumstances in which individuals may not serve as supervisors: first, those who have been criminally punished or not prosecuted for minor crimes by the People's Procuratorate or have been exempted from criminal punishment by the People's Court due to minor crimes; second, those who have been revoked of their positions in the Communist Party of China, subjected to Party disciplinary measures, or expelled from the Party;

---

[321] Liao and Zhang (2023).

[322] See the website of the Central People's Government of the People's Republic of China, https://www.gov.cn/xinwen/2021-08/20/content_5632497.htm, accessed on April 5, 2024.

[323] *Supervisor Law*, Article 12.

[324] *Supervisor Law*, Article 12.

[325] *Supervisor Law*, Article 12.

third, those who have been dismissed or removed from public office; fourth, those who have been included in the list of joint disciplinary objects for dishonesty according to law; fifth, those whose spouses have moved abroad, or who do not have spouses but whose children have all moved abroad; and sixth, other circumstances stipulated by law.[326] It is under such high standards and strict requirements that China is able to select high-quality supervisors with excellent abilities, thereby facilitating the smooth progress of anti-corruption efforts and better safeguarding the dignity of the Constitution and laws.

8.7 Emerging Legal Professions

At the end of 2019, and into the beginning of 2020, the sudden outbreak of the COVID-19 pandemic occurred. In 2021, following the pandemic, the total number of new cases accepted by courts nationwide reached 31,539,810,[327] compared to 28,283,204 in 2020,[328] marking an increase of 3,256,606 cases. Similarly, the data for 2022 remained at the same level as 2021.[329]

This surge in cases indicates a heightened demand for legal recourse among the general public, which persisted even after the immediate effects of the pandemic seemed to subside. However, accessing legal services can be financially burdensome, as these services are subject to minimum fee standards that are explicitly stipulated by law. These costs can be prohibitive for certain segments of the population, leading to a disparity in access to justice.

In response to this scenario, new forms of legal professions began to emerge, aiming to provide legal consultation, case representation, and other services at more affordable prices to meet the needs of the people. These emerging roles in the legal field offer a cost-effective alternative to traditional legal services, potentially increasing access to justice for those who find standard legal fees unattainable.

Although these new professions are not yet recognised as "legal professionals" under the official Classification Directory of Occupations of the People's Republic of China, their presence in the market reflects a practical response to a growing demand. The legitimacy and qualifications of these emerging roles seeking to provide legal services continue to be a subject of debate and scrutiny. From a practical standpoint, the emergence and persistence of these roles demonstrate their relevance and necessity in addressing the legal needs of a broader segment of the population. The future development of these professions, while uncertain, highlights the dynamic nature

---

[326] *Supervisor Law*, Article 13.

[327] Refer to *National Court Gazette 2021, Bulletin of the Supreme People's Court of the People's Republic of China*, no. 4 (2022).

[328] Refer to *National Court Gazette 2020, Bulletin of the Supreme People's Court of the People's Republic of China*, no. 4 (2021).

[329] Refer to *National Court Gazette 2022, Bulletin of the Supreme People's Court of the People's Republic of China*, no. 4 (2023).

of the legal services market and the potential for innovation in how legal assistance is provided. Whether these emerging professions will eventually be recognised and regulated remains to be seen, but their current existence is a testament to their utility and the public's demand for more accessible legal solutions.

8.7.1 Lawyer Agent

In recent years, lawyer agents have gradually come into the public eye. Generally speaking, agent refers to a natural person, legal person, or other economic organisation engaged in intermediary, brokerage, or agency business for the purpose of receiving commissions in economic activities to facilitate transactions for others.[330] Specifically, lawyer agents are supposed to facilitate the collaboration between individuals in need of legal services and lawyers, forming a relationship of agency by appointment, and earning commissions from it.

However, nowadays, in many civil cases, lawyer agents recommended by the Lawyer Agent Professional Committee of the Brokerage Association become entrusted litigation agents and are recorded in the documents issued by the court.[331] Their agency rights have been preliminarily tolerated by some courts in practice, with these courts mainly concentrated in the courts of Liaoning Province.[332] In the absence of specific legal regulations governing lawyer brokers, this phenomenon has raised questions within the legal community, primarily concerning the legitimacy of lawyer agents acting as legal representatives instead of lawyers.

From a legal perspective, whether lawyer agents can act as legal representatives depends on the circumstances. According to the Civil Procedure Law of the People's Republic of China, only three categories of individuals can act as legal representatives: lawyers or grassroots legal service workers; close relatives or employees of the parties; or citizens recommended by the community, unit, or relevant social organisations where the parties are located.[333] When a lawyer agent acts as either a close relative or employee of the party, they can indeed serve as a legal representative. However, if they are neither a close relative nor an employee of the party, and they do not fall under the category of lawyers or grassroots legal service workers, whether they can serve as a "citizen recommended by relevant social organisations" to act as a legal representative becomes a key issue.

---

[330] *Regulations on the Management of Agents* (Decree No. 14 of the State Administration for Industry and Commerce of the People's Republic of China, repealed), Article 2. Although this regulation has been repealed, its definition of "agent" still holds some reference significance.

[331] For example, Judgment No. (2022) Liaoning 01 Civil Final 10932, Judgment No. (2022) Liaoning 04 Civil Retrial 16, Ruling No. (2022) Liaoning 0292 Execution 45.

[332] In a search for "lawyer agents" on the Weike Xianxing website, there were a total of 32 documents found. Among them, 28 documents involve representatives acting as agents, and all 28 documents were issued by various courts in Liaoning Province.

[333] *Civil Procedure Law (Amended 2023)*, Article 61.

The "Supreme People's Court's Interpretation of the Application of the Civil Procedure Law of the People's Republic of China" sets forth four constitutive elements regarding this matter: First, the social organisation must be a non-profit legal person organisation established in accordance with the law or established without the requirement of registration in accordance with the law; second, the principal represented by the agent must be a member of the social organisation, or one party to the proceedings must have their domicile within the operational area of the social organisation; third, the agency matters must fall within the business scope stipulated in the social organisation's articles of association; fourth, the recommended citizen must be the legal representative of the social organisation or a staff member who has a legitimate labour relationship with the social organisation.[334] As an example, the Broker Association of Liaoning Province is a non-profit legal person organisation registered in accordance with the law. To recommend a lawyer agent for the purpose of representing the parties, it can select parties from its operational area or encourage parties to join the association, thereby recommending its leaders or staff members as lawyer agents to act as litigation agents for the parties. Thus, it is evident that the first, second, and fourth elements are relatively easy to meet in practice. However, its business scope does not explicitly mention recommending citizens as litigation agents for the parties, only referring to "mediating broker business disputes, helping brokers resolve difficulties, and safeguarding the legitimate rights and interests of brokers". In other words, the Broker Association only appoints litigation agents for its member brokers when their legitimate rights and interests are violated or when there are disputes in broker business mediation.

In summary, the role of a lawyer agent, when filled by someone who is a close relative or a staff member of the involved party, allows for a direct and immediate assumption of duties as the party's litigation agent. This proximity to the party facilitates a seamless and straightforward representation in legal proceedings, ensuring that the interests of the party are well-represented by someone familiar and trusted.

However, the scope of representation by lawyer agents is subject to more specific restrictions when it comes to their affiliation with a Broker Association. When a lawyer agent is endorsed by the Lawyer Professional Committee of the Broker Association in their capacity as a citizen, their role as a litigation agent is somewhat limited. Specifically, such a lawyer broker can only act as a litigation agent for those brokers who are members of the association, and then only under certain conditions. These conditions include scenarios where the legitimate rights and interests of these member brokers are under threat, or when disputes arise within the realm of broker business mediation.

It is important to note that, in their role as leaders or staff members of the Broker Association, lawyer brokers are not permitted to represent non-members or individuals who are not brokers. This limitation ensures that the focus of their legal advocacy remains strictly within the confines of the association's membership, thereby

[334] *Interpretation of the Supreme People's Court on the Application of the Civil Procedure Law of the People's Republic of China*, Article 87.

preserving the integrity and specific focus of their legal services within the established boundaries of the Broker Association's purview. This structured approach helps maintain clear lines of responsibility and support within the broker community, particularly in cases involving legal disputes or rights infringements.

However, in many of the relevant cases arising today, the majority involve lawyer brokers recommended by broker associations to act as litigation agents for non-members or non-brokers.[335] Regardless of whether the act of lawyer brokers being recommended by broker associations to serve as litigation agents for other parties is legal, due to the lack of clear legal regulations governing this practice and the absence of oversight by lawyer associations, as typically seen in the legal profession, and given that there are no strict requirements such as passing a National Unified Legal Professional Qualification Examination to become a lawyer broker, lawyer brokers may lack in professional competence, behavioural standards, ethical integrity, and are more likely to encounter disputes with the parties they represent while providing litigation agency services.[336] Furthermore, whether lawyer brokers serving as litigation agents will disrupt the legal service market and lower the overall quality of legal services in society has also attracted attention and sparked widespread discussion among various departments and the general public.

On 7 February 2024, the Liaoning Provincial Department of Civil Affairs issued an administrative penalty decision (Liaoning Civil Penalty Decision [2024] No. (001)) regarding the "Liaoning Broker Association" on its official website. The penalty decision states that the Liaoning Broker Association's Lawyer Broker Professional Committee exceeded its authorisation by issuing recommendation letters for litigation agents and collecting fees beyond its scope, recommending non-association leaders and individuals without legal labour relations to act as litigation agents.[337] The association failed to promptly detect and supervise the aforementioned actions of the Lawyer Broker Professional Committee, showing negligence in management, which resulted in serious negative consequences and constituted a violation of Article 30, Paragraph 1, Item (5) of the "Regulations on the Registration and Management of Social Organisations".[338] The Liaoning Provincial Department of Civil Affairs

---

[335] Cases of this nature include (2022) Liaoning 0191 Civil First Instance 3898, (2023) Liaoning 0113 Civil First Instance 6099, (2023) Liaoning 0191 Civil First Instance 610, (2022) Liaoning 0114 Civil First Instance 14282, (2022) Liaoning 0114 Civil First Instance 11829, (2023) Liaoning 0114 Civil First Instance 1520, (2022) Liaoning 01 Civil Final 17905, and so on.

[336] In case No. (2023) Liaoning 07 Civil Final 819, the appellant, acting as a lawyer agent, had a dispute arising from a service contract signed with the principal, who is the respondent in this case. The appellant neither participated in the litigation activities of the case being represented nor submitted written defence opinions on behalf of the principal to the court. In case No. (2021) Yunnan 0103 Civil First Instance 12079, the defendant, who was a borrower with a long history of overdue loans, later easily became a lawyer agent.

[337] Refer to the decision of the Liaoning Provincial Department of Civil Affairs on the Administrative Penalty of Liaoning Province Broker Association (Liao Civil Penalty Decision [2024] No. (001)), available at https://mzt.ln.gov.cn/mzt/shzzpt/xxfbpt/xzzfgg/2024020809243358225/index.shtml.

[338] Refer to the decision of the Liaoning Provincial Department of Civil Affairs on the Administrative Penalty of Liaoning Province Broker Association (Liao Civil Penalty Decision [2024] No.

imposed an administrative penalty of suspending activities for six months and sealing the "Certificate of Registration as a Legal Person of a Social Organisation", seals, and financial vouchers.[339] Indeed, through this penalty, the Liaoning Provincial Government made a public statement regarding its position: the Broker Association's Lawyer Broker Professional Committee does not have the authority to issue recommendation letters for litigation agents and collect fees, nor can it recommend individuals who are not association leaders or lack legal labour relations to act as lawyer brokers to represent litigants. In other words, lawyer brokers cannot fully replace lawyers; they can only be recommended as litigation agents for non-profit purposes when serving as association leaders or employees.

In a word, while lawyer brokers can facilitate cooperation between individuals in need and lawyers, from a legal perspective, they can only serve as litigation agents under certain conditions. However, they cannot replace lawyers, charge fees arbitrarily to litigants, and any paid legal service contracts they sign with litigants are not legally protected.[340]

8.7.2 *Legal Affairs Broker*

Recently, alongside lawyer brokers, the role of legal affairs brokers has also begun to capture the public's attention. Despite the growing interest in their work, there have been no recorded instances of legal affairs brokers acting in the capacity of litigation agents within practical settings. This absence of precedent has led to some public scepticism concerning the nature and scope of their responsibilities. The core of these doubts centres around their familiarity with their designated duties, and whether they possess the necessary qualifications and expertise to fully assume the responsibilities typically managed by lawyers. This uncertainty casts a shadow over their potential to effectively serve as litigation agents.

The public's concerns are not unfounded, as the role of a legal affairs broker is relatively new and still evolving within the legal profession. Questions about whether these brokers can offer the same level of legal representation and advice as fully qualified lawyers are significant. These doubts are compounded by the lack of practical examples where legal affairs brokers have successfully taken on the role of litigation agents, leading to further questioning of their suitability and reliability in this capacity. As such, while the interest in legal affairs brokers is undeniably growing, their ability to substitute traditional lawyers in the role of litigation agents

(001)), available at https://mzt.ln.gov.cn/mzt/shzzpt/xxfbpt/xzzfgg/2024020809243358225/index.shtml.

[339] Refer to the decision of the Liaoning Provincial Department of Civil Affairs on the Administrative Penalty of Liaoning Province Broker Association (Liao Civil Penalty Decision [2024] No. (001)), available at https://mzt.ln.gov.cn/mzt/shzzpt/xxfbpt/xzzfgg/2024020809243358225/index.shtml.

[340] Refer to the reply of the Supreme People's Court on the Effectiveness Issue of Payment Agreement in Civil Agency Contracts.

remains a topic of debate and uncertainty, reflecting broader concerns about the adaptation of new roles within the established legal framework.

Regarding the job responsibilities of legal affairs brokers, the Legal Affairs Brokers Professional Committee of the Chongqing Brokers Association provided an official explanation on 15 November 2023. They stated that the work of legal affairs brokers cannot replace that of lawyers, and legal affairs brokers act as front-end market assistants for lawyers.[341] Their responsibilities include providing legal consultation services, collecting and organising information for front-end cases, assisting clients in contacting and recommending lawyers, helping lawyers develop and maintain market reputation, and assisting lawyers in handling legal documents.[342] On its official website's introduction page for legal practice certificates, it also specifies that legal affairs brokers can engage in various industries' information, intermediation, agency representation, agency (conduct), and legal consultation work, such as enterprise legal affairs, people's mediation, and so on.[343] On 17 November 2023, the Legal Affairs Brokers Special Committee of the Chongqing Brokers Association issued a statement, declaring that the committee prohibits legal affairs brokers from soliciting brokerage business in the name of law firms or lawyers.[344] This implies that legal affairs brokers are distinct from lawyers, and their job responsibilities should not be conflated.[345] From the position of this special committee, it is evident that they do not recognise legal affairs brokers as substitutes for lawyers, nor do they endorse their signing of paid agency contracts with parties, subsequently acting as litigation agents.

From a legal perspective, the question of whether legal affairs brokers can act as litigation agents is analogous to the issue raised earlier regarding whether lawyer brokers can serve as litigation agents. As long as legal affairs brokers are acting pro bono and fall into the three categories specified by law, they can serve as litigation agents. When a legal affairs broker acts as a close relative or employee of a party, they can directly serve as the party's litigation agent. When a legal affairs broker is recommended by the legal affairs brokers special committee of the brokers association, they can only serve as litigation agents for members of the association, and this recommendation can only occur if the legal rights and interests of the broker are

---

[341] *Committee on Legal Affairs Brokers*: "In-depth Focus | Differences Between Legal Affairs Brokers and Lawyers," published on the WeChat public account "Committee on Legal Affairs Brokers," uploaded on November 15, 2023.

[342] *Committee on Legal Affairs Brokers*: "In-depth Focus | Differences Between Legal Affairs Brokers and Lawyers," published on the WeChat public account "Committee on Legal Affairs Brokers," uploaded on November 15, 2023.

[343] Refer to the Frequently Asked Questions section on the introduction of Legal Practice Certificates on the official website of the Legal Affairs Brokers Special Committee of the Chongqing Association of Brokers, accessed on April 5, 2024, at http://www.fwjjrzwh.com/h-col-155.html.

[344] The Legal Affairs Brokers Special Committee of the Chongqing Brokers Association: "A Statement," uploaded on November 18, 2023.

[345] The Legal Affairs Brokers Special Committee of the Chongqing Brokers Association: "A Statement," uploaded on November 18, 2023.

infringed upon, and the purpose is not profit-driven. They cannot be recommended to serve as litigation agents for non-members.

In terms of industry requirements, unlike lawyer brokers, legal affairs brokers must meet the requirements of the legal affairs brokers special committee of the brokers association. To practice as a legal affairs broker, one needs to obtain a practice certificate, which comes in three levels: primary, intermediate, and advanced. Each level has different requirements for obtaining the certificate. To obtain a primary legal affairs broker practice certificate, candidates must attend offline practical courses designated by the special committee, accumulate credits, and pass an online exam to receive the certificate. To obtain intermediate and advanced practice certificates, candidates must attend a three-day on-campus training program at a political and legal university, accumulate credits, and pass an exam to receive a certificate of completion from the university.[346]

To register for the aforementioned exam, candidates need to meet a series of conditions: first, they must be citizens of the People's Republic of China; second, they must uphold the Constitution of the People's Republic of China and have the right to vote and stand for election; third, participation is currently limited to individuals who are members or member units of the brokers association or its specialised committees; fourth, they must possess good political, professional, and moral qualities; fifth, they must have full capacity for civil conduct; sixth, they must have at least a standard high school diploma or equivalent; and seventh, they must have worked in legal affairs for a minimum of three months. Individuals who have been disqualified from the exam for less than two years due to violations of exam discipline or disturbances to the exam order, or those considered seriously untrustworthy entities in the legal affairs market due to violations of the Regulations on the Administration of Legal Affairs Brokers and its implementation rules, are not eligible to register for the exam.[347] The exam is conducted online, and candidates can take a practice test before the official exam. If they fail, they can restart the exam. There is no limit to the number of times a candidate can take the exam in one day; they can participate multiple times until they pass.[348]

However, the details regarding exam eligibility and certificate acquisition that were previously mentioned lack a certain level of rigour and thoroughness. Despite assurances from the Chongqing Realtor Association's Legal Broker Committee regarding the credibility and social recognition of the certificate, convincing the public of its validity remains a challenging task.

---

[346] Refer to the information on the registration process for the Legal Affairs Brokers Practice Examination on the official website of the Legal Affairs Brokers Special Committee of the Chongqing Association of Brokers, accessed on April 5, 2024, at http://www.fwjjrzwh.com/h-col-152.html.

[347] Refer to the information on the registration process for the Legal Affairs Brokers Practice Examination on the official website of the Legal Affairs Brokers Special Committee of the Chongqing Association of Brokers, accessed on April 5, 2024, at http://www.fwjjrzwh.com/h-col-152.html.

[348] Refer to the information on the registration process for the Legal Affairs Brokers Practice Examination on the official website of the Legal Affairs Brokers Special Committee of the Chongqing Association of Brokers, accessed on April 5, 2024, at http://www.fwjjrzwh.com/h-col-152.html.

Firstly, candidates aiming for the intermediate and advanced certificates are required to participate in a three-day on-campus training session at "Political and Law University". However, the ambiguity surrounding the specific institution involved casts significant doubt on the authenticity and credibility of this training information. This lack of clarity raises concerns about whether the training provided is comprehensive and legitimate.

Secondly, the entire training duration for obtaining both intermediate and advanced certificates totals just six days. This brief period is substantially inadequate for anyone to develop a deep or thorough understanding of legal principles. Consequently, the effectiveness and depth of the training provided are highly questionable, making it unlikely that participants would gain the necessary legal expertise to perform competently as legal brokers.

Thirdly, the stated "Legal Broker Management Regulations", which are cited as part of the exam qualifications, lacks any official regulations or detailed implementation rules. The Chongqing Realtor Association's Legal Broker Committee has also failed to provide the text or any reliable source for this document. This omission inevitably raises serious doubts about the legitimacy and structural integrity of the certification process.

Even setting aside questions concerning the legitimacy of the exam and the formal recognition of the certificate, the entrance requirements and standards of this particular exam, especially when compared to other examinations within the legal profession, are notably lower, both in terms of academic qualifications and requisite work experience. This lowered threshold implies that the exam is relatively less challenging. As a result, it is conceivable that an individual who has only attained a junior high school education and has a mere three months of experience in legal affairs could potentially earn a legal broker's certificate after engaging in a brief period of study and possibly multiple attempts at the examination. This individual could then be authorised to provide legal services to the public.

In such scenarios, the relatively minimal educational and experiential requirements raise significant concerns about the ability of certified legal brokers to provide high-quality legal services. This situation poses a risk not only to the integrity of legal services but also to the trust that the public places in those who are certified under such lenient criteria. Consequently, the potential for underqualified individuals to deliver legal services may ultimately compromise the quality and reliability of the assistance offered to clients, affecting the overall standard of professionalism within the field.

In conclusion, whether it is a lawyer agent or a legal broker, these new types of legal professions currently lack legal regulations and industry norms to restrict their behaviour. Practitioners in both professions may engage in work beyond their authority in practice, and the legal competence of practitioners in either profession may not meet the standards for providing legal services to others. In the long run, the overall service quality of the legal service market cannot be improved, and the quality of legal services demanded by the public is also difficult to effectively meet. Therefore, relevant departments should urge relevant social organisations to strengthen the management of such professions, improve industry entry standards, accelerate the development of legitimate industry norms, and promote the improvement of industry service quality so as to provide high-quality legal services to the public. In such time, relevant laws and regulations should be enacted to regulate practitioners' behaviour from various aspects such as industry entry, practice standards, and professional conduct, providing legal protection for the development of related industries, and truly promoting the enhancement of the public's awareness of the rule of law, improving the public legal service system, and laying a solid foundation for governing the country according to law.

Chapter 9
Information Technology in Legal Education and the Legal Profession

9.1 Information Technology and Legal Education

In today's rapidly changing world, every industry and field, including legal education, is experiencing a significant transformation that necessitates innovation and adaptation in both form and content. The driving force behind these necessary changes is the advancement and application of information technology. This technology, which goes beyond the conventional use of computers and other electronic devices for organising, storing, processing, transmitting, and controlling information, encompasses a broader field known as "information science".[1]

Information science is a comprehensive discipline that integrates various subjects such as information technology, information management, computer networks, and database management, and its primary aim is to support the collection, processing, storage, analysis, retrieval, and reporting of digital information, which is crucial for meeting the evolving needs of social, economic, and cultural development.[2] This discipline is pivotal in providing the foundational knowledge and tools needed to handle vast amounts of data effectively and efficiently, making it indispensable in today's digital age.[3]

As information technology continues to grow as a discipline, its intersection with traditional fields like law is becoming increasingly apparent and impactful.[4] This intersection raises critical questions about how legal education can be transformed through the integration of information technology.[5] The challenge lies in how to effectively guide this transformation to ensure that legal education not only keeps pace

[1] Yu (2011).

[2] Zong and Wang (2024).

[3] Zong and Wang (2024).

[4] Wu et al. (2024).

[5] Wu et al. (2024).

S. Zhang et al., *Technology, Legal Education and Legal Profession in China and Australia*, International and Comparative Law in the Asia Pacific,
https://doi.org/10.1007/978-981-96-1639-8_9

with technological advancements but also leverages these developments to enhance educational methodologies and outcomes.[6]

Embarking on a path of integrated development, where traditional legal education and information technology converge, is a hot topic continuously discussed in academic circles. Scholars and educators debate and explore various strategies to infuse legal studies with technological tools and insights. This integration promises to enrich legal education by introducing new ways of teaching, learning, and conducting research.[7] It can transform how laws are studied, interpreted, and applied, making the process more efficient, accessible, and aligned with contemporary needs.[8]

Moreover, the integration of information technology into legal education could lead to the development of new legal frameworks and understandings in response to issues arising from the digital world, such as cybersecurity, digital privacy, and intellectual property in digital contexts.[9] These are areas where the law traditionally has lagged behind technological advancements, and where legal education can benefit significantly from a closer relationship with information science.

Thus, the ongoing discourse on merging information technology with legal studies is not just about keeping up with changes but about actively shaping the future of the legal profession to better serve society. It is about creating a robust legal education system that is capable of producing professionals who are not only well-versed in law but also adept at using technological tools to enhance their practice and understanding of the law.

9.1.1 The Integration Status of Information Technology and Legal Education

From a macro policy perspective, the trajectories of legal education and information technology education in China are increasingly intersecting, reflecting a broader national agenda to integrate these critical areas more fully into the overall educational framework. In July 2016, a significant step was taken in this direction when the Ministry of Education, along with two other departments, issued the "Outline for Legal Education for Adolescents".[10] This policy initiative aimed to embed legal education more deeply within the national education system and to enhance its systematic and scientific rigour, and it signified a shift in legal education from being a specialised field targeted at specific groups, to becoming a more universal and popularised form of education accessible to the entire population.[11]

---

[6] Wu et al. (2024).

[7] Yang (2022).

[8] Yang (2022).

[9] Yang (2022).

[10] Refer to the Central People's Government of the People's Republic of China website, https://www.gov.cn/xinwen/2016-07/18/content_5092493.htm, accessed May 21, 2024.

[11] Xu (2017).

This policy orientation, however, does not imply a phasing out of traditional models of higher legal education that focuses on cultivating professional legal talent; rather, it represents a strategic expansion to promote basic legal awareness among all citizens, fostering a societal environment where the law is known, observed, and utilised effectively.[12] This approach is seen as essential for bolstering the comprehensive national strength of the country as it continues to advance its goal of governing the country according to law.[13] In this context, the promotion of legal education is also perceived as a "pioneer signal" for urging reform in the way legal studies are approached and taught.[14]

Building on this foundation, China's policy directives continued to evolve with the issuance of the "Next Generation Artificial Intelligence Development Plan" in 2017[15] and the "Key Points for Enhancing National Digital Literacy and Skills" in 2022.[16] The former outlines guiding ideologies, strategic objectives, key tasks, and guarantee measures aimed at spearheading the development of new generation artificial intelligence in China by 2030. The latter document focuses on increasing digital literacy and skills across the population, with proposals for boosting the quality and accessibility of digital education and resources, including enhancing basic education with "excellent courses", expanding e-commerce training, and improving the accessibility of key websites and mobile applications for the elderly and people with disabilities.

While these two policy documents might appear unrelated at first glance, they collectively underscore the government's commitment to elevating both legal and information technology education. By doing so, they officially mark the start of a disciplined integration where the mutual reinforcement between legal and technological education can lead to more comprehensive educational outcomes, and better prepare citizens to engage with the modern challenges and opportunities presented by an increasingly digital world. This integrated approach not only enriches the educational landscape but also aligns with broader socio-economic objectives, ensuring that both legal and digital literacy are enhanced to support China's continued development and governance strategies.

Currently, in the realm of higher education, a significant transformation is underway with some domestic universities pioneering the interdisciplinary integration of their law programs by incorporating information technology. This innovative approach reflects an evolving educational landscape where law and technology intersect, creating new opportunities for curriculum development and specialisation in areas that are increasingly relevant in today's digital economy.[17]

---

[12] Xu (2017).

[13] Xu (2017).

[14] Xu (2017).

[15] Refer to the Central People's Government of the People's Republic of China website, https://www.gov.cn/xinwen/2017-07/20/content_5212064.htm, accessed May 21, 2024.

[16] Refer to the Central People's Government of the People's Republic of China website, https://www.gov.cn/xinwen/2022-03/02/content_5676432.htm, accessed May 21, 2024.

[17] Luo and Wang (2020).

One notable example of this transformation is found at Tsinghua University, a leader in educational innovation. In 2018, Tsinghua University Law School officially launched a full-time Master of Laws program specialising in "Computational Law".[18] This program represents a cutting-edge fusion of legal studies and technology, specifically designed to address the growing intersection between the internet, digital economy, and legal frameworks. Since its establishment, the program has successfully enrolled three cohorts of students from the years 2019, 2020, and 2021, demonstrating a robust interest and demand for this specialised field.[19]

The 2022 National Postgraduate Entrance Examination Catalog has listed the Master of Laws (Computational Law) program as an independent specialty, underscoring its distinctiveness and the university's commitment to fostering niche areas of study that caters to modern societal needs.[20] This program attracts students who are keen on exploring how advanced technologies and digital transformations impact legal practices and principles. Graduates of this program are conferred a Master of Laws degree by Tsinghua University, affirming their qualifications in this hybrid discipline.[21]

The career prospects for graduates of the Computational Law program are diverse and promising. The primary employment directions post-graduation include roles in corporate legal affairs, legal positions in technology companies, civil service roles where law and IT converge, and positions as technical engineers within the internet, digital economy, and information technology sectors.[22] These opportunities reflect the program's alignment with industry needs and its capacity to equip students with the skills necessary to navigate and contribute to the digital legal landscape effectively.[23] Additionally, graduates are well-prepared to further their studies, either domestically or internationally, offering them pathways to continue their academic pursuits or enhance their professional development in specialised areas of law and technology.[24]

This interdisciplinary approach not only broadens the academic and professional horizons of law students but also ensures that legal education remains relevant and responsive to the advancements and challenges posed by the rapid growth of information technology.[25] By fostering such innovative programs, universities like Tsinghua

[18] Refer to the Tsinghua University School of Law website, https://www.law.tsinghua.edu.cn/info/1134/2605.htm, accessed May 22, 2024.

[19] See the previous footnote.

[20] Refer to the Graduate Admissions website of Tsinghua University, https://ysbm.tsinghua.edu.cn/publish/s02/s0203/detail/eebcd111-f5d7-4074-bfbd-c3b5eeb22dad?yxsdm=066&ksfs=, accessed May 22, 2024.

[21] See the previous footnote.

[22] Lin and Li (2024).

[23] Lin and Li (2024).

[24] Lin and Li (2024).

[25] Yang (2023).

are at the forefront of shaping a new generation of legal professionals, adept at merging legal expertise with technological acumen.[26]

In recent years, there has been a notable push within Chinese higher education institutions to integrate legal studies with advanced information technologies, creating innovative educational programs that respond to the contemporary demands of the legal and tech industries. A prime example of this integration is the transformation by Southwest University of Political Science and Law, which, in collaboration with key industry partners, such as iFLYTEK Co, Lt., Sichuan Yuanzhen Industrial Co, Ltd, and Chengdu Hengtu Technology Co, Ltd, restructured its Applied Law School into the School of Artificial Intelligence and Law in December 2017.[27] This newly formed school now offers specialised courses, like "Legal Big Data Mining and Application" and "Principles of Artificial Intelligence Law", which are designed to equip students with the necessary skills to excel at the intersection of law and technology.[28]

Moreover, the initiative is not isolated to Southwest University. Peking University, recognising the critical intersection of law and artificial intelligence, established the Peking University Legal Artificial Intelligence Research Center, also known as the Peking University Legal Artificial Intelligence Laboratory, in December 2017.[29] The centre aims to become a premier integrated base for legal and AI research, education, and production, both domestically and internationally, and it seeks to provide intellectual support for the burgeoning fields of legal and artificial intelligence, fostering the development of high-end compound talent in these areas.[30] This initiative aligns closely with national strategies on AI and seeks to position itself at the forefront of these pivotal industries.[31]

Similarly, Zhongnan University of Economics and Law has contributed to this innovative educational landscape by establishing a national-level experimental teaching demonstration centre. The university has also developed the "Legal Education and Teaching System (LETS)", a dynamic platform that continues to run smoothly and receive updates to enhance its capabilities.[32] LETS is designed to provide convenient and intelligent services and support for law teachers and students alike, facilitating a more engaging and effective learning environment.[33]

---

[26] Yang (2023).

[27] Refer to the School of Artificial Intelligence Law at Southwest University of Political Science and Law website, https://alc.swupl.edu.cn/index.htm, accessed May 22, 2024.

[28] See the previous footnote.

[29] Refer to the Institute for Artificial Intelligence at Peking University website, https://www.ai.pku.edu.cn, accessed May 22, 2024.

[30] See the previous footnote.

[31] See the previous footnote.

[32] Refer to the Wenlan News Network of Zhongnan University of Economics and Law, http://wellan.zuel.edu.cn/2013/0620/c1668a24070/page.htm, accessed May 22, 2024.

[33] See the previous footnote.

These developments across various universities underscore a significant shift in legal education, which increasingly leans towards incorporating cutting-edge technologies such as artificial intelligence and big data.[34] By doing so, these institutions are not only enhancing the academic experience but also preparing students to meet the future needs of the legal profession. As these programs continue to evolve, they will likely set new standards for legal education, promoting a deeper integration of technology and law, and preparing graduates to thrive in a rapidly changing professional landscape.

Despite the innovative attempts at integrating information technology into legal education, there remains a significant degree of scepticism and criticism within the academic community. These critiques suggest that the current state of integration may not be as advanced or successful as some might hope. A particular point of concern, as noted by scholars Liu Bei and Qi Hanwen, is that the majority of law schools have not adequately reformed their traditional educational objectives to align with the demands of the digital age.[35] This observation indicates that many institutions are still lagging behind the rapid pace of international technological advancements.

The critique underscores that only a limited number of universities are actively engaging in interdisciplinary integration from a curriculum design perspective, and among these institutions that have initiated such reforms, the outcomes have often been less than ideal, highlighting a gap between the intention of curriculum innovation and its practical execution.[36] Moreover, the reliance solely on updating digital devices as a means to drive disciplinary development is frequently criticised for its superficiality.[37] Merely updating equipment without a corresponding change in educational concepts, content, and teaching methods can lead to a situation where the surface appearance of modernisation masks a continued reliance on outdated practices.[38]

Furthermore, it is argued that the integration of information technology and legal education should not be simplistically viewed as merely supplementing traditional legal studies with modern tools, nor should it be narrowly defined by the inclusion of buzzwords like "artificial intelligence" or "digitalisation" in course titles without a deeper, substantive transformation of the curriculum.[39] True interdisciplinary integration requires a fundamental rethinking of how legal education is delivered and the competencies it aims to build in students.

To effectively achieve a transformation in legal education that genuinely integrates information technology, it is crucial to first clearly identify the new challenges and emerging issues posed by advancements in technology to the field of law.[40] This understanding will enable educators and policymakers to formulate appropriate

[34] Luo and Wang (2020).
[35] Liu and Qi (2023).
[36] Liu and Qi (2023).
[37] Liu and Qi (2023).
[38] Liu and Qi (2023).
[39] Hu (2024).
[40] Wu et al. (2024).

strategies and innovations that go beyond superficial changes.[41] By doing so, a new pathway for disciplinary development can be established, one that genuinely prepares future legal professionals to operate effectively at the intersection of law and technology. This approach will not only enhance the relevance and responsiveness of legal education but also ensure that it remains aligned with the evolving needs of society and the legal profession in the digital age.

9.1.2 New Challenges to Legal Education Posed by Information Technology

The impact of information technology on legal education manifests in various aspects. A summary and integration of the areas of concern within academia, can be broadly categorised into challenges to the content and mode of legal education. Moreover, challenges to the educational mode can be further classified based on different participants, including challenges to teaching methods for instructors, learning patterns for students, and organisational models for universities.

9.1.2.1 Challenges to Legal Education Content

The main challenge in adapting the content of legal education today involves finding the right balance between traditional legal knowledge and the emerging knowledge brought about by advances in information technology, along with addressing new legal issues that arise in the digital age. Law, as a discipline with a long and rich history, covers a vast spectrum of subjects, each with its own complexity and depth. Legal professionals, from their initial academic pursuits to their specialisation, are required to immerse themselves in extensive literature and integrate information from diverse fields, making their education both broad and intensive.

In the traditional framework of legal education, especially during the initial stages where foundational legal knowledge is imparted, there is a significant investment of time and effort. This rigorous approach ensures that students develop the professionalism and accuracy necessary for future legal practice. The undergraduate curriculum at various higher education institutions typically includes courses on legal theory, professional ethics, and foundational courses across different branches of law such as criminal law, civil law, administrative law, and international law. Successfully completing these courses is usually sufficient to meet the basic credit requirements for graduation. Therefore, it can be inferred that these foundational courses consume the bulk of study time for law students at the undergraduate level.[42]

However, the advent of digital technologies and the internet has introduced new dimensions to the legal field, necessitating the incorporation of courses that address

---

[41] Wu et al. (2024).

[42] Yuan (2023).

topics like cyber law, data privacy, and the legal implications of artificial intelligence. The challenge for educational institutions lies in integrating these modern topics without compromising the depth and thoroughness with which traditional subjects are taught.[43] This integration is crucial not only for maintaining the relevance of the legal curriculum but also for ensuring that students are prepared to deal with contemporary legal issues effectively.

Thus, the task for law schools is to develop a curriculum that maintains a balance between traditional doctrines and emerging trends in the legal profession influenced by technological advancements. This might involve the introduction of interdisciplinary courses that combine law with information technology, or the modification of existing courses to include elements of information technology law.[44] Additionally, law schools might consider innovative teaching methods that incorporate the use of digital tools to enhance learning and engagement.[45]

Ultimately, the goal is to create a dynamic and responsive curriculum that prepares students to operate competently both in traditional legal settings and in environments shaped by digital innovations. Achieving this balance is not only crucial for the professional development of future legal practitioners but also for the advancement of the legal field as it adapts to the ongoing transformations brought about by technology.

Table 9.1 briefly integrates the undergraduate credit requirements, total credits for traditional legal courses, and whether digital-related compulsory courses are offered in several leading law schools in China.

The current state of legal education at the undergraduate level, as evidenced by data from various universities, reveals a strong emphasis on traditional theoretical knowledge. This focus is deeply ingrained in the curriculums, which are designed to ground students in the fundamental principles of law. However, a notable gap exists in the incorporation of digital literacy and information technology skills, which are increasingly relevant in today's legal practices.[46]

In most universities, courses that cover digital skills, such as computer basics and database management, are offered, but they are generally not compulsory. They are often positioned as optional or elective courses. As a result, students, who usually have limited discretionary hours and credits available after completing their major required courses, tend to select electives based on personal interests or those that directly complement their major studies. This selection process often leads to a lack of engagement with digital-related courses, not due to a lack of relevance but because of the way educational programs are structured.[47]

Moreover, while the basic IT courses provided do equip students with fundamental skills, they fall short of delivering the depth of knowledge required to navigate the increasingly complex digital landscape that modern legal professionals face.[48] These

[43] Yuan (2023).

[44] Hu (2024).

[45] Hu (2024).

[46] Xie and He (2024).

[47] Xie and He (2024).

[48] Wu et al. (2024).

Table 9.1 Undergraduate credit requirements in some Chinese university

University	Duration	Credit requirement (theoretical course)	Credit for required courses	Credit for optional courses	Whether digital courses are required
East China University of Political Science and Law[49]	4–6 years	143	67	14	No
Jilin University[50]	4 years	152	84	31	No
Wuhan University[51]	3–6 years	84	51	22	No
Northwest University of Political Science and Law[52]	3–6 years	140	66	18	No
Renmin University of China[53]	4 years	133	67	23	No
China University of Political Science and Law[54]	3–6 years	150	63	20	No
Zhongnan University of Economics and Law[55]	3–6 years	131	62	20	No

courses are often not tailored to the specific needs of legal education but rather serve general educational purposes.[56] They are, at best, rudimentary tools that assist in basic learning and workflow management, but do not foster a deeper understanding or integration of information technology within the legal context.

Given this backdrop, the challenge of reforming legal education, to include a balance between traditional legal principles and emerging digital practices within the constraints of an already packed curriculum, becomes evident. The key issue is not merely the inclusion of more IT-related courses, but the integration of digital competencies into the core legal curriculum. This integration would not only enhance the relevance of legal training but also prepare law students more effectively for the challenges of modern legal environments, where digital literacy is just as important as legal expertise.

[49] Refer to the East China University of Political Science and Law website, https://www.ecupl.edu.cn, accessed June 1, 2024.

[50] Refer to the Jilin University website, https://www.jlu.edu.cn, accessed June 1, 2024.

[51] Refer to the Wuhan University website, https://www.whu.edu.cn, accessed June 1, 2024.

[52] Refer to the Northwest University of Political Science and Law website, https://www.nwupl.edu.cn, accessed June 1, 2024.

[53] Refer to the Renmin University of China website, https://www.ruc.edu.cn, accessed June 1, 2024.

[54] Refer to the China University of Political Science and Law website, https://www.cupl.edu.cn, accessed June 1, 2024.

[55] Refer to the website of Zhongnan University of Economics and Law, https://www.zuel.edu.cn, accessed June 1, 2024.

[56] Wu et al. (2024).

To address this challenge, universities need to rethink their curriculums strategies. This could involve the development of interdisciplinary courses that blend law with significant aspects of digital technology, such as data privacy, cybersecurity law, and digital forensics, or the modification of existing courses to include legal technology components. Additionally, legal education programs could benefit from partnerships with tech departments or institutions to co-develop courses that accurately reflect the intersection of law and technology.

Ultimately, the goal is to craft an educational framework that not only covers the traditional areas of law but also equips students with the technological skills and innovative thinking necessary for the legal profession in the digital age.[57] This approach requires a shift from viewing information technology as an adjunct, to viewing it as integral to legal education, ensuring that graduates are well-prepared to deliver legal services in an increasingly digital world.[58]

As legal education grapples with the "internal contradiction" of balancing traditional knowledge with emerging digital competencies, an "external contradiction" also emerges, posing its own set of challenges. This external contradiction revolves around how legal education should respond to the evolving legal issues that accompany the digital age. With the continuous development of internet technology and the deepening digitalisation of society, new concepts, values, and disputes continually arise, challenging the adequacy of traditional legal frameworks.

For instance, the rise of artificial intelligence raises complex legal questions, such as the determination of liability in cases of intellectual property ownership or infringement by AI-generated content, or traffic accidents involving autonomous vehicles.[59] Similarly, the emergence of new types of cybercrimes that bypass traditional legal definitions poses significant challenges for current legal systems.[60] These developments illustrate that, if legal education remains confined to traditional doctrines, it may fall short in equipping future legal professionals with the necessary tools to address and resolve these modern issues effectively.

From another perspective, the response to the challenges posed by advanced technologies and new cybercrimes has gained national attention. For example, China has been actively working towards creating a robust framework for digital law. This includes enacting fundamental laws such as the *Cybersecurity Law of the People's Republic of China*,[61] the *Data Security Law of the People's Republic of China*,[62] and the *Personal Information Protection Law of the People's Republic of China*.[63]

---

57 Yang (2023).

58 Yang (2023).

59 Chen (2023).

60 Chen (2023).

61 Refer to the National People's Congress of China website, http://www.npc.gov.cn/npc/c1773/c1849/c6680/c33634/c33636/201905/t20190521_261690.html, accessed June 1, 2024.

62 Refer to the website of the Cyberspace Administration of China, https://www.cac.gov.cn/2021-06/11/c_1624994566919140.htm, accessed June 1, 2024.

63 Refer to the Central People's Government of the People's Republic of China website, https://www.gov.cn/xinwen/2021-08/20/content_5632486.htm, accessed June 1, 2024.

These laws are continuously revised and updated to keep pace with technological advancements. Additionally, a range of supporting administrative regulations and industry standards are being developed to enhance the comprehensive legal framework addressing these new challenges.

However, the mere existence of legal norms and regulatory systems, or even the advancements in science and technology that they aim to regulate, is not sufficient. These laws and regulations lack the inherent empathy of human judgement and require real people to implement, understand, and apply them effectively. Thus, the technological advancements and the creation of new laws must be complemented by an equally progressive legal education system. This modernisation of legal education is essential to ensure that students and legal professionals continue to uphold the core values of fairness and justice amidst rapid digital transformations.

Addressing this major challenge requires a transformation in legal education that not only includes updating curriculum content but also involves cultivating a deeper understanding of how technology impacts legal principles and practices. Legal educators must actively strive to integrate new legal issues related to digital technology into the curriculum, preparing students to think critically about how these issues intersect with existing legal frameworks and how they might evolve in the future. This transformation is crucial for empowering the next generation of legal professionals to navigate the complexities of the digital age, ensuring they can adapt to and shape the evolving legal landscape effectively.

9.1.2.2 Challenges in Legal Education Models

Understanding educational models within the context of legal education involves examining various aspects: how teachers deliver content, how students engage with that content, the dynamics of interaction between teachers and students, and how universities organise and structure their courses.

Traditionally, legal education has adhered to a face-to-face teaching approach. Typically, full-time teachers with deep academic knowledge and extensive expertise lead classroom learning, following carefully prepared syllabi or curriculum plans. This mode places teachers at the forefront, where they largely control and drive the educational process. The rationale behind this approach is twofold. Firstly, the complex nature of legal studies often requires teachers to act as guides, helping students navigate through the intricate details and broad scopes of legal principles and practices. Secondly, this method is also a pragmatic solution to the efficient allocation of teaching resources, ensuring that specialised teachers can focus on imparting knowledge within their expert areas to maximise educational outcomes.

In this traditional setup, students attend classes at specified times and locations, engaging with the content delivered by the designated teachers. This structured approach allows teachers to transmit their knowledge effectively but also has inherent limitations. One significant drawback is the passive role it forces upon students, who receive information without much opportunity for interactive engagement or choice in learning paths. They are seldom able to influence the course content or the manner in which it is taught, which can lead to a disconnect between what is taught and what students may find relevant or necessary for their professional growth. This scenario often results in the under-utilisation of classroom time, where potential conflicts and contradictions between the delivered content and the students' needs may arise.

Moreover, in such a traditional educational model, the disparity in numbers between teachers and students makes it challenging to cater to the individualised educational needs of each student. Teachers, constrained by time and resource limitations, typically focus on delivering the core content, leaving little room for updating course materials or integrating new knowledge domains, such as those related to information technology. This situation underscores a critical gap in adapting legal education to contemporary demands where legal professionals must increasingly intersect with digital and technological realms.[64]

Thus, while the traditional model of legal education has its justifications, it also highlights a pressing need for reform. Modernising the educational approach could involve more interactive and flexible teaching methods that allow for greater student participation and input, aligning more closely with the evolving professional landscapes.[65] Integrating technology and adopting more adaptive educational models could significantly enhance the responsiveness of legal education, ensuring it remains relevant in the face of rapid societal and technological changes.[66]

The traditional model of fixed teaching locations in legal education is increasingly challenged by the rise of online teaching models. Since the outbreak of the COVID-19 pandemic, the landscape of education has undergone a significant transformation. Remote work and distance learning, which were once supplementary to traditional offline teaching, have become more prevalent and are now recognised as mainstream methods of educational delivery.[67] This shift reflects a broader acceptance and integration of online education into the formal educational framework, allowing it to coexist alongside traditional classroom settings.[68]

Online courses typically fall into two categories: recorded and live broadcast courses. Recorded courses, which have been a fixture in distance education for many years, offer a stable and mature form of learning. These courses are typically pre-recorded, allowing students to access the material at their convenience, providing flexibility in terms of timing and pacing of study. Educational platforms that host these courses continually innovate, improving content delivery and user interface with advancements in internet technology.

Live broadcast courses, on the other hand, have seen rapid growth in recent years. These courses leverage modern technology to break the traditional constraints of time and location imposed by physical classrooms. Online platforms providing live teaching services enhance the educational experience by offering various interactive features tailored to user needs or platform characteristics. These features include

---

[64] Xie (2023).

[65] Xie (2023).

[66] Xie (2023).

[67] Zhang (2022).

[68] Zhang (2022).

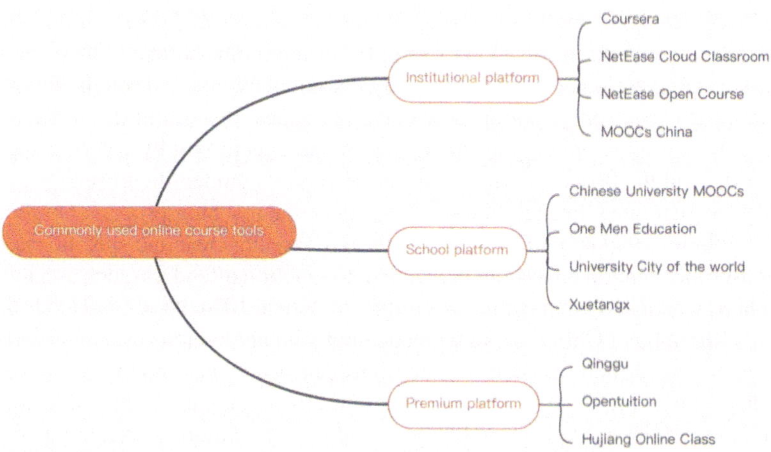

Fig. 9.1 Online courses platform in China

options for live broadcast playback, screen sharing, and interactive elements such as online polls and quizzes (see Fig. 9.1). Such functionalities enrich the learning experience, making it more engaging and interactive for students.

Several platforms are at the forefront of delivering these online courses. For instance, platforms like Chinese University MOOC, Hujiang Online Courses, and NetEase Open Courses are popular for offering a wide range of academic content. For live teaching, platforms such as Tencent Meeting, Zoom, Xiaoe Tong, and DingTalk provide robust services that support real-time interaction between instructors and students. Additionally, platforms traditionally known for other services, including video platforms like Bilibili and social media platforms such as Zhihu, Weibo, and Xiaohongshu, are also venturing into the online education space, offering live teaching functionalities.

This expansion and diversification in online education platforms demonstrate a significant shift in how legal education can be delivered.[69] No longer bound by the limitations of physical presence, educational institutions have the opportunity to reach a broader audience and provide more flexible, accessible learning options.[70] As such, the challenge for legal education in adapting to this shift lies not only in embracing these technological tools but also in ensuring that the quality and depth of education are maintained, enabling students to gain a comprehensive understanding of the law in a digital age.

The current trend of development appears to bring numerous benefits without harm to the integration of legal education with information technology. However, in reality,

[69] Xu (2023).

[70] Xu (2023).

this mode of online teaching still has many deficiencies and shortcomings, and faces numerous challenges. Firstly, there is inadequate regulation and lax requirements for certain functions of platforms.[71] For example, during online courses, classrooms, or live broadcasts, sessions can be maliciously disrupted by others through tactics like spamming irrelevant information or abusive messages, disturbing the order of the class. Although most online platforms support students to join by entering specific passwords, and the hosts have the authority to remove unidentified users, it cannot completely guarantee the stability and security of the teaching process. On the one hand, regulations and penalties for such behaviour are not clear and specific enough. Generally, only general provisions are applied to sanction offenders (such as handling individuals who insult others online according to Article 1024 of the Civil Code of the People's Republic of China[72]), but when dealing with anonymous users whose identities cannot be verified or when the nature of their behaviour cannot be determined according to existing legal norms, the deterrent effect is greatly reduced. Secondly, the online teaching mode is more likely to lead to an attention crisis among student groups compared to traditional education models.[73] This mainly refers to "the attention deficit of learners". When students participate in classes through online teaching methods, but cannot sustain their attention on course content for a long time, and instead divert their attention elsewhere due to various reasons, the course loses its meaning. These reasons are diverse, such as when students engage in self-learning through social media or video platforms, as these platforms contain content not entirely related to course materials but include many visually striking and highly appealing entertainment-oriented content. At such times, students' attention may be diverted to other content for an extended period. To avoid such situations, extremely high demands need to be placed on students' self-awareness, which is not achievable for everyone. To some extent, this is also because some platforms have only gradually differentiated themselves into online course services by their users recently, and the operators or developers did not establish specialised learning areas to reduce interference from other information when the platform was initially launched and operated. Furthermore, deliberate, artificial diversion of students' attention is often through carefully designed advertisements, with the most prominent example being the insertion of ads throughout the entire process of conferences by Tencent Meeting, which is currently widely used for live courses. As a software that provides basic functions to users for free, it is understandable that its development team earns commercial profits by embedding advertisements, and these do not suddenly pop up to interrupt meetings or courses during normal live broadcasts. However, the variety and complexity of advertisements, and even the precise targeting of advertisements to users' interests after analysing their data portraits, may lead to the dispersion of

[71] Zhao (2022), 32.

[72] *Civil Code of the People's Republic of China*, Article 1024: Civil subjects have the right to reputation. No organization or individual may infringe upon another's right to reputation through insults, defamation, or other means. Reputation is the social evaluation of a civil subject's character, prestige, abilities, credit, and other qualities.

[73] Zhao (2022), 32.

students' attention when using the software for online course learning. The resolution of the above problems cannot be achieved solely by the efforts of teachers, students, or one party of the online platform, but requires a compromise and reasonable arrangements considering the demands of all parties involved in the process.[74] Only then can the positive driving role of information technology in legal education be fully realised in this field.[75]

Another significant barrier to the effective integration of legal education with information technology within the traditional teaching model concerns the composition and qualifications of the teaching staff. In the context of legal education in China, while specialised legal education has been firmly established at the undergraduate level, most universities typically require that legal studies teachers hold at least a master's degree in law.[76] Interestingly, there are no specific stipulations that restrict teachers shifting from non-law undergraduate disciplines to continuing their studies in law at the graduate level.[77] This theoretically opens the door for individuals with interdisciplinary backgrounds, potentially including information technology, to teach in legal education settings.

However, the reality is that faculty members with such interdisciplinary expertise, particularly those with a background in information technology, are exceedingly rare within the legal academic community.[78] Research indicates that even among those legal educators who did not study law at the undergraduate level, the majority come from fields such as languages, management, political science, or economics, rather than from STEM fields like computer science, which are more directly applicable to the burgeoning needs of legal education in the digital age.[79] The transition of individuals from fields closely related to computer science into legal education is uncommon, and the progression to full-time legal educators is even rarer.[80]

This phenomenon is partly explained by the historical separation of disciplines; traditionally, law, as a social science, was seen as distinctly separate from the technical and empirical nature of STEM fields such as computer science.[81] Before the rise of the digital and information age, there was little perceived need or incentive to blend these fields within academic or professional trajectories. As a result, the current cadre of legal educators lacks substantial representation from backgrounds that blend legal expertise with information technology.

---

74 Yang (2021).

75 Yang (2021).

76 Zhang (2024).

77 Zhang (2024).

78 Wang Fujun, and Wu Shuang. "The Goals, Connotations, and Realistic Pathways of University Curriculum Systems Supporting High-Quality Talent Cultivation." *Modern Education Management*, 1–12.

79 Wang Fujun, and Wu Shuang. "The Goals, Connotations, and Realistic Pathways of University Curriculum Systems Supporting High-Quality Talent Cultivation." *Modern Education Management*, 1–12.

80 Xie (2023).

81 Wang (2023).

Given this gap, there is a pressing need for educational institutions to re-evaluate their hiring criteria and developmental strategies for the legal faculty. Encouraging a more diverse academic background among legal educators could greatly enhance the integration of technology and law. Universities might consider incentivising professionals who combine expertise in both fields, perhaps through targeted recruitment, interdisciplinary training programs, or partnerships with technology departments.

Addressing this issue is critical not only for the direct infusion of relevant IT knowledge into legal education but also for fostering an educational environment where legal studies are more naturally aligned with technological advancements.[82] This alignment is essential for preparing future legal professionals to effectively navigate the increasingly complex landscape where law intersects with rapidly evolving digital technologies.[83] Only through such strategic adjustments can legal education fully embrace and leverage the benefits of information technology, ensuring that it remains relevant and robust in the digital age.

As previously mentioned, a few universities are pioneering efforts to facilitate the integration of disciplines by establishing new colleges or research institutes specifically dedicated to merging legal studies with information technology. These initiatives often involve recruiting faculties separately specialised in legal studies and information technology to teach collaboratively. Although the intention behind this approach is laudable, aiming to foster a richer educational environment and a broader perspective among students, several challenges undermine its effectiveness and widespread adoption.

Firstly, the number of institutions embarking on such innovative ventures remains notably small, and the reach of these programs is consequently quite limited. The majority of legal education continues to be delivered through traditional channels that do not sufficiently incorporate information technology or emphasise its relevance to contemporary legal practices. This limited scope means that the impact of such interdisciplinary educational models is confined and does not significantly influence the broader landscape of legal education.

Moreover, the effectiveness of simply adding an information technology faculty to legal studies departments without rethinking the educational approach can be minimal. If the existing constraints of traditional legal education models are not adequately addressed, having two distinct types of teachers—those for legal studies and those for information technology—may result in continued separation rather than genuine integration. This separation can perpetuate the status quo, where each set of faculty members delivers content within their expertise without interlinking their disciplines meaningfully. Consequently, this setup might not effectively stimulate students' interest in interdisciplinary studies or provide them with a cohesive learning experience that melds both areas of knowledge.

Additionally, this form of integration, if not carefully managed, could inadvertently increase the academic burden on students. If students are required to meet the demands of two distinct disciplinary tracks without thoughtful integration, it could

[82] Yang (2021).

[83] Yang (2021).

lead to an overload of coursework and assignments, thereby heightening academic stress rather than enriching the educational experience.

Therefore, the real challenge lies not just in creating opportunities for interdisciplinary instruction but in fundamentally transforming the traditional legal education model to better meet contemporary needs. This transformation should aim to fully integrate information technology into legal studies in a way that enhances the curriculum cohesively, encouraging the development of new competencies that are essential for modern legal professionals. Such integration should foster an educational environment where learning is interdisciplinary by design, not just by addition, promoting an organic blending of knowledge that truly prepares students for the complexities of today's legal landscape.

From the perspective of student learning patterns, contemporary law students face a series of unique challenges that are largely a product of the digital age. The sheer volume of information available today is exponentially greater than what was accessible in the pre-internet era, raising both the learning threshold and the skill requirements for students. This escalation demands a more nuanced approach to legal education, one that transcends the mere memorisation of legal texts and focuses more on the application of law to solve real-world problems.

Legal education aims to deeply embed a solid foundation of legal knowledge, and historically, this involved students primarily accessing information through books and other printed materials.[84] In such settings, the information was curated, structured, and typically reliable. In contrast, the modern digital landscape presents a starkly different learning environment. Today's law students are inundated with an unending stream of digital content that is often fragmented and unstructured.[85] Not only does this make it challenging to navigate the information, but it also presents the added difficulty of identifying credible sources amidst a sea of potentially misleading content.

The current digital environment thus requires law students to possess advanced skills in information retrieval, discernment, and integration. They must be adept at accessing vast digital libraries, discerning relevant and accurate information, and integrating this into coherent, legally sound arguments. These skills are crucial not only for academic success but also for professional competence in legal practice.

Furthermore, the rapid development and ubiquitous presence of internet technology compel law students to either master these skills quickly or risk being overwhelmed by the information overload. This situation places additional pressure on legal educators to adapt their teaching methods. There is a growing need for educational approaches that not only provide students with the core legal knowledge but also explicitly train them in digital literacy and critical thinking.

---

[84] Yang (2016).

[85] Yang (2016).

Educators must therefore integrate training that helps students effectively utilise digital tools and resources while maintaining a critical eye for accuracy and relevance.[86] This integration could involve more practical exercises that mimic real-world legal research and case analysis, using actual online resources rather than solely traditional textbooks.[87] Such practices would not only improve students' abilities to handle large volumes of information but also prepare them to be more effective and adaptable legal professionals.[88]

Addressing these challenges is essential for preparing law students for the complexities of the modern legal environment. It involves a careful balancing act—retaining the rigorous standards of traditional legal education while incorporating the necessary tools and techniques to navigate and utilise digital resources effectively. As such, legal education must continuously evolve, ensuring it remains relevant and robust in equipping students to meet the demands of a rapidly changing world.

After evaluating the challenges faced individually by teachers and students, it is crucial to consider the dynamics of interaction between these closely associated groups, particularly the teacher-student relationship, which has historically held significant importance in Chinese education. This relationship has long been the cornerstone of the educational system, serving as the crucial link between teaching and learning, nurturing individuals, and fostering talent.

Traditionally, Chinese educational philosophies have placed a strong emphasis on the authority of teachers, often likening their role to that of parents, which underscores a hierarchical structure within the classroom.[89] This perspective has shaped educational practices for centuries, where teachers are seen as the primary source of knowledge and guidance, commanding respect and obedience from students.

However, in contemporary education models, there is a shift towards a more balanced and equitable relationship between teachers and students. This shift reflects broader educational and societal trends that favour collaborative and interactive learning environments over authoritative, lecture-based teaching.[90] Modern educational paradigms encourage dialogue, question-and-answer exchanges, and critical thinking, allowing students to take a more active role in their learning processes.[91]

Despite these advances, maintaining a healthy and effective teacher-student relationship in the era of information technology presents new challenges. The integration of digital tools and platforms into the educational process can sometimes disrupt traditional interaction patterns.[92] For instance, online learning environments, while offering flexibility and accessibility, can diminish the direct, personal interaction that is often crucial for effective teaching and mentoring. The physical separation in

86 Shen (2023).
87 Shen (2023).
88 Shen (2023).
89 Zhang and Yu (2023).
90 Wang and Lü (2021).
91 Wang and Lü (2021).
92 Xie (2023).

virtual classrooms might lead to a sense of detachment and reduce the immediacy and intimacy that face-to-face interactions foster.

Moreover, the vast and easily accessible information available online can alter the perceived authority of teachers. Students, equipped with the ability to independently verify or challenge the information provided by teachers, may feel less reliant on teachers as the sole source of knowledge.[93] This dynamic can lead to positive outcomes by encouraging students to engage more actively with learning materials, but it can also challenge teachers to continually update their knowledge and adapt their teaching strategies.

Furthermore, the rapid pace of technological change and the constant influx of new tools and platforms require both teachers and students to continually adapt to new ways of interacting and learning. This need for constant adaptation can strain the traditional teacher-student relationship unless both parties are committed to continuous learning and open communication.

Therefore, enhancing the teacher-student relationship in the context of information technology involves fostering an environment where both teachers and students feel valued and respected. Teachers must be empowered to integrate new technologies into their teaching effectively, while students should be encouraged to use these tools responsibly and constructively.[94] Effective training, ongoing support, and clear guidelines on the use of technology can help maintain the integrity and efficacy of this vital relationship, ensuring that the educational journey is mutually beneficial and aligned with the demands of the digital age.[95]

Examining the mode of curriculum design in universities reveals significant challenges in integrating information technology (IT) into legal education. Although some institutions offer IT-related courses, making these courses compulsory components of legal education or independent secondary disciplines within the law is uncommon. Typically, these IT courses are offered as electives that students may choose based on personal interest, employing less stringent assessment methods compared to core legal courses. This elective nature often leads to challenges such as low enrolment numbers and the potential cancellation of courses due to insufficient student participation. These issues highlight a general lack of enthusiasm among law students for IT-related courses, despite the growing relevance of technology in the legal field.[96]

To effectively incorporate IT into legal education without unduly increasing the academic burden on students or exceeding existing limitations on class hours, law schools must navigate carefully.[97] Strategies to enhance the appeal and integration of IT courses could include repositioning these courses to demonstrate their practical utility in modern legal contexts. For example, linking courses on cyber law or digital

93 Wang and Lü (2021).

94 Wang and Liu (2023).

95 Wang and Liu (2023).

96 Luo and Wang (2020).

97 Ma (2023).

forensics with criminal law or intellectual property courses could illustrate their applicability.

Further, encouraging interdisciplinary collaboration with computer science or data science departments could enrich the content of IT courses and provide a more robust educational experience.[98] Utilising innovative teaching methods that reflect the dynamic nature of technology, such as interactive simulations and case studies that involve digital issues, could make these courses more engaging.[99]

Additionally, law schools could improve the marketing of IT courses by actively promoting the importance of tech skills in legal practice through career talks, alumni success stories, and offering certifications for IT proficiency. Continuously gathering student feedback on IT courses can also help institutions identify barriers to enrolment and engagement, allowing them to adapt their course offerings effectively.

By addressing these aspects, law schools can better align their curriculums with the demands of the modern legal profession, facilitating a more effective integration of legal education and information technology. This alignment is crucial for preparing future lawyers to navigate a landscape increasingly dominated by digital issues, ensuring they remain competent and competitive.

9.1.3 The Future of Information Technology in Legal Education

Promoting the development of interdisciplinary integration can be achieved in two directions: updating educational content and reforming educational models.[100]

Updating educational content in the realm of legal education to include information technology reflects several critical approaches that are necessary to ensure a harmonious integration of modern tech skills with traditional legal teachings.

First and foremost, it is essential to integrate information technology-related knowledge into the existing legal curriculum by introducing "implicit courses" within traditional courses. This approach would involve embedding basic technological concepts such as big data, algorithms, and artificial intelligence seamlessly into the existing legal studies framework. The objective here would be to maintain a balance between these modern subjects and the core elements of traditional legal education, particularly in how assessments are designed and implemented. This balanced approach ensures that students can engage with new information without feeling overwhelmed, thereby avoiding excessive academic pressure.

Secondly, there should be a deliberate effort to develop new courses that address the emerging issues brought forth by digital advancements, with a particular focus on digital law. This involves not only supplementing the curriculum with foundational content on digital law but also integrating these elements in a way that they

[98] Ma (2023).

[99] Ma (2023).

[100] Long et al. (2023).

complement and enhance traditional legal disciplines. The new courses should not only address the basics of digital law but should also explore the potential for digital innovations to revolutionise other areas of law, thereby enriching the entire legal education spectrum.

Thirdly, the importance of augmenting creative and humanistic educational content cannot be understated. As we venture further into the information technology age, legal education must continue to emphasise deep, reflective thinking about humanity. Cultivating "artificial intelligence literacy" is crucial, as noted by Liu Bei and Qi Hanwen in their article, "Supply-Side Reform of Legal Education Under the Background of 'AI + Law'".[101] It is vital that, while we integrate new technological knowledge, we must not neglect the humanistic core of legal education. The curriculum should foster a nuanced understanding of how technology and human values intersect and ensure that technology serves humanity, not the other way around.

Lastly, a significant focus must be placed on the practical aspects of education following the interdisciplinary integration. Regardless of the changes in disciplinary content, the application of knowledge in practical legal settings remains the ultimate goal. The updates to the curriculum should, therefore, extend beyond theoretical knowledge to include practical skills that legal professionals need today. This means updating not only what is taught but how it is taught, ensuring that practical legal training keeps pace with technological advancements and prepares students for the realities of modern legal practice.

In essence, updating the legal curriculum to include information technology should be a comprehensive process that carefully blends new knowledge with traditional principles. This integration should enhance the curriculum, making it more relevant to today's digital landscape while ensuring it remains grounded in the critical thinking and ethical reasoning that are the hallmarks of legal education.

The transformation of the educational model in legal studies is characterised by several critical initiatives aimed at harmonising traditional legal education with emerging information technologies.[102]

Firstly, there is a significant need to adjust the faculty structure within law education institutions. This involves addressing the current imbalance by integrating "cross-disciplinary" and "dual-teacher" systems, wherein educators with professional expertise in information technology are incorporated into full-time law education faculties on an equal footing.[103] By constructing a diverse teaching team, these institutions can enhance the synergy between traditional and modern educational content, facilitating the transmission of interdisciplinary knowledge to students. This approach not only upgrades and transforms traditional courses but also signals a progressive shift towards embracing a more integrated educational framework.

---

[101] Liu and Qi (2023).

[102] Long et al. (2023).

[103] Liu and Qi (2023).

Secondly, enhancing the oversight of online education platforms is crucial.[104] Strengthening supervision and lowering the threshold for convicting disruptive behaviours in online classrooms are essential steps in maintaining the integrity and order of these new educational spaces. Alongside stricter regulatory measures, there should be a concerted effort to regularly train full-time law teachers in online teaching methodologies. This training will ensure that educators are well-equipped to manage and excel in digital teaching environments, thereby stabilising the development of online education within a framework that teachers can effectively control.

Thirdly, there is a pressing need to optimise the course system settings in universities.[105] Establishing secondary disciplines, such as "artificial intelligence law" and "digital law", under the primary discipline of law should be a priority.[106] Universities must actively explore, construct, and refine professional knowledge modules and systems that align with the deep application of information technology in legal contexts. This proactive approach will not only expand the academic curriculum but also ensure that it remains relevant in the face of rapid technological advancements.

Fourthly, enhancing the supporting infrastructure for interdisciplinary education is essential. This can be achieved by building or upgrading facilities such as smart classrooms, digital laboratories, and artificial intelligence-assisted tools.[107] Furthermore, universities should seek partnerships with research-oriented enterprises to collaboratively develop, commission, or purchase advanced "intelligent practical teaching systems".[108] These collaborations can lead to the creation of state-of-the-art educational tools that significantly enhance the learning experience.

Finally, the development of personalised new educational models should be pursued vigorously. Leveraging AI technology to refine the segmentation of legal knowledge points allows for the transformation of complex information into more digestible parts of a comprehensive legal knowledge system. This technology can also analyse data from student interactions to assess strengths and weaknesses, enabling the creation of tailored learning plans that are scientifically sound. Additionally, AI can streamline and condense traditional legal content, which frees experienced law teachers from the constraints of basic instruction. This liberation allows teachers to focus on cultivating unique classroom environments that reflect their personal teaching styles and strengthen their role in nurturing students.

Each of these initiatives reflects a strategic response to the evolving demands of legal education in the digital age, highlighting a commitment to both preserving the core values of legal training and embracing the transformative potential of technology.

Of course, all of the above are merely theoretical and simplistic analyses based on the recent development of law disciplines and the current status of legal education in Chinese universities. Considerations about how to achieve the transition of legal

[104] Liu (2024).

[105] Li and Li (2024).

[106] Li and Li (2024).

[107] Yu and Zhang (2024).

[108] Yu and Zhang (2024).

education from traditional to more modern, futuristic, and contemporary, as well as how to promote the deep integration of information technology and legal education, are still worthy of continuous and in-depth research by the academic community.

9.2 The Impact of Information Technology on the Legal Profession

The advent of the first electronic computer in 1946, followed by the birth of the internet in the late 1960s and its global popularity after the 1990s, marked the era of the widespread influence of information technology on various industries. The legal industry has also undergone unprecedented changes due to the emergence of information technology.

The changes brought by information technology in the legal industry can be glimpsed from the relevant documents issued by governments over the years and are reflected in various areas of the legal profession. The outbreak of the COVID-19 pandemic, in 2020, profoundly changed the traditional mode of operation in the legal industry, making the impact of information technology on the legal profession even more significant. Due to the needs of epidemic prevention and control, the entire legal industry had to rely on information technology to maintain its operations. To meet the demand for legal services under the epidemic prevention and control measures, the legal profession, represented by lawyers, has increased investment in information technology construction. On the one hand, law firms utilised "cloud offices" to overcome the lockdown challenges caused by the epidemic. On the other hand, law firms have fully utilised technology to improve and refine the professional service process, enabling lawyers to provide legal services online using legal information systems, in addition to offline services, as a normalised form of legal service provision.[109]

It can be seen that the use of information technology in the legal industry is not only becoming increasingly common but also increasingly important as circumstances evolve. Currently, the integration and development of information technology in the legal industry are proceeding vigorously. While information technology brings convenience to the legal industry, to some extent, it also drives the transformation and development of the legal profession. Its positive impact is evident, but at the same time, the negative effects of information technology on the legal industry should not be overlooked. A correct understanding of both the positive and negative impacts of information technology is needed to better utilise it and promote the development of the legal industry through its application.

[109] Zhou and Guo(2021).

9.2.1 Positive Impacts of Information Technology on the Legal Profession

The rapid development of information technology, both theoretically and practically, is bound to bring positive impacts to the legal profession. These impacts include enriching legal databases, enhancing the efficiency of legal professionals, creating new legal job opportunities, and increasing the transparency of legal work, among others.

9.2.1.1 Enrichment of Legal Resource Repository

The emergence of information technology has led to the digitisation of legal resources, while the requirements for legislative and judicial transparency have resulted in a rapid growth trend of legal resources available on the internet. On 25 July 2016, the 1689th meeting of the Judicial Committee of the Supreme People's Court approved the "Provisions of the Supreme People's Court on the Publication of Judgments by People's Courts on the Internet".[110] According to this document, people's courts should lawfully, comprehensively, and promptly publish all judgements that meet the requirements of openness on the internet. The publication of court judgements allows legal professionals to access the necessary case information via the internet. This enables lawyers to clarify the sentencing styles of relevant judges before litigation, thus preparing their litigation strategies and predicting case outcomes accordingly. It also allows judges to refer to judgements made by other judges in similar cases, striving for consistency in sentencing to avoid the adverse effects of inconsistent judgements on judicial authority. In addition to judgements, relevant laws, regulations, and departmental rules have also been digitised, allowing legal professionals to retrieve related laws, regulations, and regulatory systems via the internet. The digitisation of laws, regulations, and regulatory systems, along with the publication of court judgements, enriches and enhances legal big data resources. Some legal resource repositories, such as Beida Fabao and Weike Xianxing, integrate and summarise published court judgements, laws, regulations, and departmental rules and make them available on the internet. This enables legal professionals to retrieve all types of legal resources they need, such as judgements and regulations, from a single legal data repository, making information access more convenient.

9.2.1.2 Improving Efficiency of Legal Professionals

With the development of information technology, various aspects, from the internet to big data and artificial intelligence, contribute to the improvement of efficiency for legal professionals, with artificial intelligence being the most representative.

[110] See China News, https://www.chinanews.com/gn/2016/08-31/7989135.shtml, accessed June 1, 2024.

Before the emergence of artificial intelligence, information technologies such as the internet and big data had improved the efficiency of legal professionals, but still required them to invest a significant amount of time and effort. Although the existence of legal data repositories allowed legal professionals to retrieve desired legal materials through keyword searches, this method often resulted in a mere aggregation of materials matching the keywords, lacking precision. Legal professionals still needed to further review and organise the materials themselves. The advent of artificial intelligence changed this situation significantly. Artificial intelligence can assist legal professionals in completing basic tasks, freeing them from repetitive and low-specialisation tasks. After retrieving relevant content, artificial intelligence organises the materials, allowing legal professionals to obtain reports already logically integrated according to certain criteria, without the need for further organisation. In addition to data retrieval, tasks such as document proofreading and contract review can also be delegated to artificial intelligence, allowing legal professionals to engage in more in-depth legal research, and pursue more creative and innovative work, thereby enhancing overall work efficiency. In terms of intelligent retrieval, a representative example is ROSS, the world's first robot lawyer developed in the United States. Built on IBM's Watson system, ROSS possesses powerful natural language-processing capabilities and machine-learning technology to present lawyers with the most relevant and valuable legal answers, rather than merely providing a list of search results like traditional legal databases.[111] In contract review, Deloitte utilises the machine-learning contract-analysis system, Kira Systems, which can read through contracts in just 15 min, a task that would typically take a human lawyer 12 h to complete.[112] All of these examples demonstrate how the emergence of artificial intelligence has led to a significant increase in the efficiency of legal professionals.

9.2.1.3 Bringing Convenience to Legal Professionals' Daily Work

With the emergence and improvement of information technology, legal professionals are able to break free from the constraints of traditional work models. They can now provide services to clients through online consultation platforms, communicate with clients in real-time through messaging software, and reduce the time spent on offline travel, thereby providing great convenience to legal professionals.

At the same time, with the outbreak of the COVID-19 pandemic in early 2020, online conferencing platforms experienced rapid development. To meet the epidemic prevention requirements during the COVID-19 pandemic, face-to-face communication became difficult, leading to a demand for online office solutions. Numerous online office and conferencing software, developed by prominent high-tech companies, emerged rapidly to meet this demand. These software applications, such as Tencent Meeting, DingTalk, and Zoom, have been continuously adjusted and improved to meet user needs. Through these online conferencing platforms, academic

[111] Cao (2017).

[112] Cao (2017).

conferences and daily meetings for legal professionals could be conducted smoothly and conveniently, allowing legal professionals to comply with epidemic prevention regulations while efficiently completing their work.

In addition to online conferencing platforms and online consultation platforms, another convenience for legal professionals comes from online litigation systems. Influenced by the COVID-19 pandemic, at the end of 2020, online litigation, which was previously piloted in only a few courts, became widely adopted nationwide. Online litigation covers the entire process from filing a case to court hearings. In terms of case filing, lawyers who previously had to file cases in person at the courthouse, were able to file cases directly through the internet using the court's designated online systems. For example, the High Court of Gaoyou City, Jiangsu Province, issued the "Guidelines for Online Litigation Services of Gaoyou Court" on 4 February 2020, suggesting the use of online litigation services to effectively prevent and control the COVID-19 epidemic and protect public health and safety. The Supreme People's Court further affirmed online litigation in its "Notice on Strengthening and Standardizing Online Litigation Work During the Prevention and Control of the COVID-19 Epidemic" issued on 18 February 2020, which provided clear guidance for nationwide courts to conduct online litigation. The use of online litigation systems has greatly saved time for legal professionals, including lawyers, and brought great convenience to their work.

9.2.1.4 Creating New Legal Professions

The development of information technology has created emerging professions within the legal industry, with various interdisciplinary roles emerging with the advent of information technology. As information technology advances, society's demands on the legal industry increase. In order to provide better user experiences for clients and maintain competitiveness in the industry, some legal professionals are actively combining the legal profession with the information technology industry, thereby creating a large number of new legal job positions.

Internationally, some foreign law firms have initiated the construction of legal information technology. Nowadays, some international law firms have even strengthened the development of talent in the field of legal artificial intelligence. Legal developers, legal data analysts, and legal database managers are gradually joining law firms, legal database companies, and other legal institutions. In the near future, with the growing integration of information technology and law, there will be a greater demand for talent proficient in both information technology and legal knowledge in the legal industry.[113]

---

[113] Yin (2019).

9.2.1.5 Enhancing Transparency in Legal Work

The development of information technology has enhanced the transparency of legal work to a certain extent. From a judicial perspective, current courts have achieved both the openness of judgement documents and the transparency of the trial process through information technology. The public can query judgement documents that meet the public disclosure conditions on the China Judgment Documents Network and various legal resource databases. They can also watch live trials that meet the conditions on the China Courtroom Live Streaming website, and even watch trial replays anytime, anywhere. This greatly enhances the transparency of the judicial system, allowing parties to obtain relevant information in a timely manner and effectively supervise the judicial behaviour of judicial personnel, thereby better preventing judicial corruption. At the same time, judges can refer to the judgements of other judges as much as possible when hearing cases through data analysis of publicly available cases, thereby striving to achieve consistent judgements for similar cases, preventing different judgements for similar cases from damaging the image of justice in the minds of the people, and maintaining the authority and fairness of the judiciary.

From a legislative perspective, in the internet era, laws have been open and transparent from the drafting stage. In China, laws are open to the public from drafting to the issuance of drafts to the final formal promulgation, all of which are published on the internet. The digitising laws, regulations, and departmental rules allows the general public to easily access relevant content through the internet, reflecting transparency at the legislative level.

In the legal service industry, before the advent of information technology, the legal service market was more like a bilateral market, and its evaluation system was not as complete and visible as that of e-commerce platforms. This also made it difficult for parties to understand lawyers through effective channels. With the development of information technology, various online legal service platforms and self-media platforms have emerged, allowing the public to better understand lawyers through more channels, thereby choosing satisfactory lawyers and accepting corresponding legal services. In addition, lawyers can also make greater use of self-media platforms to better promote themselves, allowing parties to have a more intuitive understanding of lawyers, thereby changing to a certain extent the drawbacks caused by the lack of transparency in the evaluation system of the legal service industry in the past.

9.2.2 Challenges Brought by Information Technology to the Legal Profession

While information technology has a positive impact on the legal profession, it also presents unprecedented challenges. The emergence of artificial intelligence undoubtedly poses a significant challenge to the legal profession. Additionally, the development of information technology brings about changes in the form of evidence, which also poses immense challenges to the legal profession. The lack of comprehensive information disclosure will hinder the future development of the legal industry. These are all issues that need to be actively addressed in the future while harnessing the development brought by information technology to the legal field.

9.2.2.1 The Impact of the Emergence of Artificial Intelligence on Certain Legal Professions

In today's society, legal professionals can already rely on artificial intelligence to complete some basic tasks. However, for certain legal professionals engaged in these basic tasks such as clerks, interns, and legal assistants, the emergence of artificial intelligence has brought significant challenges. With the continuous advancement of artificial intelligence technology, simple and repetitive legal tasks that lack creativity may be completely replaced. Some straightforward cases with clear relationships can easily be handled by artificial intelligence, such as traffic accident compensation, inheritance consultation, marriage counselling, and so on. In 2019, the Higher People's Court of Shandong Province implemented a pilot project for the application of element-based, intelligent-trial systems to simplify case handling procedures, improve trial efficiency, achieve rapid review of simple cases, and specialise in similar cases throughout the province. For example, financial loan contract disputes, property service contract disputes, motor vehicle traffic accident liability disputes, private lending disputes, divorce disputes, and other types of cases were verified and applied. Nowadays, in order to maintain their competitiveness in the information age, some law firms and legal consulting companies are actively developing artificial intelligence systems. For instance, in 2023, Zhuo Jian Law Firm in Guangdong formally established the "Zhuo Jian Legal Artificial Intelligence Laboratory" in Shenzhen and signed a "Legal Artificial Intelligence Strategic Cooperation Framework Agreement" with two technology companies at the event, thereby promoting the law firm's completion of its digital transformation.[114] After the widespread application of artificial intelligence, tasks such as online consultation, document proofreading, and contract review may gradually be replaced by automation.

For courts, although current information technology only plays an auxiliary role in case adjudication and cannot replace judges, nor pose a substantive threat to the profession of judges, it is foreseeable that, in the future, with the development and maturity of information technology, especially artificial intelligence technology, some judicial support positions, such as judicial assistants and clerks, will inevitably face significant challenges, resulting in a substantial reduction in related positions. At the same time, the promotion of online dispute-resolution mechanisms is also posing a fierce challenge to traditional judicial adjudication methods. Taking the United States online dispute-resolution platforms as an example, typical representatives include Modria and Cybersettle. Modria, an online arbitration platform, was developed by eBay to resolve transaction disputes. It resolves over 60 million transaction disputes

[114] Zhang (2023).

annually, more than three times the total number of cases handled by the US court system.[115] In China, there are also similar online dispute-resolution platforms, with the Alibaba Online Dispute Resolution Center being one of the most well-known. In the future, with the increasing number of disputes and further development of information technology, there will be more online dispute-resolution platforms, and the corresponding systems and rules will become more sophisticated, which will inevitably have a profound impact on the court system.

For the legal service industry, with the widespread development of information technology, especially with the widespread application of artificial intelligence in the future, positions such as legal consulting and legal assistants will be greatly affected. With the widespread application of artificial intelligence technology in the legal service industry, the demand for some basic positions in the legal service industry will sharply decrease. Especially with the emergence of artificial intelligence lawyers, the legal service industry will face structural collapse. A customer-centric legal service market will emerge, and under the competition of artificial intelligence lawyers, the fees for high-quality legal services will no longer be unattainable, and high-quality legal services will become more accessible to everyone. By then, it will inevitably trigger a significant shake-up in the legal service industry. If legal professionals do not promptly adapt and adjust to the fierce competition in the future, they will inevitably be eliminated.

9.2.2.2 The Incomplete Disclosure of Information Poses Significant Challenges to the Legal Profession

Although, according to the relevant regulations of the Supreme People's Court, many eligible judgement documents have been uploaded to the China Judgments Online website for publication, there are still a large number of judgement documents from cases that have not been made public due to the need to protect personal privacy, commercial secrets, national security, and other reasons. Additionally, because the publication of judgement documents is not in real time, there is a certain delay, which also prevents the public from accessing the latest case information promptly. Furthermore, even with the judgement documents from courts, there are still various common problems from the perspective of legal data collection and storage. For example, "non-standardised" legal data, such as deliberations by a case's collegiate bench, will not appear in the final judgement documents.[116] Furthermore, although judicial documents are disclosed at the judicial level, there is still a considerable number of administrative documents that are not made public in practice. This lack of transparency in administrative agencies' actions contrasts with the transparency of judicial agencies, making it relatively difficult for the public to supervise administrative law enforcement actions or obtain relevant information. Currently, the vast majority of legal data in China is essentially monopolised by data collectors and

---

[115] Zhang (2020).

[116] Tong and Wang (2019).

lacks unified data standards. Data collection agencies in the legislative, judicial, law enforcement, and legal service sectors primarily prioritise confidentiality in their data collection, leading to significant delays in information disclosure and the formation of "data islands". This impedes objective data sharing.[117] Both in the judiciary and in administration, this lack of transparency can have a negative impact on judicial and administrative agencies. Due to this opacity, the public may not be able to promptly understand relevant information, potentially leading to questioning of the fairness of judicial and administrative law enforcement actions, thereby undermining their authority to some extent.

9.2.2.3 The Change in Forms of Evidence as a Challenge to Legal Profession

The advent of information technology not only brings significant disruptions to the legal profession but also presents enormous challenges due to the changes in forms of evidence it induces. The emergence of information technology has led to substantial changes in the forms of evidence, with various forms of electronic signatures and seals proliferating. While these innovations bring convenience, they also give rise to many problems, such as forgery of electronic signatures and seals, posing difficulties for legal service providers and law enforcement agencies.

The introduction of information technology enables remote control and manipulation of electronic materials by the parties involved in a case. This capability also comes with a series of security issues, including the risk of leakage of parties' information, hacking into information systems by malicious actors, and the spread of electronic viruses. Furthermore, due to the possibility of electronic document tampering, it becomes challenging for recipients to detect alterations made by third parties to incoming emails. This makes it difficult for email recipients to verify the authenticity of emails received. If legal professionals receive forged emails, the devastating impact on their subsequent work is unimaginable.[118] Legal professionals may also be held accountable for using forged evidence.

9.2.3 Response of the Legal Industry in the Information Technology Era

Looking at the current situation, it is undeniable that information technology presents a double-edged sword for the legal industry. In the future, with the further development of information technology, especially the refinement of artificial intelligence technology, how the legal industry navigates steadily amidst this tide of disruption becomes particularly crucial.

[117] Tong and Wang (2019).

[118] Qiu (2001).

9.2.3.1 Actively Adapting to Information Technology to Maintain Competitiveness

As mentioned earlier, in tasks such as data retrieval, analysis, processing, contract review, and document proofreading in the legal field, humans are almost unable to compete with artificial intelligence. However, in some areas of law that require a substantial competitive edge, such as negotiation and courtroom representation, humans are difficult to replace with artificial intelligence. This is because current artificial intelligence still lacks the ability to understand relevant ethical considerations, customs, and human emotions, which are essential in providing legal assistance. When seeking legal help, clients are not only seeking professional legal services but also emotional support. Judges, when making rulings, need to consider not only facts and laws but also social customs and ethical principles to render judgements satisfactory to the parties and society as a whole. Similarly, lawyers representing clients in courtrooms do not merely mechanically fulfil their duties based on legal provisions but also need to integrate legal principles, facts, and human sentiments to fulfil the legal mission effectively, something that artificial intelligence cannot accomplish at present. In reality, many legal issues do not have standard answers, and resolving them requires balancing interests, human sentiments, and social customs. Those addressing these issues need to possess the ability to understand the real world, a task that is not necessarily simple even for experienced lawyers, let alone for artificial intelligence, which is still in its early stages of development.[119]

Another advantage of artificial intelligence is its ability to continuously self-learn and improve as data accumulates, as exemplified by the currently popular ChatGPT. Moreover, due to the interconnectedness of data, computers can correlate specific contracts with all relevant court judgements, forming a dynamically improving relationship. In the future, with the continuous improvement of hardware and software performance as well as algorithms, advanced legal documents such as complaints, memorandums, and judgements may also be generated automatically, inevitably impacting the legal profession. However, artificial intelligence does not possess the proactive learning ability of humans, nor does it have creativity. Therefore, in certain situations, the materials involved still require review by human lawyers or judges, thus forming a relationship of human–machine collaboration.[120] Therefore, even though artificial intelligence does pose a certain degree of threat to the legal profession, as long as one can actively confront the impact of new information technologies and cultivate their skills proactively to maintain core competitiveness, they can effectively prevent themselves from being replaced by artificial intelligence in the future.

[119] Xing (2018).

[120] Cao (2017).

9.2.3.2 Establishing Connectivity in Legal Data Repositories to Eliminate Information Silos

Currently, the most significant problem for legal professionals regarding legal data repositories is the lack of comprehensive access to legal data and the untimeliness of obtaining first-hand legal information data resources. This is caused by the "officialisation" of legal data resources. The officialisation of legal data determines that comprehensive and timely access to legal data depends, to a large extent, on the extent to which legal data holders fully and promptly disclose legal information. Therefore, accelerating the opening and sharing of data in the legislative, judicial, and enforcement processes; standardising the standards and models for the disclosure of information and data by various State agencies; and achieving the docking and matching of data between various agencies become particularly important. Simultaneously, coordinating the planning of big data infrastructure construction, promoting the formulation of institutional documents for the protection and opening of public information resources, strengthening the top-level design of big data standardisation, and gradually improving the standard system are also crucial for eliminating information silos in legal data.[121] Only after the standards are clearly defined can legal data be maximally disclosed. Data that does not meet the disclosure standards must be strictly kept confidential, while data that meets the standards must be made public. Only in this way can legal professionals ensure timely access to all legal data information.

9.2.3.3 Establishing a Security System to Address the Impact of Changes in Evidence Format

The changes in the form of evidence will undoubtedly bring convenience to legal professionals, but they will also have significant negative impacts. Therefore, legal professionals need to establish relevant security systems, and carefully examine the authenticity of signatures and seals using professional equipment. At the same time, relevant information technology platforms should establish comprehensive risk-prevention and control systems to prevent viruses or hackers from modifying or leaking relevant information, thus minimising the negative impact that information technology may bring to the legal industry.

In the era of information technology, every industry is widely affected, and the legal industry is no exception. Throughout modern history, the emergence of any new factor has brought certain negative effects to the people living at that time. For example, during the Industrial Revolution, the advent of the steam engine led to mass layoffs of manual labourers. However, after decades of development, the positive impacts it brought are undeniable. Looking back, the positive impacts of the Industrial Revolution far outweighed the negative ones it produced.

---

[121] Tong and Wang (2019).

Currently, the development of information technology parallels that of the Industrial Revolution. Therefore, in the face of the negative impact of information technology on the legal profession, there is no need to overly worry. Instead, we should actively address it to better adapt to future society.

Bibliography on Australian Part

Articles/Books/Reports

Adams, Michael, 'Developments in Australian Curriculum and Teaching Across the Various Law Degrees' (Zhejiang University Guanghua Law School Forum, 28 September 2014)

Ajevski, Marjan et al, 'Chat GPT and the Future of Legal Education and Practice' (2023) 57(3) *Law Teacher* 352

'Artificial Intelligence to Help the Most Vulnerable Navigate Justice' (2021) (82) *Law Society Journal* 22

Office for Learning and Teaching, *Internationalising the Australian Law Curriculum for Enhanced Global Legal Practice* (Final Report, 2013) Re-alphabetise

Australian Institute of Health and Welfare, *Australia's Health 2022: Data Insights* (Report No 18, 2022)

Baghoomians, Irene, Emily Crawford and Jacqueline Mowbray, 'The Teaching of Public International Law in Australian Law Schools: 2021 and Beyond' (2022) 43(1) *Adelaide Law Review* 7

Barker, David, 'An Avalanche of Law Schools, 1989–2013' (2013) 6 *Journal of the Australasian Law Teachers Association* 153

Basedow, Jürgen, 'Breeding Lawyers for the Global Village: The Internationalisation of Law and Legal Education' in William van Caenegem and Mary Hiscock (eds), *The Internationalisation of Legal Education: The Future Practice of Law* (Edward Elgar, 2014)

Benjamin, Alarie, Anthony Niblett and Albert H Yoon, 'How Artificial Intelligence Will Affect the Practice of Law' (2018) 68(1) *The University of Toronto Law Journal* 106

Bigda, Jordan, 'The Legal Profession: From Humans to Robots' (2018) 18(2) *Journal of High Technology Law* 396

Black, Ann and Peter Black, 'Going Global: Australia Looks to Internationalise Legal Education' in Andrew Harding, Jiaxlang Hu, and Maarje de Visser (eds), *Legal Education in Asia: From Imitation to Innovation* (Brill Nijhoff, 2018)

Blackham, Alysa, 'Judges and Retirement Ages', (2016) 39(3) Melbourne University Law Review 738

Blanco, Felimon Bonita, 'Technology-Driven Pedagogy in Legal Education Class: A Case Study' (2023) 20(1) *Journal of Educational Technology* 36

Bradley, Denise et al, *Department of Education, Employment and Workplace Relations Review of Australian Higher Education* (Final Report, Department of education, Employment and Workplace Relations, December 2008).

Brasch, Jacoba 'Access to Justice in a COVID-19 World' (2021) 48(2) *Brief* 45

Bullows, Amy, 'How Technology is Changing the Legal Sector' (2021) 55(2) *Law Teacher* 258

S. Zhang et al., *Technology, Legal Education and Legal Profession in China and Australia*, International and Comparative Law in the Asia Pacific,
https://doi.org/10.1007/978-981-96-1639-8

Burdon, Peter D, '"Never Let a Crisis Go to Waste": The Impact of COVID-19 on Legal Education' (2022) 8 *Canadian Journal of Comparative and Contemporary Law* 1

Burgess, Paul, AI and the Rule of Law: The Necessary Evolution of a Concept (Hart, 2024)

Burridge, Roger and Julian Webb, 'The Values of Common Law Legal Education: Rethinking Rules, Responsibilities, Relationships and Roles in the Law School' (2007) 10(1) *Legal Ethics* 72

Caenegem, William van and Trish Mundy, *Special Report of Online Legal Education in Australia* (28 October 2021) < https://ssrn.com/abstract=3951659>

Cassimatis, Anthony E and Peter Billings, *Thomson Reuters Guide to Mooting* (Thomson Reuters, 2016)

Castan, Melissa and Ross Hyams, 'Blended Learning in the Law Classroom: Design, Implementation and Evaluation of an Intervention in the First Year Curriculum Design' (2017) 27(1) *Legal Education Review* 1

Chesterman, Simon, Lyria Bennett Moses and Ugo Pagallo, 'All Rise for the Honourable Robot Judge?': Using Artificial Intelligence to Regulate AI' (2023) Technology and Regulation 45

Coper, Michael 'Internationalisation and Different National Philosophies of Legal Education: Convergence, Divergence and Contestability' in William van Caenegem and Mary Hiscock (eds), *The Internationalisation of Legal Education: The Future Practice of Law* (Edward Elgar, 2014)

Council of Australian Law Deans, '2018 Data Regarding Law School Graduate Numbers and Outcomes' (2019)

Corban, Lillian and Lisa Bugden, 'Online Teaching: The Importance of Pedagogy, Place and Presence in Legal Education' (2018) 28(1) *Legal Education Review* 1

Dal Pont, GE, Lawyers' Professional Responsibility (Thomson Reuters, 7th ed, 2021)

De Maio, Carmela 'Reflecting on Teaching Law Online at Two Western Australian Universities During the Covid-19 Pandemic: Challenges and Recommendations for a Positive Learning Experience' (2022) 1 *Western Australian Law Teachers Review* 33

Dolan, Michael and Carly Erwin, 'Legal Ethics and AI' (2020) 30(3) *Australian Corporate Lawyer* 14

Dombosch, Gina, 'Green is the New Black' (2013) 11(9) *Australasian Legal Business* 62

Draper, Michael J, Simon Gibbon and Jane Thomas, 'Lecture Recording: A New Norm' (2018) 52(3) *Law Teacher* 316

Ebejer, Marlene, *Legal Practice and Ethics* (LexisNexis Butterworths, 4th ed, 2022)

Evans, Adrian et al, *Australian Clinical Legal Education: Designing and Operating a Best Practice Clinical Program in an Australian Law School* (ANU Press, 2017)

Evans, Adrian et al, 'Best Practices: Australian Clinical Legal Education' (Report, Office for Teaching and Learning, 2012)

EY, Reimagining the Legal Function Report 2019 (2019)

Fletcher, Kylie, 'Law Clinics Educating for Complexity Through Integrative Learning' (2019) 5(1) *Australian Journal of Clinical Education*

Fore, Michael and Erin Stevenson, 'The Impact of Covid-19 Pandemic on Overall Well-being of Practicing Lawyers' (2023) *PLOS ONE* 1

Galloway, Kate, 'A Rationale and Framework for Digital Literacies in Legal Education' (2017) 27 *Legal Education Review* 1

Goldsworthy, Daniel, 'The Future of Legal Education in the 21st Century' (2020) 41(1) *Adelaide Law Review* 243

David Hamer et al., Laying Down the Law (12th edition, LexisNexis, 12th ed, 2024)

Houghton, Jayden, 'Learning Modules: Problem-based Learning, Blended Learning and Flipping the Classroom' (2023) 57(3) *Law Teacher* 271

Hunter, Dan, 'The Death of the Legal Profession and the Future of Law' (2020) 43(4) *University of New South Wales Law Journal* 1199

Hutchinson, Terry 'The Transnational Lawyer: GATS, Globalisation and the Effects on Legal Education' (2006) 11(2) *Australia & New Zealand Journal of Law & Education* 9

James, Nickolas, 'A Brief History of Critique in Australian Legal Education' (2000) 24(3) *Melbourne University Law Review* 965

Johnstone, Richard and Sumitra Vignaendra, *Learning Outcomes and Curriculum Development in Law* (Australian Universities Teaching Committee, 2003)

Jones, Emma et al, 'Introduction: Defining Digital Lawyering' in Emma Jones, et al (eds), *Digital Lawyering: Technology and Legal Practice in the 21st Century* (Taylor & Francis, 2021)

Jones, Emma, 'The 21st-Century Legal Professional' in in Emma Jones, et al (eds) *Digital Lawyering: Technology and Legal Practice in the 21st Century* (Taylor & Francis, 2021)

International Legal Services Advisory Council, *Internationalisation of the Australian Law Degree Report* (Final Report, June 2004)

Urbis, *2014 Law Society National Profile* (Report, Law Society of New South Wales, April 2015) Re-alphabetise

Law Admissions Consultative Committee, Uniform Principles for Assessing the Qualifications of Overseas Applicants for Admission to the Australian Legal Profession, (Legal Profession Admission Board, 2015)

Legg, Michael and Felicity Bell, *Artificial Intelligence and the Legal Profession* (Hart, 2020)

Legg, Michael and Anthony Song, 'The Courts, the Remote Hearing and the Pandemic: From Action to Reflection' (2021) 44(1) *University of New South Wales Law Journal* 126

Lilley, Rob and Christina Do, 'What Should an 'entry-level lawyer' Look Like in a Post-COVID-19 world?' (2002) 1 *Western Australian Law Teachers' Review* 19

Lo, Vai, 'Before Competition and Beyond Complacency – The Internationalisation of Legal Education in Australia' (2013) 21(2) *Legal Education Digest* 1

Lodge, Jason M et al, Assessment Reform for the Age of Artificial Intelligence (Tertiary Education Quality and Standards Agency, 2023) <https://www.teqsa.gov.au/sites/default/files/2023-09/assessment-reform-age-artificial-intelligence-discussion-paper.pdf>

McKeith, Sam, 'Legal Tech: The Must-have Legal Technology Tools for 2021' (2021) (74) *Law Society Journal* 35

McNamara, Michael John, *Supervision in the Legal Profession* (Palgrave Macmillan, 2020)

Medianik, Katherine, 'Artificially Intelligent Lawyers: Updating the Model Rules of Professional Conduct in Accord with the New Technological Era' (2018) 39(4) *Cardozo Law Review* 1497

Moses, Lyria Bennett, 2023, 'Oversight of Police Intelligence: A Complex Web, But is it Enough?' (2023) 60(2), Osgoode Hall Law Journal, 291

Moses, Lyria Bennett, Janina L Boughey and Lisa Burton Crawford, 'Laws for Machines and Machine-made Laws', in Janina Boughey and Katie J; Miller K (eds.), The Automated State: Implications, Challenged and Opportunities for Public Law, (Federation Press, 2021)

Lyria Bennett Moses, et al., AI Decision-making and the Courts: A G guide for Judges, Tribunal Members and Court Administrators, 2022 (Australasian Institute of Judicial Administration, updated 2023) <https://aija.org.au/wp-content/uploads/2023/12/AIJA_AI-DecisionMakingReport_2023update.pdf>

Morton, Caroline E et al, 'Blended Learning: How can we Optimise Undergraduate Student Engagement?' (2016) 16(195) *BMC Medical Education* 36

Mulder, Raoul, Chi Baik, Tracii Ryan, 'Rethinking Assessment in Response to AI', (Melbourne Centre for the Study of Higher Education, July 2023) <https://melbourne-cshe.unimelb.edu.au/__data/assets/pdf_file/0004/4712062/Assessment-Guide_Web_Final.pdf>

Nicholson, Pip, 'Law School Accreditation During COVID-19: Transparency, Agility and Trust and the Australian Experience' in C Raj Kumar and SG Sreejith (eds), *Legal Education and Legal Profession During and After Covid-19* (Springer, 2022)

Nirmal, BC and Rajnish Kumar Singh, *Contemporary Issues in International Law: Environment, International Trade, Information Technology and Legal Education* (Springer, 2018)

Nottage, Luke, 'Comparing Online Legal Education World-Wide: An Overview Before and After the Pandemic' (2022) <https://ssrn.com/abstract=4128484>

Office for Learning and Teaching, Internationalising the Australian Law Curriculum for Enhanced Global Legal Practice (Final Report, 2013) <https://ltr.edu.au/resources/PP10_1789_Bentley_booklet_2012.pdf>

Pearce, Dennis, Enid Campbell and Don Harding, 'Australian Law Schools: A Discipline Assessment for the Commonwealth Tertiary Education Commission' (Final Report, Australian Government Publishing Service, 1987)

Ramsay, Ian M, 'Should Law Firms be Permitted to Incorporate? An Analysis of the Trade Practices Commission Recommendation' (1994) 10 Australian Journal of Law and& Society 245

Raz, Manda, Erwin Loh and John Fevereux, Careers in Law: A Guide for Students, Graduates and Professionals (Springer, 2020)

Ryan, Francine et al, 'The Changing Legal Profession' in Emma Jones, et al (eds) *Digital Lawyering: Technology and Legal Practice in the 21st Century* (Taylor & Francis, 2021)

Sadi, Rodrigo, 'Legal Education in the Civil Law System' (2018) 62(1) *New York Law School Law Review* 165

Smith, Marcus, 'Integrating Technology in Contemporary Legal Education' (2020) 54(2) *Law Teacher* 209

Steel, A et al, 'Use of E-Exams in High Stakes Law School Examinations: Student and Staff Reactions' (2019) 29(1) *Legal Education Review* 1

Traczykowski, Lauren and Paul Dale, 'Adapting Legal Education for Technological Changes in Business' in Christian Hauser and Wolfgang Amann (eds) *The Future of Responsible Management Education* (Pargrave Macmillan, 2023)

Triggs, Gillian, 'The Internationalisation of Legal Education: An Opportunity for Human Rights?' in William van Caenegem and Mary Hiscock (eds), *The Internationalisation of Legal Education: The Future Practice of Law* (Edward Elgar, 2014)

Urbis, *2022 National Profile of Solicitors* (Report No 6, 23 April 2023)

Van Caenegem, William, 'Ignoring the Civil Law/Common Law Divide in an Integrated World' in William van Caenegem and Mary Hiscock (eds) *The Internationalisation of Legal Education: The Future Practice of Law* (Edward Elgar, 2014)

Vijeyarasa, Ramona, 'Gendered Harms and the Regulation of Artificial Intelligence: A Comparative Assessment of Emerging Legislative Practice', (2023) 5(1) Notre Dame Journal of Emerging Technologies 114

Wang, Zhiqiong June, 'Between Constancy and Change: Legal Practice and Legal Education in the Age of Technology' (2019) 36(1) *Law in Context* 64

Williams, Anna Shavers, 'The Impact of Technology on Legal Education' (2001) 51(3) *Journal of Legal Education* 407

Wolff, Lutz-Christian and Jenny Chan, *Flipped Classrooms for Legal Education* (Springer, 2016)

Wolski, Bobette, 'Continuing the Internationalisation debate: Philosophies of legal Education, Issues in Curriculum Design and Lessons from Skills Integration' in William van Caenegem and Mary Hiscock (eds) *The Internationalisation of Legal Education: The Future Practice of Law* (Edward Elgar, 2014)

Zalnieriute, Monika, Lyria M Bennett Moses and George Williams G '6 Automating Government Decision-making: Implications for the Rule of Law', in Siddharth Peter de Souza and Maximillian Spohr (eds), Technology, Innovation and Access to Justice: Dialogues on the Future of Law, (Edinburgh University Press, 2021)

Cases

Frugtniet v Board of Examiners [2002] VSC 140

Hawkins v Clayton (1988) 164 CLR 539

R v Kirby; Ex parte Boilermakers' Society of Australia (1956) 94 CLR 54

McConnell Dowell Constructors (Aust) Pty Ltd v Santam Ltd (No 1) (2016) 51 VAR 421

Legislation

Acts Interpretation Act 1915 (SA)

Acts Interpretation Act 1984 (WA)

Australia Acts 1986 (Cth)

Australia Acts 1986 (UK)
Australia (Request and Consent) Act 1985 (Cth)
Australian Constitution
Australian Constitution Act 1842 (Imp)
Australian Courts Act 1828 (Imp)
Barristers Admission Act 1848 (NSW)
Colonial Laws Validity Act 1865 (Imp)
Constitution Alteration (Retirement of Judges) Act 1977 (Cth)
Corporations Amendment (Meetings and Documents) Act 2022 (Cth)
Court (Admission) Rules 2004 (Qld)
Court Procedure Rules 2006 (ACT)
Federal Court of Australia Act 1976 (Cth)
Higher Education Standards Framework (Threshold Standards) 2021 (Cth)
Higher Education Support Act 2003 (Cth)
Legal Profession Act 2007 (Qld)
Legal Profession Admission Rules 2007 (NT)
Legal Profession Admission Rules 2015 (NSW)
Legal Profession Admission Rules 2015 (Vic)
Legal Profession Admission Rules 2015 (WA)
Legal Profession (Board of Legal Education) Rules 2021 (Tas)
Legal Profession Continuing Professional Development (Solicitors) Rules 2015 (NSW)
Legal Profession Uniform Conduct (Solicitors) Rules 2015 (NSW)
Legal Profession Uniform General Rules 2015 (NSW)
Legal Profession Uniform Law 2014 (NSW)
Legal Profession Uniform Law 2014 (Vic)
Legal Profession Uniform Law 2014 (WA)
Legal Profession Uniform Law Solicitors' Conduct Rules 2015 (NSW)
Legal Profession Uniform Law Solicitors' Conduct Rules 2015 (Vic)
Legal Profession Uniform Law Solicitors' Conduct Rules 2015 (WA)
Local Court Act 2007 (NSW)
Model Code of Professional Responsibility 1969 (USA)
New South Wales Act 1823 (Imp)
New South Wales Constitution Act 1865 (Imp)
Northern Territory Acceptance Act 1910 (Cth)
Public Governance, Performance and Accountability Act 2003 (Cth)
Rules of the Legal Practitioners Education and Admission Council 2018 (SA)
Seat of Governance Acceptance Act 1909 (Cth)
Statute of Westminster 1931 (Imp)
Statute of Westminster Adoption Act 1942 (Cth)
Supreme Court Act 1970 (NSW)
Supreme Court (Admission) Rules 2004 (QLD)
Supreme Court Civil Rules 2006 (SA)
Supreme Court Civil Supplementary Rules 2014 (SA)
Supreme Court Rules 2000 (Tas)

Other

'5 innovation Trends Defining the Post Pandemic Legal Sector', *College of Law* (Web Page, 18 April 2022) <https://mlb.collaw.edu.au/articles/innovation-trends-defining-the-legal-sector>

'About Us', Lawpath (Web Page) <https://lawpath.com.au/about-us>

'About Us', Supreme Court of New South Wales (Web Page) <https://supremecourt.nsw.gov.au/about-us.html>

'Academic', Victorian Legal Admissions Board (Web Page, 27 June 2024) <https://www.lawadmissions.vic.gov.au/qualifications-and-training/academic>

'Accredited Law Courses', Legal Profession Admission Board (Web Page, 6 December 2023) <https://www.lpab.justice.nsw.gov.au/Pages/admission-lawyer/accredited-law-courses-plt-providers.aspx>.

'Acknowledging AI Tools and Technologies', The University of Melbourne (Web Page) <https://students.unimelb.edu.au/academic-skills/resources/academic-integrity/acknowledging-AI-tools-and-technologies>

'Acknowledging Your Use', Deakin University (Web Page, 4 March 20204) <https://www.deakin.edu.au/students/study-support/study-resources/artificial-intelligence/acknowledging-your-use>

'Admission', *New South Wales Bar Association* (Web Page) <https://nswbar.asn.au/becoming-a-barrister/admission>

'Admission in Hong Kong', Melbourne China Law Society (Web Page) <https://themcls.org/international-opportunities/hongkong-2/#:~:text=Hong%20Kong%20Clerkships&text=Clerkship%20is%20essentially%20a%20legal,and%20culture%20at%20the%20firm>

'Admission', The Supreme Court of Tasmania (Web Page) <https://www.supremecourt.tas.gov.au/practitioners/admission/>

'AI and Justice (LAWS90248)', The University of Melbourne' (Web Page, 22 May 2024) <https://handbook.unimelb.edu.au/2024/subjects/laws90248>

Artificial Intelligence Advice for Students', Tertiary Education Quality and Standards Agency (Web Page, 29 July 2024) <https://www.teqsa.gov.au/students/artificial-intelligence-advice-students>

'Artificial Intelligence and the Law (LAWS90145)', The University of Melbourne (Web Page, 3 June 2024) <https://handbook.unimelb.edu.au/2024/subjects/laws90145>

'Artificial Intelligence, Law & Society: LAWS8405', Australian National University (Web Page) <https://programsandcourses.anu.edu.au/2025/course/LAWS8405>

'At the Forefront of Practical Legal Education', College of Law (Web Page, 2024) <https://www.collaw.edu.au/about/centre-for-legal-innovation>

Australian Bureau of Statistics, *Census of Population and Housing: Income and Work Data Summary 2021* (12 October 2022)

Council of Australian Law Deans, *Bachelor of Law Standards: Learning and Teaching Academic Standards Statement* (December 2010) Re-alphabetise

Australian Learning and Teaching Council, *Bachelor of Laws Learning and Teaching Academic Standards Statement,* (December 2010) I think this is Kift, Sally Mark Israel and Rachel Field, *Learning and Teaching Academic Standards Project: Bachelor of Laws: Learning and Teaching Standards Statement December 2020* (Australian Learning & Teaching Council, 2011) < https://cald.asn.au/wp-content/uploads/2024/04/LLB-TLOsKiftetalLTASStandardsStatement2010-TLOs-LLB2.pdf>

'Australian Solicitors' Conduct Rules', Law Council of Australia (Web Page) <https://lawcouncil.au/policy-agenda/regulation-of-the-profession-and-ethics/australian-solicitors-conduct-rules>

Council of Australian Law Deans, *Juris Doctor Threshold Learning Outcomes* (March 2012) Re-alphabetise

'Australian Qualifications Framework' *Australian Qualifications Framework* (Web Page, 2016) <https://www.aqf.edu.au/framework/australian-qualifications-framework/>.

Australian Qualifications Framework', *Tertiary Education Quality and Standards Agency* (Web Page) <https://www.teqsa.gov.au/how-we-regulate/acts-and-standards/australian-qualifications-framework/>

'Bachelor of Information Technology – Bachelor of Laws', University of Wollongong Australia (Web Page) <https://coursefinder.uow.edu.au/information/index.html?course=bachelor-information-technology-bachelor-laws>

'Bachelor of Information Technology Bachelor of Laws', UTS (Web Page) <https://www.uts.edu.au/study/find-a-course/bachelor-information-technology-bachelor-laws>

'Bachelor of Information Technology/Bachelor of Laws (Honours), QUT (Web Page) <https://www.qut.edu.au/courses/bachelor-of-information-technology-bachelor-of-laws-honours>

Bachelor of Laws' *James Cook University Australia* (Webpage) <https://www.jcu.edu.au/courses/bachelor-of-laws/>

Bachelor of Laws', *UNSW Sydney* (Webpage) <https://www.unsw.edu.au/law-justice/study/undergraduate/bachelor-laws/>

'Bachelor of Laws/Bachelor of Cyber Security', Deakin University (Web Page) <https://www.deakin.edu.au/course/bachelor-laws-bachelor-cyber-security>

'Bachelor of Laws/Bachelor of Information Technology', Murdoch University (Web Page) <https://www.murdoch.edu.au/course/undergraduate/b1398>

'Barristers' Commonwealth Government Jobs and Skills, Labour Market Insights' (Web Page, 10 September 2021) <https://labourmarketinsights.gov.au/occupation-profile/barristers?occupationCode=2711#:~:text=The%20median%20age%20of%20Barristers,all%20jobs%20average%20of%2048%25.>.

Barolsky, Joel, 'The Changing Face of the Legal Profession' Melbourne Law School (Web Page, 29 October 2020) <https://law.unimelb.edu.au/news/MLS/the-changing-face-of-the-legal-profession>

'Barrister Qualifications Overview', *Bar Association of Queensland* (Web Page, 2023) <https://qldbar.asn.au/baq-cms/barrister-qualifications>.

'Becoming a Barrister', *The Law Society of Tasmania* (Web Page, 2023) <https://www.lst.org.au/home/membership-and-legal-practice/practising-in-the-law/becoming-a-barrister/>. Comes after reference below

'Becoming a Barrister', *Victorian Bar* (Web Page) <https://www.vicbar.com.au/public/about/becoming-barrister>

'Blockchain and Cryptocurrency Law (LAWS90169)', The University of Melbourne (Web Page, 8 August 2024) <https://handbook.unimelb.edu.au/2024/subjects/laws90169>

'Career Options for Lawyers', *College of Law* (Web Page) <https://www.collaw.edu.au/your-career/career-options-for-lawyers>

Cassidy, Caitlin, 'Australian Universities to Return to 'pen and paper' Exams After Students Caught Using AI to Write Essays', The Guardian (online, 10 January 2023) <https://www.theguardian.com/australia-news/2023/jan/10/universities-to-return-to-pen-and-paper-exams-after-students-caught-using-ai-to-write-essays>

Centre for Law as Protection, 'Protection From Technology-based Harms', Deakin University (Web Page) <https://lawasprotection.org.au/stream/protection-from-technology-based-harms/>

Centre for Legal Innovation, 'The Role of Client Experience Designer' (YouTube, 26 May 2022) <https://youtu.be/l5fVpfjj0Ac?si=ByqLafHS6fVGIL9c>

Centre for Legal Innovation, 'The Role of a Knowledge Manager' (YouTube, 26 May 2022) 01:15:00–08:12:00 <https://youtu.be/vq553SWEib8?si=z3U_XKOM7VxgfGTS>.

Centre for Legal Innovation, 'The Role of a Legal Data Analyst' (YouTube, 26 May 2022) <https://youtu.be/Sg72dgp-HoM>.

Centre for Legal Innovation, 'The Role of a Legal Operations Professional' (YouTube, 26 May 2022) <https://youtu.be/LDB_17lZdVg>.

Centre for Legal Innovation, 'The Role of a Legal Technologist' (YouTube, 26 May 2022) <https://youtu.be/Z2tAm2jM_hM>.

Centre for Legal Innovation, 'What are New Law Careers?' (YouTube, 26 May 2022) <https://youtu.be/q3uzjjgOkBo>.

'Changes to our Services Due to COVID-19' *Victorian Legal Aid* (Web Page, 1 July 2023) <https://www.legalaid.vic.gov.au/changes-our-services-due-covid-19>.

Chief Justice Robert French AC, 'Internationalising the Australian Law curriculum for enhanced global legal education and practice' (Speech, International Legal Services Advisory Council National Symposium, 16 March 2012), 4–5 <https://www.hcourt.gov.au/assets/publications/speeches/current-justices/frenchcj/frenchcj16mar12.pdf>

Chief Justice Robert French AC, 'Legal Education in Australia – A Never Ending Story' (Speech, Australasian Law Teachers' Association Conference, 4 July 2011)

Chief Justice Robert French AC, 'The Judiciary in an Age of Global Interdependence' (Speech, International Association for Court Administration Conference, 15 March 2011) <https://www.hcourt.gov.au/assets/publications/speeches/current-justices/frenchcj/frenchcj15mar11.pdf>

'Chief Magistrate and Other Judicial Officers' *Local Court New South Wales* (Web Page, 24 August 2023) <https://www.localcourt.nsw.gov.au/about-us/chief-magistrate.html>

'Clerkship Recruitment Program' 2024, The Law Society of New South Wales (Web Page) <https://www.lawsociety.com.au/Legal-Communities/Law-Students/Clerkship-Recruitment-Program>

College of Law, '*Alternative Careers: Where Else Can Your Law Degree Take You? A Guide for Legal Graduates*' (2023) <https://www.collaw.edu.au/resources/2021/01/21/alternative-careers-where-else-can-your-law-degree-take-you>

'Coming to the Bar', *ACT Bar Association* (Web Page, 2023) <https://www.actbar.com.au/coming-to-the-bar/>.

'Commonwealth Courts Portal', Federal Court of Australia (Web Page, July 2024) <https://www.fedcourt.gov.au/online-services/commonwealth-courts-portal>

'Complaints', Judicial Commission of Victoria (Web Page, 2024) <https://www.judicialcommission.vic.gov.au/complaints/>

Council of Australian Law Deans, *Standards for Australian Law Schools with Guidance Notes*: Adopted as at 30 July 2020 (2020)

'Courts', Attorney-General's Department (Web Page) <https://www.ag.gov.au/legal-system/courts>

'Course Overview', The University of Sydney (Web Page) <https://lec.sydney.edu.au/why-study-with-the-law-extension-committee/course-overview/>

'Cryptoassets and the Law: LAWS8338', Australian National University (Web Page) <https://programsandcourses.anu.edu.au/2025/course/LAWS8338>

'Cyber Incident', *HWL Ebsworth.* (Web Page, 2023) <https://hwlebsworth.com.au/cyber-incident/>.

'Definition of Pro Bono', *Australian Pro Bono Centre* (Web Page 2023) <https://www.probonocentre.org.au/information-on-pro-bono/definition/>

'Digital Economies and the Law: LAWS8407', Australian National University (Web Page <https://programsandcourses.anu.edu.au/2025/course/LAWS8407>

'Digital Litigation at the Court', *Supreme Court of Australia* (Web Page) <https://www.supremecourt.vic.gov.au/going-to-court/virtual-hearings/digital-litigation-resources>

'Digital Technology and Labour Law (LAWS90205)', The University of Melbourne (Web Page, 11 June 2024) <https://handbook.unimelb.edu.au/2024/subjects/laws90205>

Doraisamy, Jerome, 'How COVID-19 has Changed #auslaw', *Lawyers Weekly* (online, 2020), 7 <https://www.lawyersweekly.com.au/pdfs/LW_-_Winter_2020.pdf>.

'eCourtroom', Federal Court of Australia (Web Page, July 2024) <https://www.fedcourt.gov.au/online-services/ecourtroom>

'eLodgment', Federal Court of Australia (Web Page, August 2024) <https://www.fedcourt.gov.au/online-services/elodgment>

Federal Court of Australia, Practice Note GPN-TECH: Justice Allsop, Technology and the Court Practice Note (GPN-TECH), 25 October 2016, <https://www.fedcourt.gov.au/law-and-practice/practice-documents/practice-notes/gpn-tech>

'Foreign Laws and Lawyers', Victorian Legal Services Board + Commissioner (Web Page) <https://lsbc.vic.gov.au/lawyers/practising-law/practising-certificates/foreign-laws-and-lawyers>

'Graduate Certificate of New Technologies Law', Australian National University (Web Page) <https://programsandcourses.anu.edu.au/program/cntl>

'Ground-breaking Research Informs NSW AI Inquiry', The University of Sydney (Web Page, 18 March 2024) <https://www.sydney.edu.au/news-opinion/news/2024/03/18/ground-breaking-research-informs-nsw-ai-inquiry.html>

'Guide for Students: Best Practice when Using Generative AI', Australian National University (Web Page) <https://www.anu.edu.au/students/academic-skills/academic-integrity/best-practice-principles/guide-for-students-best>

'Herbert Smith Freehills' World-leading Alternative Legal Services Practice Announced Australian Promotions', Herbert Smith Freehills (Web Page, 2024) <https://www.herbertsmithfreehills.com/news/2024-01/HSFs-world-leading-Alternative-Legal-Services-practice-announces-Australian-promotions->

'Humans Technology Law Centre', Business and Law, Business School QUT (Web Page) <https://research.qut.edu.au/htlc/>

'Information Technology Contracting Law (LAWS 70362)', The University of Melbourne (Web Page, 25 May 2024) <https://handbook.unimelb.edu.au/2024/subjects/laws70362>

'Information Technology Law: LAWS4245', Australian National University (Web Page) <https://programsandcourses.anu.edu.au/course/laws4245>

'Information Technology Law: LAWS8445', Australian National University (Web Page) <https://programsandcourses.anu.edu.au/course/LAWS8445>

Jarvis, Paul 'Dentons to Launch Client Secure Version of ChatGPT', *Dentons* (Web Page, 1 August 2023) <https://www.dentons.com/en/about-dentons/news-events-and-awards/news/2023/august/dentons-to-launch-client-secure-version-of-chatgpt>

'JD intake FAQs' *Melbourne Law School* (Web Page) <https://law.unimelb.edu.au/study/jd-intake-faqs/>

Johnson, Liz, Helen Partridge and Philip Dawson, '1,300 Years is Long Enough: It's Pen Down for the Exam Hall' (Blog Post, 16 January 2023) <, available at: https://blogs.deakin.edu.au/cradle/1300-years-is-long-enough-its-pens-down-for-the-exam-hall/>

Galloway, Kate, 'Text to Bits: Beyond the Revolution in Law and Lawyering' (2016) < https://papers.ssrn.com/sol3/papers.cfm?abstract_id=2879220>

'Law and Technology', ANU College of Law (Web Page) <https://law.anu.edu.au/research/law-and-technology>

'LAW4545: Technology, Design, and Innovation in Legal Services', Monash University Handbook (Web Page) <https://handbook.monash.edu/2025/units/LAW4545?year=2025>

'Law (Honours) Monash University', *Victorian Tertiary Admissions Centre* (Webpage) <https://delta.vtac.edu.au/coursesearch/#/course/26/2802838/>. See note in text

Law Institute of Victoria, *2024 LIV Clerkship and Graduate Program Guidelines Providing Consistency and Fairness Throughout the Recruitment Process* (2024)

Law Society of New South Wales Flip Commission of Inquiry, *Flip: The Future of Law and Innovation in the Profession* (2017) <https://www.lawsociety.com.au/sites/default/files/2018-03/1272952.pdf>

Law Society of Western Australia, *Inquiry into The Future of the Legal Profession* (2017)

'Law Students', *The Law Society of New South Wales* (Web Page, 2023) <https://www.lawsociety.com.au/Legal-Communities/Law-Students>

'Laws (Honours)/Engineering (Honours)' *Victorian Tertiary Admissions Centre* (Webpage) <https://delta.vtac.edu.au/coursesearch/#/course/26/2802832/>bbewhmjjje/> See note in text

'LAWS77–556 Information Technology and the Law', Bond University (Web Page) <https://bond.edu.au/subject/laws77-556-information-technology-and-law>

'Legal Technology and Innovation', Swinburne University of Technology (web Page) <https://www.swinburne.edu.au/course/unit/l/law20040/>

'LLB249 Introduction to Technology Law', QUT (Web Page) <https://www.qut.edu.au/study/unit?unitCode=LLB249>

McDonough, Keely, ''World's first robot lawyer' Hit With Lawsuit for Practicising Without a License', LSJ Online (16 March 2023) <https://lsj.com.au/articles/worlds-first-robot-lawyer-hit-with-lawsuit-for-practising-without-a-license/>

'Master of Laws', The University of Sydney Law School (Web Page) <https://www.sydney.edu.au/law/study-law/postgraduate/masters.html>

'Media, Intellectual Property & Technology Law', UNSW (Web Page) <https://www.unsw.edu.au/law-justice/study/postgraduate/media-intellectual-property-and-technology-law>

'Membership Categories: Student Membership', *Law Institute of Victoria* (Web Page, 2023) <https://www.liv.asn.au/Web/Content/Membership/Membership/Member_Category/Student.aspx>

Milmo, Dan, 'Two US Lawyers Fined for Submitting Fake Court Citations from ChatGPT', The Giardian (online, 23 June 2023) <https://www.theguardian.com/technology/2023/jun/23/two-us-lawyers-fined-submitting-fake-court-citations-chatgpt>

'MLL444 Data Law, Privacy and Cybercrime', Deakin University (Web Page) <https://www.deakin.edu.au/courses-search/unit.php?unit=MLL444>

Monash Data Futures Institute, 'AI and Data Science in Better Governance and Policy, 'Monash University (Web Page) <https://www.monash.edu/data-futures-institute/research/governance-policy>

Monash Data Futures Institute, 'Flagship Projects in Better Governance and Policy', Monash University (Web Page) https://www.monash.edu/data-futures-institute/research/governance-policy/flagship-projects

Monash Data Futures Institute, 'Monash Data Futures Institute PhD Scholarships', Monash University (Web Page) <https://www.monash.edu/data-futures-institute/study/phd-scholarship>

'Monash Data Futures Institute', Monash University (Web Page) <https://www.monash.edu/data-futures-institute>

'National Practitioners/Litigants Guide to Online Hearings and Microsoft Teams', (Federal Court of Australia) <https://www.fedcourt.gov.au/online-services/online-hearings/National-Practitioners-and-Litigants-Guide-V5.pdf

'New South Wales Courts and Tribunals', NSW Government (Web Page, 3 December 2023) <https://courts.nsw.gov.au/about-us/about-the-courts-and-tribunals.html>

Niven, Kristen, 'The Rise of the Robot Lawyer? DoNotPay's Legal AI Faces Several Challenges', Lexology (Blog Post, 31 May 2024) <https://www.lexology.com/library/detail.aspx?g=fcf42316-ad93-40f5-9e10-c2aecc17cb9a>

'Our Research', Cyber Security Cooperative Research Centre (Web Page) <https://cybersecuritycrc.org.au/our-research>

'Paralegals Benefit from the Rise of Alternative Legal Service Provider (ALSP) Companies', ParalegalEDU.org (Web Page, 2024) <https://www.paralegaledu.org/alternative-legal-service-providers/>

'Practicising Certificate Conditions', The Law Society of New South Wales (Web Page) <https://www.lawsociety.com.au/practising-law-in-NSW/working-as-a-solicitor-in-NSW/your-practising-certificate/conditions>

'Preparing Documents for Lodgment', Federal Court of Australia (Web Page, July 2024) <https://www.fedcourt.gov.au/online-services/preparing-documents-for-the-court>

'Prerequisites and Professional Obligations', *WA Bar Association* (Web Page, 2023) <https://www.wabar.asn.au/coming-to-the-bar/prerequisites-and-professional-obligations/>.

'Pro Bono Partnership Models: A Practical Guide to What Works – Chapter 18: Law Students', *Australian Pro Bono Centre* (Web Page, December 2022) <https://www.probonocentre.org.au/whatworks/part-3/chap-18/>

'Register of Practitioners', High Court of Australia (Web Page) <https://www.hcourt.gov.au/registry/register-of-practitioners>

'Regulation of FinTech (LAWS90110)', The University of Melbourne (Web Page, 11 June 2024) <https://handbook.unimelb.edu.au/2024/subjects/laws90110>

Scanlon, Kate, 'Allens Launches Enterprise Version of ChatGPT, Airlie', *Allens Linklaters* (Web Page, 18 August 2023) <https://www.allens.com.au/insights-news/news/2023/08/allens-launches-enterprise-version-of-chatgpt-airlie/>

'Scoping the Establishment of a Federal Judicial Commission', Attorney-General's Department (Web Page) <https://consultations.ag.gov.au/legal-system/federal-judicial-commission/

'Specialist Certificate in Law (Digital Law and Technological Innovation)', The University of Melbourne (Web Page) <https://study.unimelb.edu.au/find/courses/graduate/specialist-certificate-in-law-digital-law-and-technological-innovation/>

'Statement on the Use of Artificial Intelligence Software in the Preparation of Material for Assessment', The University of Melbourne (Web Page, 21 April 2023) <https://academicintegrity.unimelb.edu.au/plagiarism-and-collusion/artificial-intelligence-tools-and-technologies>

'Studying Law', Queensland Law Society (Web Page, 2023) <https://www.qls.com.au/Pages/Your-legal-career/Studying-law>

'Supervised Legal Training', *Victorian Legal Services Board* (Web Page, 20 September 2022) <https://www.lawadmissions.vic.gov.au/qualifications-and-training/supervised-legal-training>

Supreme Court of New South Wales, Practice Note No SC GEN 07: Use of Technology (& September 2008) <http://www.lawlink.nsw.gov.au/practice_notes/nswsc_pc.nsf/a15f50afb1aa22a9ca2570ed000a2b08/19ae2d221b09c4fbca257483001d0781?OpenDocument>.

Supreme Court of New South Wales, Practice Note No SC GEN 15: Use of Audio-visual Links in Criminal and Certain Civil Proceedings (1 January 2009) <http://www.lawlink.nsw.gov.au/practice_notes/nswsc_pc.nsf/a15f50afb1aa22a9ca2570ed000a2b08/7bd5e80ccc50a600ca2574fc008018d?OpenDocument>

Supreme Court of Victoria, 'Guidelines for Litigants: Responsible Use of Artificial Intelligence in Litigation' (Web Page, May 2024) <https://www.supremecourt.vic.gov.au/forms-fees-and-services/forms-templates-and-guidelines/guideline-responsible-use-of-ai-in-litigation>

Supreme Court of Victoria, Practice Note SC Gen 5: Technology in Civil Litigation (2 July 2018) < https://www.supremecourt.vic.gov.au/sites/default/files/2018-10/gen_5_use_of_technology_first_revision.pdf >

Tadros, Edmund, 'Scale of HWL Ebsworth Hack Revealed: 2.5m Files, 65 Agencies', *Australian Financial Review* (online, 20 September 2023) <https://www.afr.com/companies/professional-services/scale-of-hwl-ebsworth-hack-revealed-2-5m-files-65-agencies-20230920-p5e64t>.

Tertiary Education Quality and Standards Agency, 'Reducing Regulatory Burden During COVID-19 – Important Update from TEQSA' (Web Page, 26 March 2020) <https://www.teqsa.gov.au/reducing-regulatory-burden-during-covid-19-important-update-teqsa.>

Tertiary Education Quality and Standards Agency, 'Online Delivery – Key Considerations for Providers' (Web Page, 8 April 2020) <https://www.teqsa.gov.au/latest-news/publications/online-delivery-key-considerations-providers>.

'The Legal Operations Role is Indispensable to Today's Law Firms as Well as to Legal Departments', *College of Law* (Web Page, 27 August 2020) <https://www.collaw.edu.au/news/2020/08/27/the-legal-operations-role-is-indispensable-to-today-s-law-firms-as-well-as-to-legal-departments>

The University of Melbourne, 'Assessment and Results Policy (MPF1326)', Melbourne Policy Library (Web Page) <https://policy.unimelb.edu.au/MPF1326/>

The University of Melbourne, 'Legal AI: Design and Development (LAWS90286), Handbook (Web Page, 18 July 2024) <https://handbook.unimelb.edu.au/2024/subjects/laws90286>

The University of Western Australia, 'Technology Law and Governance [LAWS5296]', Handbook 2024 (Web Page) <https://handbooks.uwa.edu.au/unitdetails?code=LAWS5296>

'Unbiased AI Could Improve Women's Rights', UTS (Web Page) <https://www.uts.edu.au/research-and-teaching/our-research/law-research/snapshots/unbiased-ai-could-improve-womens-rights>

'UNSW Allens Hub for Technology, Law & Innovation', UNSW Sydney (Web Page) <https://allenshub.unsw.edu.au/>

'UWA Tech & Policy Lab', The University of Western Australia (Web Page) <https://www.uwa.edu.au/schools/research/uwa-tech-and-policy-lab>

Weiser, Benjamin, 'Here's What Happens When Your Lawyer Uses ChatGPT', The New York Times (online, 27 May 2023) <https://www.nytimes.com/2023/05/27/nyregion/avianca-airline-lawsuit-chatgpt.html>

'Welcome to ALSA', *Australian Law Students Association* (Web Page, 2022) <https://alsa.asn.au/>

'Welcome to UNSW Institute for Cyber Security', UNSW Sydney (Web Page) <https://www.unsw.edu.au/research/ifcyber>

'What does a legal technologist do?', *Josef* (Web Page, 15 April 2021) <https://joseflegal.com/blog/new-job-what-is-a-legal-technologist/>

'Who We Are', Cyber Security Cooperative Research Centre (Web Page) <https://cybersecuritycrc.org.au/who-we-are>

'Your AI Consumer Champion', DoNot Pay (Web Page) <https://donotpay.com/>

Bibliography on Chinese Part

Journal Articles

He Qinhua, and Liu Yiyuan. "On the Inheritance of the Chinese Legal System and the Construction of China's Independent Legal Knowledge System." *China Law Review* 2024, no. 1 (2024): 1–21.

Zheng Xianwen. "Interpretative and Legislative Exegesis in the Tang Code with Commentaries." *Legal Forum* 2022, vol. 37, no. 4 (2022): 17–27.

Liu Meng. "On the Inception of Modern Chinese Legal Scholarship." *Journal of East China University of Political Science and Law*, vol. 19, no. 01, 2016, pp. 162–176.

Wang Weiwei. "Shen Dao's Concepts of 'Shi,' 'Shu,' and 'Fa' and the Realization of 'Governance of All Under Heaven'." *Studies in Political Philosophy*, no. 00, 2024, pp. 135–150, 318–319.

Zhao, Ming. "From 'Legal System' to 'Rule of Law' in the Chinese Context." *Ideological Front*, no. 2, 2015, pp. 118–122.

Jiang Peng. "The Origins of Modern Legal Education in China." *China Law Review*, no. 04 (2014): 117–130.

Zhang Wenxian. "A Programmatic Document for Strengthening Legal Education and Theoretical Research in the New Era: An Interpretation of the 'Opinions on Strengthening Legal Education and Theoretical Research in the New Era'." *China University Teaching*, no. 09 (2023): 8–14.

Fu Zitang. "Improving the Management and Guidance System of Law Schools to Enhance the Quality of Law School Construction." *China University Teaching*, no. 09, 2023, pp. 34–38, 78.

Liu Jian, Wang weimin and Liu Qiuhui." the National Unified Lawyer Qualification Examination: A Walk Together" Jurisprudence World, no. 9, 2001, pp. 4–8

Wang Jian. "The Development and Prospects of Legal Professional Education in China." *Hebei Legal Professional Education*, vol. 2, no. 01, 2024, pp. 4–12, 85.

Lian Lingwei. "On the Development and Improvement of China's Legal Professional Qualification Examination Admission System." China Law Review, no. 02, 2021, pp. 205–210.

Ding Xiangshun. "Conceptual, Institutional, and Model Innovations in the National Unified Legal Professional Qualification Examination." *China Justice*, no. 10, 2022, pp. 92–98.

Rukiya Hojia, and Jin Zilu. "Research on the Effective Connection Mechanism Between Legal Master's Education and the Legal Professional Qualification Examination." *Legal Education Research*, vol. 41, no. 02, 2023, pp. 233–248.

Yang Lili. "Constructing a New Teaching Model Oriented Toward the Cultivation of Legal Professional Abilities Under the Background of the National Unified Legal Professional Qualification Examination." *Legal Expo*, no. 25, 2020, pp. 189–190.

Gao Yifei and Jiang Wen. "Review and Reflections on the Reform of the Legal Profession Qualification Examination". Public Security Science Journal(Journal of Zhejiang Police College), no. 3, 2020, pp. 72–78.

Yang Chengxin. "On the Transition from 'Judicial Exam' to 'Legal Exam' and the Development of Legal Education: Reflections on 'A Decade of Judicial Exam Retrospective'." *Legal Education Research*, vol. 36, no. 01, 2022, pp. 371–390.

Lan Qianhui. "A Brief Discussion on the Multi-Dimensional Construction of Judges' Professional Qualities." *Legal System and Society*, no. 11, 2012, pp. 173–174.

Cao Zhiyu. "Supervisory Officials Should Also Pass the Legal Qualification Examination." *Study Forum*, no. 02, 2019, pp. 91–96.

Li Xin. "Research on the Professionalization Orientation of Legal Education in China." *Legal Expo*, no. 26, 2017, pp. 89–90.

Jiang Haitao. "Some Reflections on Establishing a National Unified Legal Professional Qualification System." *China Justice*, no. 01, 2018, pp. 23–32.

Wu Weijun. "Differentiation in Judicial and Prosecutorial System Reforms: Connotations, Reasons, and Approaches." *Journal of Jiangxi University of Finance and Economics*, no. 02, 2022, pp. 140–148.

Shi Yuanlin. "Research on the 'Three-Complete Education' System of Legal Professional Ethics Education for Undergraduate Law Students: How to Cultivate High-Quality Legal Talents with

Both Virtue and Law." *China Journal of Multimedia and Network Teaching (First Half of the Month)*, no. 05, 2021, pp. 138–140.

Liu Zheng, He Fan, and Wei Langping. "Understanding and Application of the 'Opinions on Deepening Comprehensive Supporting Reforms of the Judicial Accountability System'." *People's Judicature*, no. 25, 2020, pp. 34–37.

Li Shenglong. "Value Orientation and Pathways for Optimizing Judicial Resource Allocation." *Unity*, no. 06, 2019, pp. 51–54.

Pan Jianfeng. "On the Legal Professional Qualification Examination Aiming at the Elitization of the Legal Profession." *Modern Law Science*, vol. 41, no. 05, 2019, pp. 168–181.

Long Zongzhi, Lyu Chuan. "Problems, Contradictions and Responses to the Classification and Management of Prosecution Service Personnel." *Journal of National Prosecutors College*, no. 4, 2022, pp. 74–99.

Wu Hongqi. "Judicial Reform and Changes in the Incentive Environment of the Legal Profession." *China Legal Science*, no. 04, 2019, pp. 165–185.

Long Yifang. "Causes of Judges' Case Stress and Strategies for Coping with it." *Journal of Huzhou Teachers College*, no. 9, 2016, pp. 111–116.

Jiang Guohua, and Lai Yanjun. "The Reform and Outlook of the Judge Accountability System in the 70 Years Since the Founding of the People's Republic of China." *Jianghan Tribune*, vol. 39, no. 05, 2020, pp. 69-78.

Zhang Weiwei. "Judicial Reform in a Period of Acceleration" *National People's Congress of China*, no. 5, 2017, pp. 44–45.

Wang Lusheng. "The Risk of Involution in China's Judicial Reform and Its Governance." *Studies in Law and Business*, vol. 39, no. 03, 2022, pp. 16–29.

Zhang Qing. "Case Pressure and Its Response in Grassroots Justice after Post System Reform - Taking Three Typical Grassroots Courts in Certain Province as Examples" Journal of CUPL, no. 1, 2019, pp. 96–108,208.

Fang Le. "On the Theoretical Guidance and Fundamental Principles for the Modernization of Judicial Work in the New Era." *Law and Social Development*, vol. 29, no. 04, 2023, pp. 28–43.

Qian Dajun, and Guo Jianguo. "Analysis of the Function Realization of the Judge Quota System." *Journal of Jilin University (Social Sciences Edition)*, vol. 61, no. 02, 2021, pp. 76–83, 236.

Fan Yuhua. "Competition and Heritage of the Bar." Chinese Lawyer, no. 6, 2017, pp. 19–21.

Bai Gaoyuan. "Reflections on the Professional Positioning of Lawyers." *Legal Expo*, no. 11, 2017, p. 234.

Duan Luping. "The Evolutionary Logic and Development Path of Judicial Modernization in China." *Tribune of Political Science and Law*, vol. 42, no. 03, 2024, pp. 157–168.

Gao Yan, Ma Ji, and Zhang Jing. "Research on the Impact of the COVID-19 Pandemic on the Legal Services Industry." *Journal of Qingdao University of Science and Technology (Social Sciences Edition)*, vol. 36, no. 02, 2020, pp. 81–84.

Li Ping. "A Study of Certain Issues in Cases of Offences Involving the New Crown Epidemic." *Criminal Law Review*, vol. 64, no. 4, pp. 22–38.

Song, Jianwen, Liu Yanqi, and Liu Bin. "Characteristics, Models, and Improvement Paths of Public Legal Services During the Pandemic." Journal of Beijing Vocational College of Political Science and Law, no. 04, 2020, pp. 61–67.

Zhang Jinde and Yue Benfeng. "Development and Challenges of Online Litigation in China in the Context of Epidemic Prevention and Control." *Journal of China Emergency Management*, no. 9, 2021, 107–117.

Zhou Yitao. "Exploring the Integration of Information Technology and the Legal Profession: A Perspective on Judicial System Informatization." *China Training*, no. 04, 2017, p. 31.

Wei Bin. "The Transformation of Legal Technology: From Computerization to Digitalization and Intelligence." *Jurist*, no. 03, 2024, pp. 16–29, 190–191.

Yang Changyu. "Technological Challenges to Law in the Digital Age and Their Juridical Responses." *Seeking Truth*, vol. 49, no. 4, 2022, pp. 103–113.

Hong Dongying. "How can justice be oriented towards technological innovations such as 'Internet Plus' and artificial intelligence?" *Law Science Magazine*, no. 11, 2018, pp. 169–180.

Zhang Liang, and Zhao Dong. "Research on the Reform and Exploration of Talent Training Mechanisms in 'Artificial Intelligence + Law'" *Legal System and Economy*, vol. 33, no. 02, 2024, pp. 84–95.

Martineau, AJ 2020, "Reinforcing the infrastructure of legal research through court-authored metadata", *Law Library Journal*, vol. 112, no. 1, pp. 5–45.

Li Xiaohong. "The Connotation of the Rule of Law Professional Community and Its Construction -- A Primary Exploration of Human Resources Issues in Building the Rule of Law in China" *Journal of Sichuan University & Engineering (Social Science Edition)*, vol. 32, no. 5, 2017, 42–56.

Zheng Ge. "Rethinking the Future of Artificial Intelligence and Law." *Digital Law*, no. 03, 2023, pp. 67–82.

Preston, Cheryl B. "Lawyers' Abuse of Technology." *Cornell Law Review, no.* 103, 2017, pp. 879–976.

Zong Bo. "Directions for the Development of Legal Education in the Age of Artificial Intelligence." *Journal of Xidian University (Social Sciences Edition)*, vol. 29, no. 2, pp. 61–67.

Yi Feifei and Ma Chao. "Disclosure of Judicial Statistics in China: Current Status and Recommendations." *China Review of Administration of Justice*, no. 2, 2017, pp. 56–72.

Zuo Weimin and Wang Chanyuan. "Big Data Legal Research Based on Adjudication Networks: Reflections and Perspectives" *Journal of the East China University of Politics & Law*, vol. 23, no. 2, 2020, pp. 64–76.

Wu Zhe. "On the Authenticity of Electronic Evidence in Civil Litigation." *Journal of Hebei University of Science and Technology (Social Sciences)*, vol. 15, no. 3, 2015, pp. 48–54.

Huang Sui, and Liang Wenli. "A Survey Study on the Current Status and Development Trends of Artificial Intelligence Technology in Legal Practice." *Journal of Guangdong Open University*, vol. 31, no. 04, 2022, pp. 60–66.

Fang Tao and Li Lingzhi. "The Challenges of Artificial Intelligence to the Traditional Legal Profession and Strategies to Address Them." *Journal of Harbin Institute*, no. 9, 2019, pp. 78–80.

Huang Weiwen. "From Unicorns to AI: Should Artificial Intelligence Replace the Legal Profession? " *Law and Social Development*, no. 5, 2020, pp. 164–184.

Wang Jian. "The Origin and Future of the 'Five Institutes and Four Departments'." *Journal of China University of Political Science and Law* 2022, no. 3 (2022): 5–23.

He Zhipeng. "On the Conceptual Evolution of Legal Education during 40 Years of Reform and Opening Up." *China University Teaching* 2018, no. 11 (2018): 15–20.

Xu Shenjian. "Improving Legal Education: Approaches and Methods." *China Law Review* 2017, no. 3 (2017): 54–63.

Xie Wei. "Exploration of Reform Paths for Chinese-Style Undergraduate Legal Education under the Background of New Liberal Arts." *Guangxi Social Sciences*, no. 08, 2023, pp. 108–115.

Xiong Ying. "Research on Strengthening the Training of Master of Law Students in the Context of New Era Legal Education." *Chongqing Administration* 2023, vol. 24, no. 3 (2023): 71–74.

Deng Jingchao. "The Practical Challenges and Exploration Directions in the Training of Doctoral Law Students in China." *Academic Degrees & Graduate Education*, no. 02, 2023, pp. 64–69.

Zhan Zhongle, and Jin Lantao. "Comparative Study of Educational Jurisprudence Systematization Abroad and the Chinese Approach." *Journal of Educational Science of Hunan Normal University*, vol. 21, no. 04, 2022, pp. 76–84+122.

Li Guang'en. "Research on the Modernization Path of Legal Education under the Guidance of Xi Jinping's Thought on the Rule of Law." *Heilongjiang Education (Higher Education Research and Evaluation)*, no. 03, 2024, pp. 80–82.

Lü Xuan. "Course Implementation for Deep Integration of Education and Career: Concepts and Evaluation—A Case Study of Law Courses." *China Vocational and Technical Education*, no. 14, 2020, pp. 48–53.

Qiu Xiaoguang, and Wang, Guanxiong. "Differentiated Reforms in Legal Graduate Education under the Construction of New Liberal Arts." *Legal System and Society*, no. 30, 2023, pp. 8–10.
Wu Qianqian. "Research on the Pathways to Enhance Innovation Performance of Humanities and Social Sciences Graduate Students: From the Perspective of Graduate Student-Supervisor Relationship Quality." *Times Finance* 2017, no. 18 (2017): 192–193.
Zong Ling. "Dilemmas and Countermeasures in the Collaborative Training of Master of Law Students." *Higher Education Forum* 2023, no. 12 (2023): 94–97, 132.
Chen Canqi, and Fan Jie. "Research on the Reform of Legal Graduate Education under the Background of 'Double First-Class' Initiative." *Contemporary Educational Theory and Practice*, vol. 12, no. 04, 2020, pp. 112–117.
Yan Weilong, and Wu, Mingzhong. "Theoretical Foundation and Institutional Guarantee of Credit System Reform in Higher Education Institutions." *Educational Research*, vol. 36, no. 07, 2015, pp. 57–63.
Yang Yi. "Innovation in Legal Education under the Background of Deepening the Practice of Governing the Country According to Law." *Legal System and Society*, no. 18, 2021, pp. 166–167.
Sun Chong. "Research on the Problems of Undergraduate Thesis Writing Education under the Background of the Academic Degree Law: A Case Study of Undergraduate Legal Education." *Hebei Legal Vocational Education*, vol. 2, no. 05, 2024, pp. 45–52.
Fu Huishu. "Guidance on Undergraduate Theses and the Cultivation of Innovation Ability: A Case Study of Law Major Theses." *Educational Academic Monthly* 2012, no. 12 (2012): 30–32.
Yang Yani. "The Reform of Legal Education in the Context of New Liberal Arts Construction." *New Liberal Arts Education Research* 2021, no. 2 (2021): 80–94, 143.
Ye Jingyi. "Exploring New Paths in Legal Practice Teaching: A Review of Research on Legal Education." *Educational Development Research*, vol. 41, no. 17, 2021, p. 86.
Dai Changshu, Bao, Tiewen, and Shao, Pengfei. "The Role and Application Approaches of Practical Legal Teaching in Legal Education Reform." *Legality Vision* 2021, no. 7 (2021): 183–184.
Liu Yonghong, and Qing Xin. "Reflections, Challenges, and Responses of Legal Education in the Context of New Liberal Arts." *Journal of Sichuan University of Arts and Science* 2023, vol. 33, no. 6 (2023): 141–147.
Zhang Shengqian, and He Jingshu. "Understanding, Reasoning, and Practice of Legal Logic in Legal Education: A Review of Legal Theory: Multidimensional and Integrated." *Educational Theory and Practice*, vol. 43, no. 30, 2023, p. 65.
Liang Yanni. "Examining Legal Curriculum Reform through Postmodern Curriculum Theory." Education Modernization 2019, vol. 6, no. 78 (2019): 25–27.
Wang Chengtang, and Ma Hui. "Construction and Application of a Distributed Legal Practice Teaching System." China University Teaching 2023, no. 7 (2023): 70–75.
Lü Ting, Xu Yong, and Gao Feng. "Improvement and Enhancement of Moot Court Practice Courses." Legal System and Society, no. 17(2024):19–21.
Yang Jing. "Innovative Development of Legal Clinic Practice Teaching in China." Legal System and Society, no. 30, 2023, pp. 24–26.
Dai Peng. "Exploration of Comprehensive Social Practice Work in Universities." Journal of Liaoning University of Technology (Social Science Edition) 2023, vol. 25, no. 1 (2023): 93–96.
Ma Liuying. "Exploring the Construction Path of First-Class Law Programs in Local Universities from the Perspective of New Liberal Arts." Journal of Higher Education 2023, vol. 9, no. 32 (2023): 22–25.
Zhang Maoyu. "Some Thoughts on Strengthening Practical Teaching in Legal Education." Legal System and Society, no. 34 (2019):247–248.
Dong Yan, and Liu Shijie. "Thoughts on Improving China's Legal Education System in the New Era." Hebei Legal Vocational Education 2024, vol. 2, no. 2 (2024): 19–33.
Wang Xiaoyan, Liu Xiuqing, and Wang Hui. "A Brief Discussion on the Reform of Undergraduate Law Thesis." Legal System and Society, no. 34(2018): 194–195.

Sun Nan, Jiang Siwen, Bi Xinru, et al. "Research on the Training Model for Undergraduate Students' Scientific Research and Innovation Ability in Universities." Journal of Higher Education 2024, vol. 10, no. 25 (2024): 70–73.

Zhao Wei, and Gao Jun. "Research on the Training Model for Interdisciplinary Humanities Master's Students in the Context of New Liberal Arts." Teaching and Educating (Higher Education Forum) 2024, no. 21 (2024): 68–72.

Wang Liangliang, Wen Bo, Liu Hui, et al. "A Brief Analysis of the Educational Differences Between Undergraduates and Postgraduates." Educational Teaching Forum 2020, no. 37 (2020): 72–74.

Yang Xiuqin, and Zuo Peiying. "Policy Analysis of the Comprehensive Implementation of the Graduate Education Fee System: Goals, Limits, and Improvements." Academic Degrees & Graduate Education, no. 08(2017): 43–49.

Li Feng, Jiang Yisha, and Guo Jiangjiang. "New Trends and Implications of Overseas Studies for Undergraduates in 'Double First-Class' Universities—An Analysis Based on Employment Quality Reports from 20 Universities." China Higher Education Research, no. 03(2022): 60–66.

Mao Yufei, and Zeng Xiangquan. "The Impact of the COVID-19 Pandemic on University Graduates' Employment: Empirical Evidence from Job Board Data." Academic Research 2022, no. 1 (2022): 104–110.

Lin Runkang. "The Impact of Public Health Emergencies on the Transnational Mobility of Chinese International Students and Countermeasures." Special Zone Economy 2024, no. 1 (2024): 153–156.

Guo Erong, Shen Wenqin, and Wang Dingming. "A Comparative Study of the Legal Degree System and Education Scale between China and the United States." Academic Degrees & Graduate Education, no. 11(2020): 63–72.

Xu Li. "American Legal Education and Its Implications for China." Law Journal, vol. 31, no. 12 (2010): 84–87.

Guo Yanli. "Analysis of Legal Professional Education Relations: Insights from Foreign Legal Professional Education." Continuing Education Research 2013, no. 11 (2013): 156–158.

Yu Shanshan, and Wen, Xinhua. "In-Depth Analysis of Mainland Students' Reasons for Applying to Hong Kong Universities." Shanghai Educational Research, no. 06(2007):1–23+15.

Li Qiang, and Sun Yamei. "Understanding and Reflections on Four Trends of Chinese University Students Studying Abroad." Journal of Beijing Administrative College 2018, no. 5 (2018): 93–100.

Lin Jie, Zhang Xinqi, and Liu Yeqing. "Construction and Application of a Risk Assessment Model for Studying Abroad—Based on Evaluations in the UK and the US." Higher Education Management, vol. 17, no. 01(2023):100–114.

Chen Canqi, and Fan Jie. "Research on the Reform of Legal Graduate Education under the Background of 'Double First-Class' Construction." Contemporary Educational Theory and Practice, vol. 12, no. 04(2020): 112–117.

Zhang, Yijie. "Research on the Pathways for Aligning Legal Education with the Legal Profession Qualification Examination." Legal System and Society, no. 15(2022): 153–156.

Li Huade, and Li Yicheng. "Historical Analysis and Practical Considerations of Examination Law in China." China Examinations (Research Edition), no. 12 (2008):32–40.

Du Guoxing. "A Brief Discussion on the National Judicial Examination System." The Jurist, no. 5 (2022):125–128.

Liu Jian, Wang Weimin and Liu Qiuhui. "Bar Examination: Together." Jurisprudence World, no. 9(2001):8.

Ding Xiangshun: "The Creation and Development of China's Judicial Examination System," in Chinese Jurisprudence, no. 10(2008): 26–29.

Zhao Fuzhen. "Analysing the Characteristics and Functions of the Work of Legal Advisers in Enterprises." Coastal Enterprises and Science & Technology, no. 7(2005):182.

Chen Weidong. "Reflections on Some Problems of Criminal Defence by Lawyers in China." Journal of the Renmin University of China, vol. 8, no. 2(1994) :61–68.

He Fan. "Standards and Establishment Models for Specialized People's Courts in the New Era," Chinese Applied Jurisprudence, No. 3(2022): 59.

Wang, Jing. "The Purpose, Issues, and Improvement of the Judge Performance Evaluation Mechanism." People's Judicature, no. 16(2019): 68–71.

Wu Jinhuan and Wu Xiaoyu. "'The Examining Bowlers in the Wave of Civil Service Fever'." Honesty Outlook, no. 11(2015):34–35.

He Hengyang, "Effectively Implementing the 'Three Roles of Three Types of Personnel' to Ensure the Detailed Implementation of the Judicial Responsibility System," People's Procuratorate, no. 18 (2017): 7.

Zhang Wei, "Opportunities, Challenges, and Solutions for Prosecutorial Agencies under the Reform of the Supervision System," Journal of Hubei Police Officer College, no. 1 (2018): 25.

Jiang Baozhong, "Construction of a Criminal Accountability Mechanism for Miscarriages of Justice from the Perspective of the Judicial Responsibility System," Legal System and Society, no. 5 (2016): 74.

Zhang Jianwei, "Prosecutor Management: Judicial Regularities and Institutional Effects," People's Procuratorate, no. 8 (2023): 49.

Cheng Kai. "Functional Comparison of Litigation and Arbitration - and the Functional Advantages of Arbitration." Journal of Sichuan Police College, vol. 16, no. 2(2004):90–94.

Deng Jie. "A Brief Discussion of the Advantages of International Commercial Arbitration and Ways of Realising Them." Journal of Gansu University of Political Science and Law, No. 4(2001):26–30.

Xie Junying. "Analysis of the Cost Advantages of Arbitration for the Settlement of Commercial Disputes." Journal of Hebei University of Economics and Trade, vol. 34, no. 3(2013):86–88.

Zheng Chunxian. "Exploring the Current Status and Improvement Paths of Corporate Legal Management under the New Normal." Legal System and Society, no. 14(2021): 187–188.

Tao Guanghui. "'Seven Steps to Contract Review' for Corporate Lawyers." Faren Magazine, no. 3(2019) : 66–68.

Wang, Zheng. "Research on Strategies for Enhancing Corporate Legal Litigation Capabilities." Legal System and Society, no. 01(2021): 49–50.

Liao, Yongan, and Zhang, Hongwang. "History and Future: The Legal Nature of Notary Organizations under the Perspective of Notary System Reform—Based on the Socialization of Notarial Power." Journal of Law Modernization, vol. 7, no. 01(2023): 19–35.

Yu Zhigang. "The Transformation of Chinese Law and Jurisprudence in the Information Age." Legal Forum, vol. 26, no. 02(2011): 37–40.

Zong Guoen, and Wang Yongxin. "Research on Innovation-Driven Teaching and Advancement Paths in Universities in the Era of Digital Intelligence." China Management Informatization 2024, vol. 27, no. 3 (2024): 184–187.

Wu Di, Guo Qing, and Zhu Sha. "Why and How to Implement Information Technology Courses: New Thoughts from the Perspective of Digital Transformation in Education." China Educational Technology, no. 01(2024):59–67.

Yang Changyu. "Technological Challenges Faced by Law in the Digital Era and Legal Responses." Seeking Truth, vol. 49, no. 04(2022):103–114.

Xu Xiaotong. "The Historical Significance and Practical Strategies of Transitioning from Legal System Education to Rule of Law Education: Based on the Perspective of the 'Outline for Youth Rule of Law Education'." Educational Review 2017, no. 4 (2017): 32–35.

Luo Jianguo, and Wang Yuqiang. "Reform of the Talent Cultivation System in Universities in the Context of Educational Informatization." Educational Teaching Forum 2020, no. 13 (2020): 200–204.

Lin Xifen, and Li Zheng. "On the Global Development Trends of Computational Law." Journal of Shanghai Jiao Tong University (Philosophy and Social Sciences Edition) 2024, vol. 32, no. 6 (2024): 48–62.

Yang Bowen. "From 'Disciplinary Cocoon' to 'Breaking Out of the Cocoon': The Logical Path and Ideal Choices for the Integration of Legal Disciplines." Journal of Tianjin University (Social Sciences Edition) 2023, vol. 25, no. 6 (2023): 490–498.

Liu Bei, and Qi Hanwen. "On the Supply-Side Reform of Legal Education in the Context of 'AI + Law'." Hebei Law Science, no. 6, 2023, pp. 157–175.

Hu Ming. "Research Approaches to China's Independent Digital Legal Knowledge System." Journal of East China University of Political Science and Law 2024, vol. 27, no. 3 (2024): 69–83.

Yuan Zeng. "Rethinking the Current State of Digital Law Studies: Where Is Legal Theory Heading?" Journal of Shanghai University of Political Science and Law (Legal Forum), vol. 38, no. 03(2023):116–125.

Xie Yi, and He Bo. "Research on China's Data Legal System." Big Data, vol. 10, no. 01(2024):141–156.

Chen Yun. "Analysis and Research on New Types of Cybercrime in the Era of Big Data." China Security & Protection, vol. 2023, no. 10(2023): 104–108.

Xie Qun. "Challenges and Countermeasures for Reforming Legal Education in Higher Education Institutions in the 'Internet+' Era." Legal System and Society, vol. 2023, no. 20(2023): 166–168.

Zhang Yueqiu. "Exploration and Reflection on the Construction of an Online Teaching Quality Assurance System in Universities." Science & Technology Information 2022, vol. 20, no. 18 (2022): 188–190.

Xu Yibo. "Exploration of 'Online + Offline' Blended Teaching Methods in Legal Education." Legal System and Society, vol. 2023, no. 07(2023): 19–21.

Zhao Yuanding. "Analysis of Problems and Countermeasures in Online Distance Education." Office Automation, vol. 27, no. 23(2022): 62–64, 32.

Yang Xueke. "Research on the Construction of 'New Legal Studies' in the Digital Era." Legal Education Research 2021, vol. 33, no. 2 (2021): 61–76.

Zhang Lixin. "Research on the Implementation Path of Interdisciplinary Integration of Legal Studies in the Context of New Liberal Arts." Hebei Legal Vocational Education 2024, vol. 2, no. 6 (2024): 19–25.

Wang Tao. "The Evolution of Interdisciplinarity in Universities from a Disciplinary Perspective: From Interdisciplinary Crossing to Interdisciplinary Studies." China Higher Education Research 2023, no. 12 (2023): 71–78.

Yang Zhenhong. "Overcoming the Misconceptions of Traditional Legal Education: Creating a New Multilevel and Diverse Legal Education Model." Heilongjiang Education (Higher Education Research and Evaluation) 2016, no. 4 (2016): 8–9.

Shen Qingping, and Shen Chen. "Dilemmas and Coping Strategies of Legal Education in the Online Environment." Legal System and Society, vol. 2023, no. 27(2023): 160–162.

Zhang Ailian, and Yu Runping. "The Influence of Chinese Traditional Culture on University Students' Handling of Teacher-Student Relationships." Higher Education Forum 2023, no. 1 (2023): 72–77.

Wang Man, and Lü Jianqiang. "Teachers in the Digital Age: Identity Transformation and Value Reconstruction." Contemporary Educational Science 2021, no. 9 (2021): 35–41.

Wang Xigen, and Liu Jia. "On the Construction of Experimental Teaching Systems for Digital Law Courses." China University Teaching, vol. 2023, no. 12(2023): 46–55.

Ma Changshan. "The Transformation of Legal Education in the Digital Age." Journal of Shanghai University of Political Science and Law (Rule of Law Forum) 2023, vol. 38, no. 1 (2023): 101–111.

Long Weiqiu, Chu Dianqing, and Ji Guanhao. "The Concept and Development of Digital Collaborative Legal Education." China University Teaching 2023, no. 3 (2023): 4–11.

Liu Jinying. "Digital Governance Reshaping the New Ecosystem of Online Education." Continuing Education Research 2024, no. 10 (2024): 97–101.

Li Yuzhuo, and Li Haijuan. "Deconstruction and Reconstruction: Legal Responses and Legal Education Transformation in the Digital Society." Journal of Qiqihar University (Philosophy and Social Sciences Edition) 2024, no. 5 (2024): 22–26.

Yu Hui, and Zhang Lili. "Research on the Cultivation of Top Innovative Talents in Universities Under the Conditions of New Productive Forces." Educational Theory and Practice, no. 27(2024): 3–8.
Zhou Wei, Guo Zhilong. "Legal Professions in the Era of Artificial Intelligence: Current Situation, Limits, and Paths." Chinese Legal Education Research, no. 3(2021): 150.
Cao Jianfeng. "Ten Trends of 'Artificial Intelligence + Law'." Robot Industry, no. 5(2017): 86–96.
Yin Chao. "The Transformation of Legal Professions and the Future Direction of Legal Education in the Era of Artificial Intelligence." Chinese Legal Education Research, no. 1(2019): 104.
Zhang Endian. "Changes in Legal Professions and the Transformation of Legal Education in the Era of Artificial Intelligence." Legal Education Research, Vol. 28(2020): 111.
Tong Xiao, Wang Fengmei. "2018 Report on the Development of China's Emerging Legal Services Industry." Shanghai Legal Research (Special Issue), Vol. 11, No. 11(2019): 155.
Qiu Songmei. "Opportunities and Challenges Facing the Legal Industry in the Face of Information Technology." In Collected Papers of the International Professional Committee of the All-China Lawyers Association 2001 Conference, p. 262.
Xing Cheng. "Transformation and Challenges: When Legal Services Meet Artificial Intelligence." Shanghai Informatization,, no. 2(2018): 22.

Books

Zhou Yuhua: Chinese Judicial Studies, Beijing: Law Press, 2015.

Websites

Central People's Government of the People's Republic of China. https://www.gov.cn
the Ministry of Justice of China. https://www.moj.gov.cn
China Court website. https://www.chinacourt.org
the Supreme People's Procuratorate of China. https://www.spp.gov.cn
the Supreme People's Procuratorate of China, https://www.spp.gov.cn/spp/zdgz/201906/t20190616_421776.shtml,accessed April 5, 2024.
"Deepening the Reform of Classification and Management of Procuratorial Personnel and Further Promoting the Professionalisation of Procuratorial Assistants", website of People's Procuratorate of Fuping, http://www.sn.jcy.gov.cn/wnsfpx/dwjs/sxzz/202407/t20240730_391094.html, accessed April 5, 2024.
The Paper. https://www.thepaper.cn
Chinese Social Science Net. https://www.cssn.cn
The National People's Congress of China. http://www.npc.gov.cn
Intelligent Law Promotion Platform. http://legalinfo.moj.gov.cn
China University of Political Science and Law. https://www.cupl.edu.cn
Southwest University of Political Science and Law. https://www.swupl.edu.cn
East China University of Political Science and Law. https://www.ecupl.edu.cn
Zhongnan University of Economics and Law. https://www.zuel.edu.cn
Northwest University of Political Science and Law. https://www.nwupl.edu.cn
Law School of Peking University. https://www.law.pku.edu.cn
Law School of Renmin University of China. http://www.law.ruc.edu.cn
Law School of Wuhan University. https://law.whu.edu.cn
School of Jilin University. http://law.jlu.edu.cn
Ministry of Education of the People's Republic of China. http://www.moe.gov.cn
China Youth Network. https://t.m.youth.cn/
College of Law at National Taiwan University. https://www.law.ntu.edu.tw
Faculty of Law at the University of Hong Kong. https://www.law.hku.hk
University of Oxford Faculty of Law. https://www.law.ox.ac.uk
Harvard Law School. https://hls.harvard.edu
Liaison Office of the Central People's Government in the Macao Special Administrative Region. http://www.zlb.gov.cn
Yale University. https://www.yale.edu
Stanford University. https://studentservices.stanford.edu
University of Cambridge. https://www.postgraduate.study.cam.ac.uk

Beijing Lawyers Association. https://www.beijinglawyers.org.cn
All China Lawyers Association. https://www.acla.org.cn
King & Wood Law Firm. https://www.kwm.com
JunHe Law Firm. https://www.junhe.com
Zhong Lun Law Firm. https://www.zhonglun.com
The Third Intermediate People's Court of Shanghai. http://www.shszfy.gov.cn
Tianjin Court Website. https://tjfy.tjcourt.gov.cn
Shanghai International Economic and Trade Arbitration Commission. https://www.shiac.org
China International Economic and Trade Arbitration Commission states. https://www.cietacodr.org

Newspaper Articles

Liu Tao. "The Composition, Appointment and Removal Procedures, and Qualifications for Office in the Procuratorate," Procuratorial Daily, June 13, 2019, edition 3.
Meng Yaxu. "Integration of Arrest and Prosecution: A New Appearance of the Internal Institutions of the Supreme People's Procuratorate," Beijing Youth Daily, January 3, 2019, A08.
Zhang Weiwei. "Holding Hands with AI: Exploring the Future of the Legal Profession." Shenzhen Business Daily, December 8, 2023, A03.
Luo Sha, Huang Jinzhi and Huang Anqi: "Promoting the professionalisation of the judiciary and building the cornerstone of the judicial accountability system," China Youth Daily, July 23, 2015, edition 3.

Official Documents

Interim Measures of the Supreme People's Court for the Examination of Junior Trial Attorneys and Assistant Trial Attorneys (1999)
Provisional Measures for the Examination of Junior Prosecutors and Assistant Prosecutors (1995)
Circular of the Ministry of Justice on the Holding of the 1992 Unified National Qualification Examination for Notaries Public (1992)
Regulations on the Lawyer Qualification Examination (Order No. 61 of the Ministry of Justice)
Judges Law (1995)
Judges Law (2011)
Implementation Measures for the National Judicial Examination (Trial) (2001)
Circular of the Ministry of Justice on the Preparation of the National Judicial Examination in 2002 (2001)
Circular of the Ministry of Justice on the Preparation of the National Judicial Examination in 2003 (2002)
Circular of the Ministry of Justice on the Preparation of the National Judicial Examination in 2004 (2003)
Announcement of the Ministry of Justice No. 181 -- Announcement of the 2018 National Unified Legal Profession Qualification Examination (2018)
Announcement of the Ministry of Justice No. 4 -- Announcement of the 2024 National Unified Legal Profession Qualification Examination (2024)
Lawyers Law (2017)
Management Rules for Interns Applying for Lawyer Practice (2021)
Code of Conduct for the Practice of Lawyers (Trial) (2018)
Constitution (2018)
Organic Law of the People's Courts (2018)
Provisions of the Supreme People's Court on Several Issues Concerning the Hearing of Cases by Circuit Courts (2016)
Maritime Procedure Law (2000)
Supreme People's Court Provisions on the Jurisdiction of Cases by the Intellectual Property Courts in Beijing, Shanghai, and Guangzhou (Legal Interpretation [2020] No. 19)
Provisions of the Supreme People's Court on the Jurisdiction of Cases in the Beijing Financial Court (2021)
Provisional Measures for the Public Selection of Candidates for Appointment as Judges and Prosecutors at the Early Stage of Their Career (2008)

Regulations on the Education and Training of Judges (2020)
Guidelines of the Supreme People's Court on Strengthening and Improving the Assessment of Judges (2021)
Guiding Opinions on Strengthening and Improving the Assessment of Judges (2021)
Organic Law of the People's Procuratorates (2018)
Criminal Procedure Rules of the People's Procuratorates (2019)
Regulations on the Oath of Prosecutors of the People's Republic of China (Provisional) (2010)
Supervisor Law (2018)
Regulations on the Management of Agents (Decree No. 14 of the State Administration for Industry and Commerce of the People's Republic of China, repealed)
Civil Procedure Law (2023)
Interpretation of the Supreme People's Court on the Application of the Civil Procedure Law of the People's Republic of China (2022)
Opinions of the Supreme People's Court on Improving the Judicial Responsibility System of the People's Courts (2015)
The collection and preservation of electronic evidence is governed by Several Provisions of the Supreme People's Court on Evidence in Civil Proceedings (Amended 2019)
WeChat Articles
See the official WeChat public platform of Democracy and Law Weekly, National Legal Professional Qualification System Develops and Improves in Reform--Interview with Jia Liqun, Director General of the Department of Judicial Examinations, Ministry of Justice, published on September 22, 2017, accessed on August 21, 2024.
See the official WeChat public platform of Democracy and Law Weekly, A Look Back: The Changing Years of China's Legal Profession Admission System, published on July 30, 2018, accessed on August 21, 2024.

The manufacturer's authorised representative in the EU is Springer Nature Customer Service Centre GmbH, Europaplatz 3, 69115 Heidelberg, Germany. If you have any concerns regarding our products, please contact ProductSafety@springernature.com

Printed and bound by CPI Group (UK) Ltd, Croydon, CR0 4YY
30/09/2026
02225300-0015